# Summary of Alesia's Story

Because both of her older brothers died in accidents Alesia inherited her father's earldom of Lincoln, and that of Salisbury from her mother.

SOLE HEIRESS: After her brother's fatal accidents at Denbigh and Pontefract Castles her parents planned to send her to a nunnery. She refused. There were subsequent marriage arrangements, intermittent, due to politics.

FIRST MARRIAGE: To Thomas, Earl of Lancaster, who was later beheaded after rebellion. During this time she was warned to leave London in time, before the city opted for the King.

FIRST ABDUCTION, FIRST IMPRISONMENT: During Thomas of Lancaster's insurrections Alesia was kidnapped, imprisoned at Reigate castle and made to confess damaging imputations about her marriage.

SECOND IMPRISONMENT: With her husband dead, Alesia was imprisoned in York under suspicion. She was granted lands and revenues on conditions, and then released. Shortly afterwards she was ordered (under forfeiture of life and limb) not to communicate with any of her former husband's aides. Then she was given protection by the Sheriff of Lincoln from disaffected marauders.

SECOND MARRIAGE: With permission of the King, but without licence, Alesia married Sir Ebulo le Strange, who had been one of Thomas of Lancaster's knights. She became politically acceptable again, but with reduced social standing. Sir Ebulo having been with the young King Edward III at his coup against his mother Queen Isabella and her lover Mortimer at Nottingham Castle, they escorted the Queen to Windsor.

SECOND HUSBAND KILLED: Sir Ebulo, after eleven years of marriage, was killed in the West of Scotland. Alesia prepared for retirement by taking her vows, and receiving a habit and a ring.

SECOND ABDUCTION: Within weeks of settling down she was abducted from Bolingbroke Castle in Lincolnshire by Sir Hugh de Frene.

THIRD IMPRISONMENT: King Edward III heard of their breaking in to Somerton Castle, south of Lincoln, and ordered their imprisonment in separate chambers. They escaped. The King ordered their arrest, and made Alesia his ward. The orders for arrest were extended to several counties, and to take their lands away and to confiscate their possessions.

THIRD MARRIAGE: Alesia and Hugh married and made peace with King Edward. Sir Hugh died in Scotland within the year. Alesia's former brother-in-law, Henry of Lancaster, had to intercede with the King for her to get her lands reallocated to her.

THE POPE INTERVENES: The Pope ordered the Bishop of Lincoln to oversee Alesia, and to punish with spiritual penalties anyone who interfered with her further. (King Edward was constantly demanding that Alesia's first husband, Thomas of Lancaster, be canonized).

FOURTH IMPRISONMENT: Her late second husband Ebulo's nephew, Roger le Strange, breaks into Alesia's Bolingbroke Castle, and holds her prisoner. Horses and goods were stolen by him and his men, on a false pretext of a possible invasion on the East Coast.

SHE SUES FORMER SHERIFF: Alesia goes to court in Lincoln with successful cases against de Ledred, escheator and Sheriff, for extortions of money and rights over a period of years.

PENALTIES ON CONFESSION: Alesia's confession was accepted, with spiritual penalties. Remission at the hour of death became necessary, and had to be obtained by Alesia, because her life would be too short for completion of the penalties. Alesia was buried next to Ebulo le Strange in Barlings Abbey, near Lincoln.

Thomas of Lancaster was ultimately canonized.

The Lacy Knot. From the seal of Roger de Lacy, great, great grandfather of Alesia.

# Alesia De Lacy

## 1281 - 1348

In her own right:            Countess of Lincoln (1311-1348)
                          and   Countess of Salisbury (1308c-1337)

During her first marriage to   Thomas, Earl of Lancaster -
                           also   Countess of Lancaster,
                                  Countess of Leicester,
                                  Countess of Derby (1294-1322)

During her second marriage to   Sir Ebulo le Strange -
                              also   Lady le Strange (1324-1335)

During her third marriage to   Sir Hugh de Frene -
                           also   Lady de Frene (1337)

In her final widowhood:        Countess of Lincoln (1311-1348)
                        and   Lady de Clifford (1322-1348)

**J. G. RUDDOCK**

# ALESIA

## Countess of Lincoln

First published in Great Britain
by J. Ruddock Ltd. 1993
287 High Street, Lincoln. LN2 1AW

© J. G. Ruddock 1993
All rights reserved

ISBN 0 904327 07 8

This book is sold subject to the condition that it shall not, by way of trade or otherwise, be lent, re-sold, hired out, or otherwise circulated without the publisher's prior consent in any form of binding or cover other than that in which it is published which condition is to continue to any subsequent transaction.

Manuscript typed throughout in Canon's Garland PS2 and arranged for photographing by Mrs. Bette Draper.

No part of this publication may be reproduced in any form nor by any means without the prior permission of the publisher.

Printed by J. W. Ruddock & Sons Ltd., Lincoln, England.

Alesia's story is based on actual incidents which have been traced. Their projection is as true as seems reasonable to the author, in linking the events, and in the circumstances of the time.

The research has been continual for some years; it is based on fragments from many sources.

Where unacknowledged the sketch vignettes are derived from very old prints of which any copyright canot be traced and is believed to have long ceased.

The relevant period of the story, 1281 to 1348, was the time of the Anglo Normans in England, constantly surrounded by enemies. The Welsh fought for identity and their final homeland, having lost their northern territory which stretched up to the River Clyde. The Scots had lost some southern areas, and raided deep into England for booty and to achieve independence. The French were opportunist in challenging historic rights in France; invasions by them were always threatening. At the same time Kings Edward 1st and 3rd were trying to solve their problems by aggression and claims to Kingship over them all.

Every subject's duty was the King's. Office and Rank was achieved through being allocated lands and revenues by the King. Heredity in such was established only by consent. The King could, and did, take away everything from the disobedient.

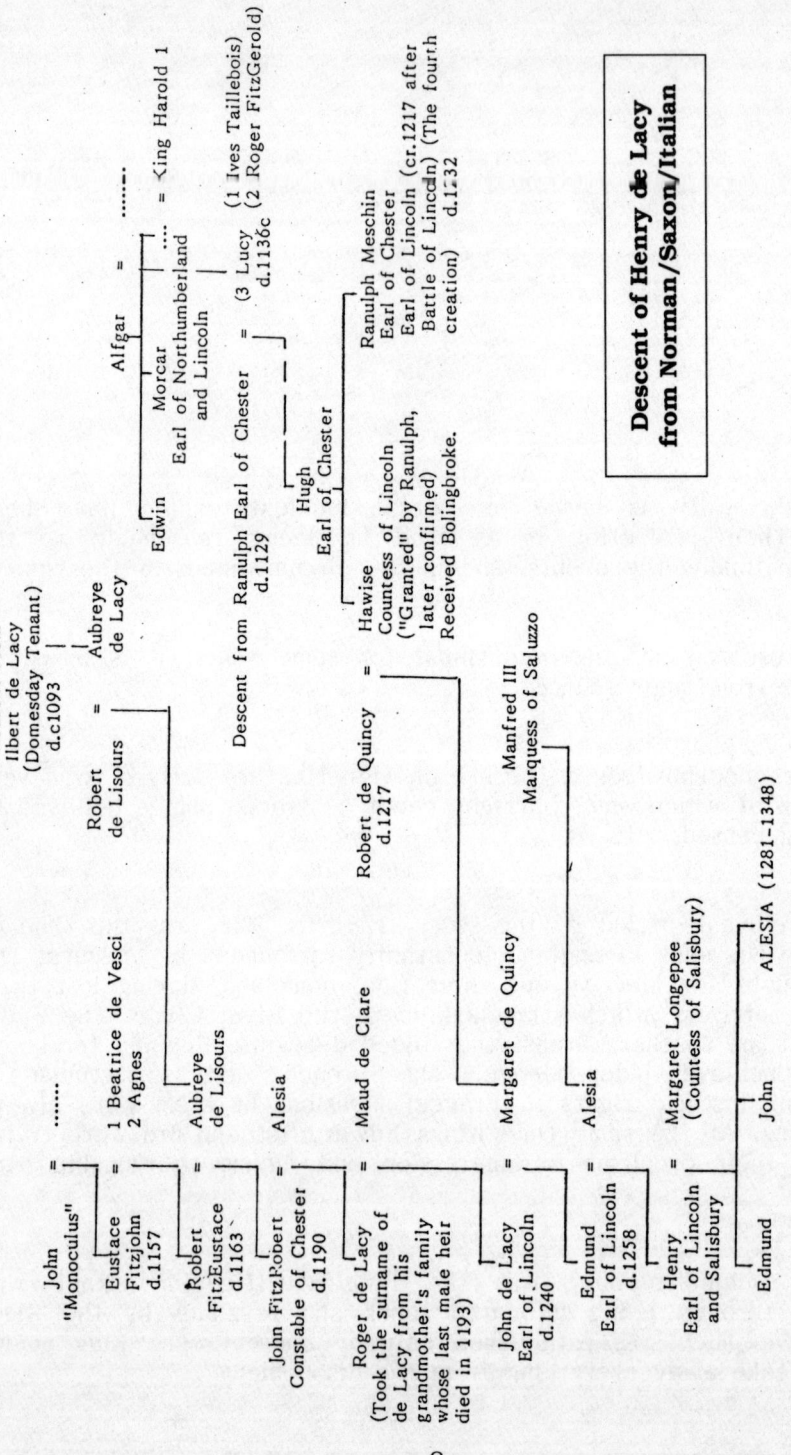

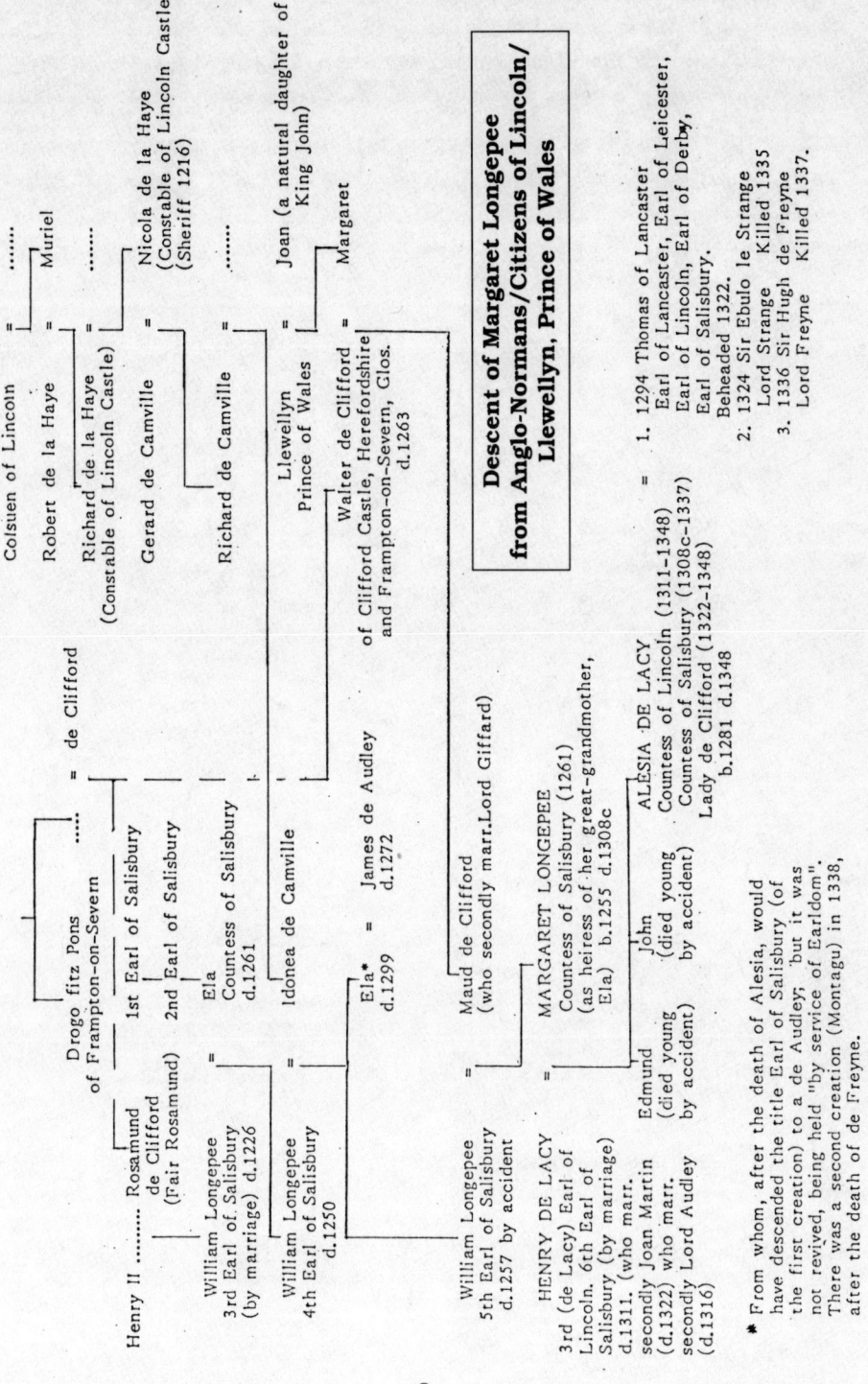

# CHAPTER 1

Heiress because of tragedies, for Alesia herself there was in her life hope, drama, fears and despair. The news of the first cries of a daughter for the de Lacy family passed by word of mouth by traveller, friar and merchant - there was sycophantic praise; there was anxiety, though Margaret her mother had survived, no further births could follow. There was already jealousy against the family by rival Lords for their great power, and disparagement from former Norman families chauvinistically proud of their assimilated England, because of Alesia's Italian grandmother.

There were those who looked thoughtfully at their own infant sons, reflecting on any past or passing connection with the de Lacy family, and how such might be suitably developed to marriage in a few years. Alesia would be bringing with her a powerful connection, even though she had two brothers to accede to the family lands and estates and privileges.

Alesia's father was Henry, the Earl of Lincoln; by position, desire, temperament, and virtually hereditarily, a right-hand man of the King, Edward the First. He expressed his joy and pleasure to his wife. The world outside could be an unfriendly influence to be met united, for without each other neither of them had a foundation on which to lean or rest. There were many, too, who based their lives and security on the de Lacy family - those near to them in their livery. The communities in their many manors could at least appreciate some vicarious prestige.

The baptism of the Lady Alesia was on Christmas Day, 1281, and the news spread far within the twelve days. In Rhuddlan Castle, where the event took place, there was a mighty cheer. This was swollen by masons, carpenters, plumbers and their labourers brought here from many counties, who were resting that day.

Shortly they would begin the building of castles at Denbigh and Ruthin. These were part of the reserve defence line of the "English" in Wales, all the time anticipating permanent homage from Llywelyn, Prince of Wales. In the meantime the former small Welsh castles were to be occupied in as much comfort as could be obtained.

While the food and drink of the Christmas festivities was devoured as gluttonously as ever, there had been a muted air in the talk and thought until the news was known. There was always that natural danger of upsetting the balances of feudal social structure if anything went wrong. Births were mysterious, and a great physical strain. Prayers had been somewhat prolonged that morning, for safe deliverance, but one or two cynical ones thought it was because Prior Meredew was gaining time, hoping to make the announcement.

The two persons more immediately affected on the day of her birth were Alesia's brothers - alive, well, and at the time bored because on Christmas Day there was no building going on. Births were by no means new to them; in the rumbustious collection of hundreds of wives of labourers, workers, soldiers, attendants, there had been much talk, much grumbling and panic and distress at births taking place at the most inconvenient places. More were short-lived or dead than remained alive. Though Edmund was but six, and John but four years old, they were fully aware of what was afoot.

Edmund himself was alive also to the feelings of many in the congratulatory company, in that they were pleased out of duty and position in their dependence on their lord, rather than from personal feeling in the matter. John was excited, more curious; but both were interested and pleased for their father and mother. Because it was a girl they had no cause for jealousy.

She was called, simply, Alesia, after her grandmother, though the antagonism of two generations before had not been entirely forgotten.

Alesia, oblivious, slept. Her mother Margaret recovering, but not too well, aimed at little except to help her husband and her family. She was but twenty-six years old, but had been nearer more campaigns of battle than many soldiers. The area was now reasonably safe, but dependent all the time on the numbers of Welsh who may be re-gathering in the north western parts, for any victory was but temporary - it was easy for the Welsh to scatter and reform again in weeks. This time, however, Edward was determined to occupy North Wales with garrisons in castles. Skilled men and labourers were called from nearly every county in England to build them. The expense was enormous. The noise on a working day was great. But Edward had had enough of broken words and revived tribal emotions - nothing would stop attack after attack other than men, permanent men, stationed, provisioned, and alert.

So here were the de Lacys, ultimately to have Denbigh Castle, strangely with Margaret herself being descended from Llywellyn the Great, Prince of Wales. Her mother had urged Archbishop Peckham to absolve the recent last Llywelyn so that he could be buried in consecrated ground. It had been a gesture from feeling on personal grounds, in respect of her mother's father.

Four years previously the campaign in North Wales had been victorious. There was the treaty of Conwy of 1277 to ratify it. Rhuddlan castle then began to be the subject of massive building operations. Henry said that Edward was coming to stay for a long time. He had never found him so firm; once and for all Wales was to be united with England - because - "Every time we go to my inheritance in France the Welsh take advantage. Or took advantage," he continued, getting used to the new situation, though it had not yet been proclaimed.

Henry, as the man himself, took pleasure at his little daughter's new life, delight so evident as he looked down at her.

"What eyes of dark beauty she has" he exclaimed, in a far from formal tone.

Henry was tall, and his oval, kindly face made him look approachable to all, as indeed he was. It also made him look influenceable, which he was not. He undertook the leadership of forces and political journeys hiding his personal fears and doubts, all with an ingrained fatalism and a sense of humour.

"I thought you might have remarked that you yourself were baptised on Christmas Day" said Margaret. He said that he had to forego that sort of thing this year in all the attention paid to mother and child.

"Thirty two years ago. Possibly things were more peaceful then." He added: "and more secure."

Margaret took up the last aside remark.

"What does that last bit mean?"

There was no-one else around, so he continued: "Just that this Kingdom" - he avoided making it personal to Edward - "already owes more to Ricardi of Lucca alone than it is likely ever to repay. There are others than them, and there's lots more to borrow, for this castle building alone."

"But the duty on wool was meant to pay..."

"It's got far beyond that. Anyway more money comes from Guienne alone than comes out of England. However, that's not much of a subject for today."

"No. But it bears much on us. Do we have to travel anywhere soon?"

It was not likely. Discussion moved to household matters. They both knew the background - that all Welsh resistance had by no means been overcome.

The waking years for Alesia were as pages from a story book, demonstrated to her by the actions and reports of others. She was not excluded from the rooms where passing discussions took place. She was not averse to listening to the doings of so many people who had to give information and to ask for decisions. It passed for her as education by observation. The learning of Latin and Writing and Sums came later. What she absorbed, albeit unconsciously, was an instinct about people in their variety, most of whom were careful to appear pleasant and helpful to her.

That there should ever be other attitudes was apparent to her in her early years because she sometimes related what she knew to lesser folk in the entourage; this resulted in some tactless desires being expressed for Alesia to find out particular things. Of course she could not do that, nor know why there would be such interest in a particular matter. But realisation grew that she was special. It stultified her free communication.

Her brothers treated affairs much more importantly, learnt of horses and fighting - and particularly from their father - that men under their command were what they depended on, and on the spirit of those men. And their forebears were their heroes - as the Richard de

Lacy who defended Chateau de Gaillard for a year in King John's time, so that Philip of France treated him thereafter with respect and civility for his personal quality. Philip still took over Normandy, however; lost to England for ever after; helping thus to turn Anglo-Norman minds to England alone.

While Edward's castles and Edward's rule were bringing some peace, Llywelyn had refused homage - some five years before Alesia was born. Hostilities had begun the subsequent year. This year 1281 Llywelyn had been killed. His brother David ap Gruffydd, captured, was condemned at a Parliament in Shrewsbury to be hanged. At Caernarfon on the fifteenth of July 1283 Edward entrusted Henry de Lacy with David's son Llywelyn for his presumed safety - but only for him to be delivered to Richard de Boys. That Richard had his orders.

Henry was reassured that no harm was meant to the boy. Through his wife Margaret he had his interest as a distant collateral, and possession of much of the land. Indeed there had been a cousin Gwenllian de Lacy, who for some years had had custody of the Castle of Rhuddlan. After this betrayal, and his remonstrance, it was but little consolation when Edward said to him that his new prince, born at Caernarfon, the new Prince Edward, of Wales, would have the Welsh connection along with Alesia, because of her own Welsh birthplace. Alesia's wide, dark eyes scarcely gave away any of her thoughts and feelings. If anyone had been prescient enough to consider the matter, they would have realised that her habit of putting her finger on her lips, and lightly stroking them, was to prevent any outward sign. For she would have much to fear, much to cry about, and much to steel herself against. By the time she was six years old so much had been spoken about wars and actions in the name of the Kingdom, so many times had she been taken away from her playmates to travel to another castle, she had to grope for security of emotion to whatever she found constant - her mother, and to the church which was reassuringly similar wherever they went.

Henry de Lacy himself, often away for days, and sometimes many months - proud as he was of his daughter, and greatly affectionate towards her, had to report stories which she could not hear except with strain. Now he was away with the King in Gascony, for what seemed ever.

These first few years brought reminiscent tales of fighting in Wales - of a private war between Henry and the Earl of Surrey over certain lands, which the King had had to resolve - of the trial of David ap Gruffydd and anecdotes of the detail of King Edward's methods of determining his sovereignty in Wales. David having been executed for his revolt, by feudal law his lands had been claimed. Henry had been confirmed into lordship of a great tract of what was now to be called Denbighshire. Caernarfon had been the Welsh seat of Government for Gwynedd, and it was the title of Prince of Wales initiated by Llywelyn which had been attached to those lands, and thus it was appropriated.

All the Bards who could be found had been put to death, through Edward's determination to allow no loyalty other than to himself. It had resulted in peace, of the type that garrisons maintain.

Alesia's brothers were too young for them to do much more for her than to patronize or tease, so she was again just left to listen, and to play with the daughters of knights, master masons, and soldiers, without discrimination. But she learnt that her father was undisputably loyal to the King; that he had been granted many lordships for his support in addition to his already extensive holdings, and even de Grey's new grants at Ruthin were under him. But what was this Edward? With such power as he had there must be some possibility of doing good, but now there was talk of expelling every single Jew from the Country. Alesia knew nothing about them, except that she had seen some in Chester and in Lincoln. They were always kept apart; they seemed to have all the money, and she'd heard that hundreds and hundreds had been hung. It was only once, about money, that anyone had been rude to her mother - a Jewish boy, from behind a wall. There had been a flung stone and a sharp taunt about Italians taking over and it would be their turn next. There was that feeling about. Margaret was very shaken, at the thought that they themselves had anything to do with usury. Grandmother Alesia would have been most voluble in response.

The Welsh Wars and French expeditions had to be paid for by borrowing. In Edward's reign wool had multiplied in price by six times, and it was in the hands of Italian merchant bankers, so he could borrow from them. Local manorial organisation continued in the ordinary way - the de Lacy retainers expanding by seven chaplains at Denbigh, one at Canford, and two at Kingston in Dorset.

By now Alesia had travelled considerably, so young as she was; she had gained juvenile impressions of castles in the North, West, North-East, and Lincolnshire, at Chester, Clitheroe, Pontefract, Lincoln, and Bolingbroke, and on returning to Denbigh, another de Lacy castle at Halton in Cheshire. She had memories of nights at priories and abbeys, camps on moors in all weathers, watching huntsmen bring in their quarry - and the excitement and bustle of new places, even down to London. But now they were at Denbigh Castle again.

It was different for Alesia this time. Instead of the comfort of a litter, or more recently an occasional scamper to keep up alongside, this time she was to ride her own pony. Their next journey was to be as far as Leicester; then the de Lacy family were to go to Bolingbroke, except for Henry who would continue to London to go onward from there to France with the King.

Denbigh Castle had made progress in the building. The outer wall had nearly completed its circuit so as to encircle a little town. The chapel of St. Hilary was completed, a haven for peace among the continuing construction works, and necessary for prayers and worship, some now to do with the forthcoming expedition. There was the silence of sullen interest in the locality from the Welsh population, at the arrival of the entourage, contrasting with the pleased attention of the masons, carpenters, plumbers, lime burners, labourers, nearly all from England. The Welsh had not all turned their loyalties to the new rule; the English felt safer with the presence of their lord.

But Henry was not remaining for long. The area was now considered safe, and Wales to be at peace. Some of his work was to do with his own affairs, such as obtaining pardon from the King for taking without licence two bucks in Rockingham forest, and another in Rotel forest; such as permission to sport along certain rivers; and, more important, protection against legislation at home in his forthcoming absence overseas. He nominated Peter of Chester and William de Vavasur to protect his interests. He enquired into the matter of Wiliam de Eyton who had had land taken from him by Peter Corbet; land, moreover, in North Wales that Henry had himself freed, in company with Roger de Mortus Mari, from the Welsh rebels.

It was going to be two or three years before he returned, so as much as possible was cleared up as had been at every castle - quitclaims to land for nuns; alienation of land to priories; decisions for master foresters; appointments for duties and offices. Enough was enough, and in due course his attitude was that the rest could wait. Leaving all that aside, he sought the report of his steward, John de Cresacre.

"We'll want to be off in two or three days, John. Apart from the usual problems, the only one is splitting up at Leicester."

"The Lord Edmund of Lancaster will no doubt let us have spare horses there; and men, sire, if required. We should have enough, but there's always the possibility of lameness."

"True. I have a message that all is ready for us, but he will have left for London."

"My lord, the only question I have is, of course, exactly which day we are to leave, and particularly who should escort the Lady Margaret and your family from Leicester to Bolingbroke."

"Three days ahead, John, on the Feast of St. Matthias. The escort -" he pondered, so many were going overseas, "de Frene may be at Leicester, perhaps."

"No, my lord, I hear he is going overseas as well. Your own sons are just too young, I feel."

"I wasn't thinking of them, no. I would be happy with you escorting them, John. I would have to do without you for the last week or two, but you deserve a rest."

Alesia was down in the outer bailey with her friend Phillipa and her father Philip de Burle, the chief marshal of the de Lacys. They were at the blacksmith's, where the roan coloured pony to be Alesia's own property, was being shod. De Burle reassured her that the pony was on the large side for her at present, but mostly because it was safer and more reliable for a journey. De Burle smiled at Alesia's obvious pride in having her own mount.

"It will be a change from borrowing a few miles as pillion on a palfrey" he remarked. "Phillipa will be beside you. Your brothers will no doubt be with you; apart from your parents of course."

Alesia wondered about her brothers' interest in her, because they were always leaving the household group, but she did not remark on it. She stood in silent interest as the shoeing was finished, with arms akimbo a picture of well nurtured authority, plain red bandeau holding tidy her long black hair, her black bodice and red skirt down to her ankles all simple and groomed, to show a composed and assured little girl.

"Has she a name?"

"So far, usually, Agnes...if that will do. Or any other, it's not too late."

"Why Agnes?"

"Because Agnes of the Stables was present at the foaling, and the men found it the first name to hand."

Alesia thought it was nice, and hoped Agnes the pony would not be quite as vigorous as her forthright namesake. At the end of the discussion the pony turned towards her, perhaps wondering why the talk had ceased. It was really what she had been waiting for - she made her number with Agnes. A short ride in the constricted space in the narrow lanes and alleys, already nearly jammed with wagons and packs and goods and people, was a difficult, certainly slow, initiation. More tomorrow, with an escort, outside the town. De Burle thought it was time to go to Hall for supper, after which night would fall. He was surprised that nurse Mary had not come yet to fetch her.

It was instinct or hunger more than timekeeping, that brought folk to their supper, all aided by the feeling from the sun and in the air that the day was at its ending hours. Most days assembly was nearly complete at the sound of the first horn. Showing an example of regularity were Henry and Margaret, and younger son John; Alesia managed it also this day. Officers of the household were present, the tables were ready with salts, spoons and cups, with mazers for the top table. There was subdued talk of John the Huntsman's day, and banter as to whether it would be mutton tonight or a more exciting animal. Such talk as there was fell quieter. The Earl Henry was getting impatient, for Edmund was very late.

Alesia stole a look at her father, just two places away, and while she knew it wasn't her fault, she knew that, kind as he was, her father was pleasant while people did, or even only tried to do, what was expected of them. If he was disappointed or crossed, then his attitude became cold and disapproving for a long time. So it was better to keep up, and why was Edmund being so stupid as to ignore assembly for supper. Margaret began to soothe the atmosphere.

"Perhaps he is too thoroughly absorbed in the construction works."

This was because Edmund had always taken a detailed interest in the defence arrangements for the castle, the style of the building, the thickness required for the walls, the possible angles of any attack, even the internal communications under siege. It was well known he had this absorption, and he may have missed the evening drawing in.

Henry did not feel he would go so far as to produce a lecture on discipline. He contented himself with a short irrelevance.

"That will all be there for him tomorrow."

Edmund did not arrive, however. So Henry began to make enquiries.

"Who was with Edmund? Surely someone must have been with him."

There was silence except for whispered conjecture, when John the Huntsman thought he had better speak if no-one else was going to.

"My Lord of Lincoln," the formality surprised the company, but John had scented the feeling of the Lord Henry, "on our return this afternoon I think I noticed the lord Edmund on the south wall with two others whom I presumed to be masons or labourers."

"You think?"

"My lord, we were too far away for recognition, and it was only by his stance and attitude that I just thought that it was the lord Edmund."

So Margaret suggested they began to eat, and to send to inform Edmund that his presence was required. Henry agreed. It was strange, though. It was only a couple of hundred yards to the far side of the enclosure. The supper horn might have carried that far. The lower table folk ate the meat, soup and boiled beef in silence. The savour of the pigeon and snipe was not the same. It would be relaxing to be assured that all was well with the lord and his family. Alesia sat stroking her bottom lip with her teeth. She couldn't think of anything to say. Margaret was asking questions about the organization of their forthcoming journey. She had her own anxieties about her husband going on a military expedition far away.

John de Lacy did not show his feelings when his father asked him to go and fetch his brother Edmund. He wanted his supper, he thought it was about damn time Edmund turned up, but he knew better than to say more than 'yes, sir'. John the Huntsman went with him, with similar unspoken reservations.

It was difficult to believe that anything untoward had happened to Edmund, but irritation began to turn to anxiety nevertheless. It was certainly strange. There had been no quarrel, nor had Edmund been reprimanded, so no cause existed for him to taunt his father. He had not been sent out of the castle on any errand. The possibility of any kidnap by Welsh marauders was discounted, for they would have been noticed. Henry beckoned the almoner, who had been out that day among the poorest. No, he had heard nothing of any activity, nor had scented any hint of trouble.

All of them now in hall were worried. There was no conversation any more, and meals were lying unfinished. None took more from the servants. The whole group tensed in helplessness without a lead, which only Henry could give. It was getting darker, and to him this meant that something was very wrong.

"Trumpeter! Go to the door, go to all corners of this place. Give the assembly call." Henry continued to his wife: "He must surely come at that. I will go out and find out what's the matter. De Monyton!"

The seneschal rose quickly.

They left the hall into the gathering twilight. Four attendants automatically rose from their places, and went with them. All would have followed if they had known what to do.

"A quick patrol, sir, round the outside?" asked the Captain of the Guard.

Henry had not thought of that, not yet thinking that Edmund was really anything but alright, but just somewhere where he should not be. This raising of a hidden fear jolted him somewhat.

"Yes" he replied and moved on.

At her place on the top table Alesia looked and wondered at the tense faces of the throng. Just because Edmund wasn't here. He always had his own interests, particularly in castles; but she herself was guarded wherever she went. For this very mealtime she had bubbled into hall, remembering her day, loving the communication with Agnes that she'd had - the look in the pony's eye, the feeling of accord when she touched her. But at this time she had to hold herself back, because she was sure that no-one was going to listen. There were tears beginning to descend.

Margaret turned to her.

"He'll be alright," she comforted, "but he has gone too far, and displeased his father."

Alesia looked up wide-eyed and her sudden realization opened her lips. So her mother thought that something was amiss. However could that be. Castles were safe. Every danger of travel, injury from animals, fighting, and childbirth and illness had been in Alesia's cognisance. But at the end of a journey the castle gate shut, was guarded, and everything was meant to be secure, to be home.

Edmund was not found quickly. The purpose of the assembly call on the trumpet was to bring Edmund forward. Secondarily it was to gather the soldiers to their stations, and to alert the townspeople, so that inquiries could be made. The state of emergency became total, as the trumpeter circulated the whole community, and word of the purpose of the search was spread from one to another. The resonance of the notes diminished with the evening light as his round progressed.

Henry and de Monyton cast their eyes round the walls of the inner bailey, from near the door of the hall.

"It is not possible, surely, for him to have gone off outside on some visit?"

"No, lord, Edmund is not foolhardy." de Monyton would like to have reassured Henry with a positive statement that Edmund must be in the castle somewhere. Any speculation might be disproved, however.

"He might have gone to the Priory and a message miscarried" said Henry, at the same time ordering two soldiers to go at once to find out.

Henry hesitated before going further, to the outer bailey which contained the beginnings of the town. Edmund would come back this way. Was that he? He caught his breath. It was his second son John, John the Huntsman, and de Burle accompanied by two men. The masons who had been noticed had been identified. The problem of the whereabouts of Edmund began to turn in Henry's mind into the serious nature of an inquiry. He had to speculate with deep anxiety that what had happened was beyond Edmund's control. Damn the darkness. Scarcely a moon. Henry interrogated the masons both together.

"Was the lord Edmund with you at all today?"

"Yes, lord"

"Where?"

"On the north wall where we're building the Bastion Tower, sir."

Henry cut the questions to the minimum.

"Did he leave alone, or were either of you with him?"

"He left alone, sir."

William de Voil, the more intelligent of the two asked for permission to describe what he could.

"Of course, of course."

"My lord, the lord Edmund took some interest in our construction work, which was to do with stones of rather difficult uneven radius."

Henry wondered if he should have allowed this because of the inevitable irrelevancies. But he continued to listen:

"We hadn't much more material, so the lord Edmund left us, just after the hunt came in. We left shortly after along the finished wall. The lord Edmund went along the wall towards the Goblin Tower where we had previously worked. Then I suppose he went down the ladder there to the bailey."

"All the way down?"

"I don't really know about that, my lord. I did just look, but he is used to it."

Henry looked up, at the word 'is', he had wondered if it had any special expression. He could trace none. de Voil assumed the next requirement:

"I did not remark where the lord Edmund went, sir, except for the first two or three yards. It was simply, at that time, as though he was going - pardon, coming, in this direction."

The other mason had nothing to add; what had been said was correct.

de Monyton asked if Edmund had been agitated, or worried, but they knew him and they said that he had been normal.

Henry was so tense with thoughts about the possibilities that he was quite ready to allow Margaret to give orders, for she had just arrived.

"There is one question." She stated. "Did Edmund come this way at all?"

The guard commander was firm that he had not, and that they had been all the time on duty.

"Then, we will retrace his way from where he was last seen."

She ascertained the name of the second mason as Godwin Fox. She had hoped that she could remember Edmund ever having mentioned them, but not.

Lit by torches, her husband, son John, and with the others who had helped, and half a dozen soldiers of the guard, they all moved off to where Edmund had last been seen. They searched as best they could in what was by now darkness with the occasional moon between the clouds.

They reached the foot of the ladder by which William de Voil had said Edmund may have descended from the north-east tower. It was an awkward route to get there, and to stay together in the narrow confines of buildings was not easy; and the groups of people, curious at the commotion, impeded progress. But there was opportunity to seek any information. It was negative. Attitudes were various. The de Lacys, however, could not notice in the gloomy light indifference in some, and a sardonic twitch on lips of others at their plight, a weakness in the mighty.

So if Edmund had not gone the straight way which they had come, wherever in this constricted place had he been? Yes, if he definitely came down this ladder, it was sometime before the evening, and it was possible for him to have made a circuitous route. Suddenly de Burle turned to the mason de Voil. He was about to ask where there was any other work that Edmund might wish to inspect. The same thought had occurred to de Voil, and it caused him a nervous gesture. It was a dreadful thought that he had had. If Edmund was really missing, lost, then there was only one other place with specially shaped stones, of unequal radius.

"Come, man, tell us!" demanded Henry, for all had now turned to de Voil. In the flickering light, held near his face, his distressed features, and attempts to utter were of themselves portentous. de Voil tried to control his fears, tried not to produce a scare. He was able to indicate with an arm that they should walk along the foot of the wall. Henry encouraged him to be calm, to say what he could, and de Voil managed a little, when Henry asked if the peculiarly curved stones had been significant. Henry knew the castle plan in detail, and he began to think that the Red Tower would have these features. But the soldiers who had been sent round the perimeter had found nothing. That was outside. Henry knew that inside there, the Red Tower, was a deep stone lined well..

He stood stock still. He would not move forward even with Margaret's utmost encouragement. de Voil whispered quickly to de Burle, who swiftly in anxiety spoke.

"Lord Henry, I beg you to go back. We will do what we can; will bring you what news we can. Please do not stay, lord."

They did bring the news. It was in the first morning light that Edmund's body was hauled up.

The next day the procession to the Priory wound its way slowly and silently to the service for the interment.

"This woe will last for life" muttered John the Huntsman. "It is not a cloud that will roll by." It was an old saying, but it served for his reading of the appearance of Henry and Margaret de Lacy. His thoughts rambled on, without utterance, as to Henry de Lacy, the Great Earl of Lincoln and of Salisbury, owner of most of Denbighshire and thousands of acres of England, holding so much power in this land. A man whose power could be taken from him by the King by nothing more than an instruction to a scrivener. A man whose spirit was invaded by an Act of God in removing from him his elder son, and removing that son in terms that carried no accolade of pride, no battle honour, but just an irrelevance in his life of missing a board over a well. Yet that lord had killed, had caused to be killed, and had led men to do the same or to be killed themselves. John the Huntsman could get no further with his ruminations, and returned in mind to his world of animals who knew no God.

That night de Voil chiselled off his carving of a goblin on the Goblin tower and smoothed the stone so that it seemed that it had never been. It was too recently conceived for comfort. His resolve to throw it, or was it him, down the well weakened as he worked. The carving of the elfish creature had been his, every line of expression did he know. In uncertainty of mind he took it to the pile of uncut stone a hundred yards away and laid it, or him, gently down. He hoped someone else would do something in due course with the material, not he.

All the people and garrison of Denbigh now had to wait for further decision on the next move in the preparations for the journey. The news had reached Ruthin and Rhuddlan, maybe to Chester. But only confirmation of Henry's duty to the King to present himself for service in Gascony could be given. All settled to their daily tasks again.

The Earl's secretary, Thomas Halton, was preparing documents for the situation as he guessed it to be. Thomas had grown up in the Earl's service, indeed had recently adopted the name of his master's Halton castle for himself, having come from that manor. From keen observation of situations in baronial households he was generally prepared with an opinion or a draft letter. As an aside now he was particularly kind to Alesia. He had noticed her pressing forward at the graveside, trying to see and trying to understand.

"I am sure, milady, that you have seen created things become bereft of life by death. We can believe only that Edmund's soul is commended by God. He can have done no wrong."

Alesia was silent. She wondered what would happen next, how could life be normal again? Her mother and father were distraught, with the imminent needs of duty impending so soon, the comfort of their being together was to be but for a week or two. It was, however, not duty, not the drafts of notes which Thomas Halton had to put before them - notes to the King, to three families informing them of Edmund's death and that thus there could be no further negotiation on a marriage contract - notes to the commissariat at places on their route that there would be a short delay - notes and instructions for prayers for his soul - it was not those which made Margaret break down, her pent tension breaking on an instant.

Into the castle, into the courtyard, three dishevelled riders, as weary as their horses, arrived noisily with messages for the Earl. To the Countess and him they told a brief story.

"Lord, I have to report at once to you that the King of Scotland has been killed." The one who spoke, a staunch and strong fellow, one Thor Boket, sensed that this news had more effect than he had expected. Usually lords looked up and treated his announcements as information to be worked on. Thor continued: "after leaving Stirling Bridge. By the shore after a boat journey. He got lost in the dark and there was an accident with his horse at Inverkeithing, where he was found..." and his voice had faded and hesitated. On a gesture of Henry's hand they all bowed and left.

Margaret banged her fists on the table by her. She breathed in deep and desperately. She crashed her elbows on the arms of her chair. She shouted - "Is it never going to end?"

"After Wales, it will now be Scotland. After killing Welsh it will be killing Scots. Alexander had only just married and now Edward will have to solve that problem. And cousin Nicholas de Audley killed, and others will be. But it is said Wales is at peace. Concussed, more like. I'm concussed."

Margaret wept. They were preparing for as much sleep as they were likely to get that night. Henry was in no better shape, except trying to put their tragedy into the context of what Antonio the parson had said - that they were one of many people with tragedies, and humble worship of God's greater purposes was the only way calm could come. Had not the King and Queen recently lost their baby eldest son, Alfonso? They would also look with greater love upon John and Alesia as the focus of their family. It had not yet dawned on Alesia the full depth of feeling the death of Edmund had engendered. To John, it had been remarkable to see such grief for his elder brother, which he could not believe within himself could ever be his own due. He was to try and adopt his brother's interests so as to achieve such worth, so little could he understand. For whereas Edmund had been practical and constructive, John was the mercurial type, with much in theory which was in but never left his mind.

Towards the later hours of night, but not the later hours of sleep, which had not come, Margaret turned and touched Henry so that he was awakened. She had had pictures in her mind of the body, in the water, and misshapen as it would be out of the water. To close her eyes clarified the horror, striking as at part of her. She and he had been in the same household so many years. They knew each other so closely thus, even more than marriage itself could blend. She had got on with Henry especially, rather than his brother John, whose wife she would have become if Henry had chanced to die. Henry and Margaret had been the inseparable ones. So there was not much need for explanations, as Margaret spoke. Her face was down towards the sheet, her shoulders throbbed. Her hand groped for him in the dark.

"I can't come back here."

Henry was astonished to find his own thoughts expressed. He knew that he had now lost interest in completing the castle, but he had been thinking more of his next two or three years away and hoping that he might be better able then to carry on. But Margaret had clarified the matter.

"No more can I."

And there was comfort in each other. To himself Henry hoped his words were final, though that depended on the understanding and goodwill of King Edward. If he really did have to return in time perhaps the vision would have been sealed over. Maybe parson Antonio was right. At first Henry had thought he was being snide because of the King abridging church powers. And what about the others? Sons had been lost, and daughters had suffered too. It was not long since the Welsh were at the gates of Chester. They burnt St. Asaph Cathedral on the way, so anything less was not expected to be saved. How foolish it was. The Welsh could not possibly defeat the larger and greater England, yet every time Edward relaxed, in they came. This time, however, in every strategic place a new castle and garrison would hold troops for control. Nothing else could be done. Perhaps they would come round to proper rule, but they all looked sour at the Nevin tournament a couple of years ago. That is, all except a few whose attitude was insincere. Damn good campaign, though, supported by sailing vessels along the north coast. The south had been easier, it had been said, just military infiltration.

Just before six this Spring morning the dawn sun illuminated the valley, the town, the castle, the people all rising and reacting to their forthcoming tasks. Henry's final decision was still required as to their day of departure.

"Tomorrow."

He explained to Margaret that this would enable them to celebrate Easter at Leicester before separating their journeys. If any administration was not done, then it would have to follow him. His order focussed the day for all. To secretary Halton alone he confided.

"Let us get away. Don't worry about ordinary furniture. Have all valuables escorted to Pontefract. There's the standing furniture at Bolingbroke and not much room. There's no time limit, but it ought to be done before there's any fuss about what people might guess is the real reason."

Thomas Halton bowed slightly to indicate understanding.

"If I stay behind to do this, may I take the conducting of the wagons on the journey myself?"

"Yes. Then proceed to Bolingbroke to see the family is properly there, and then to London."

Henry was always particular and there was a rehearsal of all the personnel necessary. There were assemblies of soldiers on foot, soldiers on horses. Musters of soldiers to stay behind. Checking of baggage, supplies and stores. Examining kit, horses, wagons. Esquires reported throughout when their tasks were done. Incomplete supplies and stores could not be made up later.

The family would be travelling with an escort of about sixty men, not a large number relative to de Lacy importance, but in accordance with Henry's usual habit. It expressed his feeling that trappings were false indicators of importance. There were Agnes brought forward for Alesia, a colt for John, a fine mare for his mother, and a chestnut for Henry - his favourite mount, which by spring and grace stood finer than all others, even to the untutored eye.

Henry usually enjoyed these travels, and the hunting on the way. They would go via Halton, Beeston, and Tutbury. The baggage train was a separate organization. Slower, escorted, taking spare horses, and cluttered with unconnected hangers-on seeking safe travel; full of bucolic jollity in the adventure of movement; and even slower at each county boundary when all the goods from the hired wagons had to be unloaded, and re-loaded into those domiciled in the next county.

In all the hours that came there had been work done to provide mourning habits, particularly for the ladies, paramountly for Margaret and Alesia. Local tailors and seamstresses were always ready for such, and with material in store, experience and ideas in their heads. Because the start tomorrow was to be at first light, Margaret and Alesia were dressed, and sat in their saddles, as practice in the late afternoon, just moving round the courtyard.

It was enough as their mounts stepped round the area for those nearby to fall silent. If the consequences of death gave compensation in pale sepulchral beauty, then this was it.

# CHAPTER 2

It was as much an event as a spectacle that the people and workmen and garrison of Denbigh castle turned out for the departure. It would be some long time, they thought, before they would see the array of the de Lacys again, not knowing that it might even be never. There was fear as well that brought them crowding to the occasion, for it was always uncertain what Welsh action might be and whether the garrison would prove strong enough, or sometimes even loyal.

Denbigh had fallen to a campaign under Henry de Lacy, and he had been given the lands of Rhufyniog, Rhos, and Dinmael, to form a large lordship. A few years before, in October 1282 the King had been there with him, accompanied by the military engineer James of St. George, planning the new castle and town. Now these extensive works were to continue under the latter's direction. He served for thirty years. He had been found by Edward the first in Savoy when returning from a Crusade, as the mason in charge at the Castle of St. Georges d'Esperanche.

The baggage train might not leave for a day or two. The Earl's own party, officials, and escort were mounted, and in order, inspected, in casual positions which would, on movement, fall into their ordered place. Young John de Lacy and Alesia came from the porch of the Great Hall to their mounts held ready. John helped Alesia to mount, the ostler moved away to help Mabota who looked after her. John himself mounted, and all waited for their Lord and his Countess. It was a short pause, but long enough for all to notice Alesia, as a statue in her still expression, lips squeezed a bit, but in her long black velvet gown trimmed with white, black feathered hat, a white chin band, on Agnes whose black mourning saddle blanket was emblazoned with the de Lacy arms. Alesia's black hair, dark eyes, and pale skin completed a picture of childhood for the silent admiration of everyone present. Robert son of Roger, an archer, was surprised to admit to himself that here was one whom he would rather save to live than he himself.

With that introduction, Margaret's similar costume did not achieve the impact that it should have done, just admiration and interest. For Margaret herself nothing could have been better, tired as she was with lack of sleep and worry. She was there, now mounted, and to her present surroundings nature by exhaustion had dulled her feelings. On the way down to the Burgess's gate she looked neither right nor left, nor seemingly looked anywhere at all. Not that communication with the party was especially expected; it was only calls to soldiers, farewells to grooms, that passed, and Alesia smiled nicely to three or four who had been her friends the last few weeks. Henry himself had said farewell solely to de Burle, his steward, who would be responsible for revenues, administration and good order in his absence. They had to ride past the outer wall where Edmund had last been seen. Neither Henry nor Margaret turned that way, nor ever looked back. They had been down to the Priory the previous evening to pray for Edmund's soul, so they did not now stop, but one matter was on Margaret's mind.

"I wonder if he should have been buried at Stanlaw."

Henry understood fully that a burial in an abbey supported by the family would be more appropriate and more comforting. It was impossible to travel all the way to North Lancashire, however, in the time he himself had available.

"Let us think about that when I am returned. I am not against the thought. Perhaps we have been..." he did not want to say hasty because that would make matters never rest, and fortunately he was interrupted by the arrival of the Captain of the Guard, accompanied by the guide. The Earl replied to them:

"Correct. To Chester, as planned. I am glad you confirm that parties have gone ahead. John the Huntsman should be at Beeston ahead of us, where we shall stay for a day's hunting."

It was his practice to lay on late morning refreshment on a journey. It was in his resources to provide for himself and his followers comparatively civilized living. There was not always a convenient castle at which to break a day's journey. Life was more often than not in the open air, at best scarcely shielded from any wind and rain. Henry, and indeed those with him heartily agreed, wanted midday refreshment above the ordinary rations which they carried.

As they approached the valleys of the Flintshire Hills, new-called, but Clwyddian to the Welsh, Henry beckoned his son John to ride alongside.

"Before long the Captain of the Guard should be coming to me to ask permission to patrol the hilltops. It should be interesting to you to do this. Go to him and detach a couple of archers and four men-at-arms. The reason is to make sure that our party is not observed nor attacked by marauders."

John knew the background, and that sometimes there was much more difficult terrain over which to act as scout for a convoy, though he was but ten years old.

"Are there any particular soldiers that I should take, father? Or not?"

Henry was impressed by his lapse being noted, but he had been thinking of their own personal problem, and was anyway assuming that the land was safe. Loyalty, however, always came into question.

"Leave that to Captain Ralf, but take specifically Sergeant Thedric. Oh, here is Captain Ralf coming up, so please deal with him."

John turned his colt, after a crisp 'yessir' which seemed right to both. Henry fell to considering the characters of the soldiers in the escort. He knew most of them well from his campaigns of the last few years. The sergeant Thedric was clear-headed, strong, and personable. Nothing but straightforward action would enter his head, because he enjoyed the life, and his status was adequate to him. The soldiers varied from that kind of loyalty and ability down to two or three of the archers who preferred to be an arrow-flight length from any possible trouble.

His son's posse had now become detached and Henry turned to see who was in it. Of the two men at arms one, Walter son of Simon, was direct and honest yet so unthinking that he would agree with one suggestion put to him one minute and the opposite the next. Yet he understood the suitable use of his strong right arm. Another, Alan Punchard, was strong enough, pushing all the time, and would not listen to an argument in the first place. Yet a good man when there was an enemy about, the nearer the better. Henry noted that at least there was none with his son who was totally against authority, in fact he was satisfied to believe that there was none such in the whole escort.

Fingering her pendant cross for such comfort as it gave her in controlling grief at the tragedy of Edmund's death, Margaret moved to her husband's side, having observed without interference her younger son being given a little responsibility. She had to think that it was wise, but that progression forward into the dangers of life for John had jolted her. She had to be consoled.

"It is part of his training. Of course I do not perceive any loose gangs approaching..." he said, instead of saying 'attacking' - "us. It will give him something positive to go for. Look - he's leading a brisk line along the top there."

Margaret had had a thousand thoughts of retreat, or retirement from this world, of her life's effort lost and unrenewable. That emptiness she felt would always be there. As she rode silently for a few miles alongside she had to feel also that these thoughts must also be Henry's, that his work was carrying him forward to all outward appearance the same man. She held up her head again; her mind became clear. She explained nothing, yet she explained all to him:

"I would have you do nothing other than what you do, nor be any other than what you are."

Henry and she exchanged a look of expressive closeness. He did not speak. He could not speak.

It was now that Alesia began to realise the void that Edmund's death was leaving in her life. People had passed through her few years in great variety and in great numbers. In a life with travel every summertime, and some winters, nothing had been settled, no relationship constant. Officials, servants, clerks, horsemen had been at different places, then a gap of months before they were seen again. Only some of the household were always with them. Even their work suffered from changing personnel. Death from illness, from cold, from injury, all these had been seen by Alesia, and much more heard of. For constancy, for security on which to rest one's mind, however, there was, she now could understand and feel within her, nothing except the family.

She looked along the hillside and there was John. There was no

Edmund. She realised that he was truly gone except in memory. Now that Agnes had been at one with her for some miles she had little need to urge her; she followed with the group. So she began to wonder about her own place. She had grown up a little more.

While Alesia had enjoyed the fun of splashing through the river Clwyd on Agnes, and loved the spring-flowered colours of the rolling landscape, the minds of the men were mostly elsewhere, not least that of her father. Movement was, however, at an easy pace, indeed that of the slowest. There was much for the men to arrange in the weeks to come, and unless at least the next six months were planned, it was difficult to keep a great household in being. The needs were those of an estate within the national estate, and effected much on the same lines as the Kingdom, the King's estate. The Steward, the Receiver, the Auditor trotted their horses with the rest, accompanied by their assistants, and their basic paraphernalia. Final instructions would come from Henry at any time over the next three weeks before he embarked.

In spite of all, Henry was looking forward to going to France, but could not prevent himself feeling selfish in the exhilarating anticipation of moving to different places and customs. As they passed near Caerwys he did keep a weather eye open for any groups of Welshmen there may be, because there was deep national feeling here. It was where Eisteddfords had been held for over two centuries. In the late morning now they were passing along the side of the river Alyn on the gradual downward route to Chester. And to England, thought Margaret, with relief. They were concluding a traverse around their scattered land possessions which they began a year before. She saw a party of men, horses, and a wagon by the riverside. She indicated it to Henry, who had already noted it, but did not say so. The Captain of the Guard detached two men to go and report. Yes, they were their own men; food had been purchased in Mold, fires had been lit, the Earl would find refreshments ready.

They all gathered in this fallow meadow by the riverside, for rest, for food; and river water for all and for the horses. Wayside picnics were Henry's sole concession to extravagance. Minor as it was, it was the only one in which he was interested, and partly because it kept military organization on its toes. And on that point, John, who had rejoined them, was told to get straight back onto his horse.

"Now look round, to check what scouts you have to post."

Then, in kindly banter, Henry added:

"They can also look out for saints or hermits. In Wales there's one in every valley."

So John observed the surroundings, but was stopped at once.

"You can tell nothing if you do it that way. Look there. Hold your head still. Examine the next bit. Stop. Move. Stop again - gaze at every point. Then you will see and perceive."

Soon John joined the family for wine. He spoke of the Welsh

defensive entrenchments he had seen on the hills, but for himself he preferred mobility.

Encouraged by the boy's interest, Henry sent him to report on the condition of the soldiers, the food they were to eat, their horses, and everything relative to what would help to make their next few hours' journey to Chester without mishap. On her own, having noticed that, Alesia told her maidservant Mabota to do the same for theirs and their ostler. All this exercise and its imitation over, the servants reported that the meal was ready; the cloths laid. All moved to suitable places on the sward, maintaining in a higgledy piggledy manner the order much as it would have been in hall. Peter Ridel, the Chaplain of the Countess, intoned the grace and all except helpers and assistants sat down. As it happened there was a suitable gap near Alesia, and Peter sat there. He felt it was fortuitous, and commenced to show that he was interested in the spiritual welfare of the child, and amiable enough for a friend. After the weather, "suitable but cool", had been disposed of, Peter pointed to the south west.

"Over there, the Christians of this area defeated the heathen Vikings - just by a great shout as that which felled the walls of Jericho."

"The Vikings here?"

"Yes, many, many seasons ago. All the Christians roared at the same time and it struck terror into the enemy. No blood was shed at all."

This raised questions as to why they were there in the first place; whether it was often tried in battles; and what it sounded like. Peter smiled, and said a practical demonstration would be difficult. He thought that here was a de Lacy alright. He did go on to say that the Vikings were then penetrating from the Isle of Man, which had belonged to them.

"Where's that?" asked Alesia, and gained some idea from the generality of the reply that Peter did not know exactly himself. She fell to thinking that dangers were likely to be anywhere. Peter realised his mixture of religious instruction and secular history had not improved his standing. He continued that he had been thinking of explaining this to all as a little homily in his grace before the meal, and at the same time putting in a word of thanks to her father that they were all properly looked after.

While Alesia was surprised at this first intimation to her that clerics had any doubt as to what should be said, her father, who had been overhearing, spoke louder to divert these matters. He was in part motivated by wanting to prevent Peter mentioning in his geographic/historic chat Bryn-ys-Ellyllion nearby, because of its being the Hill of Goblins, and would cause his wife distress.

It was about a six hour journey to Chester. A messenger was sent to Ewloe and to Hawarden castle near the route, giving compliments and advising that they were passing by. Henry suppressed the idea that this should not be done, to test if their lookouts were alert. They all then moved at an easy walk eastwards into the pastures of Cheshire. It was more relaxing where the more ordered society was so obvious, and seemingly one that cared more for their industry than their emotions. Henry was explaining to John how the English had tried to hold Wales by action at the border. Llywelyn ap Gruffydd, however, would not keep any promise, and kept raiding. Now, with Llywelyn dead these four years, and Edward's garrisons at all strategic places, let us hope it will be different.

"Who will finish Denbigh, father?"

Henry looked at him quickly, but it seemed an innocent question, just based on knowledge that he himself was to be away for some time.

"I have told James of St. George that he should do so. Whether he changes the plans or not is up to him. He's doing all the other castles."

They entered Chester castle well before the end of daylight, being welcomed by the guard outside, partly mounted with the dual function of presenting respect to the Earl as Constable of Chester castle, and of preventing entry to any party that was not his. Last year they had been at his main base, Pontefract castle, for much of the summer, followed by a move across the hills to Clitheroe where the de Lacys had lands and a smaller castle, down to Halton castle, on the river Mersey, then to Denbigh. Now, Chester was his own last chance to assess the state of the North, before leaving the country. What a difficult position England and its Continental dominions were in. Encircled by Scots, Welsh, Irish, and the French. If one looked after the North then the King of France took a province from the Anglo/Norman inheritance. Go south to France to maintain the boundaries, and the Scots came in. Or the Welsh. And the Irish help whoever caused the trouble. So what's the forecast this time? That night Henry suddenly hit the straw-filled paillasse which was on the settle. It popped up the other side. Then he hit it again, and a corner rose in reaction. He roared with laughter.

"What on earth are you doing?"

"Margaret, my dear, I am studying international politics. When they are cured in one place they just pop up in another, like this paillasse. That's all they are."

The next morning was enough for reports, collected by de Grey, Justice of Chester. There was time to examine the new choir works in the Cathedral, to order financial contribution to it, but not to wait for bowing respectfulness in exchange. That afternoon they reached Beeston castle. It was not a place for a long stay, unless of necessity. In an astounding position, perched hundreds of feet up prominently on a rock commanding the plain. Defended by its difficulty of access, that also dictated what it could provide for living, which amounted only to a gatehouse which doubled as a keep, with towers along the walls for followers.

There was plenty to talk about. Henry being taxed by his son John as to what did really happen some fourteen years before when he had had to besiege the castle. Illegally taken by Robert de Ferrers, the previous Earl of Derby, it was Edmund of Lancaster with Reginald de Grey and Henry whose forces had got him out. Henry gave a reticent description of their surprise attack, and suggested that at Leicester would be Edmund of Lancaster, and so John could ask him. He did add another note, however.

"It was ten years later that we received our pardon from the King for the deaths we had to cause, and those rebels who repented got it too. It is always some time before the written parchment catches up, and in the meantime one has to assume one did right."

Their immediate host, the Constable, Hamo le Strange, fully assured all that the effort had been most praiseworthy. He had had his appointment regranted.

A message arrived from Edmund of Lancaster, hoping they would enjoy hunting in his forests, and would stay at Leicester long enough. He would now be there to be their host. In such pressing terms was it couched that Henry continued to that castle without any delay at Tutbury. That was also a Lancaster place but it looked as though John the Huntsman had made a poor report of the present state of the surroundings, from his point of view. Game there was to eat, but at least he was not wishing to risk his reputation in the chase.

Another long day on the road would perhaps not matter, and Henry would contain his great desire for complete relief and outgiving excitement which came to him in the hunt. Their welcome at Leicester castle more than made up for their tiredness on arrival. Even Alesia was uplifted, she and Agnes having traversed forty miles since dawn.

Refreshed and settled, Henry and Edmund were deep in talk of all that had gone before in which they had shared, and in Henry's report on the state of the North and of Wales. Edmund, the older man, a son of King Henry III, was Earl of Leicester, Derby and Lancaster. His first wife had died some dozen years before, and with them now was his second Countess, Blanche, daughter of Robert, Count of Artois. She was speaking with Margaret, with great sympathy over the news of their son Edmund. It did not seem the moment to project what she really wanted to say, that is that one of her sons Thomas or Henry might well do for Alesia, but Margaret guessed something from the signs. It was not, however, her position to press her daughter forward, the offer had to come from the boy's parent, and no doubt if she waited it would come. The next day when all the ladies stayed indoors it was expressed. Blanche suggested the tentative consideration of a marriage contract in due course between Thomas and Alesia. Margaret expressed pleasure at the possibility, said that they had not really considered anybody yet, because it was early enough.

"I know nothing about what dowry and land arrangements there could be. We have not yet been able to think of the new position with

John and Alesia."

"Let's think of her just as a girl, then. My husband is so modest, and thinks he possesses far too much, anyway, and it is not property we are looking at. For myself, I am worth myself alone, and no more."

Next evening Alesia asked her mother a question to which she had a fair idea of the answer.

"Mother, why do you keep looking at me and then at Thomas?"

As it was, Thomas was more involved in a group discussing the day they had had. It had been long, tiring, and tough, thoroughly exhilarating to the strong and forthright youth that he was. They had hunted deer in Leicester Forest. They had runs to Glenfield, beyond Desford, down to Thurlaston with much untouched for the morrow. They had begun hard by Bromkinsthorpe in the west field of Leicester township. Over all this the hunting and warren were reserved exclusively to the Earls of Leicester. The foresters and keepers effected the double task of sport of the chase, and consequent provision of venison for the sustenance of the household. They had their instructions from Earl Edmund not to interfere with folk collecting small firewood, but those who took venison and large timber were tried before the Woodmote at Heathley. This conformed with Henry's own way of administration and the attitude of staff and rural folk in the clearing was pleasant enough to have enhanced the day. At daybreak grooms had located deer. Huntsman Hugh had inspected deer droppings in several runs, and had recommended those to put before Earl Edmund. His pack of hounds was, in variety, in colour and in appearance from greyhound to bloodhound, but each was tested, and worked together to make an effective pack. The needs were various, to flush deer from woody thickets, woods and marshes, and then to trace and follow them as they strained in hysteria to escape. The tracker dog, held by a rope tied to its collar, soon completed his task. The huntsman Hugh, now mounted, drew up his horn in its leather sling, and with the Earl's permission, all the hunters were informed by a deep blare, that the hunt was begun. The grooms in their tunics, hose, and boots, were armed with either stick or spear or knife, and most with horn. They moved on foot to keep hounds on track, or to find them when lost. In time they would help to divide and load the quarry on to a pony. The vivid life and excitement of the pursuit affected all so that fatigue was forgotten until the end, enhanced by the tang of the compulsive feeling that there was some tasty delicate meat at the end. Henry de Lacy's huntsman John was just assisting today, giving his opinion only when asked, because it was not his territory. He felt always an extra pride after a good day, and this was no exception. It was his added pleasure that the lords and gentlemen by their aggressive action in the hunt were the better prepared for war against England's enemies.

The exchange of views in the early evening was favourable to the day. The young Thomas, but four years older than Alesia, had shortened his day only through the fatigue of both his ponies. He saw Alesia before the others had returned, and weary and needing some communication, spoke with her.

"I understand we are being discussed, Alesia."

Alesia bobbed.

"I have been told about it...sir. I did have to ask. I hope that I may please you.... if it comes about."

"It seemed firm to me. What is your doubt... if what."

"It is a long time to pass, and much can happen in a few years."

"You sound a bit cautious, my dear."

Thomas was quite taken with the girl, but had no reason to be committed in his emotions. He was hardly yet a young man. There were other English and Foreign possibilities. He smiled, which was rare, and a pleasing beginning for Alesia. She asked if he had had a good day, and it seemed it was a subject on which at least he was happy to expound. He even promised to tutor Alesia something of it on the morrow.

That evening the talk of Edmund, Henry, Blanche and Margaret was all about the forthcoming years, and what they had to arrange. About Bolingbroke Margaret's opinion was clear:

"Safe, supplied with food, dull, but my children with me. Oh, Henry, I do not like your absences. I have to say that."

Henry said nothing about his tasks which made him travel. He was not expected to; he was not sure himself whether he liked them or not. It was something which had to be done, which had reward in achievement.

Edmund brought the conversation to practical matters. He, brother of the King, and both of them being sons of Henry III, was the first Earl of Lancaster. Now forty one years of age, he was always loyal to his brother and had no special ambitions for himself. At the early age of nine the Pope granted to him the Kingdom of Sicily. The assessable links with past Viking marauders had almost withered, and four years later the next Pope cancelled it. By the age of twenty four he had accumulated extensive lands and the earldom of Leicester, forfeited by de Montfort; the earldom of Derby forfeited by de Ferrers; the new Lancaster one; and by marriage those of Albemarle and Devon. Experience including a Crusade demonstrated little military ability but an easygoing and trusting nature. He was pleasant enough to all so as to have achieved a nickname. It was Crossback from the crusading garb of his one action which could demonstrate initiative. He was to be Regent while Edward was in France.

"I hope, Edmund, you will maintain a good peace for us while the King is away."

"My dear Margaret, all reports are to that end. I shall be holding a full meeting tomorrow. Wales can hardly rise, or not much, with so many garrisons to catch any trouble before it develops far. I do sometimes believe that we should have retained the Gascons we used in the campaign."

"Unbiased loyalty, you mean?"

"I do. It provided an unprejudiced and professional reserve. However, there can hardly be any bother."

"Scotland?" asked Margaret.

"The Scots have not moved south for a time."

"I know that, but I also know... perhaps I'd better not say it. I'll just put it that with no heirs near to the throne of Scotland, anything England does will be one more division in a disputed situation."

"Suitably vague," Edmund replied, and smiled, to Margaret's relief. "We know who you mean by England. Don't worry, dear, I shall not start anything. You will of course come to London to join with Blanche and me?"

"Of course, if it can be arranged. But we may wait the year of Henry's absence, and let the young have the fresh air and sport of Lincolnshire."

"Well, let us hope. I think my greatest worry is going to be money, money, money. There's been the Welsh war, the building of castles at great cost, but above all the Jews are apprehensive, with us using the bankers of Cahors, and the Lombards. However, I expect we'll get by. In fact, we've got to, haven't we?"

It was more the function of lay clerks than barons to worry about where money came from, though the King's indebtedness had already gone far past any point of repayment. Not that his followers were very much better, but there were political jobs to be done and that was the priority. Henry de Lacy preferred laymen rather than ordained priests to keep his accounts, and required them to be done by two or three constables, bailiffs or reeves jointly.

Now it was the day of the feast of St. Cecilia and the column was formed for the journey of Edmund and his family, along with Henry de Lacy, to the south. Bravery and dried tears were the lot of Margaret, in her chamber with Eustachia de Cantelupe, who was as comforting as could be. Sir William de Cantelupe had been deputed to escort Margaret, John and Alesia to Bolingbroke. He had arrived a couple of days before with his wife, and men-at-arms, from his main manor at Griseley in Nottinghamshire. With all this gathering the castle facilities were at full stretch, until this day when the main party had left. Sir William spoke with Margaret. It was a relationship of friendliness and detached respect, based on the de Lacy position as Earls of Lincoln and the Cantelupe family having held office for generations of previous Earls of Lincoln, including those who had forfeited the honour by misdeeds. There was strategic connection between the castles they held in southern Wales.

"We can leave when you say, Lady Margaret. We will be ready as required. The weather can surely only improve."

"A few days then, Sir William. I would like to get settled. Which way shall we go?"

"Presumably to the de Ros castle of Belvoir, then maybe to Tattershall for a night. Or perhaps to Newark for the night, Lincoln for another. It depends who you may wish to see; or there's the d'Arcy's of Nocton," which he added with a mischievous smile.

"I want to go the shortest way, and I'm quite sure you know about the d'Arcy's."

"There are reports of trouble in the area sponsored by him, but I thought you would be immune."

"Belvoir, and Lincoln, please, where we will stay a few days."

de Cantelupe felt that there would be plenty to occupy her mind in the absence of her husband, and as much coming and going of officials as usual, and some neighbours. Indeed the young would need supervision and encouragement. He indicated that he was always available to escort her on any travel. Then he fell to complimenting her pretty daughter who had come in to the chamber. He withdrew, as Peter the Chaplain entered. A slightly querulous look from Alesia made him reassure himself that he was a priest for adults and not for children, so he gave Margaret his respects with a mustered confidence.

After a prayer and a reading, on request he intoned to her with persuasion, from one of St. Paul's letters to the Romans: "When trials come, endure them patiently: steadfastly maintain the habit of prayer. Share the happiness of those who are happy, share the sorrow of those who are sad."

He kept some homily in reserve in case there were questions to answer, but the simplicity of the message was adequate. It was appreciated that it was the only way to be drawn from constant self examination, the most enduring release of tension.

Almost the same message as that of Brother Antonio at Denbigh. Could there be any other? Had the tragedy of John's drowning been punishment? Peter could hardly say that a de Lacy lady was being punished by God for anything; leaving unspoken, of course, his doubts on that matter. He produced an answer of his own.

"In accordance with St. Paul's charging us to look at others, try and find any special sin in those who have also suffered, and it is rare so to do. The condition of man on earth is fraught with tragedy, but the Lord's mercies are new every morning."

It was the best that could be done. His position was detached yet had to be approved; he could utter the truth with subtlety or directness, yet had to be accepted. It seemed to satisfy and to calm.

"A good fellow. Doing his best. I thought he had an answer" John remarked, on Peter taking his leave. He was prepared to accept what parsons said. It always struck a chord in his sensitive mind. The last thing he wanted to do was to discuss, or examine the basis of religious influence. He wanted to believe, and to thrust himself into the security of the atmosphere that total trust provided.

Margaret fell to thinking that she must make sure in her husband's absence that their manors were run properly, that their castles maintained, their lives preserved, and that all was to be in good order for Henry's return. She permitted herself a twitch of a smile when she realised how little that immediate thought accorded with what her Chaplain had just urged. Doubtless that could all come later, or perhaps it was there all the time. There were things to do. Then there was the present decision required.

"We will depart the day after tomorrow. We hope to be home to celebrate Whitsuntide."

The second sentence gave the journey some purpose. But Alesia was speaking.

"Uncle Edmund has never worn his red cross when I've seen him."

"He got it for the Holy Land, darling, not for England."

"Why do they call him 'Crossback' then?"

"Men together seem to play at nicknames," replied Margaret.

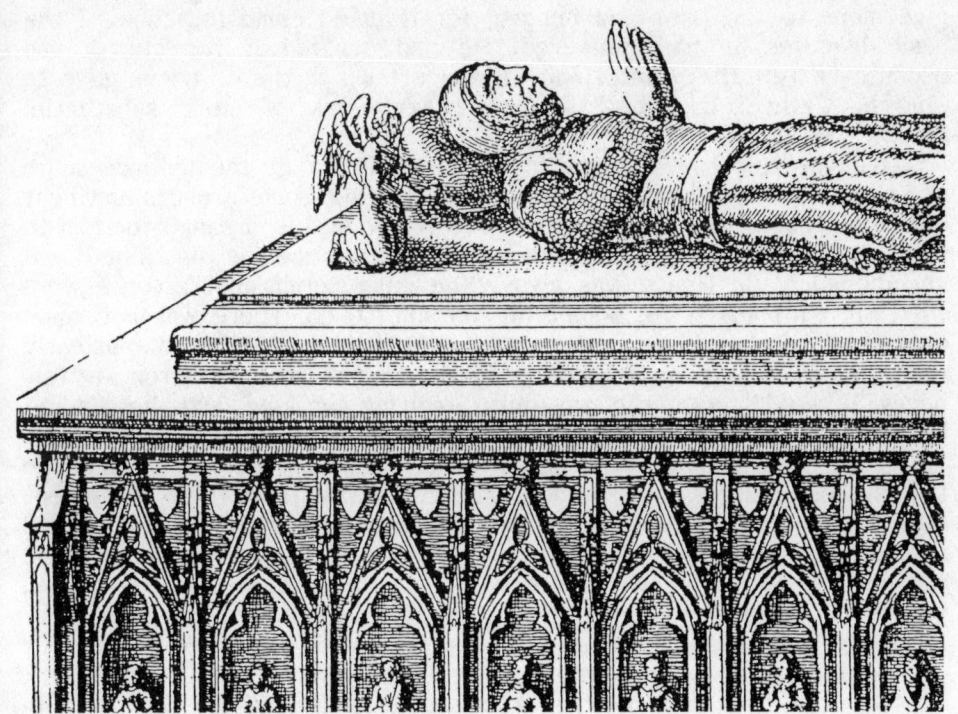

The tomb in Old St. Paul's Cathedral, London, of Alesia's father, Henry de Lacy, 3rd Earl of Lincoln, 6th Earl of Salisbury.

# CHAPTER 3

Between the impersonal but polite farewell of Richard de Coleshill, Steward of the Honour of Leicester, and the effusive welcome of Robert de Ros at Belvoir, was a day spent in the saddle. The officials who had accompanied the de Lacys had gone on to London with Lord Lincoln, so the party of Countess Margaret was her immediate household. The officials of the Honour of Bolingbroke were at that castle already, being for the most part based there. Even Pontefract and Clitheroe reported to them. So the de Lacys and the de Cantelupes were accompanied only by chaplain, secretary, messengers, standard bearer (it gave Margaret a lift to have her personal banner on these occasions), grooms, maids, archers, and men-at-arms. The colourful cortege was fronted by the dun coloured clothing of the guide.

In village after village the usual knot of staring rural folk stood by the way, wondering who, expecting news, and closing in after a picnic stop to acquire any scraps or vessels left behind. Beggars would appear from seemingly empty countryside by any ford in the guise of helpers in the hope of charitable reward.

Peter the Chaplain wondered if he should have urged Margaret to give more to the poor and hungry, for it could come into one of the basic homilies he had delivered. He had omitted it for clarity and because he felt the great financial support which the de Lacys gave to Church, Cathedral, Abbey and to prayer was of more substantial effect.

After Belvoir they passed to the open heath of the uplands south of Lincoln. When John sought permission to take some archers and hunt hares, Margaret took thought that she really should arrange for him to live at some other noble house, rather than he be untrained and unoccupied while Henry was away. She gave permission, after a word with Sir William. It was something for him to do. There was not much chance of success while on the move, not much possibility of patiently waiting and watching, creeping forward, and shooting from a few paces. It would be on the run, quite exciting for John, and there might be luck. There were certainly plenty of hares.

In the closing miles of the journey to Lincoln it led to John and the two archers halting by a wood, some two miles from their party, but still in sight over the heath. They were hailed, they reined in, and turned. Seven men rode towards them. It was a surprise, and at first not possible to assess whether it was a simple encounter of passers-by. It was not. John's group of three was at once hemmed and penned by a horseman close each side.

"You will give us reward!"

This was from the seventh, a commanding fellow. He continued in contemptuous amusement.

"A boy! A-hunting!"

John himself was conditioned by his rank, and his nurturing, and class, at least for a while to feel power and ability superior to such as these could hold. His two archers were looking to him for a lead, but in the circumstances there was no possibility of ordering either resistance or flight. His sword was lifted from his saddle scabbard.

"It's a start. Failing much more, it will be used on you!"

John was too proud to turn round, to see if his predicament had been seen. He sat still, given the slight movement of the horses, and hoped there would be an opening which he could exploit.

The men decided to take the horses. That the Darcie gang really existed had seemed incredulous to John, but it was clearly active, and this lot must undoubtedly be part. To his own surprise he did not like to say who he was; in fact he felt that if he did so he might well be kidnapped for ransom. As he perforce stayed still, he looked closely at all the seven men, and resolved later to identify those responsible for this lawless behaviour.

"Wilmar!" called one to his leader - to draw attention to a posse approaching from a few hundred yards.

"Take the weapons, take the horses!" Then they pushed the party into some thorn bushes, with a threat at sword point to carve up one of the archers.

Where there were virtually no folk as on Lincoln heath, and little cover other than bush and scrub of elder and hawthorn, Sir William de Cantelupe had not felt the need to be alert. Although visibility was extensive, such growth as there was did obscure. It was in the spirit of investigation that Sir William had orderd a posse of a dozen men to ride towards the distant group, to see if they might be harmful. Thus sergeant Bunting and company arrived to pull three humiliated people from thorns which gave resiliently at each attempt they made to free themselves, the while unattached spikes penetrated sharply further.

They all met again in a clear part of the heath. Margaret and Sir William moved to the group of rescued and rescuers. Chaplain Peter noticed that she crossed herself, and he began to urge his palfrey forward in case he was needed to listen. He was not. She made the gesture as the thought of forgiveness in all the one body of Christ came jumbled into her mind, tensed, anxious and furious as she was. It was a reflex gesture after seeing her son was well and unhurt, and preliminary to the expression of vitriolic vituperation about the gang of outlaws who had attacked her son and stolen her horses and arms. Sir William tried to hide his wonder at the emotional expression directed to the distant gang. It was said that Darcie sheltered and maintained these predators, profiting from them to increase his low income as a Knight.

"Sir William! We will go to Nocton now."

"My lady, my lady, we have but three or four hours to get to Lincoln and to get settled there, before nightfall."

"We have plenty of men! Seek this gang at least! I am not going by here doing nothing."

She noticed that Alesia had come forward, which reminded her of her responsibilities, and John spoke.

"Mother, dear, this must be done properly, flushing them out with a suitable force. I would dearly love to go now. We are alright for the moment; now they have disappeared. All we had better do with this group is to go past that wood and be ready if we chance across them."

Sir William saw that matters had taken a calmer turn, but was not prepared himself to be responsible for escorting the de Lacy family if it included offensive action which was the proper duty of the Sheriff of the County. It was not possible to contemplate arrows flying about with a party made up as was this one.

Alesia thought it was going to be like a good chase, hunting people. Mabota was told to take her to the further side of the group. Sir William and John exchanged a shrug which gave understanding between them that the men would have gone far off anyway.

"Very well, ma'am, we will cross the river at Washingborough. It will cause little delay. We will thus reach the castle along the north side, which may well be better than approaching through the city."

It was the very next morning that Margaret gathered to herself all her authority as Countess of Lincoln and Salisbury. A sheriff was sent for, Lincolnshire by its extent being work for two.

"Sir Simon de Aston."

"My lady, greetings."

"Sir Simon, law in this county is not being maintained when even my family can be humiliated with impunity..."

"Ma'am I have heard the story from your messenger. The Darcie gang..."

"You are fully aware of these people. My own son, and they would have been after anyone else who would have been around. It was only our numbers, when they saw them, that made them flee. That is not what order should depend on, Sir Simon."

"Ma'am, I know..."

"Kindly inform me what you are going to do about it, why you have done nothing apparent, and I see no evidence that the Statute of Westminster of last year has had any effect at all."

She went on to detail the incident. Sir William de Cantelupe nodded general agreement, and when Margaret had seemingly concluded, broke his silence, suggesting that they might learn from Sir Simon the possibilities in the matter. Indeed, what support the Countess could in fact herself order.

Sir Simon de Aston spoke slowly. He was prepared for interruptions and having to give explanations. Such as were necessary he gave with patience. There were three points, he said, so far as his colleague and he were concerned.

"The Statute of Westminster was passed last year, and its detail has been known here for but a few months. It is not directed to me...

except that somehow... I have, in due course, which cannot be yet, to ensure owners demolish this brushwood and scrub it speaks about, all of it, for two hundred feet each side of the highway. I am not an owner of land affected, not myself. I have to wait to see if owners are going to obey in a reasonable time..."

It struck him suddenly that in any case it would have made no difference, because the incident was far beyond that limit.

"Sir Simon, let me have clarity in what you are doing, not why you cannot. My son has been assaulted, and I have had horses and property stolen, I remind you."

Sir William de Cantelupe interjected, with what he hoped was a calming familiarity.

"Lady Margaret, Sir Simon cannot take on people like Sir Norman Darcie without superior assistance."

"He is the sheriff, or one of them. They have men, arms; they can act at any time in accordance with law."

Sir Simon de Aston gave a slight snort.

"I appreciate your impatience ma'am. I too, am impatient in this matter. I make not excuses. If I can have a few moments I can tell you what can be done, and what not."

He was not answered, nor was he interrupted, so he continued.

"These predators and vagabonds in this gang have the patronage of Sir Norman Darcie. It is not an unusual situation, however regrettable. With respect, indeed, ma'am, you presumably know that Sir Norman has been arrested before."

"He was young then."

"Maybe, twenty eight years of age according to the record. Yes, since then he has done certain duties for the King, such as at Shrewsbury three years ago. His son is now about twenty seven and probably the one behind this trouble. There are two main points, one of which is that they can be apprehended and they will run for, and obtain, sanctuary in Nocton church. The other is that if I - no, let me put it another way - if Sir Norman or his son Sir Philip are disturbed by me, the sheriff, then after that all the more powerful people will condemn me for antagonism towards the authority of their kind. May I ask what would be said among those you know and meet should I..."

"I understand you. But the law, then?"

"Ah. The law. Words ma'am, rules ma'am. It needs tangible power to enforce. I have to repeat, someone greater than Sir Norman Darcie must give the order and power to me."

"My son and my property?"

"I can only suggest, and submit to you ma'am, that you yourself demand it from him, because he would laugh at me and beat my messenger."

Margaret, John, and Alesia had come across many situations in talk and hearsay. This time, having been present and insulted by bravado and theft even as lesser folk, even the young Alesia shared the unspoken understanding which impacted upon them now - that the urge and passionate activity of Henry for law and order was a more than worthy cause. Their unity was increased by sharing the same deep feeling. Margaret pondered, and the two men stood silent until she spoke, which was after she had thought rapidly on several factors which she could not, or did not want to, express aloud.

The church and sanctuary. Henry and she had spoken often of this power. They thought secretly that it was overgreat, interfering in the punishment of wrongdoers, even preventing it. The patronage of the lawless by those in high positions. That was foolish at least, offensive to the peaceful running of manors, it was irresponsible, encouraging anarchy from villeins at worst. The sheriff, what he said was correct, and he was in office only for a year. If Henry were here, he would authorise a county force. That may still not get Darcie himself, whichever one it was, and within months he would start again, when authority had gone away.

"I authorise you to send a strong posse to Nocton, with a letter from me. Bring back my property and let us have a report. Perhaps there can then be further action."

"In your name, I can agree to that, my lady."

Sir Simon added that he would report to her, when some conclusion had been reached.

He did so, three days later.

"Sir Simon, that is not the whole truth."

"My lady! That is the report!"

"I tell you it is not all there is to be told!"

"But..." and he wondered if she had other sources of information. Somewhat apprehensive, for he did know that there was more to say, but which should be omitted, Sir Simon thought desperately that maybe Sir Norman Darcie had communicated with her, or had she had gossip from his men.

In fact, all she had been working on was that his tone of voice had been a little contrived; plus the fact that such reports in these situations were usually glossed.

"Shall you start again?" suggested Margaret. She wiped her nose and chin to give an air of casual strength in relaxation. She was tempted to prompt him, but remained silently waiting, as hopefully being more effective.

"My men brought back your horses, that is true. They brought in three men, that is true. That is all. Yes, I have to add that the d'Arcies were not there. Neither of them, was the message, but if I may say so, I did not think it was true. There were horses in the stable that were warm of recent use. Good horses, not vagabond ones. Your horses were identified by their gear, milady."

"Was there no resistance? Where did you capture the three men?" It was Margaret's resentment about being refuted by the d'Arcies which put a penetrating edge on her voice. It was the latter question that Sir Simon had been trying to avoid, and it was her tone which made him believe that she knew already the answer.

"Ma'am, may my men be forgiven. By you I beg; by God, I hope. How else can this work be done? How, just how, in what other way? Yes. Those three whom I have were dragged from the church, and now I have to find a charge against them, to save my men, and probably to save myself."

"Do what you can with them. I will speak with Bishop Sutton tomorrow. In time let us hope my Lord Lincoln in Council can urge improvements."

She hoped that she had not gone too far in revealing their own increasing feelings against the overweening surge of the power of Church and Pope.

And what the Lord Bishop, Oliver Sutton said, was:

"The three men who were kidnapped from the sanctuary of the church of Nocton shall be returned there to be exactly as they were, unharmed."

"Oliver!" Margaret almost shouted in her astonishment.

"It is only because you can call me Oliver, and I can call you Margaret, that when that is done, I will close the case."

Oliver Sutton had been the Bishop of Lincoln for some six years, and had he not sound reasons for pride, confidence, and assurance in his interpretation of his power through his religious office? In the first year of his appointment the body of St. Hugh, glory of all that was holy, that was right, that was sanctity in preparation for life after death, had been re-interred in the magnificent presbytery erected for the purpose, at the east end of Lincoln Cathedral.

It was a structure of inspired beauty and daring in expression, garnished with angels, admirable in its skill, and awesome to the people. Archbishop, Bishops, Abbots, had been present, and more - the King, the Queen, their children, and multitudes asking for protection of Saint Hugh. Oils of the most healing quality emanated from the body and could be touched as they exuded from his shrine. It was he, Oliver Sutton, who had officiated at the ceremony.

Was not Lincoln the greatest diocese in England? With all that temporal power in decision, in counsel, it was now that of Oliver Sutton. Was he not building further this church which was the house of his throne under God; building further to Glory, expression on earth of man's puny ability to show how great was His influence. Why, it was more than a day's ride before one could not look back and marvel at the distant sight of the great Cathedral at Lincoln witnessing God's presence. From Humber to Thames, under the Holy Father and Archbishop alone he was the mediator for every soul.

There was no need for the Bishop to speak further. Margaret was stunned into silence. She now knew how puny was the power of such as her husband while the church rode without a single doubt upon the simple credulity of the people. So the sanctity of the holy church had been trespassed upon in Nocton. The Bishop was not unkind in an aggressive sense, and clearly had no intention of offending the de Lacys. He would, however, leave things as he had spoken. He had decided that he had said what was right, and that was how he must be spoken of in de Lacy circles.

"I am of course in favour of the apprehension of criminals. Do please believe, Lady Margaret, though, that one task of church and God is to keep their places holy and without conflict."

Margaret murmured some not very coherent reply, being a little tremulous at her own position in the initiative she had taken with the sheriff. This was assumed by Oliver Sutton as the end of the matter, concluding that his order would be implemented.

"It is unfortunately a fairly usual situation with Knights" continued the bishop. "They are wrong, but many have to find more money or property by illdoing."

Bishop Sutton could hardly go further, in that he himself was as materialist as anyone - in the name of God - and His work - and His House. Oliver himself was now beyond self-doubt, though in the past he had wondered if teasing the populace with relics and flowing oils had Christian reality. By now, however, he knew - he knew that people were calmed with hope in these beliefs and experiences - he knew that there had to be the expression on earth of as much mystery and glory as man could devise to show God's influence. He knew that the more material resources the church had the more that expression could be fulfilled. Where was to be found any other answer? What a glorious age it was in which to live.

"What do you like best in church, Alesia?"

She replied to the bishop that she liked the sermon and the men singing best. The bishop did not pursue that one, but elucidated from John that his real interest was military, and he only hoped that there would be something at Bolingbroke to occupy him. Should they stay in the county for the whole year the bishop trusted that they would celebrate the Christian festivals with him.

As they left the Bishop's manor of Nettleham for Lincoln castle the early orange twilight sun sought the pinnacles and towers of the Cathedral. The new church of St. Mary Magdalen was on their short route, on the corner by the market place which lay just outside the castle gateway. It had just built so that the local parishioners could have their own place to worship, having been allowed a corner of the cathedral since it was built over two centuries before where the previous parish church had stood. John supposed that Bishop Oliver Sutton must be a great and good man.

# CHAPTER 4

An early day was spent travelling from Lincoln Castle to Bolingbroke, with a break at Baumber in the middle of the day, a manor of a sister-in-law. Margaret intended to have a full and proper period of mourning for her elder son, and for her grandmother, Margaret, whose soul left her body last year. She had to go into retreat to reassess and to regain strength to look upon the world. All this without her husband, now far away. For a while the more serious affairs could be left to bachelor brother-in-law John de Lacy in London, certainly if the King could leave the whole country in the hands of his brother Edmund of Lancaster. When Sir William Cantelupe returned to his manor of Griseley, she pursued no more than contemplation and prayer in chapel, reading her Book of Hours to devour from it purpose and meaning, and sought daily to know but that John and Alesia were well.

One day John asked if he could go to be an esquire in some noble house for his further education. Margaret did not agree, with the remark that he was just like his great grandfather John. Since that John had been the founder of the greater fortunes of their family neither John nor Alesia could together decide whether he was being complimented or not. His great grandfather had married his daughter to Richard, Duke of Gloucester, to the fury of many barons, and he and Simon de Montfort as a consequence had to leave the King's council. His own marriage had been to Margaret de Quincy through whom he became Earl of Lincoln. Sometimes he had acted against and sometimes with the King, the last being thought to be due to a bribe from the Bishop of Winchester. Alesia soon lost interest, but John did think more than once on this example of achieving ambition.

Messengers were despatched to Henry with frequent regularity with humdrum reports of daily affairs, above all the question continually put about the length of his absence. Henry's messages were about the campaigning way of living. No comfort came in such words.

Then there was delay in Henry's return to England, and more delay, and Margaret's demand to know why. In weeks she received a messenger of more presence and expression than the usual silent simple carrier of a pouch of parchments. He was able to say that delay there would be, considerable in months. And a full communication would follow. With dignity and calm Margaret dismissed him. She sent for chaplain Peter.

He had been taxed often to the depths of his learning, and more than once he had asked for advice from others of his calling. He wanted to do what he could for Margaret as a person. It was not his wish to have a charge who was a religious shell.

"The other day, Peter, from the Holy Gospel of St. Mark, you read about Bartimaeus son of Timaeus, the blind beggar. Speak to me more of that."

On explanation to him of the present situation Peter had been expecting something different. With near desperation he had tried to think of a new text or lesson which would bring her back to living, in the name of the Lord, but certainly living. Why this approach? At least questions were easier to answer than it was to initiate discussion. So he proceeded, and he himself came to understand as he continued. He arranged his voice with a median sound between heavenly authority and earthly equality.

"Jesus was with his disciples in a large crowd, leaving Jericho, when blind Bartimaeus called out - he had to call out twice, against the throng - 'Son of David, have pity on me!' Jesus asked him what he wanted, which was to be able to see..."

Peter paused, having assessed the significance of the reading.

"...Go, said Jesus, your faith has cured you. At once, it is written in the Gospel, Bartimaeus recovered his sight and followed Jesus."

Peter made deliberately another pause, watching Margaret carefully, as impersonally as possible, but she now obviously felt the way to relaxation and renewal, and his own eyes near-filled with tears.

"His message can come to be seen, ma'am. It is not sight, not eyes, it is understanding that is meant. That the way of Jesus is not to ignore him and his teachings - to do things, human things in this human world, but always in his name. Open your eyes, look outwardly, Jesus will act it out for you."

John and Alesia had come into the Chamber when they heard the rumours about the latest message from Gascony. Margaret hugged them and hugged them and cried out, with tears in her heart.

Upon the fading of the sun on the day after the Feast of St. Gregory the Pope, a rider arrived with the promised letter from Henry to Margaret. The messenger insisted on handing it to her personally, achieved after some difficulty with secretary Halton. He did, however, also have a verbal communication from the Earl. He spoke quietly, uncultured, but with sensitivity to the feeling his words would induce.

"Milady, the Earl presents these words through me, in that he did not wish..."

With relief Margaret realised that it was not, then, her husband's death about which he was going to speak.

"...to commit to parchment in case they fell into false hands, and I am able to say that my words are those exactly as his lordship gave to me. My lady, he considers with great regret, and good wishes under God for you and his family, and your welfare and health, that he is forced to the opinion, rumours and statements notwithstanding, that there will be further delay in the return of the King and himself to England."

The man spoke slowly and deliberately, as if recalling every correct syllable. Margaret was about to ask for the meat of the matter, as he continued. Away from his brief he expressed some calming and warming words, and concluded: "...in his opinion is the like of two more years."

"Two!" she gasped,

"My lady, may I put it strongly that my lord was much affected as he spoke. But, yes, ma'am; two. Others are of different, shorter, opinion, but that is his lordship's considered thought, concerning the difficulties."

Two. Two? Margaret assimilated the purport. For the moment there was no more to say or think than that there would be a message to return. Upon that the man withdrew. The confidential nature of the Earl of Lincoln's opinions had been agreed. Shortly Margaret took the children into this confidence, and she had to tell them of the possibility of their being at Bolingbroke for two more seasons; at least they had to plan for that eventuality. They would not move far from there in this period, certainly she did not feel like going to London for social life without her husband.

"Might it not keep us in the eye of those who govern, for our future good?"

"Your father is with the King, John, and nothing could be more important."

"What are we all going to do, then?"

Margaret sighed, with half-shut eyes, to relax her tensions, how grateful and glad she was to be climbing away from despond to regained mental strength. She was now forced to have some purpose. She had to become strong enough to live with this news from her husband, and to link it with a confident look to the future.

"What are we going to do? We are to prepare and be ready for your father's admiration when he does return. There is much to learn, to practice, and to do. Alesia will start with her latin; you, John, will be taught everything that can be done with the people here and in Lincoln; and, of course, develop your military interests. There is something to achieve."

"I think we should go to London to meet father," said Alesia.

"For that reason, when it is time, of course we will go. It must be borne. We must, we must prepare for your father's return, as players rehearse for a scene."

So Margaret took stock. Firstly by sending for Sir Laurence Leidet, the Steward of the Castle and of the northern estates. She excused herself slightly in her first remarks.

"Sir Laurence. You have perhaps been working this last year feeling that we have let you pursue your tasks with our interest being slight. Our affairs in the south are being supervised by Sir Edmund, as appointed by Lord Henry, and my mother is looking after the Salisbury interests at Canford. I am inviting them here to stay a while, so that I may be fully apprised of all situations. So now I wish for discussion and report from you, on all aspects, but more especially for the education of my son John. He is now old enough to absorb these things with responsibility. Now, further, as you know, he is vastly interested in army matters. In fact, he was only sharply distrained from accompanying his father. I want him, in effect, to be trained to be ready to go with him in, say, three or four years' time. You will appreciate that the standard has to be high."

Sir Laurence had been thinking while Margaret spoke. He suffered from constantly having to use untrained persons in every aspect of his duties. Get a good clerk, get a good blacksmith, and they usually went or were summoned elsewhere, or fate took a hand.

"Milady. I can find suitable people to train your son John to a fair pitch. Let us then go as far as we can. I will tell you when we can go no further, and then we will have to find some tutor or example more worthy. I take it that this will go on, even may Lord Henry return?"

On confirmation of that, Sir Laurence became his most diffident, and with care introduced a sensitive consideration.

"There is, however ma'am, one item which needs your support, above all."

"And that is?"

"Training, and practice, milady, in hunting, in archery, in tactics, in jousting, in horsemanship, in endurance - may I add, perhaps specially, in personal relationships with others who are direct in manner and do not respect persons except for what they can do, and for their personal attributes - all these things - if done effectively - can be a painful process, even if just mentally. That is why boys are usually sent to other households - where there is no-one, may I say, to complain to..." He paused, clicking his tongue "...training should be slightly more robust than the life for which it is preparation."

"You mean, Sir Laurence, can it be done - with me here?"

"I would not say that there is harm in all this, but there is strain. There has to be. There also has to be trust that the effort would work towards an effective future lord."

"I will support you. Of course we will discuss from time to time. Of course I shall watch John with your statement in mind."

She hoped she could keep to that resolve.

By May, 1287, Henry was given protection against all crown needs in England, because he was staying beyond seas with the King until Michaelmas. In August his prophecy of greater delay was reinforced by further protection for one year. And after that, in October, for a further period; in April 1288 until All Saints; in October - with the King until Easter. Thereupon Margaret made preparations to take John and Alesia to London. It looked this time as though it was somewhere near finality. There was oh so much to talk about, the children were more than eager to see their father again.

They made their confessions with an air of clearing all before this future. A few days later they arrived in London. Margaret took as much notice as she could of affairs that were placed before her by Peter de Cestre and William le Vavasur, nominees of Henry. It was their opinion that summer would be well through when the King and Lord Lincoln and all the forces had returned. And it was so. It was August when they landed, four days more to their reaching London. It would be about the anniversary of young Edmund's death.

It was Alesia who glimpsed first against the lowering sun the silhouette that was her father. From his new mansion, Lincoln's Inn on the northern edge of London, he could shortly be seen more clearly across the fields, with a few attendants, the centre focus of an escort of a score of mounted soldiers. Football, wrestling, running, games in the fields all ceased; way was made, as much to see Lord Lincoln pass as of the need to give them room.

"I shall not wait up here! Mabby!" Alesia was away. This time Mabota did not reprove her for the diminutive of her name. John was quietly excited. He deferred to his mother, who followed with decorum Alesia's undignified rush. All the tensions of fear and hope of the last three years were loosing from her. Whatever she could say would be inadequate. She hoped that she had proved her worth to Henry. In the courtyard now Mabota would not let free Alesia's hand until her father had dismounted. Alesia was jumping up and down.

"Daddy!" in excitement.

"Daddy!" as she reached him.

"Daddy!" as she hugged him, to which he responded, lifting her up, looking over her shoulder, also smiling happily at Margaret and at John.

Henry encompassed nearly all of the three in his arms. In this little scrum he gave as much indication as could be done to indicate priority and affection to Margaret, enough for her alone to understand. The news of all their doings was going to take some time. One thing he could say at once.

"How wonderful you all look! How grown up you children have become!" A long embrace enabled him to say to Margaret alone that it was not possible to have done a better job on those children, and he could see that at once. John and Alesia stood by, modestly quiet in their appreciation of the parental warmth they felt. Now Henry spoke again.

"If you ladies will proceed indoors, John will come with me. There are these men and these horses to be given some attention. We shall not be long. Then there's dirt and dust to remove, whereupon I shall be a bit more civilised."

Much candlewax guttered to the air that night. Alesia showed off her latin, eager she said to speak further and at length with more than her country tutors, with ambassadors and prelates with whom they could now again have social contact. Henry looked fondly at his so animated daughter.

"Rara avis in terris, nigroque simillima cygno," was his comment to her, a compliment comparing her beauty to that of a swan, and colloquially a prodigy.

He and John together talked of what they had done, and of a small part of Henry's activity, movements, and purpose in the last three years. Margaret herself took pleasure in these exchanges, but with the late hours come she had to insist that all retired. There would be time in future, for, thank God, they would be together. Besides, Henry was very tired. It was a way of closing the evening. He turned out to be not so tired as she first thought.

The house had been built only ten years previously. Henry had bought the property from the Black Friars, the Benedictines who had found greater space down by the river. His Lincoln's Inn was made partly from the remains of the friary and partly from an old house of the Bishop of Chichester who had supported the friars. This new and large establishment suited Henry well. Their domestic apartments were new; accommodation for retainers, servants, soldiers was amply provided by study rooms, dormitories, refectory, kitchens, library, chapter house, cloisters, church, and gardens.

It was a healthy location. The adjoining fields were important for the horses, and the water conduit was capacious. For short periods it could accommodate as many as five hundred folk. It all contrasted with Chancellor's Lane on its east side, in such a foul and miry state that John Briton, custos of London, had some years before ordered it to be barred up, and still it so was.

A sunny day; with a small escort and Mabota, Alesia exercised Agnes. There were always knots of folk in the fields, but this day a larger gathering than usual grouped near the gate of the Earl's domain.

"They're down by the river!" called out one of the soldier escort as they trotted out. A certain hostility in the small crowd was subdued by this shout. As they all looked up Alesia noticed desperation in their faces, worn by anxiety, not the usual sort of look in peasants hungry but resigned to making the best of any distress. They were expressions from which hope had gone.

"Your call means what?" she asked. "Do you mean they are looking for the Friars?"

"Yes, lady Alesia, those Friars help the Jews, now they're banned from their usual trade. Or any trade, I suppose. There are Jews here nearly every day now."

Noticing that Alesia looked anxious, he added that they never seemed to get violent. As the Jews had not dispersed on their return, Mabota made their escort take them into the grounds by another gate.

"I didn't know you had some subtle strategy in you, Mabota."

"It has saved you at least from insult, Lady Alesia."

"What insult? Why me?"

"Alesia dear. You did not hear their remarks. Some called back."
"All right, what?"

It was difficult for Mabota to pass on uncomplimentary oaths, and she wished she had kept her mouth shut. She escaped by dissimulation.

"They were of course angry and replied with swearing, and I meant only that they were clearly against us."

The episode made Alesia nervous. It looked to her like a personal attack by the disaffected. She would speak to her father, who replied:

"Jews do not follow or obey our laws. The coinage of the realm has to be kept as firm and trustworthy as possible, but what do they do? They clip it, they sell the gold, or lend it, and use what's left as though it had not been reduced in value. Nothing stops them, not the hangings, not punishment, not confiscation of goods; authority seems to mean nothing in this regard. Their own religion, or whatever it is, prevents them from more ordinary ways of earning their keep."

Margaret intervened to show the seriousness of these affairs, but also to prevent Henry working up to the death of Jesus Christ.

While Alesia fell silent, she herself was surprised to realise that she felt more shock at her father than anything else. Her dear and kind father was respected by all classes. How astonishing to know how calm straightforward rectitude had this side to it. Punishment including death to recalcitrants to prevent the sullying of the even tenor of the daily lives of others. But Alesia knew that there was not a noble in the land who was not indebted to Jews, for the most part unable to repay.

"Now," continued her father "it is thought best that they be sent away from the kingdom for ever."

"I had heard that more of their goods were to be confiscated.

"They are allowed enough for subsistence on their journeys. It will relieve the state of a great burden. France has done the same, and has persuaded us also."

"How many?"

"Some fifteen thousand, I understand."

Alesia was now on unsure ground to make any reply, but she thought it seemed an awful lot of people. She tried to ask where they were meant to go, but found within herself that it was only curiosity from the practical point of view rather than from sympathy. She did just reflect that her family had been borrowing money from Italian bankers, but she had assumed that it was through her Italian grandmother's connections. It had not been much, because her father was frugal, and generally used state exchequer money for his state business.

Her father smiled at her quiet acceptance of his basic description of the situation, not reaching her process of thought. That night,

Alesia sought further clarification from Mabota.
"What did that Jew say?"
"I told you, lady Alesia."
"Tell me again...and properly...I want to know exactly."
"He said two words only, against you, lady Alesia, or your family. I think not personal." At least she hoped.
"Very well, what!"
"S-something about Italians, milady."
"Something bad about Italians, you mean."
And so Mabota admitted it.
"I am not surprised." Alesia's calm reply left Mabota gaping.
Alesia was also wondering when that rapacious giant, the state, would seize the money of the Florentine and Lombard bankers which they were now lending with so much trust, based on their expanding maritime enterprise, even in to Flanders and England, in great galleys from Genoa and Venice.
"I shall never understand this money business Mabota." It was a true and genuine statement, which ·Alesia took no further. Mabota would have liked to have done so, for had not the King and Lord Lincoln just been fighting about the revenues of parts of France?
Alesia slept that night and dreamt with fear that it was she herself alone in penury, seeking food in woods; without a soul who knew of her, her fate; for relief she grasped the trees and embraced the oaks, for there was no other life. Except she had been hearing breath. It was a swan. Behind her. At her left side. Now the right. Just looking. She held out with hesitation first her left hand. Then her right. Was the swan really there, or was it... In panic she turned. The swan stretched forward, hissing. It tore at her, ripped her clothes. She felt no breath of a living thing. She turned as she struggled on the ground, which opened her to further attack. It was never she but only her clothes at which the animal tore. Naked, she was left alone. She breathed hard and deep. Her right hand was tightly in her teeth, as gripped as painfully as teeth can do. Loosing the hand, she covered herself.
Slowly lying back on the bed, Alesia's breathing consciously came down to normal. With the relief of peace, she absorbed her surroundings. Fearfully creeping to the window, she looked at the gate to the fields. There were no Jews there.
That day she looked outward from herself with wider eyes. She conversed with Mabota to try and discover her worth, her loyalties, her fears, the basis of her living. She went to the stables and interested herself in the dogs, their kinds, their qualities. She spoke with grooms and ostlers, wives and children from that day forth, all as in the same world. She felt affinity with every living thing. Realisation, interest, contrasting with her inward childhood; awareness now, but often detached, without sympathy.
In the household Margaret had entertainment to organise. The

family together, the King in England, and links to reforge. Indeed, to reassess. Under Edmund in the last three years authority had been weak, partly by temperament, partly by lack of final power to act. Corruption had grown in the activities of the justices. Who else but Henry to adjudge, with chancellors Robert Burnell and a few others. Many of the people were resentful, not only of the government but particularly against the activities of judges and ministers in its absence. It was to be a long task, with drawn out investigation. Henry was horrified to find the miscreants to include Thomas de Weyland, Chief Justice of Common Pleas, and Ralph de Hengham, Chief Justice of the Kings Bench. How foolish people were to stray from law and equity as soon as superior restraint was absent.

The circumstance amended Margaret's invitation list. There would always be tension at a political gathering, but it made a better afternoon if the guest list were sifted. So not Ralph de Hengham, and not Thomas de Weyland, and not a good few others. Just: "not, an order my dear," and no explanation would Henry give. To him, after long experience and some excesses in his youth, a social gathering was of no interest unless he learnt something.

"So who will be here?" he asked: "Just to know what I can expect to discuss, or even answer."

"In your sphere, darling, Edward, the Warwicks, the Badlesmeres, Grandisons, de Greys. The two Edmunds of course, Lancaster and obviously I have to invite the Warrene family."

This last was true, and Henry knew it was so. Strange how social life can get cluttered up with people whom one did not want to see, and yet it was necessary to put on a smiling front and to cover the wariness. Unspoken and unreasoning competition between the Warrenes, Earls of Surrey, and their kin, and the de Lacys had gone on for two generations already. It did not affect either of their positions relative to the King, but there were disputes about lands which the Lords Surrey coveted or claimed. Their fathers had acted similarly.

"Ah, John Warrene. Of course." mused Henry.

"Then Bishops Anthony Durham, Roger Carlisle, the Dean of York is in Westminster, Henry de Newerk. Then le Stranges, Cliffords, Audleys; do you want the whole nominal roll? Everyone from my Cliffords to foreign Ambassadors, in fact."

"All I want is to assess the amount of diplomacy needed, so that's enough. I will exude goodwill in all directions."

"Do you think we should mention John and a possible bride, now he's nearly thirteen. We haven't done a lot about it, except between ourselves. Then there's Alesia; shall we talk with Edmund and Blanche about Thomas again?"

"I think it might be a good idea to wait, to delay. We're in circulation again and let's see what fields may open. Same for Alesia I would have thought at present. Better wait anyway to see if Edmund's interest on that keeps up."

"I gather then, you did not meet some dark lady in France with a beautiful daughter and an eligible son."

Into the garden went most of the children, leaving behind only those who wished to cling to their parents as being too young, and those who were old enough to believe that games were behind them. Thomas looked at the young group and then returned to hall. He spoke to Alesia briefly, more in a probing curiosity than in conversation.

Alesia and one or two others thought he didn't like them very much, but that was a shallow judgment. He spoke mostly to little Prince Edward. But he did draw Alesia's attention to Elizabeth de Ferre, the daughter of King Edward's chief seneschal in Gascony.

"What's the matter with her? They say she's a bit stupid."

"I hadn't noticed, really. She hardly talks. In fact I don't think she's said anything at all. But we've only just met."

"They say she's unfortunate and bewitched into dumbness."

"Well, she may not have played these games before."

So Alesia watched. After dancing Green Grow the Leaves, for which the garden provided several suitable hawthorn trees, someone suggested Oats, Beans and Barley. Elizabeth stood and watched and then joined in. She wouldn't make the responses to say she "must obey" in this dance of courtship and marriage rites. The more impatient pushed her out of the way. So Alesia moved to her and spoke, but there was no response but a few tears, hidden as best they could be. Alesia drew her away. Elizabeth did not speak. Alesia tried some dance movements for Elizabeth to imitate, which she did most effectively and in detail.

"Come with me." said Alesia, who realized suddenly that it was useless talking. So she looked closely at Elizabeth, first at her mouth. Alesia said something. Elizabeth moved her lips but nothing could be heard. Alesia turned away, and quickly back, and something made her do this and then to shout out loud. Again, an inch from Elizabeth's ear, who, with a look of surprise and disbelief had felt a stirring. Grabbed by Alesia they both ran to the buildings, through the groups of guests, to the de Ferres.

"She's only deaf!" roared Alesia "she's ever so bright!"

"Good God! you mean Elizabeth?" Neither of the de Ferres had ever thought of that possibility.

"She's never heard anything, so she can't repeat anything" was the straightforward analysis that Alesia produced. At least knowing the problem, so possible now it had been stated, might find someone who could help Elizabeth to face the world. It was the best party they had ever attended.

Henry himself saw this commotion but was occupied with the detailed chatter of Philip de Sechevill whose unfortunate main interest was fortification and that of Denbigh in particular. He reported that the walls of the town were just finished. He praised the fascinating plan that had been devised, the placing of the walls, the gates so defensive in their entrance angles, but wondered why the halls and chambers were not as luxurious as they might be.

"My work there is finished" was Henry's terse reply, and he would not be drawn further. de Sechevill had begun the conversation hoping to be recognised for his worth, but saw that he was going the wrong way, for a reason he did not know. He then simply passed on what he had heard, on a forced cheerful note, that the people of Denbigh were relieved that they were to be exempted from toll, and other taxes.

"Yes, the works are paid for," explained Henry. "There was a tax on oats to pay for the church of St. Hilary. They seemed to dislike that less than paying for their own defence."

de Sechevill wondered if it really was their own defence, but silently inclined and withdrew.

Margaret herself was busy enough in subtly moving people to converse with the different guests. After a chat with Thomas, John was detained for some time by the Bishop of London. Discussion between them about people made the Bishop talk of persuading John to become a priest. John demurred.

"The church" grinned the bishop "is organized very much like the army."

As the sun set over the western fields only those remained who were to spend the evening at a dinner, the King and Queen, Edmund and Blanche, Thomas and Henry of Lancaster, and the family. After Queen Eleanor had expressed her regards and thanks to Margaret for an enjoyable and interesting occasion, King Edward lisped charming compliments. Shortly all guests had been lit and escorted away. Margaret could hardly wait for her exhausted children to be taken to their beds.

"How is it possible, I am amazed - actually about you too; how can Edward and you act as though you had no care in the world when you know all the difficulties and hazards you've got to steer through?"

Henry was no philosopher, thoughtful though he could be. Only simple answers occurred to him.

"One cannot think of everything all the time. If that's not a sufficient explanation - put it this way - there's always something to do to improve matters, but most of it goes right. Of course I should have said your arrangements for our guests were totally disarming."

"Yet shortly there are going to be thousands of people expelled from England for ever, there are important people to be condemned, Scotland looks a thoroughly dangerous situation. Guy de Ferre thinks that Gascony will be in ferment again in a few years. To say nothing of Wales."

"All that, my dear, may be true. It has gone on like that for a long time, and probably always will. If you mean - is this state threatened with something with which it cannot cope, the answer is I wouldn't think so for a moment."

He stayed silent, out of what he thought was tact, over the whisper from Edmund of Lancaster that Thomas was being considered for marriage to Beatrice, the daughter of Hugh, son of the Duke of Burgundy. He was helped in his decision to say nothing at this moment by a whispered hint from Margaret.

"Idoine le Usser went overseas with Roper, on your expedition, she said. For a year, anyway."

"Ay. And she came back with one le Usser extra."

A game of Hoodman Blind.

# CHAPTER 5

Alesia's ninth year, in the calendar 1290, was the one when education, experience and dreams for her future coalesced to form lasting impressions. It was to Peter, her mother's chaplain's regret that education did not appear to rank as the greatest of her interests. To be adept at Latin and French conversation were exceptions, but these now needed only practice. Alesia herself could only suggest that because she felt the detachment in her family's position she consequently took more interest than most in the native tongue of developing English. That could have been because she felt safer with lesser folk in their own mode of free communication.

Apart from religion that was about as far in discussion as the chaplain could get. Alesia accepted his pursuing his subject at length, but absorbed only the need for honourable conscience and the hope for good. She had observed enough on this earth already to doubt the translation of ideal love down to its surface. Whatever else she was, she had inherited within her, except that a statement overheard of her father seemed to clarify a lot.

"Sir chaplain. Do you understand that we have to live a double life?"

Because this produced no sound, but only the sight of an open jaw, Alesia rephrased this to refer to a split life. She was informed that one had a soul for oneself and that it was indivisible. It began to be dangerous ground as she continued, albeit after a pause to gather her confidence.

"Take my father. In his duties he is a Christian and I believe of the highest order. But without a split from those Christian duties how is it possible to do much of what is required of him. Many men are hurt by military actions. Men are hanged or imprisoned by order. This year fifteen thousand Jews are ordered to go - just to go. We see them herding past here every day. It is said they have been allowed money for sustenance but it doesn't look like it. No-one will agree to sort out the Scottish Crown without killing."

Alesia would have gone on but she began to think she must be wrong to doubt so much.

"The church has much to do. Its work is scarce begun. But leave that to us to do our best, even if it be many centuries, for the Truth is being revealed slowly."

Having received that reply, Alesia realized there was to be no discussion, nor real communication, so she said no more. She omitted to ask why the Pope took money from prebends in England to pay for religious foundations in Rome. Her father and other barons had written to protest most vigorously. She would not discover what Peter thought of that. Her great grandfather had been ex-communicated for being one of those who pressed King John to seal the Great Charter so she began to feel the solid power of the church.

Alesia's and her brother's education was always being interrupted by travel when Henry was at home. This year was no exception. The experiences of journeys and new scenes were preferable to both of them. John was taking charge of escorts, or at least riding with and discussing matters with captains-at-arms. It was his true intention to learn strategy for military use, realizing that upon the usage of an army in battle was what the crown and the state depended. Alesia was pleased and absorbed by the generally benevolent and confidental talk of those who accompanied them.

This summer the Bishop of Carlisle and John, Earl of Warrenne travelled north with them to Pontefract. Alesia was a little scared of Warrenne. There was always tension when he was with them, so she had learnt to respond with inconclusive monosyllables, much, she thought, as he did himself. Sad that the brisk and forthright Bishop of Durham, Anthony Bek, had diverted to business other than this expedition. Alesia knew him from meetings in Lincolnshire, he so expansive on his new castle of Somerton at Boothby.

The family were to go as far as Pontefract Castle, the main body was for Scotland to enquire about the state of things to do with their Queen and realm as they might affect King Edward, his son, and the people of Scotland. Pontefract castle stood high, occupying a rock outcrop, the construction encircling the level area at the top. Strong and virtually inaccessible were the walls, towers, and the protected approach. As comfortable as possible were the family quarters, almost luxurious, as was fit for this great de Lacy seat. Whatever happened in the North - a Scots invasion, the treachery of Northern lords, it was here that the incursion would have to be finally stopped. On the place the Romans chose, on their main road to the North, the garrison's remit was to hold the gate to Southern England.

"You'll be alright when you yourself have to hold it," was the comment of John the Huntsman to young John de Lacy.

"But you, John, are a huntsman."

"You've been out with me these last few days, Sir John, and I can tell the worth of your handling the chase. I've been in fights, and there's scarce a difference between running hounds and running men. If there is, I'd like to know it." He paused, "and I'd use the knowledge."

"Maybe I see what you mean. I'll watch more. What about castles, though?"

"Castles is the kennels. But start at the beginning. The stag, the wolf and the like is the enemy. One or a dozen. Dogs don't catch them or harm them by stopping in kennels. Men don't harm their enemies by stopping in castles. You've got to be on the chase, with shouts to encourage, with whippers in, with more than one group to use. You look at it that way, Sir John."

"I certainly see the resemblance."

When that day they had killed and were resting before returning to the castle. John the Huntsman looked up as the boy made to ask a question.

"It's personal."

"Alright, sir. I am your servant."

"It's your affair, though, John. But why are you still John the Huntsman, not, say, John Huntsman; or Hunt; or Hunter. Most folk by now have taken a name. Or been given one by their neighbours. Some have changed them from a village to a calling, or otherwise. In fact, it's meant to be compulsory."

John the Huntsman was a long time answering. He rather deliberately moved his knife in and around the meat in his hand, ridding himself of irritation he must not express. At last he spoke.

"My missis is always saying that."

John de Lacy was slightly upset to have fallen onto an old subject which to him he had thought was new.

"Ay. She's on to me to do as the others. You done it about a hundred years ago. Your great great grandfather, that is. Alright. Nearly everyone has two names, that's how it is now. Let me tell you then, sir, why I do not. At least, I suppose I can explain it to you. Simply, I prefer the old ways. I like the firmer things of the past. That's one of 'em. My grandfather was 'John the Cellarer', my father 'John the Carter'. And I'm proud of being John, that is, John and my occupation, the Huntsman. Besides my sons may not be huntsmen, so why should they, and theirs, be called wrong?"

With his extra stab at the venison, John the Huntsman's aristocratic companion John gave a short friendly laugh. It ought to be us, really, who take that view, he mused. In fact he knew that their choice of surname had been urged on to them because otherwise it would have died out. "de Lassi", in Northern France, which had only a thin connection. There was more to listen to as the day ended.

"We've done deer today. If there's enough I'll bring out all the tricks for wolves tomorrow. And you, sir, tell me what compares with military things."

"I'll learn more than tell," replied John, whose next month became the best he'd known.

It was always a trait of the de Lacys that their importance was tempered with modesty. While it was a natural consequence of their personality it was of itself prudent to listen and understand what lesser folk were thinking, even though their power was miniscule. But there was power in the people together, and certainly in groups of folk as needed for wartime and the greater civil tasks, and collective dumb insolence was easily occasioned. The office of Earldom of Lincoln had been achieved only some two generations before, and had not been especially sought. It was the consequence of a second marriage on both sides. The main value of the de Lacys was their calm honesty and steadfast belief in what was right. This almost entirely meant that in their eyes the lawful king was the only king, and they would serve him.

Occasional dissent served but to contrast their firm reliability. Henry was now the greatest of them all, and the most accepted.

Henry had reason for satisfaction in his position of respect and trust and authority. And he had reason for quelling within himself the dangers of pride. For pride meant slackness, and when he felt it entering his mind he always began to feel uneasy. A middle grade of family, of Normandy, their place had been to serve ordinarily, elevated as far as the constableship of a castle, albeit to such importance as that of Chester. Their marriages were sometimes to lesser daughters of greater folk, and on occasion, a de Lacy daughter to someone more important. Henry's grandfather, John, had, however, been admired by his second wife's uncle, the great Earl of Chester and Lincoln, who by two wives had achieved no heir. Upon such natural vagaries can greatness rest, was Henry's constant contemplation. John by that second marriage became connected with direct descent from the Saxon Earls Edwin, and Morcar, brothers-in-law of King Harold. Margaret de Quincy, his wife, was descended from their sister Lucy. After the forced marriage of Lucy to the Norman Ivo Taillebois, then her second, then her third marriage with Ranulph Meschin, Earl of Chester, this link with the pre-Conquest Royal House had come to the de Lacys. To that John de Lacy from his mother-in-law came the Earldom of Lincoln, and the castle and lands of the Honour of Bolingbroke. It was also well in Henry's knowledge and feeling that the reason why they were Earls of Lincoln was because some seventy five years previously the titular Earl, Gilbert de Gant, had chosen the wrong side against the lawful king.

Why his father, Edmund, married an Italian, by the arrangement of Peter of Savoy, Henry was never sure. Peter was Queen Eleanor's brother, so she was either helping Alesia de Saluzzo or Edmund, or matchmaking as her wont. While it improved the de Lacy position in England it also served to offend some nobles. As a domestic marriage to an excellent and lively lady it prospered; for influence at home it showed the usual de Lacy modesty, and feeling that any national duty was but a trusteeship. Clearly there was little communication between England and Saluzzo, south of Turin, only on the occasional delegation to Rome. At home, it was necessary to override snide gossip about bankers of Italy being connected with the family, which they were not.

With his own marriage, albeit arranged long before he had heard the word itself, Henry had entwined everything needed for completeness of the base of a dynasty. His Pontefract castle was built by Ilbert de Lacy, of whom indirectly, he was the surviving heir, some two centuries after. He possessed the same lordships and the more than two hundred manors. Margaret his wife, although Countess of Salisbury, brought to him direct connection by descent from pre-Norman days with the city of Lincoln, and hereditary constableship of Lincoln castle. Upon all this Henry based his life on the establishment of law as the foundation of the church and of the kingdom. In practice he put them in the other order.

Now, this early Autumn, the expedition was returning southwards to Pontefract, then shortly to meet the king at Clipstone in Sherwood Forest. Edward would have to decide on action to do with Scotland after receiving their report. From York messengers were sent ahead whose news of their impending arrival was greeted with pleasure. Preparations were stimulated, stocks of food were checked and further were organized. John sent out scouts from the castle. Signals were arranged so that their welcome could be warm and immediate.

Messages had come in advance asking if the de Lacy family at Pontefract were well and unharmed. Twice in the last two days Henry had sought reassurance, disguised as it might be in other requests. Messengers had been told to see his family and to report in confidence. It was only at his arrival that Margaret saw the concern upon his expression. It was not long before there was an opportunity to speak, the family together. There was not only Henry's anxiety to be explained, but some of Margaret's interests were pressing.

"You look a little better after food and rest, Henry; it worries me that you have some distress. What went wrong. Is it you, or us, only? Bishop Carlisle seemed the same as ever."

"I'm sorry to be so transparent. Yes. I was anxious about you. About John. About Alesia."

The chorus was that there was nothing at all amiss.

"It is unusual for you to be like this. You must know we are well cared for here. I know there can be accidents..." she added bravely, thinking of Edmund. And she saw that it reflected in her husband, more deeply than it had before.

"My dear. Children. I thank God you are as you are. Forgive my state. Perhaps I had better tell you. The expedition to Scotland is another story. That was alright. At least I myself think it is."

The three waited patiently in silence over further hesitation.

"In York on our return I had a dream. Often I dream and it is gone. I sought an interpretation of this one, because it remained firm and alive. It was vivid. I see it now. There was a dog. A small brown furry dog. It walked towards a fire. A good burning fire with much flame and red hot embers. I knew it was getting too close, but it went onwards. It got into the fire. I must have been gaping at its action, but that turned to horror, when I saw - I saw that it did not mind the heat and flames. It just did not mind. It was not affected. The dog walked in and then out again."

Henry paused because of the feeling that this had induced in him. He then recounted further.

"I had woken, but turned and fell asleep again. Once more, even clearer, this dog walked to a fire. Maybe the same fire, I do not know. Certainly the same little dog. A friendly little animal. The fire burning even stronger. It walked in, turned round, and sat right on and among the searing fuel. It's hair was longish, and was burning, or lit rather. Certainly not burning away. It just sat, almost lay down, in all this without pain or hurt. It took no notice of my calling to it. It just looked and looked at me, without any special expression I could describe."

Margaret moved to hold his hand. Henry looked round at them, calmed through this relationship with normality.

"I'm glad I didn't have that dream" said Alesia.

"Thank you darling" Henry replied, "I'm glad you didn't."

Being prompted he explained he had tried to achieve an astrological explanation, which had to come from a secret visit to Maria of Echewell, reputedly best of all such exponents in York.

"After many questions, the dog, she said, represented me. I feared I might have been looking at my own soul in hell. She denied that possibility quite vehemently. She denied any other interpretation which I suggested. The point is that I was seeing myself amidst disaster. Yet surviving myself. I am desperate to know what disaster to come."

It was all Henry could do to confess to what he himself considered weakness in the face of nature. They began to question him.

"Is it not, perhaps, in the past, as an event?" asked Margaret.

"Would a different soothsayer have given the same answer?" asked John.

"I can see why you were anxious and sent messages, daddy. But what did Maria elucidate, as might be less frightening?"

These questions Henry had to brush aside. He had been into it in detail and at length to the point of cynicism, till he dare go no further.

"Perhaps" Margaret aimed at comforting "this event may not happen to you or us, but to someone else. Some person near to you."

"To whom?"

"Tragedies happen also to others, indeed to all. You said you appeared to be unaffected yourself."

"It was difficult to analyse the mind behind the dog's expression. It was bland and plain. I hope to God the interpretation may have some error."

To emphasize normality Margaret began to speak of the future of John and Alesia. She knew now that never would John be allowed or encouraged to live in another baronial household. It was not vital, but within the year or so more positive steps would have to be taken towards a marriage contract. In the past the de Lacys had never forced partners on their children, without their consent. But, yes, they would think about it, so that John himself could in due course be the final decider.

For Alesia there was a little more time, although this subject was the perennial one. Thomas of Lancaster seemed likely to be free again, for the negotiations about Blanche of Burgundy were drawn out. Henry thought the reason was simple. Thomas and his brothers, Henry and

John, were meant to inherit Provence from their grandmother Eleanor, and the Duke of Burgundy was quite sure that they would not achieve it. Charles of Naples, nephew of Louis of France, had virtually taken it over already.

Alesia had been in a waking reverie in the cosiness of their closeness and atmosphere of love and concern. She wondered if this could come from such detached placing of people together. She had to suppose so. In these moments her eyes glazed in suspension of feeling, the trust for her whole body and soul in the hands of others. Looking up at her father, she could see he was abstracted too. Before they all retired Henry had to clear his mind and calm his soul.

"In the morning I will tell de Hutford to draft a charter for my monks of Stanlaw. They have been asking long enough to be moved because of encroachments by the sea. I am going to grant them Whalley. And some churches and chapels for their living."

With this decided, preparations made, it was in a more relaxed frame of mind that they moved south to join the king and court. Messengers had been despatched to make their manor of Knesale ready for their arrival. In the middle of the county of Nottinghamshire, it was convenient for attendance at the council.

Reticent as Henry always was about affairs of state, there was usually something to say about the general way things might go.

"We certainly discussed Scotland in detail, and for once there was no dispute between Edward's advisers. Even Warrenne concurred that there's dispute enough possible among the Scots. Today we concluded that the kingship is between Baliol and Bruce. Edward's influence for either would decide."

"All this just because little Margaret died. The answer should be clear."

"It should be."

Margaret analysed the situation in a sentence.

"Knowing Edward, I reckon he wants to do one thing, but Eleanor and Burnell are moderating him."

"Moderating?"

"Edward has always to be moderated, as you know. I mean prevented from charging in himself."

"Edward himself as King of Scotland! Impossible! Or is it?"

"You think a minute. As a man, he is losing all his ancestors' lands in France. He has got to push on somewhere. He'll go for Scotland."

"But it's not necessary to him."

"It's necessary for himself, though."

"Well, my dear, he did make hints at one time, but I'm damned if I dare utter them as you have."

Nothing was clarified in the next few days; then the court was to move to Lincoln. Queen Eleanor was always kind to children, and Alesia and she knew each other well. On this journey, however, Alesia saw her but once, for a short conversation at Marnham, where all had to be ferried across the River Trent. The Queen had spoken to few that day.

"She's not well, I think." reported Alesia "She did not seem cheerful. She was pale. I left upon a nod. Of course I curtsied first. She seemed so tired."

Margaret had not been called to speak with or accompany her, so what Alesia said must be true. After all, they agreed, it was a cold November day. Perhaps the medicines which had been fetched from Worksop priory could cure the troubles.

Henry himself had been keeping an eye on the marshalling of the ferrymen and the arrngements for his own staff and escort. At the same time he was avoiding any reaction to the loud asides of the boatmen as to why the devil the monks of Newstead and Rufford should always have their ferrying done for nothing.

It was but one hour later that Edward demanded to know if there was a manor house in Harby, and who was there. To that, the home of Richard de Weston, they turned. Eleanor was too weak to move further. What de Weston could provide was comfort and warmth for one, the Queen, Eleanor of Castile. The love and helpmeet of King Edward the First was prostrate. Portent and fear stunned all.

It was hastily arranged for camping for as many guards as were needed; no court business was expected and only close companions remained. Medicines were sent for from Lincoln.

The bells of the church hard by were left unrung so as to have no disturbance to the Queen. No prophecy was possible for the life of Edward's devoted loving wife. Advice was taken of their chaplains as to where hope might be found, whereupon it was thought that Edward only could give expression to sufficient piety and conciliation. It was also his own feeling. He passed a desperate visit to Rufford Abbey. Solemnity and prayer served little to rest his soul. Towards the end of the month he returned. Prayer for her life had to change to prayer for her soul in heaven.

"I do not cease to love her now she is dead."

Queen Eleanor's heart was interred in Lincoln Cathedral. A funeral cortege was to be prepared for the journey to London.

The procession in Lincoln moved from castle to cathedral to the new eastern end constructed in the memory of Hugh of Avalon.

However confused were the thoughts of others those of Alesia were clear and strong. It was a couple of hundred yards from inside Lincoln Castle to the Cathedral. The King distraught; the reliance he had placed upon Eleanor's judgment, on her advice, and on her companionship had been deep, genuine and the subject of talk, if not always of admiration and wonder, by his adherents. The day she died at Harby, some seven miles away, had given the King's enemies some hope of a regime less strong and certain of itself.

There were usually crowds in the market by the castle entrance. Today they were swelled for the sight of what was the main itinerant administration of the land in all its finery, escorted by the best soldiers and servants. It was not a matter of complaint by stallholders that a way was cleared for them - it was not for long compared with the extra business about, and the dues to the Earl of Lincoln stayed unchanged.

Alesia walked with her brother. Their father and mother were by the King and his nephew Thomas of Lancaster.

The lesser or greater fears that are felt when something established changes gave thought to all those present. Would their own position alter, perhaps improve? Had they relied too much on the Queen's favour; or maybe too little, which would help now she had gone. The church would of course make a material gain. The merchants and citizenry of Lincoln were free of restraint in their thinking. Some were sympathetic on human grounds, most were there for curiosity, some had seen all these people several times, and there was some discussion as to whom the King would marry next, and so he should, some women said. But to Alesia de Lacy, nine years old, one thing stood out leaving no space for any other thought. The King in distress. Sooner rather than later she herself would be betrothed to someone. What hope, what perfection, the marriage of Edward and Eleanor had shown - as ambition and dream of that sort was hers to be. She would play her part. Several names had been discussed by her parents, some of them known to her as persons. Her own parents were friendly and pleased with each other. It would all be done as though she were a symbol; an estate; castles; a step to power. She accepted it. It seemed to work as well as anything. Everyone she knew jockeyed for some position, even servants, gatekeepers, reeves and squires wanted to move a notch up. Above all she felt she was equipped with more female armoury and strategy than nearly every woman she met.

The pale morning sun illumined nothing in the mind of King Edward. His queen was dead. She could do no more to be his companion. He moved where directed by the standard form of funeral occasions, followed and accompanied by prelates, earls, knights, chaplains, esquires, the families of some of the greater folk, many local inhabitants discreetly distanced. Below the great east window Bishop Sutton intoned the service for "...Alionore quondam regine Angliae uxoris Regis Edwardii filii Regis Henrici..."

Alesia stood stock still. This death was different. There was drama in the scene itself. The resonance of the bishop's voice, pitching evenly far along and up the cathedral beyond the presence of these persons here. The dignity expressed by the formal movements of the clerics contrasted with and emphasised the bowed figure of the broken king, the wondering faces of his children.

Alesia looked nowhere except straight forward. The angels of stone high above in their heavenly choir were not in her thoughts. None of the anxieties of the rest of those in attendance crossed her mind. She was full of Eleanor the departed queen. It gave her ambition and trust that for such a unity as they had had she herself could hope. And further, for that, once married, would she work. It was possible, because she had seen it to be so.

Down her left cheek, from a dark eye framed in her black long hair, a tear ran, followed by another. She felt relief at their cool passage, in closer understanding. Her unmoving expression did not change, and yet standing so still, a few had noticed her, and then had watched. The grave ceremony concluded, they remarked how pious with grief she had behaved. Alesia was silent for reply. She knew that it was for herself she had been communicating.

The emotions of the King in his sadness were that evening touched by Alesia in the sweet gravity of her demeanour towards him. She was affected by her admiration of him in accordance with her own hopes. His brother Edmund of Lancaster was most benevolent towards her, and Bishop Sutton was amiably inclined.

Next day in Lincoln castle Henry gathered his family together to discuss his own forthcoming movements. Because he began with the need for him to go overseas again in February there was a stimulus for them all to talk at once, Margaret, John, and Alesia. In resigned despair, it was Margaret who prevailed.

"To where? And how long?"

"We will celebrate Christmas at Ashridge with Edward. He has just so requested. He has also hinted that I am needed to go to Spain for certain discussions. Perhaps not until February."

"Can't we all go to Spain?" interjected Alesia.

"Certainly one day. I'm afraid you've got to grow a few years yet. Of course I want to take you."

"Then," interposed Margaret "can I hope that there will be our usual summer peregrinations?"

"I fully expect so. The Spanish business may not be long. Robert de Hutford and Thomas de Fishburn will have our affairs in hand."

"It all sounds very pleasant, calm and organized doesn't it, yet it does nothing for my anxieties and worry about you yourself. There are storms at sea, dangers on land, all which you know of because you're there, and maybe safe, but we do not know."

It had all been said before, and they knew that nothing could be done about it. There were other subjects in mind.

Alesia was interested about her future.

"There are still possibilities of Thomas of Lancaster being your husband, but naturally we have to wait for Edmund and Blanche."

"Why?" asked Alesia, mindful of the fact that her parents had been discussing her brother's future, and whom they might ask.

"It is different with boys. Don't ask me why", spoke Margaret.

"Somehow it became me," Henry grinned at their long continally friendly companionship. "As for girls they are meant to attract like flowers do bees."

"Well, I haven't heard the buzzing" responded Alesia with some fervour. "The bees fly near, gaze, and remain silent."

"Thomas is mixed up with political possibilities at present. As you know, they are hoping to get the Duke of Burgundy's support over his Provence inheritance, by marriage to his daughter. Also, Burgundy would no doubt like England's support. Thomas is the real heir, from Queen Eleanor of Provence, our late Queen Eleanor's mother. There are other whispers around, but nothing firm. I think we keep you up to date."

Alesia was fully conscious of the looks her way at social occasions; looks of unconcealed examination of her physical development. She was not ambitious to marry into the family of Edward the King. She was a bit afraid of Thomas, though, and his straight, thin, taut lips.

It was arranged that they would stay at the manor of Canford in Dorset while Henry was away. It would be anyway the place to collect the funds for his journey, and to organize any necessary despatches. John stated that he would take an interest in this organization.

"You, father, are a sort of military lawyer. I think I'm tending that way. It seems to be a way of getting on."

"True each has to make his own way. I must admit I think sometimes a local official with a more settled job has a better life. As settled life goes if you want it, that is."

"Like uncle John, in the King's administration? No, thank you sir. I'll settle for this type of life. By the way, he is suggesting to the King that I be granted the wood of Clyve in Shropshire. It makes a start."

After the hopeful discussion between father and son it was the latter who thought he should introduce a warning. He spoke in part for reassurance, in part to seek his father's confidence. John reassured himself with a quick look round that only the four of them were in the chamber.

"I know the dangers, or at least some of them. I can see why you are so firm that it is only law, and laws that are kept, that holds people to reasonable behaviour."

"But?" his father waited, smiling.

"But this. We have enemies, or at least people who do not like us. For example, after all the years Warrenne and his men remain detached and wary. Do I do the same, and to what end? Why do they detest us? That's only an example of the submerged antagonisms, as I am sure you know better than I."

Henry had to pause for thought. This was one subject which he hoped would go away. False counsels to the King, constant needling in state affairs, always by somebody an effort to undermine his position. As Henry had grown older he had met this situation by taking as little advice as possible, relying on the King's trust in his integrity, and in battle on his leadership and strategic ability. Warrenne and he had often been together, at least in comparative peace. Perhaps he was getting older too. In the most prominent case there was however young John Warrenne, the heir.

"Is it going to continue with their sons?" John concluded.

"How can I say? If you want some cautious wisdom, as I expect you do, I am sorry to say that I think the answer must be that it is. At least you should not be surprised if such troubles recur. It is part of court life, where success can come only from one source."

This openness of a part of Henry previously concealed astonished them. It frightened mother and daughter. Henry could not, of course, prophesy. Just that caution was needed, as of course in all state affairs and relationships. John accepted what was spoken as a straightforward organizational possibility but felt that he must know more, if his father was now prepared to speak.

"I had better tell you then. In a word, it is the rise of the de Lacys. Of us. But remember that the Earls of Surrey, the Warrenne family may be the more powerful militarily. Perhaps you thought I was. Not so, except that I take more part in administrative affairs, so may have more actual influence. But there's more to it than that. Leaving aside past jealousies I have offended Warrene, in the King's name of course, by our trying to bring in a new Domesday Book to regulate proof of purchase and sale of land.You know the result of that -"

"Warrenne wielding his grandfather's sword as proof, and a quarrel with King Edward."

"He did, however, submit in the end."

"Exactly. But he has not forgiven me. His son John should forget it, but he may not."

"He hasn't."

"Well, there was a compromise generally with the barons. Edward was then diverted by foreign matters. There are a few small disagreements of course, there always are; but Warrenne takes our measure from the larger one. Other persons are affected by other measures."

Margaret added that there were other things which made the Warrennes bristle. One was that Henry had been made an executor of Queen Eleanor's will, which he was not.

"As to your grandfather's quarrel with the previous Earl, it was started off by the Italian connection."

"Not for that of itself, so much" Henry added to Margaret's remark, "but it looked as though we were trying to begin a political dynasty or gain influence with the Holy Father. Of course, incidentally, Warrenne would not have been made an executor, because he knows nothing of legal processes. His behaviour has made that obvious, but his assessment of himself is a different matter."

Later, when Henry and she were alone, Margaret meant to ask a further question on a matter which had been unresolved. When they were together, however, it had become the time for bed. They prepared for their night's sleep, and she turned towards her husband. She felt him and their mutual responses transcended conversation. So any further, indeed lesser, communication waited until the dawn.

It was at first light that the household was always wont to stir, in the opportunity of accord with nature's timing, from which it was not possible far to fly. There came shortly recollection of what Margaret wanted to ask.

"That day. The one in the fire. Is it all now resolved? I am wondering if the death of Eleanor is its propitiation."

"May it so be. I wonder, but I do not really think so. It has some of the elements, but I cannot see that dear Eleanor's death is direct enough to us. Close, but not personal. The comfort I muster is that the possible event may have passed unrealised. Perhaps the conjunction of forces has changed to veer us from the passage of a disaster."

"If the burning were symbolic, also the expression on the little dog, I gather a sweet one, might it not express our - your present position, my dear? I mean the position of having more authority, more duties, which is producing more enemies - above which you ride with equanimity."

"I am not convinced that it was equanimity. Plaintive stolidity, with a look of loss..."

"Loss!"

Margaret wished she had not exclaimed. She stopped at the one word. It had been understood, though, that might it have referred to their previous loss - of their son Edmund. And if it was not a past event in reference; dear God, could it surely not be a future one.

"We do not know enough about these things" was how Henry buried thought and stopped that conversation, but there was a further word to be uttered by his wife.

"I know it is not in your mind, nor in mine, but I beg you not to get too powerful. I know what you have is all for what you do. I know you're frugal compared with others. But not everyone sees it that way."

Henry did not demur, but thought that he could scarcely deny the King's trust in his abilities, nor requiring the revenues to sustain the offices. Nor could he control what other people thought, and he would ever believe and work for the regulation of their actions by law. Of course, he felt, what his wife said was true. Some spoke as if the lawyers trained and housed in his Lincoln's Inn were for his manipulation.

The power of England, however, was stretched. It was becoming logistically too strenuous a task for Edward to maintain his authority in his French possessions. The King of France was constantly making penetrating moves to increase his influence. Time was on his side, for a long term policy of undoing the connections of the former Normans now across the water in England. The links of marriages were not now strong enough by themselves to maintain unnatural boundaries.

Wales may well have been united with England these eight years, but it had strained the treasury to all but bankruptcy. Philip of France was intriguing with little honour to gain Guienne, without which Edward could not pay his way. Pope Boniface had been declared Sovereign of Scotland. Edward threatened that he would now destroy Scotland from sea to sea. Then he prepared his own claims to that throne. In all this the barons stood for England, not for the Pope and the exactions of his church, and they would not fight overseas for their own King's French lands.

The death of Queen Eleanor, the year 1291, King Edward's mother, at Amesbury brought to him a second blow, as at the end of an era. Provence taken by Philip of France in spite of all the inheritance rules, made Edward seek once more to continue with the old methods.

"At a favourable moment I will open negotiations for Prince Edward to marry Isabella, Philip's elder daughter. It should enable retention of what I hold."

In almost the last moderating statement he was able to make before his health failed unto death. Burnell agreed, but suggested that Philip of France would make other moves on the pretext of unity of France and Provence.

Henry de Lacy himself noted at this council that Edward constantly referred to his French lands as his own, as personal property. This was true in essence, but did not and never had encouraged barons to cross the water and fight for what thus was not their feudal responsibility. King John had trouble that way. King Henry III had. Edward was now having the same problem. Henry remained quiet, however, on that point. Afterwards Edmund addressed him, obviously as previously agreed with the King.

"Henry. Your daughter Alesia. We would like to talk more formally about a marriage to our Thomas. What do you think?"

"I am sure we both would be delighted, Edmund."

King Edward moved near, and joined in the exchange.

"Enchanted. Such a pretty girl."

Thomas himself was pleased enough. The loss of Provence being a blow to his pride and material expectations, his latent character was developing more towards that of his forceful acquisitive grandfather. Edmund, so easy-going, saw in his son an energy that in himself was lacking, and admired him for it.

"Marry France to his son Edward, and leave the stability of England to his nephew Thomas is therefore now the King's plan," was brother John's remark.

"So far as I am concerned he would marry me" was Alesia's rejoinder. To make it fully understood, she added "myself." Her father just smiled.

Mabota suggested to Alesia in private that with lives as uncertain as they were, then one day by marrying the King's nephew, she may well be Queen. Prince Edward looked healthy enough to Alesia, though. It was true his elder brothers had died young. It was better not to bother about such a possibility, even if she wanted to. Alesia's mind was full enough, of hope, of anticipation, and at the same time diverted by family preparations for a journey north. Henry was to be with the King on Scottish business. The arbitration of who had the best claim to be King of Scotland was to be concluded at Norham Castle on the river Tweed. The de Lacys were to ride first as far north as their castle at Clitheroe in Lancashire, then across the Pennines to Pontefract, where Henry would join the King, and leave his family to await his return.

How fortunate it was that Henry was at a King's council when a messenger from Burgundy was able to give him private information. His master had not yet ceased to think of Thomas of Lancaster as a future son-in-law. Negotiations may have seemed to have been of little more than correspondence, but the Duke did desire connection with England. Pressure from the King of France was strong to prevent it. Any firm prophecy would be guesswork. To Edmund of Lancaster it was again a matter that his son would have to marry Beatrice of Burgundy if state policy prevailed, to have a mutual alliance against France.

This all was of realistic consequence to no-one but Alesia, so far as Henry was concerned. They were leaving on the morrow, and all doubts could be explained as rumour. He knew the strength of the King of France in these matters. He would put it out as kindly and obscurely as possible when he had to. He was certain that the King of France would win. An English King's nephew at his eastern flank was more than Philip would tolerate.

Thomas, Earl of Leicester,
Lancaster, Lincoln, Derby and Salisbury.

# CHAPTER 6

They were to spend little more than a week at Clitheroe. It was quite enough for Margaret. The restricted size of the castle allowed no social life, even if the weather did. The comfort was minimal, excepting the fires for warmth, which, having less space to heat than in many castles, did their work better. Nevertheless, it was a valuable territory of the de Lacys, producing hundreds of pounds a year, from land of beauty of natural features, of much soil which seemed unpromising, and all under frequent wandering mists, and peopled by those who would as like resort to a witch as listen to the parson. However, it served as excellent terrain for breeding and exercising horses, and from that much revenue was received. It was part of his inheritance which Henry had thought of devising to Thomas.

The founder of the castle, Robert de Lacy, had intended only a place to fall back on from the depredations of the Scots. Half a dozen acres of bailey were flanked by a lofty wall. The keep itself was but twenty feet square inside walls ten feet thick. The secret spring of water was what decided its precise location. The Norman gateway tower, already nearly two centuries old, was conspicuous in the valley of the river Ribble, goal for the convoy which was the de Lacy household on the move.

A dozen clerks worked at this seat of the Honour of Clitheroe, Henry de Lacy being the lord paramount following previous generations back to that Ilbert de Lacy on whom Pope Alexander III had conferred the lordship of Blackburnshire and the Honor of Bolingbroke. Bowland was granted by King Henry III. The forest of Pendle itself was in the jurisdiction of the de Lacy manor of Ightonhill, which included Burnley. At Easter and Michaelmas there was the forest court at Higham.

Out of pride and pleasure, and wonder at this vast and varied property, and the unusual effect the locality had on the people, the first Henry de Lacy perambulated the forest himself. The present Henry had no intention of doing that; all his movement would be incidental to hunting in the forest. For this he exacted a renunciation of those rights from the Abbot of Whalley. It was thus that Alesia now began to know this place, and how she found it accorded with her mood.

Rumours had reached her that Thomas may yet be betrothed to someone other than she. Her father would only answer a doubting question with an unfirm answer, such as "Surely not. There is always gossip." There was, however, not a single communication from Lord Lancaster. That, too, she was told, could as well betoken final decision. So in what had become uncertainty to her, and yet based on a feeling of future responsibility, Alesia rode with the hunt looking more at the land and its people than at the quarry. Two days she further spent escorted in the area.    Her leader was Ric de Merclesden, the Greave of the forest, and Master Forester of

Blackburnshire. He and his Warden and Keeper of the forest of Pendle, William de Tatham, knew it all so well.

Alesia found the great wide promontory of Pendle a scene to love and to fear. It was better to halt in the drifting mist, to look down where a shaft of sun illumined habitations and their crops for sustenance far below. Up on Pendle Hill was remoteness, changing texture of the air, varying nature of the light. On Pendle Hill was all feeling that the soul must be sought outside oneself. The short acidic grass spread as far as one could see, even with clear and distant visibility, yet its dark green surface gave no message, at least to the living. Alesia reined in; the escorting party halted with her. She stretched her arms fully outwards in a gesture encompassing this wide spread of nothingness which lay at the mercy of nature's elements. de Merclesden understood but uttered not at all. It was how Pendle was. It often caused him to yearn to take flight up into the elements.

They had made sure that at this time there were no remains of delinquents at the place where they were done to death, on the highest point. Moving downwards to Higham to see the courthouse, Alesia was stunned by the contrast between the free outgiving of the soul on top of the hill and the steady workaday look in the vale below. There are indeed two lives to live, she thought: the roots, and the flowers of their toil.

"There is not much revenue from the summit area, de Merclesden."

"Lady Alesia, that is true. There are losses. I can't say I would trust even every forester. Venison is taken. There's nothing we can do about timber thefts if folk take it within a bow-length of their own gate. There are the usual revenues - the Honour of Clitheroe, though, is only rich because of the horses. Perhaps however, ma'am, the revenue in the spirit is greater on the summit."

Turning in Higham to go north again to Clitheroe, Alesia was conscious that she had not spoken to any of the inhabitants, but she was not sure how to effect it. Bedraggled as folk were, it was not easy to make a random choice. There was a cry, from a group of three, who rapidly slunk round a corner, then the next one, to disappear.

"You never will be Queen!"

And as Alesia looked in astonishment, without a ready answer:

"Not Lancaster! Not Lancaster!"

Soothing words came from de Merclesden. It takes people that way here, he explained, and Alesia could well believe it.

"There are witches in the remoter corners. I expect my men know these."

"What did they mean, though? 'Queen' doesn't come into it."

"You are expected to be in the succession, Lady Alesia, but it was probably not that."

"So people say, but what was it then? Alesia answered, to both parts.

"Witches are always trying to prophecy things; and this is no exception. Most of the prophecies are meaningless, and then forgotten about when they are unfulfilled."

de Merclesden was clearly going no further, and Alesia remained silent over her dislike of the several implications of their first shout, and the implied warning - or was it derision for the ambition they assumed of the second.

The family were now to move for a few days hunting to Ightonhill - the legal capital of Pendle forest, and fortunately also the best hunting. Alesia remained quiet to the end, as the custodian, Parker, in a proprietorial way narrated so much about Pendle and his horse-breeding, his salmon and his trout. Her father let him continue. After all, the de Lacys were there only now and again. Parker's pride was momentarily halted by a question from Alesia herself.

"What has the Lord Lancaster to do with Pendle?"

After some hesitation to come to earth and remember detail the answer came.

"He has a manor house here, and certain rights to game, warren, and so on."

Alesia did not explain why she wanted to know. Henry's light smile was to do with her oblique way of clarifying Parker's position to him. Parker felt it prudent not to reveal the attitudes of people who were already cautious about Thomas of Lancaster.

With the departure of the de Lacys for Pontefract, Ightonhill reverted to Parker's authority. Once at their huge towering stronghold of Pontefract their arrival was made known to Henry's mother, Alesia. She was in tears, which some regarded as the over-expressive emotion of her Italian temperament. It was her granddaughter Alesia herself who by her bearing comforted her, and reassured Henry and Margaret. A message had come from Edmund of Lancaster. Thomas had now been officially betrothed to Beatrice of Burgundy. Alesia alone knew that she had harboured her own doubts. Some showed their disappointment, and their thoughts that politics should interfere with her happiness. They marvelled that she accepted the tidings with such composure. But the tautness of Thomas's expression and the thrust of his nature that was developing had seeded in Alesia some anxiety. She gave a big and special hug to her father, reassuring him that there was no cause to blame himself, nor to worry about her.

"Return from the north safe and sound. We wait for that, impatiently."

As Henry rode off for Norham castle on the river Tweed, he felt blessed indeed by the devotion of his daughter. His problem now, as Edward's closest adviser, was to perceive what reason his King had for what he was about to do. No Queen Eleanor, no Burnell now. Edward was extrovert, a hunter, persuasive, and passionate in his duty to render England's dominion safe. And they were to confront the Scots with Edward's claim to their throne. One God, Henry thought was easy to support, for He changed never. One King, well. Anointed certainly, stability vital, but sometimes earthly actions were unexplainable. Perhaps Edward's actions were in his make up, not in the logic of his circumstance.

The gaunt fearsome aspect of Pontefract Castle stayed in Henry's view for a long time, silhouetted against the early morning November sun. He had turned again and again to wave, though it was uncertain whether he could be identified in the column of guards and men-at-arms. Left behind, once more, were his wife, his remaining son, his daughter, and his mother. Their life in his absence was above all to make sure of their own wellbeing. As much gossip and information of what was happening outside the castle walls helped to that end.

Discussion was sometimes on money. This was especially the subject of Henry's mother. A dozen crosses for the memory of Edward's Queen Eleanor were being erected on the route of the journey of her body from Lincoln to London. They were costing more than estimated. So was everything.

"But every cross is taking a year's revenue of a dozen manors already! At the same time there are meant to be controls on prices of food!"

Other talk was of the pardon of Henry's bailiff William de Coden and his foresters over their actions in Wales; this was commented on by Robert Heppale, steward of Clitheroe and Ightonhill, who had reported to Pontefract. Margaret's cousin Nicolas Longepee had been translated to the position of Bishop of Salisbury. Above all, the messages that mattered were those on the fate and progress of their own Lord of Lincoln. Then that day dawned which was to yield the written parchment saying that they would be together to celebrate Christmas. Henry would manage to return in time. The man had come from Durham, so Henry must be in York by now. Perhaps he would be detained there by King Edward. Whether or not - preparations for relaxed and joyous feasting and worship gained full purpose.

Welcomes produced much the same activity as farewells. To the battlements all climbed to watch the retinue wind closer until individuals were identifiable. Waves and shouts showed all were well. Up the slope to the high promontory rode the entourage.

To gain a further and uninterrupted view John had to see round an interrupting tower. He, young John de Lacy, future Earl, was loth to lose his feeling of joy at again seeing his father.

Disaster at this moment of excited apprehension could not be comprehended. As one fell silent on the walls, so did another. In the total silence Margaret's scream of incisive pain echoed on the walls of the Keep itself. From others there escaped sounds of fright amid disaster. Alesia had seen her father down below change from open cheerful mien to ashen grey. He had been down from his saddle, over to the rock upon which had fallen John, his only surviving son. Alesia herself slumped unconscious, crumpled against a crenellation. Those below in the compound gasped in fear at the unknown reason for apparent terror.

There was suitable material for a rough stretcher in a baggage wagon. They carried John into the castle. Dead. Henry was supported as he walked beside him. Dear God. God? One accessible God. Accessible? No, let that not be denied. Where was the response of God for mental comfort. How could such response be felt? The Black Friars' house in Pontefract, founded by Henry's father received the body but their words gave no feeling in return. Not only is there influence of God, but also there are works of the devil.

God answered the de Lacys only in the strength that they had within themselves. There was a moving funeral oration, but the de Lacys heard it not. Throughout the castle and the lands of the Honour of Pontefract, there was personal grief, compounded with the fear of an unknown next Lord. Only Alesia remained as sole young representative of the de Lacy family. Unique in proper dealing and fair arrangement, one could not do better than with a de Lacy. That Christmas for the de Lacy family the great log fires produced no warmth. The celebration of the birth of Jesus changed Alesia. Not yet a wife, but within her alone was the element of the de Lacy future.

Pontefract Castle, main stronghold of the de Lacy family, devolving to the Earls of Lincoln, until Thomas of Lancaster's execution in 1322.

# CHAPTER 7

Alesia felt alone. It was solitude in all the press of attention upon herself in the crowded days subsequent to her second brother's accidental death. Now fate had made of her an only child. Her parents were shattered into silence with their grief, while looking askance at Alesia as the only one left to love. In days and weeks they gave no reaction to the sympathy and attempted understanding of so many others. The healing of their hearts would be long, if it ever came; morale engendered by hope was for ever gone.

There had been the funeral, and it was followed by their journey to London. Lodged at Lincoln's Inn in Holborn, more reminders of the tragedy arrived in many further condolences as the news spread further. Alesia wept alone, or in the presence of Mabota. Try as they would, feeling they must indeed rebuild their lives, her parents were not able yet to communicate with her other than to have her close to them, but in silence. Others had lost children, certainly as babes; many as sickly adolescents. These accidents of Edmund and John had occurred out of their enthusiasms, and because of their full vigour.

That dog's eyes, that dog in Henry's dream, haunted him. They had been calm, unfearing, looking straight forward. In the fire the dog had given the air of being still alive, yet it must have surely died. Contemplating quietly of an evening Henry knew that that was himself. A calmness was coming over him. It increased his wonder at the holy mysteries of life; of the unfathomable ways of God working in his creatures. Margaret had no such thoughtful ability. Although there was Alesia, her pride and perfect sustenance had gone to the grave. She made sure that prayers were said and resaid for the souls of her sons. She refused to leave her husband's side on all possible occasions. She tried to maintain him in his duty to God, the King, and to his daughter. The future of the family was now Alesia. Some arrangements must be considered. But every required thought sent through her whole nerve structure the savage strain of fear that John must have felt as he was falling.

"That is one thing you must not do" Mabota had chided Alesia when she had expressed the thought that she should try to be a new son to them.

"You must be the feminine beautiful daughter that you are. They do not want you to be what you are not, and could not properly be." She continued: "You will soon have much to consider. Why, Thomas may be back again."

"Thomas? I don't know that I mind. Who said?"

Outside her family there were many who did not mind. Assessments were reassessed, because now whoever married Alesia would in time become Earl of Lincoln and of Salisbury.

But Mabota continued:

"Sometimes your grandmother speaks to me. She has said she is sure that the King of France won't let Burgundy get away with this marriage of his daughter to Thomas."

"It is agreed."

"Lady Alesia, Kings can unagree things."

It was not easy for Alesia to know about that. Her own experience had been from her father's record of keeping a word once given. For herself she could see that in a volatile and unordered world his principles must be right. He was in the councils of King Edward. She, however, had to decide what she wanted, a decision though it might be which would have no influence.

"Mabota, there must be a moment when all seems right, or proved, or, if you see what I mean, everything is clearly focussed?"

Mabota, lady's maid, waited quietly.

"My father and mother must regain meaning in life."

"Lady Alesia, to me they appear to seek it through the church, which alone can explain the certainty of all things."

So long now had Henry and Margaret retreated into despair, and so long had chaplains tried to comfort, to divert, to show the whole of life in one spiritual context that Alesia could see no return of their former attunement to life on earth. Henry was continuing with his state duties, as coldly as duty could be; but he was able to hide the brain's compartment of his personal grief. His exertions and travels for his King and Country now fully absorbed him. Margaret's duty was to him, to further him, to sustain him in accordance with such truths as could be found in her mind after prayer and communion.

Alesia began to feel unwanted. Not for Thomas. Occasional talk but no arrangement. She thought the family should have a future through her. She would have to wait. Grief, pain, disease, death in families all around - even the King himself with sons lost and now his Queen - and how poignant it became when it was one's own. Shock. And Alesia now the only one where hope had been nurtured on three. Through the ordinary activities of the Earl's household Alesia moved, more with her bodily existence than with her intellect. She was in no position to ask about her future. She had to be patient until she was told.

There was enough chatter to sift, if there had been anything about her in it. Henry back to Scotland with the King. His return. Edward's genealogical claims to the Scottish throne, too strongly put, thought Alesia. Then, Baliol to be the King's puppet king. There were frequent references to land and markets, which was nearer to Alesia's interest as to what lands might be her dowry. There was land and courts given to Abbot and Convent, land and rent to a chaplain, and on the incoming side another manor or two and another Hundred. Margaret achieved an order to Roger Lestrange, justice of the forest this side of Trent, to have fifteen bucks and does from the New Forest to stock her new park in Canford, Dorset.

Then some strange news fell to Alesia. Master Halton was writing and listing and checking again. He was working on roll after roll. She acted as if she knew all about it.

"That's a long job, Master Halton."

"The grant, yes, Lady Alesia."

"Seems to cover everything."

"It's meant to, Lady Alesia. Indeed it has to."

"I've never seen it written down before."

"No. It's all on separate pieces of course. Nor dare I miss anything out. The law lasts so long."

Alesia could not yet divine why every single holding and right of her father's vast possessions were being the subject of a legal document. Perhaps it was that King Edward was repeating his former plans for proofs of ownership.

"The King will be pleased at it all being tidied up" she said, in a matter of fact tone.

"More particularly his brother the Lord Edmund of course. Or indeed yourself Lady Alesia."

"Me?" This was certainly a surprise.

Master Halton spoke carefully, for when one astonished one's superiors there could follow too many explanations.

"I meant only that your interests are preserved, as I presume you knew, Lady Alesia."

This was enough for them both. Alesia assumed wrongly but satisfactorily that the document was purely an estate deed. She further gathered, correctly, that it was nothing to do with any possible marriage arrangement for her.

It needed only another hint or two for the whole process to clarify. It came at a gathering, from Edmund of Lancaster himself.

"I don't want you to think that your rights are in any way affected. It's only a precaution. Your father agreed that it should all be certain. Everything is re-granted to your father, and his descendants, which means you."

Alesia noted in her mind the necessary precaution. She was the descendant. She might then not marry at all and have none of her own descendants. That appeared to be the thinking. Her eyes filled with tears. She curtsied so as to lower her head. She sidled away, at least herself believing that her feelings were not noticed.

"You are being astonishing. Really, Lady Alesia, please. Whatever do you expect?"

Mabota was beginning to be bolder in her personal expression, now Alesia was older, and needed support. With a naturalness which Alesia had rarely seen, Mabota expressed her own views. Alesia could not expect to be party to any preliminary talk as to whether she would be married to anyone. She was too valuable for that in herself and in what she stood for. She was very marriageable indeed as a person. Probably, most likely her parents were fending off unsuitable suitors. Of course they were. She had just herself seen that her interests were protected. So the man had to be exceptional for herself and for her responsibilities.

"Then, Mabota, I'm down to a handful of possibles."

"Certainly. But you can't know them all. There are foreign princes, too."

"And why not a handful? No-one is eligible to everybody."

Then Alesia continued:

"I'll stay a handful to you, anyway, dear Mabota."

Mild jocularity did not, however, clear the matter in her mind. Everything, absolutely everything, given to the King, then granted back again to her father, and failing heirs, to Edmund of Lancaster and his heirs. All this because her brothers were dead. Alesia had heard of little except the law from her father's lips, so she knew much of its trifling precision. Was she an heir? If she was, a female heir, why go through all this, it being clear that its basis was that no males were left. Edmund was dear and imprecise, so his words may well not be true. Alesia's environment had always led her to believe that her position was assured. Subject of course to life itself, and particularly to keeping on the side of the King. To gain knowledge of her future it was still more than necessary to wait and see and listen for a breakthrough on the point in her elders' conversation. She became adept at sitting quietly while people spoke their thoughts, she appearing occupied in some sewing task.

So few knew of any legal arrangements, and not an iota had changed in the running of the manors, that unfortunately it was not a topic for anyone of importance to have to discuss. Margaret, however, in her own detachment from affairs, noticed the same in her daughter. It came better for Alesia thus, that her mother enquired of her.

"We have all been very quiet these last months. We mustn't let it sadden us for ever. All has been done that can be done. It is for our prayers to help now. There is none other. We must keep up hope on this earth. Perhaps its my fault that you have seemed withdrawn. Shall we talk about you?"

"Mother. What is there to say, for me. I am well. I am quiet. I pursue day to day tasks. I learn nothing of my future, as a daughter, as a wife, or... well, I suppose that's it."

"Oh, Alesia, we're always looking to settle you in time. You are still young, of course."

"Looking? It has all changed, and it is as though I cannot represent the de Lacy family."

"Oh, Alesia, is that what you're thinking? It is I suppose a world of men..."

"Women defend castles, and get imprisoned sometimes like any man."

"Yes, darling." Margaret hesitated, "but they don't do it for some aggressive principle. They do it for love of some man."

"Then, mother, who do I know whom I am to love; and..." in a hasty bold tone..."and what I'm meant to live on."

"Alesia!"

"Well, what is it and where?"

"I see you do not understand. Or understand too much, but not the whole. Now we are both confused. We must have your position explained. By your father."

"I would rather you explain, mother. Not much, just enough. I only want to know enough."

"Darling, yes, all right. I had no idea that you did not know all. For a start, on my being, well, no longer here - you receive all my lands and titles."

"Yes, mother. Thank you. For the assurance, that is. It is part of the family continuance. But.."

"I think you mean why all this change in the Lincoln inheritance. Yes? To be quite clear, Alesia darling, I do not know, except that it was meant to clarify things. But Salisbury is unaffected."

Alesia had not realised this.

"Am I to marry Thomas?"

"It is not arranged, no. They still cling to the other contract. The House of Lancaster came into it only because of getting the Lincoln lands ultimately into the King's family, instead of them being held too far away."

"So I am still the de Lacy heiress?"

"I understand so. Yes, of course. To everything." Then in a moment of inspiration "That's why your husband needs such secret and careful choice."

Strange, though, that her mother's lands had not gone through the same legal process. Was Alesia not to pass the Lincoln and Salisbury titles on to stand alone, by marriage to some minor scion?

In her depression of what seemed to Alesia as apparent abandonment of her place in the family she felt that there was but one person to whom she could speak, to discover, and to make an oblique approach to her parents. It was her grandmother Alesia, who had been making guesses of her own. Her Italian nature, full such as it was, had caused her as much jealous insult from others as its use and expression had beneficial effect for the de Lacys. Having arrived to marry Henry's father, she at once, for no fault of her own, usurped a position which others coveted for a daughter. She appeared also as a harbinger of Lombard and Florentine bankers, desperately useful to every noble house as they were, and unpopular for that. The association had no material basis at all, with the minor exception that her attitude to the frugal use of money resources made it appear so. Henry followed his mother's attitude on this matter with ingrained care.

Knowing as much or more as any other lady of experience in a burgeoning household of scores of humans, grandmother Alesia was pleased to listen and talk at greater length and with more privacy than was usual.

"Dear Alesia, you are still tender of complexion and fair of bodily disposition. I can also say you have guile, laughter and loving more than a woman needs. Of course you have also envy and malice and anger. They too have to come out. You need not be worried at all. Men begin to take heed of you, for yourself. You can speak Latin and French and some Italian. You read. You can write if you want to. Do not take it to heart when you hear men say - some men - that they would rather women could not read, nor delve into the scriptures. There must be knowledge to withstand the perils of the soul. Above all, I am proud of you as a granddaughter."

While Alesia was comforted by conversation with her grandmother, she still sought for more.

"Oh, that document, and the law. Now, Alesia darling, there never is all that certainty in spite of all men's laws. Look at me - simply by goodwill, and love I suppose, as a dowager I have manors and rights granted. It is usual. It is the method. You will be in the same position. If you really want to know why your father's properties have all been granted to Edmund of Lancaster and confirmed back again, then you will have to learn that from your father. Or maybe you know a young lawyer. No, that would not be right to reveal your ignorance on the matter. To my mind, it is only a confirmation of what Henry has, and his rights in new circumstances."

"That's my point. New..." Alesia emphasized the word "...circumstances."

"My own observation, my dear, is that it is a legal safeguard, for the family, including you. It's like making a list of everything, and giving it legal backing."

The tensions returned to Alesia. It was her lot these months, that new thoughts came forth. She tried hard not to give her mind to passing things of the earth but to find more in heavenly things. Listening and pondering in church services was indeed instructive, but minor as palliative. More and more the thoughts tingled that she desired the serpent to slither towards her as it had to Eve. Perhaps there was no haven but the church to keep her dark thoughts at bay. That was where all looked for eternal truth and comfort.

Confession to her mother's personal chaplain was not such a close affair to her that Alesia ever revealed much of any inner thought. She was more likely to tell Mabota of any problem. Bath time was usually as good as any other. It was usually fun, relaxing in the hot water, and self-indulgent. One grey evening the water surface lay flat and still, inviting Alesia to enter and disturb it. As a mirror it was in which she was reassured at what she saw. Her own rounded limbs, her shapely waist, firm and jaunty breasts, her long black tresses coming over her left shoulder towards them. Her face showed beauty in its lively contrast with its dark waving frame of hair. As she knocked her knee on the side of the tub the glassy reflections all wobbled away and disappeared.

Alesia put both her hands up to her neck to gather her hair up and away. If only she could be seen and praised as herself for what she knew and felt she was. Mabota helped her hair into position. Alesia turned. They embraced. They kissed. They embraced hard. It passed as suddenly as it had begun. In wonder, Alesia was relaxed. This was not the way. She knew. It was never mentioned by either of them. Just a little trembling for a while.

In the sudden consciousness of her adolescence Alesia was reassured. She looked where she could find reflections; in puddles and quiet water here and there. The best were in her bath and in the dark windows of her chamber, where she could contemplate her own naked well-formed shape. She thought perhaps that she was slightly plump. Withal she felt alone, though in the midst of a considerable household.

Henry being away, down south, for a few days, Alesia saw fit to join the hunt again. Not too far, in the inclement weather, were her orders to John. It was a casual group this day, relaxed because there was no urgency to replenish the food supplies. Alesia was in a chatty mood, resulting from some days of exchanges with young lawyers at the Inn and some visitors. She was sad that there were none to accompany the hunt staff and her this day. Apart from hounds, however, and the commands to them, there was babble enough coming from the dozen participants, in which Alesia was delighted to join. Peter the Chaplain was with them, helping to exercise a horse. A couple of the men had stayed on from the visit of Felicia the Prioress, for their further improvement in the science of the hunt. Being unfamiliar with the Lady Alesia they were by no means as free with their exchanges as were the others. They had both the same baptismal name, the one was Richard in the Lane, the other Richard le Brazur. It was not the habit of the former to give deep thought to much that happened. His intellect was small and needs were minor. Richard le Brazur comprehended a great deal, though, being contemplative in wonder that the Lady Alesia should exude such responsive cheerfulness. It had seemed to him that those set above him must be of different clay than he.

They walked their horses easily northwards from Lincoln's Inn, to make for the wooded hills. In all they made a loose and constantly varying grouping, and at a summit Richard le Brazur and Alesia became side by side, as the hunt paused for assessment of the next line to take. This Richard was especially detached in his manner, as was his habit when in the presence of the ones who had authority. If it seemed like lack of interest in her, it would have been misjudgment. But it had to be left to the lady to speak first.

"You usually hunt in the west, I assume."

"Indeed, only for the Priory, Lady Alesia." It seemed welcome to say more, and having noticed the general communication with this young lady Richard le Brazur thought he would try to clear what was niggling in his mind. So he continued:

"I think this is the first time that on the hunt there has been a lady present, my lady. In the service of the prioress, of course, we are not accompanied."

"Never?"

"The prioress Felicia is strict, possibly somewhat old now, but I believe she never hunted. She forbids her nuns to do so."

"She misses much." Alesia smiled and added: "I, too, miss much, but when I do achieve a hit, it is especially satisfying."

Before they all moved further onwards, Richard le Brazur remarked that in future the Lady Alesia herself would no doubt be allowed to continue. The hunting group devolved into another changing pattern. Before they had moved down the side of a small valley and up the other side, Alesia began to wonder what was meant by that last remark, 'no doubt continue?' Why any doubt? An improperly formed sentence? 'Doubt' because ladies gave it up? Perhaps. But she did not think that that could be near to her years. But the word 'allowed' had been uttered in an even tone, of straightforward factualism. Maybe Richard had insufficient knowledge of de Lacy ways, for no-one had ever 'disallowed' her or any other woman hunting. It had been the other way.

In a few moments it happened to be Peter the Chaplain who was alongside, a movement in part contrived to check on her safety.

"Ah, Peter, we seem to be uncertain in our direction; what is your opinion as to where we should seek some quarry?"

"Lady Alesia, I feel sure my opinion on that is no better than yours, but I would hazard that there'll be more than one deer in that wood further north on the hill."

"We are veering that way; in the most unplanned day I've had. Almost only a reconnaissance. That might even suit the canons of prioress Felicia, I understand."

Peter the Chaplain was amused and pleased at the aside; it had to be his policy to propound as much religious tuition and respect for God that the family was likely to absorb. He replied in the same vein, and at once set to move forward:

"I do not know what she will do with you, I'm sure. But I expect all will be well."

With one sharp move Alesia reined in and to them all she cried:

"Halt!"

Upon the instant as they all turned to her, hesitating in astonishment before they closed in, at once she shouted more:

"Peter! You mean something by that! What? and you Richard! Tell me at once! What is that about the prioress Felicia? John! Come here! Something is known about affairs which concern me! What is being talked?"

A silence of astounded surprise ensued. A number of the party knew nothing at all, and waited with eager interest to hear the resolution of the situation. It should have been Peter the Chaplain who spoke, as the closest to the family, the nearest to their counsels, and in fact the only other educated person there. He sat stunned, however, with the dumbness of fear that he may have broken a confidential undertaking. So it was Richard le Brazur, being not of the immediate de Lacy retainers, who first opened his mouth to speak. To John the Huntsman this did not seem right that an outsider should have this expression of intimacy in family affairs; so he at once reined closer in towards Alesia. The moment of silence from all now seemed so long to her, the astounded looks towards her so unwavering, she began to fear that she had made a foolish misunderstanding of innocent conversation. She was at once affirmed, however, by John's quick explanation.

"Milady Alesia. With respect..." and he gave a minor salute with his hand towards his forehead "...we have been speaking for a day or two - in our interest for you - of what we hear about - well, you, milady. Your future, or at least what reaches us, of course, which may be wrong. It is not intended to be without...."

Alesia rejected any idea of adopting the useless air of displeasure about their gossiping, for it was a permanent feature of the life of underlings. The tension she felt came out as a statement, given slowly in a tone at once of dignity and of inquiry.

"I know of no plans."

All the men felt deeply that there must have been a trespass on her affairs, and again it was a tardy matter awaiting one to take the initiative. Peter the Chaplain now felt it was up to him.

"Lady Alesia, I am sure that you must realize that whatever we speak about must in a sense be second-hand at least, and our comments must be therefore from imperfect knowledge."

Alesia now knew well that there was something in plans for her from somewhere about which she apparently knew nothing. Her temper was rising.

"Be quick, now. Tell me."

"Ma'am, how can we believe that we can..."

"I know the excuses. Tell me what is going on."

With an audible gathering of breath, Peter stated flatly:

"It is being said, and we assumed that you must know..."

Alesia glared towards him at that interpolation.

"...that ... come, milady. Surely the arrangement for the nunnery is known... to..."

With one swift turn and spurs deep into her mount Alesia crashed her way between the mounted men behind her, all helped by her horse Cresselly trying to rear up at this sudden painful command. She was away. To the south, to Lincoln's Inn. Across the valley, up to the summit and on. Rad de Kilburn, in charge of the guard, with some presence of mind, ordered his men at once:

"Follow her!"

Peter the Chaplain and the others crossed themselves. In the name of dear God, thought Peter. Oh! Save the family from another accident, to their last child. Is that what it was to be? Scared of what he may find, he began to ride slowly back to the Inn. The others had asked him what they should do. He could only reply in bewilderment that he did not know. John decided that he could not continue the hunt until at least he had the news of Alesia's safe arrival.

Her journey had been seen so far to be swift. Riding astride, which was fortunate for her stability, in her stimulated taut unthinking condition Alesia urged her mount to the swiftest gallop he could attain. As sure-footed as any, Cresselly himself absorbed the feelings of his rider and let nothing deter the urge for speed. There was experience of each others ways over a period which might co-ordinate their unconscious movements into a safe successful ride. Down the side of the hill to the fields, only by good fortune Cresselly placing his hooves without mishap. Nearer to the Inn there were more to gape than had stood staring in the further fields. In the open the cattle had been disturbed and had run aside, in Highgate children escaped but felt some flying mud. Geese would have brought Alesia down if they had been pottering nearer the church; the sharp turn left was fortunately clear. So was the gateway into Lincoln's Inn. Seeing that they could not catch her, the soldiers had fallen to a more modest pace, to avoid such dangerous flight, and in the minds of more than one, to avoid looking as though they were the cause of the trouble. There were many games in Lincoln's Inn Fields which ceased as Alesia galloped past, followed by as many remarks and ribaldry at the escort tagging behind.

The crunching beat of Cresselly on the loose stones drew a sentry to peer from the guardroom, and as soon to withdraw to safety. Alesia ignored all reaction; she jumped off in the open yard, ran to the solar behind the hall, expecting to find, and did find, her mother. The peaceful, quiet embroidery which Margaret was slowly pursuing was thrown into irrelevance. Alesia was still carrying a whip, augmenting thus the force of her attitude:

"What, mother, is this about a nunnery?" her words came deliberate and forcibly.

Margaret had never seen her daughter like this. Before being able to gather a reply, Alesia continued:

"There are plans. For me. I am told by servants!"

Margaret managed a faint nod. She herself was attempting to assemble persuasion and the justification.

"It is true? It is true? I say it is not so. I will not go to any nunnery. Am I so unmarriageable? I hear it from gossip. From gossip overheard at that. I object. I will not be imprisoned as a delicate object for life."

Margaret had to react involuntarily to that: she stood, and cried out:

"A bride of Christ! A prisoner! Alesia!"

"The truth of this has been kept from me. Many knew it, but I do not. I tell you I will not go, and you must undo it. You say a bride, I say a bride in a coarse covering, and swearing hatred of all that is alive."

Margaret was accustomed more to smooth arrangement of the lives of unquestioning persons, and she, with Henry, had not considered other than their plan was the right one. So she had first of all to calm her daughter, and either to take refuge in her husband's feelings, or to insist on the rightness and acceptibility of such a course. At this moment she knew not which.

Alesia remained red, forceful, angry, and asweat.

"I have returned from the hunt..." she spoke through clenched teeth "...on hearing what is news to me, in believing that my interpretation of their chatter might be wrong. Now you have managed to say it is right, I have to tell you that I will make it wrong, for I refuse."

"Oh, my God, Alesia. How will you not do..."

"I-will-not-go. I refuse. Let that be known at once."

Alesia espied a reflection of herself in glass. She held out her dark long hair. "You would condemn these flowing locks to be shorn? At least my brother monks would contemplate on what had been!"

"My dear, I did not quite mean...I know not what...Your father..."

"Do you think I cannot guess? Of course I see him desperate in grief for Edmund and John. Of course I am too. I have seen his mind moving on nothing except absolutely necessary work. I know he can hardly bear to go back to Denbigh. I know his thoughts when at Pontefract. But understand this, my mother - I am not a sacrifice."

"Whatever do you mean?" Margaret tensed in astonishment.

"I am not to be buried into the depths of bereaved despair so that my soul has to match in life that of my brothers dead. I have life. I am going to keep it.

"Your father..."

"He must find some other way of conciliation."

"Enough!"

"Enough indeed! I am the authority for my body and my command is 'Never!!"

"Alesia" The word came more calmly from Margaret than she had hoped. She perceived the depth of Alesia's utterances. She and Henry had hardly considered her reactions, and thus had not spoken of their proposal to her. It had been a plan emanating from their fear and despair.

"Alesia." The tone was meant to indicate calm explanation. It had now come to Margaret that they had been putting off this moment. It would have been better to have been open about the matter. Margaret closed her eyes. She was too taut to achieve a coherent argument. The hesitation was long, and the silence was broken by Alesia herself:

"Do you accept that I am quite clear and firm on..."

"Yes, yes." Margaret found a voice.

"...and is that an end to the matter?"

Margaret knew that Alesia's future had been under much discussion, and not only between Henry and herself. It was a question as to where she could best be placed politically. The field was narrow, because the King was unremitting in his urge for greater centralization of resources.

"The nunnery was founded by my great grandmother, darling..." her mother faded, to continue:

"There have been difficulties in arranging marriage, darling." Margaret put forward an arm in the subconscious hope that affection might cure and calm. At once she realized that the attempt at confidence aroused more adverse emotion.

"Me! Difficult for marriage?" This incredulous question from Alesia was followed by her statement giving clearly her set ambition:

"Are there no others in this world apart from Thomas of Lancaster, now to marry for politics? I, in God's good time, and long away may that be, to hold Lincoln and Salisbury, and who could thus espouse a strong and loyal person to those offices, and thus could forward our line for generations - you mean that that is difficult? Now look at me, and on that other count of my own person, you mean that I, too, am difficult?"

Margaret could explain no more without inducing further fury from her daughter. She faded into a slumped position. Of course Alesia was right. It was all overlaid with what would be allowed, and what suited. They were not their own masters in this. Alesia had not been looked at as a person. Perhaps that was partly because of Henry trying to do things for the state, thus becoming embroiled in failing negotiations which negated any other course. Alesia could not be married without the King's permission, and for Thomas she was only a reserve.

"Shall I answer my questions myself?"

All Margaret could do was to temporize:

"I will see what I, indeed we, can do. I suppose there is hope. We have thought that this was right. I imagine that we cannot force you, nor do we really want to. Shall we leave it till your father returns in a couple of days or so?"

Margaret had struggled through the sentences. It gave to Alesia, who frowned with thought, that her mother was speaking from a background that was not of her own feeling. With a touch of kindness Alesia took her leave:

"I will go out again..." She had changed her mind when about to speak further. She had made herself clear. Because of her mother's obvious distress, she kissed her on the cheek. Margaret made to restrain her, desperate in her lack of influence, to no effect. Alesia was going out again. Whither? Her mood turned to helplessness. Alesia moved swiftly to avoid the reaction which would have brought her to apologise to her mother, perhaps to agree even to be obedient to their wish. Closing her eyes momentarily as she walked slowly along, she began to reinforce her thoughts - no, she could not temperamentally, physically, nor by discipline become a nun. She became calm, certain and confident in her stolidity against the idea. To avoid the dominance of the knowledge that if she was not to be married then there was no alternative than the nunnery, she had to find some human beings with whom to talk.

It would be as well, she thought, to check Cresselly with groom Nic, son of Robert le Wine. Passing not far inside the gateway she did not fail to hear the calls of the knot of interested folk gathered there in the hope of more news of Alesia de Lacy's gallop home. The best shout was to do with the excellent skill of her riding, and she did not forbear to turn and smile. Her escorts were waiting for further orders, it still being early in the day. Perhaps later, she would rejoin the hunt. They would be informed.

Alesia wanted to do nothing other than make sure that in a calm atmosphere she could stolidly and quietly maintain her point of view against her parents.

When Lord Lincoln returned, he at once sensed the atmosphere. The scene before him was the result of two days of perseverance in sewing and embroidery by Margaret and Alesia. Not much had been spoken, and certainly nothing on the main subject of their thoughts. Their lack of communication appeared to inhibit them outwardly yet their minds quietly together on the same task brought unspoken attachment. As the shouts below indirectly announced Lord Henry's arrival, Margaret rose, and made one short comment:

"Leave it to me."

In private, Henry digested his wife's report of Alesia's action, which was smoothed into sounding like a discussion in depth. Very well, they would have to try further. He did not wish to say how fearful he had been for Alesia's safety, body and soul, unless confided to God. It was fortunate that there was no occasiion for him to learn of her prowess at speed on Cresselly.

Further hope for Alesia and the constant consideration of the possibilities all devolved to the difficulties. His feeling of sadness and failure returned, to what it had been before he had conceived the satisfaction of offering his last child to Jesus Christ for life. In due time Alesia spoke to her father, suddenly interrupting his long drawn out reverie.

Henry moved his head slightly upward, dredged into alertness. Alesia held her lower lip between her teeth in worry that he had been disturbed too much. Henry had but felt that his attention was required somewhere. He looked slowly round to discover some confirmation. On seeing Alesia he felt a flash of contrition at what he knew in himself had been a period of emotional withdrawal. He knew he had been wrong. He awoke from mourning. With caution he wondered how Alesia was going to approach him. To her great relief, he smiled wryly.

"Father. You're going off to Scotland soon, no doubt." She hesitated, and instead of quite a long sentence, all that came out were three words.

"What about me?"

So Henry, to her surprise, began to say it all for her.

"You mean your future, your tasks which have to be learnt, your place now. My total and darkly beautiful heiress."

Henry always thought out his words with care. He said Margaret would catch him out years later if he did not. So he continued, after a pause, and after he had rejected the expression of all sorts of mild philosophies about his present position, and hopes for her and fundamentals of life and its organization. He felt sometimes that he was too near to the sight of all the problems of keeping the country going. It kept him from the day to day understanding which was all that nearly everyone needed.

"It might be Thomas, yet."

"Oh," which Alesia said on a rising middle tone, including in it all surprise and caution and a desire to show respect.

"Do not tell anyone at present. You won't, will you, darling. It does of course affect you, more than anyone. So I tell you early."

"The Burgundy affair?"

"The Duke has been prevailed upon by Philip."

So with Thomas she would be sharing her life and the de Lacy possessions. A few weeks later it had become semi-official. The nunnery was never mentioned again. On the next occasion when she was alone with grandmother Alesia, that lady's opinion was clearly put.

"Oh no, you're not."

"Grandmother, good heavens, not what?"

"Not going to share your inheritance with him. You must have your own manors, and keep them separate. Always."

"How can..."

"And you mean, why. I will have a word with your father. I have been waiting for this. I am not talking about Thomas as a husband. But you must have your own organization. Because once a man gets hold of all this, the de Lacy inheritance will melt and disperse. I've seen it dozens of times." She veered her statements from the man to the situation, but she really meant the man. It was an understanding which she alone seemed to have.

"I am a little young to be encompassing all this."

"I tell you, partly because no-one else will, but I tell you now because I am getting older. It cannot be known how long I have to live. God may decide my life span is done. I am nearing sixty. It has been a fair time already."

"Well, grandmother, I don't want to remember you just for this, of course. I hope you live a long time yet."

"Yes, yes. But do hark back to my stricture sometimes. How do I know?..." for Alesia had appeared to be about to ask a question..." you will I hope be happy enough with Thomas. But all we women have to watch for ourselves - and Thomas is like his grandfather - aggressive, little restraint - yes, that was fine for that generation - there were the de Montfort lands available, and others. Thomas pushes and wants, wants and pushes, and always more. There is nothing spare for him to take. But I've said enough."

Alesia bobbed lightly to her grandmother. Any words would have had to be profound, and her mother had just entered. She was promptly brought back to the daily, existing world. Margaret was full of something to say, which diverted her from noticing the close rapprochement between her daughter and her mother-in-law.

"Henry, thank God, is coming back to his former self. He has some plan, which he won't yet tell me about. It has comforted him. It seems to me that however hard I myself have tried I haven't got far with him. Whatever it is, it needs that we go to St. Paul's on Sunday instead of worshipping here."

While there was some relief that life may go forward again, grandmother Alesia had to speculate with some doubt.

"My dear Margaret, if he is better then you can also be. You have taken God's will so well. I hope you can share in whatever his plan is."

"If Henry can look forward, then only can I."

"Yes. Henry always had to come to a conclusion in his mind before he ever activated. The process was always a period of detached dreaming."

None of them could make a satisfying guess as to how Henry was going to thrust from the forefront of his mind the losses of his sons.

That Sunday mid-morning Henry, his wife, and his daughter dismounted at the northern door of the great Cathedral. Nothing had been spoken on the way. In the minds of the two ladies was only silent curiosity. Their small escort of mounted men in their routine had needed no commands. The family was expected, was met by two clerics, and four of their guard came with them into the building. All this was so far as normal as it might have been for a service. The whole structure and its appurtenances were familiar to all of them. The de Lacy family had contributed great sums of money to its construction. They followed the Earl along the transept, and up the dozen steps and through the door into the choir. Along the centre, between the two opposite rows of canopied seats, and up five steps, to kneel before the great altar. This was just for a prayer to attune them with the place and the occasion.

Assuming their quiet compliance, Henry gathered his wife and daughter close, by hand on shoulder. Together they moved from the choir to the south aisle. At last he began to relax. He stopped them by the doorway and turned round.

"Margaret, Alesia. At the far end there is the chapel of St. Dunstan. Forgive me, but I have to do this now, and there I choose to place my tomb and monument."

The sharp cry from the ladies was no more than he expected. Henry continued. "Such decisions have to be made. I want to make mine now. I have made it, in fact. The certainty of it calms me."

Alesia looked about her. They were by the grave and monument to Eustace de Fauconberg - Justician - Bishop - and then Archbishop of Canterbury. Nearby, the Chancellor and Bishop Henry de Wengham. Neither she nor her mother could comment. It was plainly action to ease and conclude his grief. It had to be allowed to run. As they moved along the aisle to St. Dunstan's chapel, they knew at least that a great anxiety had gone from him. It was to be Margaret who took up the new, or revived, era.

"Of course this will be. You more than deserve permanent memory. What is it going to look like?" Yet she wondered why her sons were not to be so much honoured. As they knelt in the chapel itself for private communion it was enough that she felt that mourning had had a definite end. She herself would follow. The clerics had prepared something for this occaion. It was almost a funeral service again, but with the hope for living in the mercy of God and everlasting life.

There was to be a design sketch produced - however long it might be before it was needed, was Henry's smiling comment as they left. Passing down the north aisle the lesser tombs of Roger the Black, Bishop of London, and the panelled coffins of Sibba of the East Saxons and King Ethelred did not please Henry.

"I prefer workmanship beautiful in itself. Although it might all be finished in Henry's lifetime, Alesia felt it was up to her to make a mental note. Glimpsing the tall nave was of itself inspiring with its clustered pillars, some reaching right up to the clerestory. It was a place for glory forever.

They were leaving now, gauped at as usual by the lesser folk, with most who made obeisance as they passed. The fresh air outside seemed to yield acknowledgment to the change induced in Henry's mind, now so clarified. Alesia felt deeply that it was an action well taken. As she mounted, she glanced across at the charnel chapel on the north side of the churchyard, so full of generations of disinterred bones. It had been provided by Lady Dionysia de Montchensie for the health of her soul. Alesia preferred her father's idea of a monument. If it falls to my responsibility, she thought, I will make sure his effigy is in armour, shielded against earthly peril.

The very next day the de Lacys were present at a ceremony after service in their own chapel representing the other end of life on earth. There was Ismena, wife of Caret the cellarer, to be churched. Alesia wondered if it was a subtle lesson for her that this time they stayed to hear the whole process. Ismena had done her best to appear smart and clean in a robe for the occasion. It was made up and altered from one used by members of the household. Ismena's own curiosity in the ceremony had long since ebbed. This churching followed her sixth child. But it was an occasion for being the centre of attraction. She repeated the words:

"I am well pleased. The snares of death compassed me round about. The pains of hell got hold upon me, trouble and heaviness. Deliver my soul."

Father Reginald intoned humble thanks that this woman was delivered from the great peril and pain of childbirth.

Ismena went on:

"I was sore troubled. I said in my haste: All men are liars. For all the benefits the Lord hath done unto me I will receive the cup of salvation. I will pay my vows."

She felt better, through His help to faithfully live and walk according to His will in this life present in hope of partaking everlasting life. Caret gave a penny, glad that it was not he who was being closely examined by the chaplain this day, in that it had not been too honestly acquired. A passing thought about his six children smothered his conscience, and the parson seemed to feel goodwill. Though outwardly the formality of routine had prevailed Father Reginald was inwardly calmed by the repeated births of the Caret family. It was a reassuring symbol of the continuity of life and of the church, amongst the plethora of babies' lives short lived, and adult lives cut off in mystery nowhere near their natural span.

Ladies hunting deer.

# CHAPTER 8

There had been no formality within the family in passing information to Alesia on the renewed progress of her betrothal. The certainty of having Thomas as her husband had evolved, as much through changing outside factors, as indecision on both sides. As friends there were few closer than Henry, King Edward, and his brother Edmund. Their political needs at home and abroad swayed the possibilities of any marriage cards that could be played, for either of the young people. Their marriage would have to fit as many circumstances as could be assessed. By the midsummer of 1292, with a Parliament to be in London, all would be present to effect the announcement.

"Mabota, I am not sure I agree with my grandmother; I am coming to believe that Thomas is someone I could love. Only occasionally until now have I wondered how it would feel to touch him, to have him near and close."

"You've kept your eyes open I think, Lady Alesia; and I think also you've decided he's the best."

"He seems more forthright than almost anyone I know. Take Guy for example; I couldn't marry him. He's far too weak."

"Perhaps you should ask Gran Alesia again."

"No, Mabota; it is to be. I am quite sure it will be alright. People are always giving warnings. I am looking at the strength of purpose he seems to show."

Since the faithful Mabota looked quizzical, Alesia continued: "Of course he hasn't much to have purpose about now. But in the hunt he's always in front; in his conversation he's always clear and to the point."

"Oh my dear Alesia, I do hope indeed that it is a great and happy success."

Mabota herself had not had much chance to marry in her youth. She was always on the move with the de Lacys, or in their household. She lived vicariously with their continual events, problems, and meetings with the great. Respect from others was reward enough, as she carried the mantle of her noble employer. Even though her intellect encompassed little more than the mechanics of life and its maintenance, she once made a remark which focussed a matter for Henry, Earl of Lincoln.

One day she happened to hand his belt to his esquire, Walter le Freeman, who was fitting up his lord for departure for France. Henry turned to her with a smile of thanks, and saw that she looked somewhat thoughtful. She must have something worth expressing, he said. Henry would not accept her answer that she was going to wish him a successful expedition.

"There was more than that. Come, Mabota. It could be interesting." He was half-teasing, with forced jollity at departure for many weeks.

Mabota, having thus to trespass beyond what was her ordinary station to speak, moved forward, watched with trepidation by a few, and wry amusement by others. She gathered the confidence of her long service. She curtsied to the ground, and looked up. "My lord. We have our opinions, usually may I say agreeable ones. On this matter, which is not my concern, I am sorry I looked as if I was presuming..."

"Please proceed."

"...simply that I, ...we, servants, feel that, having left France two centuries ago, our Lord King should stay in England."

With Mabota's tongue now dry, Henry would like to know more of what must have been a discussion by the lesser folk.

"For ever, do you mean?"

"There is England to look after, my lord. Especially after the Crusades."

With a tolerant smile, Henry read more than that. He spoke indirectly to help things along:

"It is meant, I suppose, that France makes it too much?"

Mabota had gained confidence: "The lord King of France will ferret at every corner without cease till it's all his." She rose and hustled off, giving Henry but a second to show her that he had taken no offence. Strange that he himself had never thought that this would go on for ever. There were laws on inheritance and connections by marriages. Of course there were ambitious men, and men who only respected law when the King's army was on its way. Perhaps Edward was living in the past, but maybe the people did not understand where revenue came from.

On his return it would be Alesia's year; when the parents began to look forward again, when the future of their line was accepted as being the future of their daughter. To be merged with the family of their lord the King was appropriate to ambition, but its reasoning was more in service and respect for the Kingdom, and for the organisation of monarchy. Henry was part of the Royal scene, with many others, Earls, Bishops, and their retainers of descending rank, all accompanied by stewards, attorneys, constables, and receivers of revenue, by clerks for their messages and organization, by soldiers for their protection, cooks for their feeding, others to tailor, buckle, ostle, shoe, fetch and carry, so many that maintaining the head led to the employment of the more needed to maintain the maintainers. For all this, Henry was not one who inflated his importance by employing wasted personnel so as to impress. He had as yet made no legal settlement for Alesia's betrothal, though he had put forward a promise of his estates in Cheshire and Lancashire, but then only on his decease. Thomas's father Edmund of Lancaster then borrowed four thousand marks from him, to acquire and improve the Palace of the Savoy. It was two-fifths of Henry's annual income, and he was not expecting it back again.

In all this consideration on a grand scale, from Alesia came a request intended as no more than the scuffle of a mouse, but producing the reaction of an explosion.

"I would like my own huntsman."

Deep in the mental satisfaction of much having been achieved on Alesia's behalf, Henry remained quiet if rigid for a moment. Alesia, grown up?

"I would like to have Torkill of Saxby as my huntsman. My own huntsman. To begin my household."

Grandmother Alesia also showed surprise as she heard this. She had given a slight start at Alesia's choice of her first symbol of independence, not at the fact of it. Henry had noticed this situation, but put to it a different reason, namely any demand by his daughter at all.

"It is up to your future husband" was Henry's firm statement of dismissal. Alesia, however, had now new strength and purpose.

"I require experience in the next year or two of controlling a household. I thought I'd start with the basics, and with dogs" she added with an ingenuous grin. Her grandmother exercised her tongue to stop herself interrupting, and prayed for Alesia. It was to be her initiative in her life from now, or from never. Grandmother thought back to her youth in Saluzzo. She always recalled the stifling attitudes concerning the formalities of living, the orders of procedure, the rigidity of social action over any incident away from the mundane. It was better in England, with fewer rules, even jokes about social behaviour, and plenty of rough jostling with lesser more natural folk. She hoped she had encouraged Alesia enough to avoid once and for all submission to any authoritarian trap. She had had no succcess in her own modest efforts on that with the Countess Margaret, because her daughter-in-law's preferences had always been entirely for submission.

"Thomas may wish to have a say in these affairs" counselled Henry, in hope of diversion if not cessation.

Margaret was leaving it all to Henry. She needed time to consider this sudden demand. For herself, ever since she was small her total ownerships, of vast extent, had been given over to her husband, with trust complete, and a say allowed in their administration.

Alesia having uttered, was waiting, silently. Instinctively she knew it was the best way to persuade.

Torkill of Saxby was a freckled Lincolnshire lad. His mien while hunting was determined; in manner he was philosophical, and in comment objective. Known to the de Lacys for several years through his parents being foresters, he got the job. Henry had always assumed that a clerk would have been the first requirement, or a chaplain, or a steward. He at last assimilated in his mind that these days the young had to be listened to. Perhaps he had better discuss more with his daughter.

Lincoln's Inn hummed and clattered with preparations for the betrothal feast. The stables staff got little sleep. The horses had for weeks gone out and returned and been augmented in numbers for more and more invitations to be despatched for this semi-royal, political, and social occasion. Clerks, stewards, cooks and cellarers were on their mettle.

King Edward, widower, would be the principal guest, or perhaps Edmund of Lancaster and Blanche, if the young Lady Alesia herself and the Lord Thomas were not. The Earl and Countess of Surrey, and a son and daughter, William the Earl and his Countess of Warwick and their son Guy, the Lords de Grey, Herefords, de Bohuns - these were to be but a few of the higher ranks of guests. The Lord Audley, the Bishop of London, William Bishop of Ely, Deans of London, Lincoln and Chester, sheriffs, justices, priors, canons and chaplains, were tailed by others, the Knights Robert Tibetot, Richard de Heron, Thomas de Sancto Vigare, Peter Malore, Walter de Wik. John de Hatton compiled and recompiled lists of court, government, household and foreign personages, ambassadors and City merchants for Henry and Margaret to make a final decision. Should he invite on their behalf John de Bytoria, Martin Guidysa and Peter Rotherici, of Spain, all now in England? They had acted for Henry in Aquitaine - John de Hatton's memory was capacious.

Having been with Henry in Scotland there was Geoffrey de Welles, William de Bryvill, Robert de Ros, William de Ros of Hamelak, Robert de Pynkenye, Walter de Bek.

Henry began to think of the cost, and the security of the country, with everybody in London for a Parliament. He put on a limit. On the day it was exceeded. Servants of the guests came in greater numbers for the show. Others, uninvited, but dressed in sufficient finery to be unchallengeable by the guards at the gate. Their task was difficult enough in excluding the press of bummers from the Fields. There would be food and entertainment well worth the off chance of being thrown out.

"Let matrimony, like other sacraments, be celebrated with honour and reverence in due time."

"Where mutual consent is not, there is no marriage."

"Those who give in marriage boys and girls effect nothing unless the children consent in their years of discretion."

"Plight not your mutual faith except in an open place, publicly, as in the presence of these persons assembled for this purpose."

Both Alesia and Thomas were well past the assumed dawn of will and consent, the age of seven. So espousal was assumed. Infancy had ended, though the marriage must wait till she was twelve, and he fourteen. Not a soul present considered that there would be any repudiation, which was in any case prejudicial to the State and the capacity of the law.

"The blessing of peace..." included the acquisition of friends, wealth, the wife's beauty. This last was this day admired by Thomas. Alesia's shapely figure showed well in her velvet gown of Lincoln greine, with drapings of lace; hanging upon her bosom a jewel elaborating the Lincoln arms. As an escort she was a prize for herself. Thomas was happy in the prospect of this matrimony, and delighted to listen to Alesia when the routine of those religious intonations had blessed their future contract. With some guilt at previous doubts Alesia curtsied lightly in submission.

"I have read much of wives, Thomas, and I hope never to be one to you that could displease."

"That is my feeling to you also, dear Alesia, though I have not read of it. Let us hope it is natural to both of us."

"My feelings are growing to know pleasurable solutions to our problems."

They both laughed, and the company was reassured, and felt secure in the rightness of things.

"Where did you get this Torkill from?"

"Torkill of Saxby? He's a promising young hunter, and I know him to be honest. We can rely on him."

"We? He's yours, I understand. I haven't the vestige of a household myself yet."

"We'll build one up. There's always room for good huntsmen, and for more than one team."

"I suppose I shouldn't put it this way, but thank God you didn't start with a chaplain."

Thomas paused, and resumed:

"I've never noticed that you were obsessed with hunting, though."

"He was the first to be suitable in any office required."

Thomas was at present content to have their needs arranged in any way, his own inheritances having been so far frustrated. He did not bring himself to utter the thought which arose in him - that he had not even a field of beans to give to an abbey in celebration. Besides, the de Lacys irritated him a little in that they seemed ever to have resources. The Lancasters were always borrowing, even as they did from Alesia's father, a subject of his family's realm.

"Alesia darling" came from Blanche of Lancaster, Thomas's mother, as they moved across the throng. "How pretty you are! I think Thomas is very lucky" - ignoring or forgetting the years of other possibilities and hopes and efforts. She continued, a little more thoughtfully: "You girls do something these days to make yourselves more attractive. We in my time didn't have to bother or try - we were just told not to."

Alesia smiled. She rather thought that generally she had been more told than free to choose.

Up to them came a tall smiling gentleman who, acknowledging Thomas, to Alesia stated that he had indeed met her when she was but four years old. She would not remember, of course. He continued:

"That is the sort of thing you have to hear on these occasions. I am honoured to meet you, Sir Thomas. I am Hugh de Frene, of Moccas in Herefordshire. May I give you my best wishes."

As he moved to pass on, Alesia was able to reply:

"Sir Hugh, I do remember hearing that you were going to fortify your manor at Moccas. I met some of your family a short while ago. My mother and I were at Clifford," she added as de Frene looked somewhat surprised.

"I am sorry, I have been absent a long time. That news had not reached me. The crenellation is to make my property a bit safer for my growing family; not because I'm expecting anything from the Welsh."

After generalities on the matter, when alone again Thomas was constrained to observe to Alesia:

"It looks to me that the de Lacys have a great household and that the Lancasters have a great number of relatives." Then: "Can we walk round outside and see some of your staff. I had better make a start in knowing them."

"Aye, Thomas, and they, you."

Escorted by two esquires they left the reception unobtrusively, the guests being engaged in eating, drinking, talking and grouping with those they knew or wanted to know. In the compound was the throng of servants, guards, gardeners, and as many staff as were not cooking or serving, all with their families. They were also at their own celebration of eating and drinking, and all hoping to see, perhaps meet, the young couple together. Thomas reacted to the informality as though it were disorder. No forms, no stools, servants helping each other to everything, the cooks having eaten and drunk enough as they had prepared the feast. Their courtesy and cheer brought him, however, to some enjoyment of the occasion, which he had approached with awkwardness.

Torkill of Saxby was nearby.

"Master Torkill" said Thomas, glad indeed to be able to communicate with at least one face he knew.

"Lord Thomas, sir."

"I am told you are to be huntsman to the Lady Alesia, which probably means to both of us. What have you hunted in quantity for a large household?"

"Sir. May I say that success, such as it may be, is in tracing the quarry, and shifting it towards the hunters. That brings it directly to the quality of the lurchers."

Alesia intervened to say that that experience was probably the most valuable.

"I have not yet been in ibex or wolf country, my lady Alesia."

It was a formal exchange, a little distant. Alesia and Torkill knew they liked each other, and they knew they must not go one step beyond their positions.

"Odd" Mary Saxton, laundress, remarked to her husband, groom, when Alesia and Thomas had gone from earshot. "She never mentioned children. The lord Thomas looked over at ours, but not she."

"Seven was probably more than she wanted..." he faded there.

Banter was also not absent from the throng of greater people.

"Bit young for you" taunted Guy de Rodrigues to the older Hugh de Frene. "She smiles nicely, though."

Sir Hugh was only mildly amused at this reducton to banality of a pleasant meeting with Alesia. He cursed himself for making an explanation.

"Alesia is related to the de Cliffords, who have a castle near me in Herefordshire."

"de Clifford, eh? Of the Fair Rosamund?" de Rodrigues would not miss that tone.

Hugh murmured a confirmative noise of dismissal.

However adult Alesia and Thomas had begun to feel, it was fun to have the attention of all - children but a year or two younger than themselves, and of so many others, much older, from King Edward downwards. When his father Edmund, and Alesia's father Henry came up to them later in the day, they spoke almost casually and in matter of fact tones.

"To you, Thomas, we have agreed that you will be granted the de Lacy possessions in Lancashire and Cheshire."

At least that cleared Thomas's wondering doubts. It would bring him to adulthood, power and respect. This was the system and the method and Alesia was impressed how it influenced her affianced. He seemed to have missed the deferment of the grant until Henry's decease.

Had Alesia not been born to her status and grown into separating some praise and adulation from its real basis she could well have had her head turned into an excessive belief in her own importance by the excess of pleasure expressed on her behalf as to her future. She had also observed over a few years how attitudes changed depending on whom people were talking to. Thomas was surprised at her easy familiarity with cooks, cellarmen, ostlers, servants and clerks, which amounted to an apparent freedom on both sides to communicate as persons above just words. Yet no barrier was crossed. It was hereditary in her that what is heard is truth if it does not come from fear, and the de Lacys were always eager to know the truth, instinctively for their own social stability. While Alesia did just feel that Thomas could not go as far, silent as he mostly seemed to be, she hoped that what seemed a barrier between him and her own surroundings would in time disappear.

"I suppose, Alesia," Thomas muttered as they returned to the great throng "you realise these people will say something different now we are gone."

Alesia was shocked at this cynicism, in that she had herself loved the chat which had just passed among the retainers and what had been for her alone in spite of Thomas's presence. She did not reply to him, though answers came. She felt them inadequate to a man who could so detach himself from people who were the basis of their life. It was new to her, and with her future husband she was unable to begin putting forward an opinion without his receptivity, nor a starting point. She knew that he was perfectly correct in what he had just said, but that likelihood was to be expected, and as it was not objectionable to her she had to fall to silence.

After they left, Mary de Lettres, heavy bosomed cook, put it that Alesia 'traded to stud as a cow' had her sympathy in the situation. She meant the same as Eleanor Cobeldick, laundrywoman, when she urged, but not very loudly, that 'I'd rather be me than a hundred thousand acres'. The men were cooler observers of the couple, for all were thinking in the terms of their security and their future. With no de Lacy heir, just Alesia the heiress, perhaps there was no better, more certain, arrangement, than to hitch on to the King's family. After all, Thomas's father was easy going; Thomas took after his more pushing grandfather, but it was just as well. They were not to know that he would come to the same ignominious fate.

As they returned to the throng of visitors, up to Alesia and Thomas came Anthony de Bek, Bishop of Durham, a militant and political prelate if ever there was one; related to the de Greys who were next after Henry de Lacy in campaign commands.

"Now which of your father's lands do you prefer" he began as conversation, with no significant intent. The forthcoming answer did enliven Thomas's interest, however.

"The Honour of Bolingbroke" grinned Alesia with juvenility suddenly returned within all this adult ceremony, "the food's by far the best."

They all laughed.

"Is the venison tough on Pendle, then?" asked the Bishop.

"Indeed no, Sir, I love Pendle, but for its dreaming mystery which makes me afraid of the supernatural. But for living on this earth our Lincolnshire lands are prolific."

The Bishop was not looking to make a point relative to his calling. He responded:

"My new castle of Somerton in that County has nothing like the resources there which you have. It is often a problem catching a rabbit. The ground's too damp for them."

He had built it when Archdeacon of Durham, on land given by his aunt, who had married a de Grey. The de Beks as a family had considerable land in Lincolnshire, but:

"Wrong part," he went on, having told this several times before, "not convenient for the journey north."

In the hubbub of the formal feasting, sitting next to each other, Alesia and Thomas began to develop mutual feelings in the situation which had been directed upon them. Thomas decided that she was a very nice girl to have around, and felt confidence in their future circumstances.

"If Uncle Edward goes on like this," he added with a rare smile, "the nation's problems will be solved before I have to do anything. You solved one, didn't you, Bishop, by capturing Dirleton Castle?"

Bishop Bek gave a short laugh, projecting genuine modesty: "You have heard of that, have you now? Well, it took a long siege, and it was helped by being more or less the same plan as Somerton."

By the hour the good wishes, the feasting and the joviality had dwindled, the King had gone, prelates, lords and burgesses had departed. Those who felt they had a duty towards the Earl of Lincoln, and wanted to be noticed, had stayed, perhaps too long.

The focus of being the main purpose of the gathering had faded; the horses and litters had drawn up to the doors in order of precedence; the attendants had all assembled correctly for their own lords without instructions, as jealous as they of their superiority over the next one. Thomas and Alesia were together, the farewells being made by their elders. They looked pleasurably at each other.

"Did you really mean all those amiable things you said to the envoy from France?" asked Thomas.

Alesia wondered what tone this question contained.

"Just conversation" she replied.

"I think I know a look you have when you are dissembling." And he added, with a grin: "I hope he himself does not."

"Naturally I was mindful on your behalf to listen and be pleasant, and not to provoke - not even..."

"No, not even about their machinations on Provence. A pity there is no-one in France to uphold the law like your father does in England." Then he turned to whisper that he wished his uncle would lay less stress on wanting the throne of France. It was a far different affair than Ireland, Wales and Scotland.

"Money, I suppose," Thomas continued, "but defence of the realm is easier without that stretch of territory."

Alesia expressed surprise if not some alarm. It was but three generations back that the French had been marauding halfway up England, being defeated at the gate of Lincoln Castle.

"I understand that before long I am to go with your father to Gascony. I shall learn more for myself, and possibly also learn his opinion."

Alesia changed the subject as their parents returned.

"Joan was a bit sharp I thought when she said that here at last was a marriage which was not arranged by Queen Eleanor."

"She only arranged them for her French kinswomen so far as I know; Fiennes, Beaumont, and people. We must be, and I presume we both want to be, of England."

The others were near enough now for Alesia to take the opportunity of this remark to curtsey to Thomas as a little show.

"I shall be together with you on that and with all things" she demurely uttered, to his pleasure.

To the others for their diversion from this scene she descried:

"Strange the envoy of France should try and make me believe I was named after Alesia, the very starting place of his country's being."

Thomas and his father and mother and their attendants departed. They were all well satisfied that the marriage to come was appropriate and right. Henry and Margaret were quietly pleased with the arrangement, confirmed by over-interpreting the curtseying scene as they had entered. To Henry the betrothal had done more than that, however. He began to behold a future for the de Lacys. His affection and hopes had long been frustrated, his motivation for building a secure realm had had the feeling taken away by the deaths of his sons. He would not care to admit that words from his chaplain had been of no comfort. He had accepted all in grace in his belief that life could hold for all as much as they could take. Happiness was illusory, respect and continual effort was all.

"Before we go to Gascony I will conclude arrangements for your stay at Bolingbroke. Thomas will come with us. It is thought that your marriage will be in a couple of years. There is much to arrange, although it is a nuisance that another foreign tour has to intervene."

The ladies accepted this without comment. Margaret was used to it. Alesia had seen enough of it to expect none other, except to wonder why women were left behind. She was too young to feel she could say that now. Henry continued that the period would be an excellent opportunity for Alesia to be shown more of what was expected of a wife, and to learn the organization of a great household. He was ashamed to say that latterly all this had been neglected. It was also useful to know who was for one and who against.

Before they retired, Henry asked Alesia who impressed her most. Apart from Thomas, of course.

"Impressed? The one I perhaps found nearest to my comprehension was Paulin de Paris..."

"Who?" asked Margaret.

"I assume he was correctly a guest, a Dominican he said he was."

"He would be on the nuncio's staff."

"Maybe" resumed Alesia struggling through the interruption "but he announced to me that because he was going to be a Dominican monk he would not be allowed to marry - and he said it in such a tone that I thought he would be scared stiff to marry anyway."

Henry hoped that it showed a nice ability to study character. Alesia's experience of people was in fact far more extensive than her parents imagined. The area by Lincoln's Inn was a place to absorb much knowledge of folk by simple observation. She did not admit to her nodding acquaintance with some of the rabble, with the mountebanks who harangued them, those who had bears dancing for them, and the owners of dogs being set at oxen for their entertainment. Her escorts were always prepared to watch those, and the football and the wrestling. She wasn't going to say that she knew idle vagabonds were nicknamed 'Lincoln's Inn Mumpers', nor that 'Rufflers' was the slang for beggars and cripples who tried to look like maimed soldiers. Alesia was able to see the real world, but also to be determined that she never sank into it; nor to be one of the effetes for which she had contempt.

The great hall of Lincoln's Inn became a buzz of workers under Seneschal Blewpett. Without his urging they would all have moved at once to their sleeping places on the floor and in the alcoves. Yet they did feel better when they woke to see it tidy and the straw fresh, for as much as some could firstly discern after the brevity of their night, and the condition of their heads. But the day was meant to be as normal as any other, if it could be. With the crowded hall and the candles and tapers, lanterns and lamps Seneschal Blewpett was relieved that his fear of fire had been quenched at least for that night. With the dawn he was about again to get the day going by these worn-out servants, for the Lord Lincoln would appear as though nothing had happened.

Mabota awoke Alesia, with little need in her excited state.

"He's firm and determined, a fine young man" propounded Mabota. The severalth time she had so said over the last few months. "He's got the rock hard temperament to lean on a man should have."

"You seem to think I am a wild emotional thing, Mabota."

"I don't know what it is, dear Lady Alesia, but a woman needs the strength of a man's mind and his counsel of correction."

It had however been Alesia's observation so far that it was the man who needed the woman's counsel. In the close knit couples of her acquaintance it seemed so, and King Edward without his Eleanor had lost his charm and confidence. As Mabota did not have a man at all it seemed, however, that only upset could follow if she said anything.

"So where will you marry, do you think, lady Alesia?"

"Well, Mabby, I hope at Woodstock, where granny was married."

"You like her and if I may say, I think you have much of her."

"I like the idea, anyway. I would like to travel to Italy to see her family. Father goes on the way to Rome, but for women it seems to be different. But it wasn't different for Eleanor."

"I am sure you can persuade someone" smiled Mabota.

Outside and away to far beyond the confines of this chamber the betrothal of Thomas and Alesia became known, as a rumour being confirmed. It was approved in the Lancaster and de Lacy manors, castles, and religious houses. Caution was in the minds of those dependent on the Earls of Surrey in their ancient rivalry. Political convenience and de Lacy family ambition had strengthened themselves in the name of the King, some said. Others scoffed at Thomas's father Edmund, trustful and generous and knightly he was, unambitious, politically little, guileless and weary in negotiations with the French.

"No! Henry, you do not! Nor you, Margaret! Where are the

documents? Some land and revenues of course, maybe most, but not all, not all to Thomas. Alesia must hold her own direct, to her alone."

Grandmother Alesia de Lacy would insist, and insist again, that so much as would maintain a de Lacy household must go to Alesia. Henry had described his proposals for passing his all to the Lancasters, subject to his own life interest.

"You think your laws are so strong and firm, Henry. Yes, and what happens if Thomas gets all, and dies, or even falters against the King, what then of your daughter? Depending on goodwill of whom? She must have of her own."

Grandmother Alesia rat-tatted on about the hazards - they were not married yet anyway - nature was such that they may never be - and how do you undo your document then? She persisted from what she had so often heard of so many dealings among her own in Italy. She never mentioned her main force of argument that backed her feeling - just that she did not trust Thomas.

Henry and Margaret agreed with her ultimately. After all, Margaret herself had had her own complete inheritance, although on a different route in the law. Further than what he had already done, he took no action on his sixty thousand acres in Lincolnshire nor on his many other dispersed sources of revenue. He had never been strong on claiming his wife's lands, and left them alone now.

Grandmother Alesia was satisfied. She herself, living on the revenues of the town and honour of Pontefract, its manors and hamlets, then did not demur when Henry proposed to leave all that to the King on her own decease. No-one but she informed Alesia.

The family's journey to Bolingbroke, and the long sojourn there, once more assumed the character of education for Alesia. She felt that she had been rediscovered in her father's new attitude, which reflected upon her mother, grandmother and indeed the closer persons of the household all began to feel that they had knowledge to offer. She was their future. Fortunately she was quite prepared to be the centre of attraction, and to ask questions whether it was about horses, domestic affairs, revenue, politics or religion.

"I hope I am not expected to remember all these things I'm told" she confided to Mabota.

"Lady Alesia you will not be alone in any decisions you might have to make."

Alesia supposed not. It was clear that Mabota was a confidante for her childish past only. Perhaps life would be nicer if she herself were allowed to consider only the simple things.

# CHAPTER 9

The decision had been made to travel north, after several days of waiting upon the weather. By the colour of the sun these last few evenings it looked now as if the roads might be drier than of late. Henry had not minded much for himself, but the movement of two hundred men was always sluggish. Alesia noticed that her father was smiling amiably, it seemed to himself, as they left the chapel to join the waiting convoy.

"I hope we have a good journey" she ventured, believing that her father's mood presaged just that.

"Certainly. We'll settle for Berkhamstead for the first night."

There was more to his even temper that morning, but it did not come out. It was the commanding Earl of Lincoln who sat his horse watching his banner unfurl for the company to move. What he was thinking was, however, that great decisions depended on the uncontrollable changes of sun and rain. This particular order to move this day had further been inspired by his realizing from their quality that London was running out of decent vegetables. For as often as he was sardonic about the strength and purpose of man this moment was an example. He would command that which could be commanded, but his followers leaned upon him for absolute control. King Cnut had not been wrong.

The groups of horsemen devolved into order. The procession formed section by section, under the eye of the mounted column commander ouside the gate, but who had little physical ability in the circumstances to rearrange anything. Precedences were, however, known and were self-correcting if necessary by any whose position would be pre-empted. Soldiers and guides preceded the trumpeters, then servants, the clerks and administrators, the chaplains and secretaries then the standard aloft with the Earl's red lion rampant on golden cloth, accompanied by pages. Father, mother and daughter in a row behind were followed by their personal aides. Knights and Esquires were the last group as far as the rearguard.

Captain Ywein Pothened reported that the column was in order. Henry was able to follow many of the accents which he came across, but Ywein's usually required repetition and analysis, a mixture of Breton and Celtic. He took the message from the tone and the expression, and ordered the start. It was a mystery, but others always seemed to understand him. He hoped the baggage train would be moving well, but as it had left the day before there was no news. The gates of Lincoln's Inn behind them shut, the staff looking forward to a few months of doing very little after they had cleared up.

Alesia was astride Crust, so called after what had pleased him since a foal. A medium sized roan, he matched her new feeling of adulthood. She fell to thinking that she must spend the next two years learning much about revenues as about other wife's duties. It seemed to be what Thomas was interested in, for he spoke of little else but the power he needed to take his place as close relative of the King and his heirs. Her dowry was now to be finally settled by documents and laws, but the lordships and possessions were never to Thomas to be enough. Already he had protested about alienations by Henry to Abbots and Convents and Chaplains of rights to courts, wrecks, warrens, and rents of land. Alesia asked her grandmother for advice, and she agreed on this point with Thomas - it would not happen on this scale in Savoy - people in England think they can give material things away and live just the same afterwards. Even still alienating revenues to the church when it owned more than half the land already. A personal feeling, she supposed. But she still did not like Thomas's attitude of greed, she mused.

From the dawn departure to mid-morning little was spoken. Riding in the group was not conducive to conversation, and Henry was more concerned to observe the company and to savour the freshness of the day. Margaret achieved some communication, expressing satisfaction that she was riding with a feeling of freedom and not in her litter which had been at her request sent on with the baggage.

It was different when they paused for refreshment in mid-morning, up on the heather covered hills. By now several other travellers had joined them at the rear, following at a respectful distance. Henry had them summoned to him.

"They call me Thomas the fowler, my lord, because my father was, but in truth I am now a stonemason. Tholi here and Simon Tres are both also stonemasons on a summons to the King's works in Wales."

Henry frowned at his own recollections of Denbigh. Thomas seemed then fearful that he had been forward in his approach, but felt that he should explain why they were tagging along behind, that at least he was on the King's business after a fashion.

"We have no other protection on the way, Lord, from people; nor the elves and the nicers and the ores at night, but that we group together as we can."

"But you have lived through many nights already" rejoined Henry, knowing that they would be shut out of any castle at which his own retinue stayed.

"At night we sing, Lord -
Now the owle is flowne abroad
for I hear the croaking toade
and the bat that shuns the day
through the darke doth make her way.
Now the ghostes of men doe rise
and with fearful hideous cryes
Seek revengement (from the goode)
On their heads that spilt their blood."
He hesitated, as Alesia intervened:
"Come some spirit, quicke!  I say

Night's the devil's holiday."

All laughed in pleasant surprise at this participation.

It was the road also to Chester, but they were advised that because of the de Lacys' diversion to Leicester they should soon try and link with others.

"We are going to Northampton only to buy wool, my lord," then spoke one of the two merchants. He thought this was rather dull after the colourful and rough stonemasons, and he knew no songs.

"And what is the wool to be used for?" asked Alesia.

"We have customers for cloth mostly among the townsmen of London, my lady."

"Indeed, some Aldermen" added the other trying to gain a little importance. "And some ladies, too, milady."

"Where did this wool come from, then, of my cloak?"

The merchant spoke confidently on his own ground:

"Not from Northampton. Not us I am sorry to say, milady. I would say from Lincolnshire by its texture."

Alesia decided she would not tax them as to whether it was better or not.

"While correct, how can you tell?" asked her father.

"My lord, experience of looking at many wools, but also I thought the colour was of a Lincoln dye."

"True," said Alesia, "perhaps you will expand your business to include our sheep."

As the journey resumed Henry said in an educative way that one learnt far more by such conversations than by official contact. It was a way of finding out what the people really thought.

"You were lucky this time" interpolated Margaret, "that you didn't get a lot about their family illnesses and poor food."

"We would have done sooner or later, I'm sure. The others looked ready for that. But it is no use complaining to me of what is the work of God."

And tragedy can strike all and anyone, thought Alesia.

The night at the King's great castle of Berkhamsted was but the prelude to the further journey, a time for review of the condition of the horses, the fitness of the men and wagons for the further miles ahead. In the morning early the company was assembled ready to move off.

The marshal approached Henry, who sat awaiting him with an air of patient authority.

"Ready to move off my lord."

"I do not think so, master marshal."

"My lord?"

"I suggest you examine the company further."

This was Lord Lincoln's known way of exerting his command, and which made the recipient uncomfortable. The marshal was in divided mind as to whether to seek clarification. He decided to move away to examine further, having noted Henry's unmoving features. As he turned his mount, saluting, he was addressed:

"You will find nothing, master marshal, by riding along the company. That grey in the eighth row was lame late yesterday. Is it any better now? I think not. Also I see four soldiers without water - why?"

Those soldiers themselves thought they could not be seen from where Henry was.

"We will wait a few minutes, and I will then inspect."

Thus guided, a hot pace was set towards the castle of Leicester, of Alesia's future father-in-law Edmund of Lancaster. There would be time there, indeed necessity, for hunting.

"I want the sport as much as to help fill the store."

Henry enjoyed the chase, and was not one for the trapping of boars and hares. They would seek venison.

One hunting day Henry had about him again his benevolent air, though it may not have been much noticed in the general turmoil of the assembly of the hunting party. It was clear that the easy-going temperament of the Earl of Lancaster spread through his estate's administration. It was quite necessary to hunt hard for these three days, so as to replenish the stocks necessary at Leicester castle. Such unexpected or half expected difficulties always quietened Henry's attitude, for he seemed to gain strength from what was ranged against him.

All had been active since daybreak; doubtless by now grooms had located deer at pasture and had tracked the best antlered specimen. They would be marking with twigs where it returned to the woods. The hunters began to move slowly in the general direction as arranged, awaiting the grooms' return with their report. The splendid and noisy cavalcade would too soon disperse any herd if it were not in specialist groups. Soldier escorts had their duties, so did those of the commissariat, assistants and pages, but direct involvement in the hunt was not included. Up in front with Lord Henry were officials of the castle, a couple of clerics, and several esquires. The Lady Margaret stayed to organize for their return. Alesia was towards the rear of the hunting party with John and Torkill the huntsmen; she would take what part she could.

The rendezvous in a grass field by the river Soar gleamed damply in the morning light. Servants quickly laid a table for Henry and Alesia and the chaplains, with cloths on the ground for the others of rank. There was no doubt, thought Alesia that fresh air sharpened one's appetite if not one's wits, and she hoped upon hope that she may show some prowess with her bow.

"Torkill" she asked, as she heard faintly a snatch of tune from him, "what are you singing?" Then she continued without his answer, because it could have been embarassing, she noticed. Her father pretended not to have heard that it was:

"Lady, he said, I promise duly,

That all my life I'll serve thee truly."

Fortunately any question whether he was going to continue on the next few lines was answered by the arrival of the scouts. It had, however, never crossed their minds that Torkill would have gone so far as to pass complimentary remarks on the beauty of his maiden mistress, which comprised the remainder of the lyric.

The reports from the scouts were received by gathering round the lord's table. Henry's decision as to which deer to chase was made by a quick examination of the various droppings brought in. The humans fed and aled, the horses and hounds watered, in the stimulus of the sounds of horns, neighing and barking, the party moved to the wood called Twaite. The twigs which marked the way the chosen deer had entered the wood were identified. The forester of the Twaite whipped in to make sure his fences were not too damaged by over-eager hounds, helped by the park-keeper of Tooley Park, who was certain the hunt would ride across country to his area later. The Earl Edmund of Lancaster never troubled about trespassing by poor women for gathering dry wood for sale, but he would not appreciate paying for any damage which produced it, whatever the station of the person causing it.

The hounds were straining to chase as fast as possible, urged or no by the horn, by the striking of boots with leather thongs, or by the encouragement of them, bloodhounds and greyhounds, each by their own name.

The lord Henry loved it all for the excitement and as much for the organization of keeping the pack on the scent, or re-finding the scent, for the revival of tired hounds by bread, always alert for any occasion when he felt advice should be given, or to show his own interest in the matter. Not much if any stimulus was required - the hunting of protected deer with full permission in the presence of a great lord had its own privilege. There was reputation to be got by the appointed men; for the younger there was skill and promise to be shown for future recommendation. There was Alesia, the betrothed of Thomas the King's nephew, their future lord, to impress.

Jungwin, the groom who had found this particular stag, and had picked it well, could no longer follow. He had done his main task from before dawn. His dog had found the droppings on this trail, had led the hunt to hoof marks and footprints of the deer. Urged by Jungwin's tone of voice, which promised many things to him which he could not understand, his lurcher in silence with his guile had urged the deer towards the pack. His master was, however, on foot, and they had both been overtaken by the mounted hunt, leaving them in a frenzy, with hope only that the deer would make a circular movement and return to them. In this they were both to be disappointed, and Jungwin followed as best possible, looking the while for any lost hounds. The chase took to the north, then west, and round southwards out of Twaite wood to near Thurlaston, at full speed to the centre of Normanton Turville. Not an unusual happening; hunting itself was always worth watching, and so often dispersed and far away that months would pass sometimes without this spectacle, or any other in a village. Such as were quick enough to notice were spattered by the deer charging through the muddy street. The straggling field that followed was seen by all. Information as to who was the lord and the finely dressed, if dishevelled, young lady was at last obtained from a soldier in the escort in the rear.

Sharp right to Tooley Park stag and hunt wheeled, the latter by now with fair certainty of success. The frightened deer had done well over so much soft ground. Tired now, by noon it was possible to outmanoeuvre it. The noise of the hounds in their fury at being whipped off diverted them from the swathe of the huntsman's sword which brought about the kill. The death was sounded. The riders replied. They rode round the body. The Lord Henry ordered the skinning and the quartering.

Torkill the huntsman noticed that Alesia gulped, exhausted though she was; he had seen that her young eyes closed at the stroke of death. As, near her, they moved to leave for Leicester, he spoke.

"Lady Alesia, Holy Church saith that animal hath no rationality."

Alesia did not reply because at that moment she could not. Henry joined them just then.

"I was suggesting, my lord, that we may have a chance for the Lady Alesia to use the bow on the ride back to the castle."

Which pleased Henry. Sport it was, as well as the necessity to cull, and to eat. The men were, however, now fully occupied, which prevented any idea of another full hunt in force. Deer also had to be killed for practical reasons by easier stalking methods. He looked back to see if his attention was needed, but all seemed well. Branches were being cut to carry the meat, a bed of leaves was being laid on which to skin the animal. Then the testicles and the tongue would be removed, the stomach opened for the liver and the kidneys, viscera and entrails. The pieces of good meat would be cut for the kitchens. In war and peace, Henry supposed that sooner or later he would get used to what it was necessary to do to creatures.

"Alesia, your Torkill seems useful, he did a couple of times turn hounds where no-one else had noticed the need." Without waiting for a reply Henry asked his daughter if she had noticed the young man de Twici for his keenness.

"He didn't seem to stop at charging through streams, at least" agreed Alesia.

"We'll watch him a bit then. The young Edward needs a good apprentice and maybe he will do."

Alesia was more interested in her own feelings of warm and sensuous exhaustion.

Fortunately, by nightfall, dogs and lost hunters had managed to return to Leicester castle, and detached followers who had joined as closely as they felt they would be allowed had all reached home.

Two days more hunting in the Firth to the north, and Barne Park to the west, but Alesia did not join in. Suitably escorted, she followed the more leisurely pursuit of camouflaging herself in green with hunting esquires, to await game urged in their direction. To her great relief it was not she who only wounded a deer, which had to be pursued to the death by the attending dogs.

Their journey next day seemed tame.

Henry had not really expected to complete the escort of his family to Lincolnshire. Any day there could be a messenger riding up to bring news that the Continental journey had been brought forward. He had attended the King earlier in the year on his visitations in the Midlands, and felt reasonably up-to-date on the possibilities of political needs. It was to be a journey to Norham again, and to Berwick previous to travelling to France. Balliol was to be confirmed to the throne of Scotland, and was to do homage to Edward.

The dangers of possible trouble all round England's boundaries made for a wary temperament. It also had made this journey of the Earl of Lincoln, his family, and retinue take the longer route to Bolingbroke, via Lincoln. It was a better, firmer way in bad weather, but its attraction this time was that it kept Henry's options open, the quicker to join any forces to the west. Between Lincoln and Bolingbroke the reality of the task of those in government became to Alesia more clear. It was not because their distant relatives, the Tibetots, had disputed and gained the manor of Horncastle, but because the Bishops of Carlisle had a house there, indeed giving homage and service to the manor. It was a principal place of their abode, even further south than Howden in Yorkshire; an escape from the border contests which made Rose Castle in Cumberland uninhabitable. Because of this expense devolving upon them the inhabitants of the manor and soke kept demanding exemption from payments and services.

The necessity for a Bishop from the North to seek continual refuge so far south was illustrative of the turbulent state of affairs. Henry explained a little, with not much more than confirmation, rather than reveal his mild contempt for someone who wished constantly to be safe. 'Illustrious in counsel, undaunted in the fight, chief among the warriors of his country, the brightest ornament of the reign' is how he himself was regarded. The Earl centred the nation, right and duty upon himself, and let others utter their opinion of him if they wished, and that was the opinion they gave. Long ago he realised that any talk could not be stopped. Fundamentals and not the froth were the only thoughts worth considering.

So they proceeded in the later afternoon to take the final few miles to Bolingbroke, up and down the rolling southern end of the Lincolnshire Wolds. Such procession always gave the locals a rare show, to enliven the day, and mental relaxation in submerging oneself in a bow to the great. To an extent Henry's peregrinations disappointed. It was his personality which made his reputation. The size of his retinue did not warrant much more respect than could be given to a couple of travelling knights with their men. But Lord Lincoln's banners proclaimed that his presence did not need the outward show.

They came upon the castle, looking down towards it from the barren open ground of the chalk hills, which encompassed it on the three sides except the south. There stretched out the extended distant view of fenland. The castle sat solid in its moat, which was fed by springs. A uniform structure, about an acre and a half in area, it had four projections with rooms and lodgings, and two watch towers. It was the strong gatehouse on the north, and its drawbridge, to which the column took their direction. It all looked peaceable down there, strong as it was, but much of the view from the castle itself was abruptly into the hillsides, and to feel safe it needed patrols. It was the de Lacys' favourite home. The variety of soil yielded many plants for food and medicine. Prolific aquatic birds inhabited the watery south lands.

Wayside Ale House.

# CHAPTER 10

The shadow of the dawning sun crept over the eastern hill to bring Bolingbroke to the life and bustle of its Tuesday market day. This, their first morning after their long journey, contrasted with the peace and quiet sought by the de Lacys. It did help, however, by drawing off so many castle staff and folk that some privacy was easier to find. Henry knew by information now that he had two weeks to spare; Margaret once again had somehow to feel calm in support of his departure on another and then another mission; Alesia was set to compose herself for her future, to suppress new dreams, to be ready for her forthcoming step into adulthood. Of the three it was she who rose first and gazed southwards through her little window. In the distance she could just discern the distant tower of Boston church over a dozen miles away. She marvelled at the power of man, for it was said there were plans to pull it down and to build a new really tall great church. Her maid was disturbed into alertness by the movement.

"Mabota, I mentioned I wanted to tidy my hair. Now."

Mabota, having become used to this new show of authority, was amused and interested.

"It can all be ready in a few moments, Lady Alesia. You mean the cutting of it straight."

"I do. I have to look plain and serious until I marry."

"You are certainly being deeply thoughtful, Lady Alesia," replied Mabota, wondering whether she would have so expressed it herself.

Nevertheless, the preparation of Alesia's hair went forward; the bowls of hot water arrived, the maid Elvira who was so good at cutting hair worked on the damp locks. Alesia was calm, serene as her mind latched securely on her intended future. Her brow was crossed with a thick deep glossy fringe. The sides were cut plain and straight around.

Mabota dare not say, but by the time Alesia was complete with dark gown and surcote she had not achieved the quiet demure effect she had intended. The pale pink-white of her face showing smooth as framed by the hair, with her dark eyes set therein. The beauty restrained made nothing other than an attraction and challenge to any man.

"If I may say, Lady Alesia" and Mabota spoke after some desperate thought, "at this time of day, perhaps a crespine."

It was not as if Alesia had not sensed some of this thought, having seen herself in the polished metal mirror. So she submitted to the netted crespine, to wonder if that was itself enough. She would do it gradually, then, and also have the barbette. By the fitting of this rimmed white hat and wide ribbon under the chin the effect did become subdued, at least modest. Mabota felt relief.

"Dear Alesia, you are not yet allowed to be a private person enough."

Alesia agreed by just a look. When she joined her parents she knew her appearance was satisfactory. No surprise or special looks were passed as she walked across the bailey to the great hall and up past the end of that to join Henry and Margaret in the chapel. Then, after the bread and fruit of their breakfast, Alesia waited in the solar for her father and mother to supervise the projected day's arrangements, in their separate spheres of estate and commissariat.

Joining her, they walked together to the bailey, and up the steps to the top of the wall, where there were seats and they would be alone and unheard. There was much to agree between them, and information to impart to Alesia for her future. As she turned to see her husband reach the parapet, Margaret observed with anxiety that he had begun to look grim, and had steadied himself twice on the low stone battlements.

"It is a little chilly still up here." she uttered in a deliberately low and unexpressive voice. Henry did not know that she had seen his slight loss of control, and demurred that he felt sure the weather would improve. Margaret certainly did not want their precious few days at Bolingbroke to be overshadowed by the memory of happenings to their sons on the walls of Denbigh and Pontefract.

"Let us go to the solar, and return later, when what sun there is becomes stronger" she virtually ordered, noting that Henry had not been able to take a positive stand on the matter. Alesia followed them, eyebrows metaphorically raised at the apparent muddle. The lady Margaret's maid, Edeline, was posted at the solar steps to hold up any who might have wished to communicate with them.

At last in the right atmosphere where she could express herself, Margaret had to say with foreboding, but evenly:

"Once again, to Scotland;" She paused. "The joy of your return ceases all my tensions. Keep safe. For my soul, keep safe."

"It is not so much a journey with any danger this time. We have finished the negotiations in Scotland."

"There is always someone undoing what Edward tries to do with Scotland."

"For Scotland we should say," rejoindered Henry, smiling, "if they were not such opportunists as soon as Edward's back is turned I doubt if he would give them another thought. That seems impossible," he had to add. He could not say here in Alesia's presence that in due course he would hope that Margaret would travel more with him. He was in any event not sure that it was a promise he wanted to make, because journeys were not always pleasant. But for some comfort he did say that Thomas would in future travel more with him on his state expeditions. Margaret had another point needling her mind, yet trying to avoid giving Henry anxious thoughts for his tour.

"Bolingbroke will be here when you get back" she smiled.

"In your capable hands, of course." Henry divined that there was some extra worry somewhere. He recalled that recently there had been a raid on Boston, causing fire and destruction of dwellings and meeting halls, all caused by wild men and outlaws - disguised as wandering friars and men of the church.

"You are really safe here, my dear. There are scores of men at arms loyal to us, who will remain. I suppose I shall be only a few weeks this time."

"Yes, dear Henry, I know. Perhaps I'm getting older! But I do think the people are more restive than a few years ago."

"Unfortunately when Edward demobilises some men from his forces they do not all go back home peaceably."

"What with that, the Darcies and their kind, and you never know who." She turned to Alesia: "Of course I shall properly command here when your father has gone."

"Yes, mother, I have seen you do so before. I will play my part too" Alesia replied with eagerness, to help her mother in her depressed state.

"Even so" continued Margaret, "I'm damned if I can see how the Darcies can pray and raid and support a priory at Nocton all so close together. If one patrol of mine gets so much as challenged by them I'll advance upon them myself."

"That's better" smiled Henry. Alesia rather hoped it might happen. It produced exciting knightly visions. It was then decided that they would visit Barlings Abbey before Henry was to leave, and would inform nunneries nearby that the ladies were to be here. Two days later a messenger was despatched to Barlings that they would arrive there for the mid-morning mass on Sunday, and for such hospitality as could be afforded.

In the mist of the early morning the day showed promise to improve as the sun rose higher. The de Lacys rode without haste, for there was ample time to arrive by ten o'clock at Barlings. Chaplain, guards, escort and the guide formed up the rear, his only job on this occasion being with any stragglers. It was a casual arrangement in the quiet countryside. It was a pity, thought Henry, that they trotted through Horncastle at the moment when early mass had just finished. They would think that he and his family were avoiding worship. He was also having further thoughts. They concerned Margaret. Of course he would like to stay more with her. Of course they both understood the position. His family duty had continued for centuries, hers for perhaps even longer than his by one of the stems of her lineage. They got on well, had never questioned their unity, because of the force majeure of their parents' planning to put them together. Perhaps they got on so amiably because he was so often away. His lips stretched slightly at that. He had his command outside. The authority at their homes was hers, it seemed to him.

Barlings Abbey had been founded a hundred and thirty eight years before by Ralph de la Haye, from whom much had devolved to the Lincoln inheritance. In those distant years there had been such a thrust to prayer in its hope, and to Abbeys for their seeking after learning.

Where else was truth to be found? The increasing awakening of the spirit was searching desperately for answers. Other than through their mediation, where else could the deeper questions about life on earth and its preparation for death be pondered? Henry felt sometimes that the growth of secular law countered church teachings, yet he had become an outstanding instrument of it. The church was as firm as anybody in holding to its rights, written or unwritten. The souls of Henry and his family must surely, however, rest in greater peace in eternal life only if they supported abbeys and priories and churches and cathedrals. It put their work and position in society in balance. It provided worship and prayer for the souls of the generality of people who did not have those responsibilities.

In a couple of hours they saw the square tower of the abbey, with its corner crocheted pinnacles. It gave to the de Lacys a personal pleasure as the mass of the nave grew larger at their approach. To them there was comfort in the constancy of the continuing thoughts of the monks for their sponsors. The family could never resist the feeling of relaxation in the atmosphere of permanency induced by being within the abbey.

It was at Oxeney, a place with a name, but consisting only of hovels and byres clustered in a few fields. It had been started at Barlings further up the Barlings Eau, a little river. After a few years it was re-started further downstream, because of there being more water for sustenance and transport.

The mid-morning sun illumined the clean buff stone, the quiet river reflected as much as it was able of the great abbey buildings. The composition of the scene was enhanced by the working boats drawn to the far bank, some angled on the shore, for the tide was low. One monk only was to be espied, moving smartly to the building in as pious a manner as possible for his speed. A messenger, no doubt, to report the arrival. No boatmen were to be seen anywhere. Attending at the service to demonstrate their devotion, Henry assumed. The party splashed its way through the water and climbed the far bank. They wheeled round the southern side of the complex of buildings, to turn towards the western entrance to the abbey.

"Welcome, my lord. Welcome, Lady Margaret, Lady Alesia." Abbot Bencelin was at his most amiable. Then he began to bite his lip until the mood of his visitors and patrons had been established. He could never seem to bring himself to welcome the Lady Margaret first, though it was really her family's abbey foundation.

If the de Lacys had noticed, they made no showing of the fact. Even so, the Lady Margaret led the way into the building. After some moments in the abbot's quarters to refresh and refurbish after the journey, they proceeded along the beaten rubble floor of the nave to their allotted places before the altar, in the choir. Because of their visit, folk from all the surrounding area had come in, to see them, in a sense to be associated with them. Thereby the nave was well filled.

Alesia always liked such occasions. The quiet crowds gave her confidence, the ritual gave her security and relaxation, the music and singing brought her a sense of participation, perhaps in something greater than herself. Today an anthem was to be sung by a new brother, Ywein, of whom the abbot had already spoken highly. The pleasant expectation which this had induced was now to be resolved. The de Lacys, the abbot and the monks, and the people all composed themselves, and Ywein moved to the step of the Sanctuary, to wait for all rustling to subside.

He began to sing.

He was the first basso profundo that any of them had ever heard.

The deep transporting key of those reverberating notes affected all with admiration, for their own received pleasure, and for their extra sustenance from such submission of this work to God's glory. But to Alesia it was more. Deeply influenced by the performance in sound and atmosphere, three times throughout she was penetrated by Ywein's voice, which made her physically vibrate. How vulnerable and frightened she felt to be so influenced by a man, a monk. It had crashed through her ordinary defences. She thought desperately about the walls of Jericho. It must have been like that. Surely Ywein would not, could not, have done it on purpose. But he had noticed her little shakings. How could she come here again? How could she explain anyway, to avoid being brought here in future?

Alesia realized her mouth was open all this time. So she dropped her head to be as natural as possible. She hoped she could cobble up some explanation in case she had been seen. And if seen, understood. Ywein's eyes had just moved to her left, after noticing her. Perhaps to Mabota. Alesia turned slightly that way. Clearly from the look of enquiry, she had seen. Maybe no-one else was taking any notice of her. They were all now to kneel for prayer. Alesia began to wonder if it could ever happen with such intensity again. Whatever tension remained in her as they progressed to the abbott's lodgings for their dinner was gradually dispelled. The talk was all on organizational matters. They varied from earnest and expected pleas from the abbot for support for further improvement. All in the name of the efficacy of prayer. Henry had long before made up his mind to go some of the way. The abbot realized that he was to receive no more than had been decided, and turned to more general affairs.

One was almost mutual. He enquired about the perambulation ordered by the Sheriff in that a dozen knights were to certify the bounds of Henry's land in Bolingbroke and Sibsey. Additionally that of the abbot of Kirkstead in Coningsby.

"Only a minor administrative tidying up," said Henry: "It will be decided by the Justices at Westminster before Michaelmas." With tongue-in-cheek demeanour he concluded: "I expect they know that at

Kirkstead."

Exchanges such as this were frequent with her father. Alesia always found them of interest, just for the verbal feints they always contained. On the way home she thought she would seek to enter her father's world. The weather turned, however, to the attack with rain and wind. With drying and washing and dressing to regain comfort and dignity back at Bolingbroke no spare time in the evening remained, and it waited for the next day's conversation in the solar.

There were things which Alesia wanted to know. They were all about her future. She had been elated over her betrothal, and the fuss over her at the ceremony. Quite moved at the homilies in the name of the Holy Trinity on her new relationship. It resolved into one question. It had to be diffidently put, linked as it was with the emotional relationship of a child and parent. But why was she not sent to live with the Lancasters now? It was not that she wanted to leave her present life and her mother and father, but was it not usual? Her mother replied.

"Often usual, yes. Most often, probably. We just thought that it would wait till all the legal formalities were ready. Land and the arrangements for it, I mean. Perhaps wait even until after the wedding. It's really undecided."

"The marriage must be certain, though?"

"Yes, darling, indeed so. If you're thinking of the beginnings of your father and me, I was a special case on the death of my own father, so it was thought best that I move in almost as a baby. Your father grew up at the Court of the third Henry."

Margaret smiled, and added: "There were still negotiations. It is our lot. We have to be linked with revenues so as to carry out our work. I suppose it is better than having no fixed way in life." With a tact which surprised herself she refrained from expressing that she rather thought that the Lancaster establishment was not yet separate enough from that of the King.

"Please understand I do not wish to fly away. But I have to look to what I have been appointed." Alesia then added - "willingly."

Her father joined in.

"Yes, partly a matter of finalizing estates, partly, well, just feelings as to when you should go. We shall see the Lancasters at Christmas so it will come up again. The main point is the Settlement, and then to arrange it."

Henry was hoping to be light on the matter, because he thought Alesia was upset. Not quite so. It was herself and her situation and need which gave rise to her thought. None other than an intriguing relationship yet existed between Thomas and her. Without being able to explain that she was perfectly happy to remain as now, she spoke no more about it. The talk turned to her father's forthcoming journey, and veered through that to what she should do, and absorb in the meantime. On request, her father tried a summing up.

"Management. Patient management. You cannot expect everyone to see your point of view, nor guess what you want. Nor, unfortunately, are many good at carrying on without constant interest being taken in them. Or supervision. It's a matter of what you ... or Thomas .. want to achieve."

Alesia took the opportunity to ask about the country's affairs.

"Is it then Edward's desire that you go to Scotland, to Wales, to France, and organize the land?"

"Fortunately I am wholeheartedly in favour. It's the job to help run the country. Thomas will have to take it up. If we didn't, there would soon be chaos. Why all these people attack England at every opportunity I do not know. It seems to be a fact of man's nature."

"Can they ever win?"

"My dear girl, that's a very deep question. Given alertness and action on our part I do not see how they can. And given support of our own nobles and people. Without all that, yes, of course they would. The shadow of the Scots alone affects as far as our castle of Pontefract."

Overlaid in that was Henry's thought that though the state would doubtless survive, he was not so certain about individuals in these encounters. It was clear in her expression that Margaret was considering that unspoken fear again. News would be continually sent by messenger. They would all meet in Lincoln on Henry's return south. He had meant to tutor Margaret and Alesia on the reasons for his journey, and on the political state of things, but formality was inappropriate. That was usual, and information passed in conversational snippets.

On the appointed morning of the departure, the early sun glanced across the fen. Even as it contrasted the light on dyke and crop it shone on Henry's entourage of riders as they climbed Horncastle Hill. The ladies stood on the north-west tower to watch the departure. A small ceremony had developed for the final farewell on these occasions, including a last visual signal between them. As they reached the summit of the low hill Henry wheeled the forward party leftwards, and all turned to look down towards the castle. Not till that moment was his banner unfurled. Then they went about again, to move away to the west.

This time, after that, Alesia determined to pay more attention to a lady's responsibilities in the absence of her husband. It was not a difficult resolution, for that was exactly what her mother had in mind. Margaret welcomed the possibility of discussion and support, rather than herself shoulder the decisions to be taken. She certainly set about the accustomed tasks in her usual manner, with sighs and yet determination to sort out matters which could never be done when the place was full of retainers, chaplains, soldiers and clerks. Her own household was enough to be going on with.

The steward awaited them in the bailey. Alesia soon realized that her mother's sighs were not all for her lord's absence.

"Sir Richard, the alleys on the walls are as messy as this bailey. You will be including them in the clearing of all this, I presume."

It had been in Sir Richard's mind that cleansing would be done, but that spoken assumption stimulated him to get it done quicker.

"Lady Margaret, by tomorrow there will be four carts and several women at the task. A start will be made today," he added as that did not quite appear to satisfy.

"There is every reason to have people standing by at once, on my lord's departure."

Sir Richard avoided saying that there was work in the fields and her lord's departing was never fixed to a day. He bowed slightly and somehow his stick moved a little backwards along the ground, to increase the acknowledgment of authority. His lady Margaret stated that she would go through the wardrober's accounts for food and wines as a first supervision that day.

"Will you also, my lady, also be, er - when will you be requiring to see the others - almoner, clerk, marshal, and ..."

"Day by day, but falconer this afternoon."

Somehow they had relapsed into formality, instead of names. The tension that gave rise to that would fade in a day or two. Sir Richard was always cautious of the immediacy with which ladies in authority wanted everything solved, being used to the lord Henry being patient so long as he felt things were going to be done. He bowed, and absorbed the fact that for some weeks things would be enlivened. He had better see that the carts for collecting all this rubbish were really on their way.

He nodded acknowledgment to the guards at the gate, his footsteps squdged along the dirty drawbridge, bringing him at once into the village. At this stage it would not be effective to check the bailiff on the matter. Strange, he thought, that after all these years of experience on estates, that the arrival or not of a cart or two was the standard of his being judged. He could supervise wheelwrights, coopers, carpenters, harvesting, stock feeding, salting, which were some of the things which needed his control. He was reasonably fair with reeve, villeins, and with the share for tithes; he could tell good food from that just too old. Yet when it came to Robert Wandard bringing his cart and the rest of them it all seemed to depend on something beyond his ordinary power because they always seemed to embody their own mysterious inertia.

It was with surprise and relief that his eyebrows rose as he passed the west door of the church to observe one cart moving slowly his way. His heart sank again when the driver turned out to be Will Boidin. Sir Richard nearly twanged into ordering its immediate use, but instead began:

"Where's Robert?"

Will guessed the situation on sight, and noted the urgent tone, but he himself had never hurried in his life. Sitting on the front edge of the cart, he moved his left foot off the rump of the ox on the left and rested his right foot on the rump of the ox on the right. This was received by the animals as a signal to stop their progress abruptly from one mile an hour.

"Sir Richard?"

It was said with an air of commencing a long period of conversation. Sir Richard mentally allocated all his reserves of patience to getting this cart into service.

"Where's Robert?"

"Robert? Wandard?"

"That is so" said Sir Richard with a faintly barbed air which slipped out.

"I'm instead of 'im."

As soon as Sir Richard asked why, he knew what error he had made, and sharply set to undo it. It took three efforts to cease the explanation. That Robert Wandard had had an accident was all that need have been said.

"To the castle, then" - to Will.

"Now! To the castle, on!" - from Will to the beast.

"Your work's at the castle, Will."

It had not reduced Will's exposition on why Robert had not appeared. But now he himself was ready and he took his right foot away from ox contact. These animals clearly had some unknown means of communication because they moved forward, and with a short tug on a string rein they turned left round the church to make for the castle gate. Sir Richard thought he would get this one to the castle before he enquired about the other three carts.

Thankfully he ceased to wonder why Will never replaced his left foot on the left ox. He had learnt that Robert Wandard could not use his arm after it had been crushed, and the bailiff was there with him to see if anything could be done. Particularly, hoped Sir Richard, the bailiff was trying to achieve three more carts. There was no effective encouragement he could give to speed up Will or his oxen. Will might have been urged to accelerate them by using well placed sensitive persuasion with the foot, but Sir Richard was certainly not going to tell him to do that. It only increased their speed to an irritated trot for about twenty yards anyway. Such action seemed to be usually for boredom on the driver's part, and Will had never indicated that he wanted to avoid that simple stolid state. The wagon therefore now proceeded on the track to the castle at the more cautious pace of one half a mile an hour.

Sir Richard did not wish to be seen escorting ox-carts to work. He turned into the church as being the nearest handy alibi to make any watching villagers believe he was on more appropriate business. He had often noticed that even walking around had impressed the lesser folk that he could be on a task of importance, even when he was thinking of nothing at all.

Will and his wagon moved without much noise across the drawbridge up to the gatehouse and through it without any change of locomotion. The oxen had been there before, Will had been there before, and as he passed the guard he spoke one syllable to him:

"Will," he said, without much of a glance. In fact he had summed up the situation some yards before. Lord Lincoln was up to his tricks again, in putting on guards and leaving men who did not know the locals. Will regarded himself as having more right to the place than any foreigner and thus was not going to make effort to communicate.

With casual alertness in the same measure the guard made no move, to speak, nor to stop the wagon. He had seen Sir Richard speaking to Will. He was not interested in making acquaintance of an ox-cart driver. Above all, he thought that if these beast were stopped they may never start again. He thus appeared to take no notice, which caused Will not to worry; his responsive feeling was occasioned into a frown.

Having done nothing in the church for what he judged to be more than a suitable length of time, Sir Richard de Duay, steward of Bolingbroke Castle, emerged with his morale and importance recirculating in his veins. He too entered the castle with no more than a monosyllable about the time of day, but he did receive a conventional respectful reply. He was relieved to observe that clearing work looked as if it had started, by Emma, Roheisia, and two boys. He observed also that the lady Alesia was sitting on a lower step of the solar stair. With no inkling of his inner illogicality he assumed at once that she was there to make sure that this work, and maybe other tasks, were going to be done. Thinking thus about her in the way he knew that others wrongly thought about him, he approached her, adopting a suitable attitude.

Alesia herself was indeed thinking about nothing in particular, and what was going on was part of general castle bailey activity. After over two hundred folk had been there the reduction to a third of them would enable and need a lot of rubbish, litter, ordure and the like to be cleared. Horses did not mind where they were; the oxen didn't help.

Sir Richard did not mention the clearing process, for it had obviously been begun. It would take two or three days. His was only the responsibility. Most often, of course, the whole family had left by the time it was being done. A new attitude to Alesia struck him, and caused him to look at her with fresh eyes.

Heiress of the sixty thousand acres by Bolingbroke in particular, Sir Richard knew now where his future lay. It was necessary to treat her power seriously to maintain and increase his worth in her eyes.

"Ah. Lady Alesia. A pleasantish day. May I hope that during your stay here that I can interest you in the workings of these manors and perhaps the people here."

Alesia had been stroking one of the dogs which had wandered up, which then having received enough affection and no food had duly strayed on. She was feeling thus relaxed and comfortable in the sunshine.

"Perhaps the people?" she answered.

Sir Richard examined in his mind the tone of voice in which this question was set. Did she mean why bother about the people at all, or that it was so important that she was surprised that he had said 'perhaps'. With some rapidity he assumed that Alesia would have much the same attitude as her father.

"The people. Indeed. We can do nothing without them, Lady Alesia."

He then added after this inconclusive moment: "The King himself begins to ask more and more of them. The advice of the greater, the work of the lesser. It is not easy to manage people, and it helps to know them; and may I have your permission to add, Lady Alesia, for them to know those in command."

Which last sentence he decided suitably avoided expressing that knowing such as the de Lacys would be an exercise of the mind and certainly not emotional closeness. Alesia understood, and she nodded before her reply. Her world was her father and her mother; her future was Thomas. Maybe Mabota and John and Torkill the huntsmen had shared more of her ordinary self. Casual and brief acquaintance with children, soldiers, masons, priests, grooms, and the whole gamut of many manors had made her feel she knew the people. Her security of feeling was in social occasions when the King and his followers were all around. In that political world, however, among those present enemies were to be noted; indeed absentees might also be such.

Hesitation in her reply almost made Sir Richard bring up another subject, and would have so done if he could have conjured one.

"As and when my mother will spare me from her tutorials of a woman's duty I will certainly accompany you Sir Richard. I would like to know what is to be known. Villeins and cottars doubtless have their problems."

She was not being very close to Sir Richard. She automatically was taking her place above him. It was inborn, he decided. He would play the useful factual servant. It would have to work with Alesia de Lacy, for it was already being spoken that Thomas was unapproachable. He did not get off to a good start, however, though he did not know that.

The next morning Alesia had to say to her mother: "For myself I would have thought that if I had a castle to clean, and the owners were there, then I would have ordered that where the owners were likely to go would be cleaned first."

Margaret quite agreed: "But in all of my life I have never yet managed to get that message across without a specific instruction. One wearies in the end. I assume that there is a mysterious reason unknown to women. In fact, if it weren't for women I do not think the place would be cleaned at all."

"Sir Richard suggested I go with him on his duties sometimes."

"Certainly. Perhaps you'll ask him the answer. Though he will at once forget it himself. For a time, however, stay with me while I interview our almoner; I am not even sure who's doing it at the moment."

"Did you ever get tired of learning, learning, and then learning, mother?"

"It didn't seem to apply to me, darling. It just gradually arrived in my head. Such as I do know, that is. I am so very sorry, darling, we have not done much for you..."

She trailed off, because it had been because of her two sons, now lost; so Alesia hoped the almoner would not be long in coming. He was a new one. A young priest, Hamo Pechin, who explained that he had adopted the name of Hugh. He hoped in time to be able to enter a monastery. Margaret noted that it was not the usual attitude that Henry liked in his administrators.

"Which order do you find attractive?" she asked.

Giving no detail in his reply, he clearly found the close community and the inhibition of his earthly feelings a calming influence. Hugh spoke like that, perhaps to relate to what conversation the ladies might think appropriate or which approximated to a feminine point of view. He felt he had achieved some ingratiation. This was because Alesia reacted with her eyes to look up at him more closely as he stood there. It was, however, interest, and some surprise that had caused her to do so. She was intrigued by a tone of voice which she had heard before. She wondered if her mother had noticed. The poor young man was looking for refuge. What could be the perfection for a young man in that imprisoned life? Surely they must change when they achieved their place?

"I do not know how long you are going to stay, then" continued Margaret, hoping that that would not be taken as a promise for anything at all; "But the almoner's duties while here are of course the same."

Hugh was interested enough in ensuring that the poor and the infirm and the aged were fed. He would rather buy them food than give them money, which appeared to conform with his monkish tendencies. Thin and fair in complexion as he was, Margaret felt at heart he would not waste much on the greedy. They would need further talk in due course. He may go.

"In the name of God. Amen." Hugh departed.

Margaret looked to Alesia and smiled and spoke loudly: "As you go round I hope you will find that he really is the best almoner one could ever have."

When she was certain that Hugh was out of earshot she spoke her real thought in a lower voice: "As far as the people themselves are concerned, what can we do? We only distribute food, which grows in the fields. No-one except God can increase the crop."

As well as food, money also seemed to be short. Thomas never had any, but he was not yet in an inheritance. She did know that her father was about to request once again that debts to the exchequer be cancelled.

"Obviously," explained Margaret, "your father cannot be expected to finance expeditions everywhere entirely by himself."

Alesia looked quickly at her mother, and expressed that it all seemed to work very well.

"Do you really think then, dear Alesia, that I am a good firm administrator-in-chief? I suggest you prepare for your tour round with Sir Richard. In a few days I will come with you."

"Why is this castle here?" asked Alesia suddenly. She knew well that wives would stand in for husbands in their absence, but checking one's staff and workers was included. From her mother's tone she saw now that for all her poise, her mother's outward reassurance was just the cloak over her waiting for her husband's return. She had had a thought about a stalwart defence of the castle as would befit a heroine. Margaret did not quite get the point.

"Yes, mother, but castle defences assume an attacker. This place is much stronger than an ordinary manor warrants. Is it the collected revenues of the Honor stored here? Surely not."

"Whatever it is, it has so far never happened. Against any invasion, I believe. When Ranulf built it, then it would be the Danes or the Saxons. Now the French; but when they came it was from Dover and London. Maybe the Flemings these days. There's always somebody. So far the Scots haven't got as far as here."

Margaret smiled: "Perhaps I had better talk with Peter the Armourer next."

Alesia began to think that running manors and castles was going to be interesting, and in the morning she greeted Sir Richard with the thought. He took it as being complimentary. The little group therefore set out in good humour. There was Alesia and Mabota, Sir Richard and his aide. Two clerks, four armed men, and two messengers. The very minimum. Sustenance was hoped for as a result of messages sent previously to the reeves of the villages they would visit.

Sir Richard judged folk in straightforward terms. His attitude to them assumed that they were in character either melancholic, phlegmatic, irritable or sanguine, all of which he assumed had no mixture, and all of which he treated distantly. Alesia found it was based on medical theory, but Sir Richard felt it made him understand their minds. Though her travels had been extensive, in an uncanny way, Sir Richard made Alesia feel she had better open her eyes, and abandon what she now could see was an upbringing in a cocoon. In the saddle she sat at the village of Bane, gazing thoughtfully at the Master Carpenter and his men preparing wood for a cart wheel.

Her Latin and her Greek, music, church and the clerks in Holy Orders did not bring out her mind as warmly as the sight of these strong men at their constructive work. The men were pleased by her obvious interest.

"Perhaps, Sir Richard, the church with all the knowledge has the theory. These men have the practicality."

Sir Richard was always a little upset by the de Lacys not being intimate enough to call him just by his Christian name, and that thought cropped up again at this moment. His mind diverted onto this because he had no conception that there might be two aspects to life on earth.

"I believe, my Lady, that degrees between people are enduring."

Alesia supposed he had to think that way, or he would not have been a steward. With detached observation she watched the freemen, cottars and villeins at work, the smiths, the bakers, the priests, the women. And after several days of such exploration, Margaret noticed her quietness in the evening.

"What did you find today, Alesia?"

She really wanted to keep it to herself, to savour a little what had impressed her, such a tiny fraction of life as it was. There seemed to be no real reason why she should not say, except that she did not wish to be the subject of ridicule, however kind. She tried to occasion surprise and defence by jumping right to the point.

"I came across a hovel. One which surprised me."

"It must have been remarkable if there was a surprise in a hovel. A not unpleasant surprise I hope."

"It stunned me. In all villages the hovels and tofts are untidy, the floors are rough, the food is not clean, the comfort is small, the ...."

"Yes, but what..."

"But in this one... Do you know of Widow Helen, for that was her hovel?"

Margaret did not.

"On the way out to Keal. I only got a glimpse as we passed. It seemed to shine with cleanliness. I just saw her. She seemed to glow with the rightness of her own self. In all these drab dwellings and so many who drag themselves through life, she seemed to embody a principle for living. It is a light in the greyness."

"Perhaps one day, you might go and look again," said Margaret. Alesia knew that she would, and would not be disappointed. It had presented to her an image of a lonely person holding her head high. It accorded with her mood as she looked in the morning across the marshes. Observation of village life was one thing with its anxieties about weather, animals and their illnesses, and folk with their disputes and tragedies. It could, however, all be put under a few headings and fitted into routine of what had always happened before. Perhaps Sir Richard was right about people. There must be more in life. Suddenly

Alesia thought how strange it was that as the future Countess of Lancaster, Lincoln, Salisbury, Leicester, Derby and Ferrers, she at this moment was bored. Whatever she could think up she must do. Here there was no expression possible, even though she felt the local people appreciated her presence. That might be because they found it reassuring, and not for her personal value. She was becoming tense in finding that the stimulating potential of her situation had to be matched by an even stronger patience. It was not in her to enquire if her mother felt the same, because she guessed that the answer would consist of a homily on women's lot in a world dangerous with marauders. She looked at the jewels in the casket by her, pursing her lips slightly. With wry expression she considered that men called women precious, locked up as jewels as they so often were. Embroidery that afternoon with her mother drew her concentration close, until Margaret said:

"I think it's about time we invited some people here, to know our neighbours better."

Alesia gave a start, at the idea which so suited her mood.

"Not if you feel not," continued Margaret, "but I thought it was rather quiet for you."

Alesia was constrained to discuss more factual matters with her mother, now that the atmosphere was more relaxed.

"I do not think mother, that I shall ever have such an ordered mind as yours. First things first - you pursue them, to the exclusion of everything else."

"It's the only way I've seen to do it. The basis has to be got right first. The staff, the stores, without that nothing goes right. I can assure you it's not my natural way. It had to be hammered in. But surely you saw that with Sir Richard on your rounds."

"When one thinks of it, what I saw with Sir Richard was Sir Richard himself. He told me at the beginning that he dealt entirely with trouble and things which had gone wrong. Then he spent every day showing me what was right. Anything distressful never got a mention."

"Well. That's a good beginning. The biggest problem with staff is getting at the truth behind the facade."

"I've got as far as the facade, then."

"Poverty, disease, bad crops, ageing bodies all have to be borne, darling. There is no palliative except hope and prayer."

Margaret softened her remark by adding that at least she had never come across any other.

Alesia fell into silence. She rose, to look through a small window to the castle bailey, over the far outer wall, up to the open fields on the rising hills beyond. All she saw provided evidence for fear. Man, horse, ox could be struck by illness without warning. Sight, hearing, movement of the body could inexplicably become impaired or useless. The works of man even in stone wear in the elements. In wood and thatch as in man there was decay. From strange forces out there beyond crops grew or not and man was sustained or not. The earth itself needed, and got, its fallow rest from growing food. The reasons were not known to man. Even the planets, where doctors sought talismans and answers, were hidden in the daylit sky, which made the darkness in the night so full of portent. The supreme power above had to be conciliated in the hope of His love falling upon oneself. With a hasty correction of her thoughts Alesia desired the love for all and not just for herself.

These deep impressions lasted long enough for her mother to grasp her daughter's contemplation, which resulted in a kind and quizzical look in her direction. As Alesia turned towards the centre of the room she was humbly inhibited by wonder to respond. In a sort of connected way, she said:

"Sir Richard said more than once that he had heard that all the Jews had not yet left the country. He reckoned there were still some at Boston and maybe a few in hiding in Lincoln."

"God knows what they're living on, then. They're meant to have gone eighteen months ago. They'll be rounded up. Try not to tell your father. He always thinks every law is perfectly effected. I am always telling him to have patience."

"Why was it all done, anyway?"

"Money, darling. It has not made our relations with the people any better; worse in fact. They've no-one else to blame, now. But it gets too dark for sewing."

Activity next morning was hunting again, finding Alesia in an improved mood.

"You grin, John, why?" demanded Alesia of John in the early sun of the morning. She had decided that with more provisions required for possible larger numbers she herself would join in the hunt. She so informed John and Torkill that in a week or two guests were expected to visit.

"If I did, lady Alesia, I am sorry. I did not mean to grin."

"Very well. You reacted one way or another. Do you mean you know already? I suppose such talk does get round."

"Indeed lady Alesia. A whisper in the castle comes out in the market at the gate. In days it is at markets in Horncastle, Spilsby, Alford, Tattershall, and not long to Lincoln. Although I dare say the message is not quite the same on each repetition."

"I would have thought there were better things to talk about."

John would have liked to enlighten her further.

"There is one point, however, lady Alesia" he made to say: "that it is stated, rumoured perhaps, that your father has reached Pontefract on his way back here."

"That does not accord with what we know, in fact" replied Alesia. Messengers, she supposed, often misread what they should not even see.

The hunting that day was vigorous and aggressive. The sounds were glorious, stimulating in the achievement of replenishing a great game larder. Alesia killed a deer herself. She shot it from a little too near for full pride, though there was praise enough. Peter the chaplain who had accompanied them was able to act with fair modesty. He had killed one himself. He joined with a little fear in the general excitement. 'Up, Peter, kill and eat' the Lord had said. But the Peter of the Holy Book had remonstrated. Peter the chaplain added to himself that a clean hunting kill was as good as the slaughter in the byre. God would count them all clean to assuage man's hunger. He must check the sayings of that other Peter.

It was a successful day. When the venison reached the table, sometimes the rabbit, and particularly the goose, Alesia lowered her face towards it and whispered to herself a little prayer. The smiling indulgence of Peter was not much help on these occasions.

This closing of the mind to an enormous number of God's creatures was not for Alesia to dispute, nor to affect her, other than to feel that she must discipline her emotion. At least she looked more closely at human acquaintances who arrived, stayed a day or two, and returned to their manors.

"Mother" from time to time she raised the question of Margaret: "do father and the King really want to know about the people who are around here? de Welles, Willoughby, Copledyk and those? They all seem to me to be completely uninterested in National matters. They can't be a bother to anybody. They want just the life they've got."

"Well, le Strange ought to be well satisfied as Justice of the Forest this side of Trent. He is, I think, more ambitious even so. As to all the others I admit I find it more relaxing here than in London. The Court is full of people who think they are worth more."

"And not minding against whom. But mainly they all asked where and when I was to be married."

"I hope they also gave you due good wishes."

"Not all. Some seemed to believe it was a personal matter to me. Anyway, is it yet decided?"

"Briefly, darling, we do not know. It might be London. If in the country it would be most likely Woodstock. It all depends where the King is going to be in a year or two."

Margaret read the still questioning look in her daughter's face, so she added:

"If in London at our Inn I suppose. A lot depends on Edmund and Thomas, and come to that I'm sorry to say, the mood of the citizens. If they are quiet and we are in favour, it could be in St. Paul's. Westminster is perhaps too far, but God knows we have paid thousands over generations for building it."

Margaret rarely brought the Almighty into her conversation, and Alesia felt from the tone of her mother's voice that she thought that the living God did know of these payments to provide a house for Him.

Her mother then carried on:

"At least you found out something about the squires of the district."

"Above all I found that they were trying to know more outside their own dull lives, but to do nothing about it. de Beaumont pumped me about Thomas Wayland. I just said that as the King's chief justice he shouldn't harbour murderers even if they were his own men. I think he knew that, and he seemed amused at the rumour that Weyland disguised himself as a friar. That's true, though, isn't it?"

"They seem up-to-date enough round here. Yes, he was seized at Bury St. Edmunds and that took a two month siege. He was only one of several sent to the Tower. Sad, but they get up to their own lawbreaking when Edward and Eleanor are out of the country. After four years' absence, however, Edward should have expected to have to sort things out on his return."

It was the season when the tints of autumn began to found the thought that the ladies were to be at Bolingbroke throughout the coming winter. Some questioning of the latest messenger from Lord Henry evinced his surprise that the rumours of the party returning from Scotland were not believed.

Margaret stated with some acerbity: "I believe but firm notes."

"Milady. I know only that 'tis said. But also milady I know that milord of Lincoln will not speculate on these matters."

For a moment Margaret wondered if Will de Hackthorn could actually read the parchments he carried. His eyes had never revealed such clarity as he looked at them, however, and once again she marvelled at the spread of communication among the lower orders.

Will de Hackthorn understood that within a day or two there could be a message of certainty on the matter.

"If it's William de Puy who rides it could well be here tomorrow, milady. He has right to better horses."

Margaret told Will to rest and to be available from the next afternoon. She ignored the hint about the horse. She moved off to read the despatches, by now accompanied by clerk and chaplain and secretary. Faint forecast did they give to her of what Will said might be on the morrow. Yet next day early in the afternoon William de Puy clattered without hesitation over the drawbridge into the bailey and the urgent message was that they should all make rendezvous in Lincoln to save time and journeying. Margaret ordered at once that they would move on the morrow, and Lincoln castle should be sent confirmation. Reaction from steward, seneschal, marshal and captain was little more than a nod from each, to the extent that Margaret wondered if her order was getting across, even whether there was some difficulty or trouble. Then she realized that, as so often, she was speaking to men who knew what she was going to say. They had heard all the gossip and read all the signs and the carts and horses and palanquins were already half prepared.

She should have felt comforted in being served by staff who were ready in anticipation. Yet it seemed to take from her the command of her affairs, leaving her uneasy. Tensions in her arose, this bringing to a head all the anxieties and fears in the absence of her husband all these weeks.

"Alesia" Margaret informed her daughter a few minutes later, after confirming to her the latest news "perhaps you will accompany me to chapel to pray again for your father's safe return."

In the chapel with its faded patterned walls they knelt. Not this time did Margaret give any outward show or gesture, nor had she brought Peter the chaplain. Alesia glanced towards her as best she could without being noticed. She had seen this mood before and it had always puzzled her. Her mother there, with her hands over her eyes, not uttering, not moving. Alesia did the same. Without knowledge of what her mother may have been thinking towards her God, Alesia in the same attitude and silence began to feel, and surmised, as her mother did.

There was no need for positive thought. Enwrapped by the structure of the chapel room, in the presence of the symbolism of the spirit, the poisons in her soul slowly faded, to relax her finger by finger, foot by foot, till the body and the mind were calm in the security of the belief in something eternal.

How private it had all been.

"I am so looking forward to the journey tomorrow," remarked Margaret as they left. Alesia was surprised to realise that no priest had told her that in such a way equanimity and confidence could return. She looked back at the chapel, turned again and took her mother's arm.

Bolingbroke Castle, Lincolnshire, in ruins.

# CHAPTER 11

"We will ride to Barlings by midday, Sir Richard. I want a smart turnout." Margaret nearly added that she would delay departure until she got one. It served as it was to crisp up the excitement and pleasure of the armed men at being on the move again. Some produced a suitable grumble.

"This time" added the Countess of Lincoln "tip the wink to chaplains and secretaries and all." "Perhaps there should have been more notice" was the mildest comment among the esquire and clerkly classes as they made their extra effort until the evening had dimmed into darker night, for they themselves were too used to rumours to act upon them.

In the morning it was with some feeling of amusement that Margaret mounted Goodbrook, firm in her determination to present a fine company to her husband at Lincoln. Start this way and even if Henry did not arrive for a day or two it may endure. Start badly and they would be all the time an untidy crew. Alesia observed her mother with quizzical interest, not herself having felt the need to prove herself.

Margaret and she rode along the line of assembled company.

"I am not convinced Sir Richard, that all is prepared as it should be." Having spoken in those terms, Margaret realized that it sounded more like an instinctive emotional effort to find some fault, she must needs correct this, and so looked carefully at the detail. A few specific corrections would reinforce her authority, as well as improve discipline.

Though the marshal had his responsibilities, it was only Sir Richard who could wield the authority over the Earl's men. To him Margaret indicated lack of cleanliness on two cloaks, loose girths on four horses, incomplete provisions of three men.

The next conversation with the Lady Margaret that Sir Richard had was as he turned to leave Barlings to return to Bolingbroke. He had done his work, but felt that he had not pleased. With a wan smile, therefore, he listened to her saying:

"A pleasant ride, Sir Richard. Keep the castle well for our return."

Had she emphasized 'well' he pondered. He saluted the Countess, and Alesia, who forbore to say anything. It was clearly the moment for a small smile of farewell, rather than a remark from her about desiring next time a deeper look at the life and struggles of the people.

It was full of hope and joy that the party got near to the eastern wall of Lincoln. Unity again in the family of three was their only purpose, and their need.

The group rode slowly along the summit of the northern side of the deep river cleft at Lincoln. The central focus of the city being the bulk of the Cathedral of St. Mary. The land falls away on three sides. Its drama had been before them for the last twenty miles, its bulk silhouetted on the two hundred foot high hill.

Lincoln castle was reached unimpeded through the remains of the city gateway on the east and passing the north side of the cathedral. In the open place outside the castle gate the public interest in purchasing at the market stalls waned rapidly, way being quickly made for the Countess, Alesia, and their retinue. No hindrance at the castle entrance gate. Indeed, hushed as were the people in the market, unspeaking as were the castle guards, attendant in silence the ostlers, Margaret began to feel a notion that there was unease. Alesia and she dismounted. In the troop the standard was lowered, and on the instant one was raised on the castle.

Just inside the western gate stood a Captain of Horse, visible but not prominent. Undecided whether to come forward now, or until the Countess would be refreshed from her travel, he had chosen his position so that fate may decide the point. If Margaret were alert, she would notice him now. If she was tired, then he would seek audience later.

Margaret noticed him.

"Who is that?"

"Captain le Gaoulher, milady" answered Seneschal de Root. "I understand he has a message for you."

de Root stumbled over the name.

"Who? What is his name? Do we know him?"

"No, Lady, I do not know him. He arrived yesterday, late in the evening, in the King's livery. He was tired, his horse lathered. His name marks him, I understand, as a Breton."

"Well, where is he from?"

"He says he is from the Earl. His message is for you, and he would not reveal even its subject to me."

de Root then realized by Margaret's expression that she began to fear bad news of her husband, so he added:

"There is no hint, ma'am that he brings distressful news. Perhaps I had better call him to clear it up."

He was to be brought to her at once.

"Not letters, Lady Margaret." Captain le Gaoulher was crisp with a disciplined mind. His request for permission to pass his messages to her in private was granted, except that de Root must stay. They moved to the small solar at the west end of the hall, Alesia with them, and their personal maids.

"There are two parts to my information which I am to tell you, Lady Margaret. Both come from the Earl himself. I was sent as his personal courier. My lord presents his compliments and states his regrets that he has to ask you to journey further. He cannot reach here yet, and desires that you proceed - in due convenience, of course - to Leicester..." on observing the effect of this le Gaoulher gave the rest of his news with haste: "...there is more - about my Lord - he is in excellent health - but at York with suddenness the King - I am told to say - decided to travel to the eastern parts of Yorkshire. I was there - ma'am - we were expecting to travel south when all was changed that morning."

"Why no letter, or this in writing?"

"There was no time I assure you, my lady, but such note can be expected. I was ordered to travel fast."

"Captain le Gaoulher, if I have your name correctly" spoke Margaret in measured tone "I have to ask, why you? Alone?"

"My name is Breton, it is not French at all, and does, I have to say, sometimes cause difficulty. Is not the livery of the King enough? It is because with the extra journey and some illness among Lord Lincoln's messengers that I was the only one available. Our numbers are too few to accommodate fully these extra - er - excursions."

"Do you know anyone here?" persisted Margaret.

le Gaoulher stiffened.

"I offer again the King's livery."

Alesia could see that it had all been enough for her mother. A look to de Root, and he caused the withdrawal of le Gaoulher from the chamber. Neither mother nor daughter liked this situation.

"Surely, Henry would never send such a message by a stranger."

"It was said that none other was available, and that they are short of men."

"So they send one of the King's captains?"

"The King has sometimes sent messages by word of mouth, but of course usually by an educated clerk. I must add that I am suspicious. We have had Welsh hostages held here, and I am fairly sure he sounds like one of them." Margaret and Alesia fell to discussing where to wait for further advice from Henry. From le Gaoulher they had discovered only that it was felt best that they travel to Leicester now, to Earl Edmund's castle there. The personal part of his message sounded the least personal.

Margaret, tired, from instinct only uttered: "Let us get through this night. Tomorrow we will confer with the Sheriff for advice. Put le Gaoulher in a distant chamber, and have him discreetly watched."

She agreed with de Root that it was to be a restless night. He, however, wanted to say one thing more:

"There is a strong loyalty - alright my lady, not among all, but certainly with most - to one's lord in this castle, among those stationed here, and among those who have come with you. With diffidence I hope you will understand me when I say that there may be friction, arising between Sheriff's men and Lord's men, so any task must be clear and separate."

Margaret and Alesia fell silent. They wondered what error they may have made. de Root paused, and then spoke again:

"You will be safe here. I will see to that. I was already putting rumours together of marauders outside the city when le Gaoulher was waiting by the West Gate. We were already alert, ma'am." He finished with confidence in his voice.

"Why the West Gate?" asked Alesia.

"le Gaoulher would be expecting you to go round the north of the city and enter there, but you came through the upper town instead."

Alesia did not feel up to asking about the marauders. There were always some around. The Close was being walled all round for protection. The population was growing too fast, and there was not enough land to occupy them all. de Root gave comfort.

"It is not a siege. Only the possibility of noise and shouts, now that we know all is guarded."

"We will wait here for further news. I will despatch a note within the hour to Lord Henry."

Mabota whispered to her mistress, who turned to her mother:

"The alerting of Leicester castle, and requesting an escort would be a good idea, and quick."

"Thank you, Mabota. Yes, Alesia dear. And indeed you do it. As the betrothed to Thomas you should have the authority."

They both managed to laugh.

Mabota again whispered to Alesia. It was a somewhat lengthy sentence.

"Come, come, tell me, Mabota," interpolated Margaret, "let's have it out loud."

Mabota curtsied and excused her presumption, and continued "...but Lady Margaret, Lady Alesia, may I say I do not believe that the Lord Henry would send you words by a mouth that you can scarcely understand. And why not Pontefract, which is his own, and nearer to him?"

The clarity of this enhanced their own chord of doubt.

"de Root, send for Sheriff de Novo Mercato. He should have been here to meet us, anyway. He is to bring a posse to interrogate this Breton."

"A King's man, ma'am?"

At best Margaret realized that his remark was advice given in astonishment and fear. Her expression of her own surprise was taken at once for her confirmed command.

It was over an hour before Novo Mercato arrived, link lighted through the darkness, Margaret's first words of greeting had to be about how tired he looked.

"We have been towards Sleaford today, milady, trying to apprehend some felons."

Before she had time to ask further, indeed to sympathize, the Sheriff expressed his anxiety about the safety of the two ladies, and requested to know the facts. They were meeting in the Great Hall, which had been cleared, with guards at the door. In the candlelight and waving shadows it was easy to magnify fears, and to bolster their own thoughts with asides, but sifting evidence was well within the Sheriff's experience.

His fingers tapped the table in a minor rhythm as he thought, but not for long.

"His horse? How was it caparisoned? Do you know whether it was one of the King's?"

No-one recalled.

"With your permission, milady, I will arrest this man. I cannot do so without it. This is Lord Lincoln's castle, and I would most certainly..."

"...be in trouble without any agreement. Very well, I agree. Then perhaps you will tell us what is in your mind."

The sheriff requested de Root to arrest le Gaoulher, and to confine him in the north east tower. He further ordered a report on the horse on which he had arrived. He returned to the centre table:

"Is there any reason why the King himself should send one of his men, with a message?"

The import of this focussed the whole story. The explanation at once was shown to be paltry. To Margaret a sudden increase in her fears brought her hands to her face, in her imaginings of disaster. Alesia had to give the answer.

"No real reason, since father is with the King. Except, of course, that father himself may, perhaps, be ill."

"It would, however, be in writing. But this man said that Henry was not ill."

"I am beginning to believe that his whole attitude is false."

"Lady Lincoln, I must clearly express my feelings on this matter to you at once. I am sure there is no danger any more to you. I also am certain that Lord Lincoln is himself not connected with this at all. But none of this can be proved at this moment, and certainly not at this time of night. Let me put your mind further at rest. Firstly, I do not believe that this man is either a Breton, or from the King. I surmise that he is one of the Welsh soldiers, disaffected or discharged, now marauding the countryside. He may have been in the forces to Brittany, or he may just have picked up a Breton identity in Wales from a Breton sailor or an onion merchant. They are of course still virtually the same race. I think he chose a too dramatic message to ring true. Particularly, if he had been genuine he would have entered the castle with some confidence. His bearing sounds to be otherwise."

"So there was little danger. But what was, or is, his purpose?"

"A reward, presumably. With respect, however, ma'am, may I request returning to this matter tomorrow?"

"Indeed, sir sheriff, you are tired. So are we. I understand."

In fact Novo Mercato wanted to make an investigation, but this moment served to relax the ladies in a feeling of safety for the night. It was half an hour before the sheriff was able to leave Lincoln castle for his own lodging. le Gaoulher had made off. Every corner had to be examined. The guards were briefed again.

In the early hours next morning search was begun in the city, without much hope, because the ruinous walls on the western side would not prevent any wilful escaper. Two posses were despatched - one due north to the river Humber, the other to search north-west along Tillbridge Lane, with which the sheriff went himself. Earlier than expected, by mid-afternoon, he had returned. He hastened at once to the castle, and requested audience. The Countess of Lincoln was impatient.

"All day, de Novo Mercato, we have waited for you. Here is some evidence we have found. Of course I understand that you have been out to search for this man."

The sheriff was shown the garments of the King's livery which had been abandoned in a dark corner, so that le Gaoulher could escape unidentified. The sheriff showed little surprise, nor much enthusiasm.

"Yes," he explained, "it pieces together. I suggest his plan went wrong. Less than a dozen miles from this city today we found the body of the real messenger. There was enough scattered around to prove his office. The parchments are for the Tower of London. The man who called himself le Gaoulher wanted the livery only, to deceive you. Why? His message to you was fabricated. An afterthought. Something to get him out of a difficult position, such as explaining his presence here, or trying to."

He paused to see if his story was being accepted or was doubtful. The Countess and Alesia wished for the rest.

"I have now unfortunately to come to the difficult if not dangerous reason for him being here at all. I have to suggest that it was spontaneous that he stole this disguise, and that he had a target which he could approach in the confidence that it would induce."

"My husband."

"The Earl, precisely. He expected him to be with your party, I imagine. There is trouble coming in Wales, it is said."

"A dispossessed and disaffected Welshman."

"In my opinion, yes. The Earl should be warned. We will continue our search."

Margaret and Alesia found some reassurance in the calm attitude of the sheriff, though not much in the possibility of the apprehending of le Gaoulher, if that was his real name. It sounded too much like the word for Welshman itself, though they were told its real meaning was a falconer.

It was in the chapel in early morning that their retreat from fear began. Rarely had Margaret and Alesia seen daylight gathering with such relief.

"Be merciful, Oh God, unto me, for man goeth about to devour me. Mine enemies are daily in hand to swallow me up. Though I am sometime afraid: yet put I my trust in thee. We thank thee Lord for bringing us safely to the beginning of another day."

From the Chapel they walked across the bailey back to the Great

Hall and to the solar, accompanied as they were by chaplain, steward, seneschal, and three esquires. It became an early lesson for Alesia in sensing among the staff and household as they passed by those who were in sympathy with them.

"One can also tell," Alesia spoke quietly to her mother, "those who are a little bit pleased about our problem."

"The difficulty then," rejoined Margaret, "is remembering who was what. Your father is very good at that."

"He'll be coming soon?"

Margaret had already sent the news by two couriers, to find him, and to send word quickly about meeting. The incident was now gossiped in the town, and by mid-morning Margaret and Alesia were asked if they would receive some merchants. A group of respectful citizens was duly received. John de Blyton introduced himself and John de Fenton, Thomas de Carlton, William de Baiocis and Ralph de Kyme.

"We are here to show our homage to you, my lady, Countess of Lincoln, and to the Lady Alesia, at the same time as our sympathy to you in the unfortunate incident of last night, of which we have heard. We were to request to see you in any event, to show our joy at the betrothal of the Lady Alesia. It is my humble duty, milady, to offer from ourselves to the Lady Alesia a present on this occasion. We pray that it may be accepted."

"Of course" Margaret replied, "it will be to our great pleasure. But what is your calling?"

"de Fenton and I have shops on the High Bridge, milady; jewellery for myself, and cloth for John. Thomas, William and Ralph are licenced to deal in wool. These days that has to be within the realm, and..." with a tolerant smile..."not with anyone within the power of the Countess of Flanders. If I may return to our offering, milady, it would give us all happiness for the Lady Alesia in respect of our good wishes if this could be accepted. In our name and others from our city."

It was an epergne of gold made by Walter de Karliolo, goldsmith, of Lincoln. With an involuntary gasp, Alesia exclaimed at its beauty as it was uncovered. She flushed at the attention of these citizens to her. With profuse thanks she pleased them by telling of the prominent position in her household that it would occupy, and for so long as she may live.

In their minds were pleasantries about progeny, but they were not uttered. It was one of Alesia's minor amusements to guess what would have been said by underlings if they had the nerve to be their natural selves.

It was the next day, that Alesia showed her present to another visitor, Roger Lestrange, Justice of the Forest this side of Trent. He had come to give his sympathy and sought assurance that the ladies were now well and confident of their safety.

"It astounds me, Roger, that a King's man can be killed so casually. It must signify deep unrest."

"My dear Margaret, no. I am sorry to say it is not infrequent. You may recall that I was sent to the Pope with John de Sancto Johaime, and what were we charged to return with? The Holy Father's complaints that his letters to ecclesiastics did not reach them - the bearers were often seized, he thought. There is no real way of stopping wild marauders."

Perhaps it had been just money, but to Margaret this was not a comforting note, it even concentrating her thoughts on the danger to her husband. Further, it demonstrated Roger's shallow understanding, though his office implied the opposite. Roger's further chatter was all on his papal trip, and the Pope's complaints that his ecclesiastics were imprisoned for light offences, and his taking umbrage that prelates and clerks were forced to answer to lay justices.

"John and I" he rambled on "told him that the King was at peace with his prelates and clergy and is ready to do justice to all; but the Holy Father still demanded rectification, and even an answer."

Margaret had been hearing but taking in only the general line, but felt she must make an intelligent reply.

"It is not my recollection that Bishops and Abbots produced the correct funds for the Crusades, which was left to their consciences by the Pope..."

"No, I..."

"...in fact Bishop Oliver here is totally absorbed in strengthening the wall round his close, and in planning cloisters - where there is not a single monk to walk through them. He counts more carefully than anyone the fruit, the vegetables, flocks and herds for his tenths for his fabric fund."

"With ecclesiastical censures for non-payment" added Alesia, emboldened, but surprised at her mother's openness in her distressed state of mind.

On Roger's departure next morning they had hope of an early reassurance from the Lord Henry. That evening it seemed that there was nothing left to say. They sat by the fire, just looking. The stillness of their heads, the immobility of their faces expressed the suspension of hope, and the uncertainty of the fear that was still with them.

Then the message of assurance from Henry did arrive. He could come to Lincoln very soon. He sent a captain and men to guard them further, and with that trusted escort they would meet earlier if they would make their way to Pontefract, where they would be joined by the whole royal party. If they felt not able to make the journey then he would haste to Lincoln from there.

So for Pontefract they left, so oddly not unlike the message of le Gaoulher. Margaret did not want to upset her husband's duties; he seemed to be cleverly soothing her shock by diminishing its importance. She remembered one of his sayings once - referring to her father's accidental death while jousting at Blyth. She had asked, when she grew up, what the others then did.

"They mourned. Then they had to carry on. It is to continue then or never; one has to keep one's balance, one's morale, one's confidence."

The Justices of Lincoln, Adam de Crokedayle and William Inge could see small chance of le Gaoulher being apprehended, in spite of the sheriff's optimism, and Margaret cynically and fully believed them. Such calming words that Bishop Oliver Sutton produced came well from his office, but above all courage came from another source. For public show they took communion in the chapel of St. Mary Magdalen in the Cathedral. Thereafter Margaret and Alesia moved down the nave and past the choir to the brilliant new tomb of the late Queen Eleanor. In the presence of its inspiration there was no doubt of confident belief.

The Savoy, of the Earls of Lancaster.

# CHAPTER 12

At Pontefract the King and Henry were highly amused at the recounting of the visit to the Pope by Roger le Strange. Edward was not surprised at him inflating the matter somewhat:

"The Pope considered my envoys not good enough for him - that they were of insufficient rank, and that letters of credence were not fitting for great and grave matters. He said he nevertheless received them with paternal affection. He did, however, also think that one thousand marks a year for my submission about Scotland were not enough to be agreeable to the honour of the apostolic See."

Then he turned to Alesia, modestly standing nearby.

"Now, my dear, the great subject for you is when it can be arranged for your marriage to my nephew. Yes? Well, now, when can I guarantee to be at Woodstock? Given no emergencies - you'll need some notice, Margaret, - I would think that the court can get round to there by late Summer. How about that, Henry?"

"On present plans, yes, Edward..." for the benefit of the ladies he continued "...to London now, Canterbury, then there are matters in the west. I think late Summer will mean the end of September. A very nice time in the middle of England."

Margaret was used to receiving decisions in this way, oblique clarification of something about which she had been wondering for ages. To obscure the suddenness by which she felt projected into another step in life, Alesia lowered her head and dropped a curtsy in acknowledgment.

As the court moved southwards from castle to castle more and more gathered in the King's entourage. Henry was granted the right for some weeks to sport along any river in the realm where he happened to be passing. The birds and the fish were a fine dietary supplement. Henry and his men, and his wife and daughter all enjoyed the catching from the living stores of rivers and woods. There seemed little interest concerning their adventure in Lincoln with le Gaoulher, and Alesia never did discover whether it was humour or his own personal interest that made King Edward forbid the flying of falcon on the sporting licence.

Mabota, however, had other matters on her mind. "Who will marry you then, Lady Alesia? If it's the Bishop Sutton he always does his ordinations on Holy Cross day. It ought to be Bishop Sutton. Not that I'm against the Archbishop which you might want, but you are of Lincoln, aren't you?"

"Let's not leave out Salisbury, Mabby," smiled Alesia, "and our cousin Bishop there. Though his health is not so good, he tries to be active. Neither does Bishop Sutton travel so much now."

Mabota frowned. "It's the Lincoln diocese at Oxford and Bishop Salisbury would have to have Lincoln's Bishop's permission."

Alesia surmised that she herself would not have any say in the matter.

"At least Woodstock seems decided, and there's all Summer to prepare for the rest of it."

They were well on the way to London by now. The castle of Berkhamsted was their last sojourn before all dispersed to their residences in the capital. There would be much administration waiting for decisions, there would be more councils and meetings. The King was more accessible in London to Ambassadors, the Papal Nuncio, and to City merchants. An air of seriousness settled on the party at the approach of their greater responsibilities.

"Why, mother, do you always smile when Woodstock is mentioned for my wedding?"

"Do I?"

"You have done the last few days, ever since you knew where it was to be. I know all about Fair Rosamund, if that's it."

First Margaret wondered if Alesia really was so sophisticated as to know more than hearsay about Rosamund Clifford, an ancestress of hers, mistress of King Henry II, and of her dwelling at Woodstock. Rosamund was generally considered to have been badly treated. They contributed much to Godstow Nunnery, near Oxford, where Fair Rosamund was buried. Margaret could never quite decide whether to be open about Rosamund, or to ignore the kind of fame which it brought. To the empty gossipers it still provided fuel for salacious disrespect. But it was not that. Alesia might as well know why an unconscious atavistic pleasure gave rise to her feminine reaction.

"Yes, I suppose I have sometimes looked a little droll. I must stop that. It is, however, that it was at Woodstock a dozen years ago that I told your father that your life had begun. It was on the eve of St. Mark, strangely, on that lovers' day.

Alesia was silent, with eyelids lowered at the aptness of this, but moreso of the wonder that so short a time ago she was not. Such was the prolific spread of nature in field and byre and in the home that there was nothing related to birth that was not normally around her. But this referred to her alone, without which she would not be there, nor would she have being to see this world. And yet it was treated and spoken of by so many in rude terms. Yet it must be wonderful to produce another life, and for that Alesia began to look forward with hope of fulfilment. To lift folk up in spirit of course it had to be sanctified and blessed.

"Let us hope that is a good omen" was Alesia's comment.

Margaret hesitated a second before agreeing, having to decide that Alesia was not referring to Fair Rosamund. Sometimes she wanted to laugh, or alternatively speak out, all about man's hypocrisy. That was a strong word, which she would not use aloud, but the consistency of rightness was often hard to find. The menfolk in her family had helped England forward for generations; they had worshipped; they had supported great Cathedrals and churches and abbeys and nunneries. The

Crusades had been attended.

Yet - it was necessary and conventional publicly to ignore the existence of Peter de Cestria. Kinsman of Henry, the mother unmentioned. Peter himself being given clerkly duties, paid for by various church stipends, though he was not ordained. At least thought Peter himself, I am more protected than they as ordinary clerk of the diocese of Coventry. So church rules were supported so long as they fitted, yet were propagated as a means of disciplining the population. Margaret wished she did not have these whimsical thoughts, and certainly that they did not make her lips relax into revealing them. From the social order imposed seven generations before by William the Bastard, from churches built to achieve revenue from the people, and outlets for ordinands of monasteries, came rules all overlaid with men's ideals, yet challenged to contempt by their behaviour.

Fearful of looking down at the lapses of man, she knew she had to raise her eyes, to the hope engendered in the marvel of existence. The mystery of it all had to have the reassurance and explanation of the Holy Church. May Alesia's life be towards perfection in its eyes.

All thoughts other than those of rectitude were to vanish as Margaret joined the assembling group for the last day's ride to London. She crossed herself as she passed the altar which accompanied them. A portable one, for use on their travels, under faculty from the Pope to Henry, some four years before, to give comfort in his bereavement.

The King had left the previous morning, with William of Louth the Bishop of Ely, and Walter Langton Bishop of Lichfield, which gave opportunity to Henry to meld his own household closer to himself. Henry always felt more secure in their loyalty after there had been apparently equal interchange with wife and daughter, chaplains, clerks, almoner and treasurer, knights, esquires, huntsmen, escorts and guide. As there was still some talk of le Gaoulher, as a representation by that incident of Welsh disaffection, Henry was constrained to explain the situation. His expositions generally were given to the few around him, leaving them to spread down the ranks. He assumed that there was thereafter little diminution of what he said, about which he was only sometimes right. Mostly it was embroidered.

"The Welsh are a kindred of free tribesmen. In Denbigh they say they are all descended from Canon, son of Lawburgh. They subdivide everything through bodies of joint tenants, which they call gavels. In some cases there are even half-gavels, but all the tenants derive their rights from their kindred. They share the wood and the waste, but the pasture is in common. It all works well when there is plenty of land to accommodate those needing it, but it is now out of balance, with too many people. Also redivision takes place only on the death of the grandfather, except that free tribesmen can claim a share. So, there are more and more Welsh with no livelihood."

The captain of their escort asked surely they could change the system.

"The Welsh do not change" replied Henry, and then added a point which he had been hoping to avoid mentioning:

"These people thus have nothing to do except make trouble because of disaffection. In England we change slower than we should - look how long it is taking to alter village fields from pairs to threes. Yet it would give more space for labour and much more food. Again, the Welsh being so close-knit denies a man his own identity, diminished again by our conquest. Identity is what they really struggle for."

Henry felt he had perhaps hinted at possible disaffection in England. He, of all persons, though he was more aware than most. Captain le Jane acknowledged the courtesy of being answered, and expressed no further point. He wondered whether the Earl would be surprised at what his soldiers would say to that. It would be from the narrow picture seen by their relatives. It was that there had always been food and always would be, and more work was for more tithes to the parson and more dues to the lord and his bailiffs. Maybe one or two saw the force of the idea, but were afeared of altering the normal natural way, for nature would revenge itself in the soil.

The Lord Henry thought the new arrangement would have to wait until a bad year made the people cry out for and then agree with the remedy. Not too bad a year, he hoped wryly.

Before he gave the instruction to move off, Henry beckoned John le Hunt and Torkill of Saxby to discreetly keep station with Alesia just in case there should be some unpleasant situation. The saffron silk banner was raised; the slow moving column of some two hundred in all gave colour and spectacle where it passed. There were plenty in the groups who watched so as to assess the standard of the men and the horseflesh, with the bonus of seeing, and doffing to, the Earl, his lady and their daughter. Whoever chose that animal for the earl knew his horses. The extra smoothness of its carriage was clear even to those who had only ever got an ox to move. The better holding of its head implied self knowledge of his superiority.

Between Alesia and John and Torkill an easy conversation developed. Still not twenty, and not considering that they would ever be huntsmen to anyone else, they related themselves totally to the team that made the household a close and friendly group.

"The way you're looking alert, Torkill, there's a hare under every bramble."

Both huntsmen laughed.

"Hit 'em sideways with the arrow, at the shoulder, is best," Torkill mused aloud. "There's plenty of sign of roebuck on the saplings, too."

"I can see you to are alive on the matter. You're a natural for a huntsman, so I imagine that is why you are one, John."

"It runs in the family, lady Alesia, so far I can't see any extra problem like that in Wales. There's plenty of game. So long as it is properly reserved, may I add. And, of course, so long as the arrows travel right."

Alesia laughed again.

"With you John there's thus no difficulty."

"I hope not, lady Alesia. I do like to feel there's something there for the future."

Alesia pondered on that thought. What of herself? The last representative of the family, now named de Lacy, over two hundred years in England and who knows how long before in Normandy. She was to be wife of a man who would be one step higher. Perhaps that made it harder to feel at ease, not like John and Torkill who were content in their abilities. Thomas himself was the grandson of the Earl of Lancaster who had achieved the lands of Simon de Montfort. Having got onto the wrong side, Simon had lost all. The family and all their friends were in England, anyway, just because Harold had lost a fight. But long before that they had all been Viking raiders. Within all this context Thomas seemed potentially strong and forthright enough to look after her and himself.

There was another way to feel secure, like Burnell, so recently deceased. Edward had so strongly relied on him for the soundness of his advice, sometimes telling him, with amusement, that he'd got the council to gang up on him. A remarkably confident man. Bishop of Bath he was, to give him revenue, and chancellor. Alesia smiled slightly to herself, having lost any logic in her musings, for she had heard that Burnell would have been an archbishop, except for one obvious flaw. He had too many illegitimate children. Yet he had complemented Edward, and his loss was badly felt, indeed noticeable. Eleanor had been Edward's vital helpmeet too. Alesia perked up her head - perhaps Bishop Burnell's sources were his lady friends.

Alesia rode on in the mood of taking what would come in life and hoping for the best. She would hope to goodly manage and to achieve camaraderie with her husband. The huntsmen had fallen back, not having received further hint that their talking would continue. For themselves, they would lose credibility with their own comperes if they did not maintain their servanthood. Nor were they envious of their lord and the ladies, who showed a happy face to all, but did they perhaps not make shift to do so? They seemed to arrange their lives relative to duty, to fiefs, indifferent to the warmth of any personality. Give them pals and ale. Upper class folk needed to examine the reality in the minds of the lower orders, and these two huntsmen enjoyed the dual position and interest which it gave them.

The company reined to at the de Lacy Manor of Edgware. Food and drink were prepared for all. To be in a great household made proper sustenance the more likely and perhaps most of the troop were somewhat perfunctory in thanking their God for it. Lord Henry took the opportunity to hear from bailiff and reeve of progress in the fields and the results of courts. Once again John Dyber had been fined twopence for brewing ale without a licence. Henry had to look away to prevent himself catching Margaret's eye at this annual repetition so solemnly given.

Hovering nearby, a little detached from the differing groups, was William Maengot, marshal of the goods wagons, which had also got as far as Edgware. Clearly there was something he wished to say, and he had some hesitation.

"Well, Maengot?"

As one who felt that confidence would be restored if a point could be cleared from his mind, William Maengot moved forward.

"Pardon, lord, but a wagon has broken a cross-tree, and there will be a delay. I assure you, lord, it is being mended now, but I cannot give the length of time. It must be a day or more."

Henry interrupted any further statement, to gain the relevant points.

"Which wagon?" He could see a fair way away what looked like timber work in progress.

"The one, lord, with the heavier domestic furniture. We could pack them up in part on the other wagons."

"A few hours may not matter, but why so long for mending a cross-tree?"

"All we have, lord, is old Dryknotter, who..."

"What is Dryknotter?"

"I am sorry, lord. It's how we call him. His real name I can't remember. He's particular about perfection in his timber that he'll never hurry or make shift."

"That has advantages," mused Henry, "but not so much now."

He decided to look closer at the work, and Alesia accompanied him.

"He's the only man available, lord," excused Maengot. Then he added, for further explanation of the necessary submission to Dryknotter's character:

"I have a young carpenter with us, but - er - Dryknotter - will not let him touch his timber."

The Lord Lincoln stood casually by when he saw the work which was being done. A poor piece of wood had been half split for some time, where the fault had not been visible, and it was having to come out. Old Dryknotter acknowledged with respect the presence of the Earl, but made no further move that would divert him from his work. Henry noted that the job could have been satisfactorily effected for the present need just by added splints, to keep the baulk together long enough. It was strange to the small group of his entourage looking on that he did not use authority to get this done, so as to get on. Henry had no intention of doing so, as soon as he had been there a moment.

What the great lord marked, where a spoken word would have intruded from either side, was an equal personality, deserving of equal respect. Dryknotter was at one with his materials, his tools, and the task in hand. He seemed mentally to embrace the problem as a friend. Nothing would be done temporary or second-rate. Henry thought it would be an experience to sell him some timber. Dryknotter would know more about it than the merchant. He turned to go back, and returned acknowledgment. It was to Maengot he spoke, drily, and loud enough for Dryknotter to hear.

"Have the cart brought along later. Retain four men as escort for it. The cart is more valuable now than the contents."

To London, then, with the Summer to prepare for the wedding. In early Autumn, it would be to Oxford for Woodstock, for the uniting of the great houses of Lancaster and Lincoln, which included four other earldoms.

The midday after their arrival at the Earl of Lincoln's Inn, Thomas rode over from the Lancaster house on the Strand. He thus surprised and pleased them, reassuring Henry of the young man's will and personality, and of the fitness for the association. This mutual trust was to last to the end of Henry's life, but not long after that with his daughter.

"This coming Autumn, Thomas, perhaps you would join me on the tour to Gascony? The usual troubles and showing of authority."

Thomas would. There was no better way - his father was no general, no manager of people. It was his grandfather whom Thomas had to emulate, a man of some force. Experience with the Earl of Lincoln would equip him better than with any other.

Alesia received him, while she was alone. Fortified by a view of his future, and dressed for the horse, any brittleness in his make-up submerged. Thomas marched up to her with confidence. Alesia smiled as submissive feelings overcame her. She lowered her head slightly.

"I'm glad" she whispered.

Thomas took both her hands and looked closely at her. He felt now personally accepted by the de Lacys. The question of lands and revenues was being resolved, but he felt that they were no more than his due. Perhaps less, but it was a good solid arrangement and the girl who went with it all looked well worth having. The background made her more interesting as a person. The picture had a frame. Suddenly he crushed her to him, to say:

"Let us look forward together."

Slightly bruising as it was to her, Alesia sagely accepted the enthusiasm behind this gauche approach. She listened to Thomas enthusing about his forthcoming association with her father. It would be after they were married. In a few years he would have his own household. She assumed that she was included, and only a young man's naivety had prevented it being expressed. She could perceive as much by his manner.

Another day it was arranged for a visitor, for whose arrival a certain briskness was induced into the establishment. Instructions from

Margaret for the house staff were insistent, the guards at the gates were inspected more closely. The Bishop of London, Richard de Gravesend, was to see Alesia. Her kirtle of white and surcote of black were correct for this formality. The unnoted doubt was that when set against Alesia's clear skin tone and long dark hair it appeared too feminine for a bishop's interview. The effect was, however, subdued by a dark green kerchief as a wimple on her head, waving down to her shoulders, her sleek hair bunned and netted under it. A matter was to be discussed with Alesia alone. It was not fitting that the bishop should be the only person with her, so with him was Canon Edward Lissett. Further, Peter, Margaret's chaplain, in attendance for Alesia's reassurance, and private report. Thus, Alesia was alone, albeit with bachelors of the church, for a fair minded meeting, with the background of righteousness.

The Bishop had had some difficulty in deciding the line he should take, and how serious he should be in his purpose of discovering if Alesia was fully apprised of the purpose and meaning of marriage. It seemed self-evident from previous acquaintance, but a duty had to be done, which in this instance he had taken on himself. This young lady before him was in her twelfth year, and was as grown up as most. With diplomacy in the background, however, the Bishop was aware of her potential power - to be of the King's family, her father the force behind the growth of law, her relatives including bishops - it was well that he himself should take the opportunity of being well thought of. He deemed it the wrong occasion to urge support for the Church of Rome. The de Lacys supported English resentment about the levies of 'Peter's Pence' being multiplied in its exactions to support the Holy Father instead of just the English College in Rome. No, it was an occasion for friendliness, and for assumption that all was well unless some fundamental hitch appeared.

Only the bishop and Alesia sat. They were sideways on to the windows, because Alesia had rearranged the chairs. She did not want to be dazzled talking to a silhouette. Canon and chaplain flanked his lordship, standing. Alesia looked towards Peter the chaplain with a faint raising of the eyebrows, and looked back demurely more or less towards the bishop's cross hanging above his somewhat spherical centre. With a sideways gradual silent movement Peter managed a yard or two towards a neutral position. The bishop began to feel that he had already had his assessment, so he would raise the level of his questions.

"Now that marriage preparations are beginning, Alesia, I am sure you know we have to talk a few minutes on the matter." He continued without waiting for a reply. Alesia observed that even nodding was not necessary. "Your betrothal was a sponsalia de futuro, and thus marriage can follow - if both you and Thomas so wish. Or need not if you both mutually wish that. I have to add that point, I'm afraid, because I understand that there was no actual blessing at the betrothal."

Surprised, Alesia responded at once.

"I am sorry to interrupt you Lord Bishop, but I thought there was a blessing. We went to our chapel, and we took communion."

"Let me hasten to say, dear Alesia, that the point I make is not a great matter. I am told, however, that in the canon terms of which I have to speak the precise blessing was not given, in fact because it was not requested. May I...."

Alesia looked to Peter to check the substance of this point. He nodded slightly, with the air of an invisible mediator. The bishop continued as Alesia made no remark.

"There is just this church law, which is as firm for all as civil law," which addition he silently regretted as a weakness, "...that blessed or not a betrothal is the firm intention. It can even be broken if blessed - if I dare mention that, but that might mean excommunication." He gave a light laugh.

Alesia smiled, to help the bishop at his attempt at the humour of what he thought was such a situation which would be quite impossible.

"Let me clear such points as I understand, Lord Bishop" spoke Alesia, "I am tutored as far as our pledge with our exchanging rings, joining hands and, er, kissing - there were a large number of witnesses, and we could hardly help sealing it with a cup of wine. I know also that at my age the holy church must assure herself that I know what I am doing."

She showed the ring, holding forward her hand with all the demonstration of an actor. As Richard of Gravesend looked briefly towards it, Alesia glimpsed with more perception the bishop's cross, with its pearls and rubies set in a patterned gold. Munificent, and with presence, a former King's clerk, he was known as a great benefactor to the church, to the poor, and to Cambridge University. For himself, he felt by now that he had done his duty.

"Surely the banns may be published when appropriate. I do have to bring in these formal statements. May I say, Alesia, that I am sure Oliver Sutton of Lincoln will be sorry this pleasurable meeting has been passed to me."

He began to raise himself from the chair, so Alesia did the same. The bishop continued most amiably.

"Then there is your kinsman at Salisbury, Nicholas, but I am afraid he cannot carry out much by now, he is so full of years."

With civilities the Lord Bishop departed, murmuring final words about the success of Nicholas of Salisbury's mother Ela in founding the Abbey of Lacock. Most valuable for seeking the ultimate truth. Alesia curtsied at his retiring form, as it disappeared through the doorway; with the two priests close by him. Momentarily the light from the doorway was blocked.

Rules, formality, keep to that as a front, thought Alesia. Nicholas of Salisbury was directly of her mother's family. He was the grandson of Henry the second and Rosamund Clifford. Sometimes it was inevitable to smile to oneself. The marriage of Llewelyn Prince of Wales, and a natural daughter of King John was included on the other side. Ah, but the church had wanted the taking place of subsequent marriage to legitimise bastard children, but the barons would not allow it. She could have had a much more interesting conversation with Bishop Richard of Gravesend.

Mabota considered him to be a very good man, and Alesia had to ask why.

"He's devoted to practical acts of good to the people, they say. He is said to believe his monument is what he will leave behind, and it won't be made of stone."

Alesia diverted to simpler questions. She looked again at Mabota, and her clean and pleasant motherly plumpness. Her amiable if plain face showed calmness and honesty.

"I've often wondered why you are not married yourself, Mabota. Of course I do not want to lose you. But life is that for a woman, and I'm sure you would be a wonderful wife. You've never asked me to do anything to arrange it for you, however."

"Ma'am, even at over thirty years I know there are possibilities. It's not as though there haven't been hints. Do I want to? I don't think so. At least I have the choice by being with you. That's a strange idea maybe, Lady Alesia, but moving about so much is something I appreciate. I can change my mind before I see them again."

They both grinned.

"It's an angle on the subject, anyway" rejoindered Alesia.

"Whatever my instincts look as if they ought to be, ma'am, they are fully occupied with you. And of course with what the future holds."

Mabota had hesitated a fraction over the words of her last sentence. She had wanted to utter the thought. She smiled while she was speaking. What with nature being in the hands of God, and her instincts also, sub-consciously she had wished to steer between hope, pleasure, instinct, and the fear of failure if God decided otherwise.

For Alesia the theme for the late Spring and Summer was set. Growing more alert to the renewal of life, her eyes in chapel strayed constantly to the Virgin Mary, her interest in the swallows making homes under the eaves became proprietorial. It seemed more difficult for her, she thought, when continual visitors came and went for talk about what she should have and own and her servants and household and numbers and the wedding itself.

"One thing, mother, if I were to live at Edmund's house it might enable you to travel with father. You sometimes seem to want to, as you once did."

"Thank you darling. But I've done enough of that. This year, anyway, there's a good reason, apart from the fact that I don't want to lose you. The Lancaster household is in a state of turmoil at the moment. Blanche is to travel with Edmund and your father to France, so they will not be at home. One reason for that is that Edmund has achieved a licence to fortify his Savoy Palace on the Strand. He'll do it so lavishly that it will be unliveable for a year at least."

There were several other places, where the Lancasters could reside but not very near London, nor did they often use them.

"You yourself take father's absence with equanimity, mother, it seems."

"Do I dear? If it looks like that outwardly, then I am better at it than I thought I was. Do you know, after your father has been away a few days, my feelings nearly take the better of me."

Margaret paused, hesitating before she revealed her inner thought, but she went on.

"I can tell you, Alesia, that I have the idea that I'm being neglected and unwanted when Henry is away. I smother it of course. It's wrong. Perhaps silly. But it's there. What he really wants is the sound background. Me looking after things. Me just being alright. It is not, however, awfully interesting just being for the sake of being. Waiting is an art I have never quite perfected."

"It cures as soon as father comes back, of course."

"Of course, but there's always that feeling of - well - deferring communication until those little remembered things seem useless."

Margaret laughed a little.

"I am not one who prefers their husband to be away, but I'm sure you've come across some who do."

Alesia regarded her mother with deepened interest, a human failing having become known. Henry's mission was about the seafaring men of Normandy and England who were disputing again. It was about fishing and rights and antagonism which often fell into fighting, hanging of each other, each encounter revenging the previous.

With the going and the returning the summer would pass, and the wedding at Woodstock would suddenly be nigh. Perhaps they would have time to get out of London down to Canford in Dorset. There they might be able to meet her father on his return, if he could sail back to Poole. It was certainly not convenient for the de Lacy family to stay at any of the Earl of Surrey's places on the King's present itinerary.

So it was the task of this Holborn household to keep Alesia and her mother, the chaplains, clerks, guards and servants fed and comfortable. More than once John and Torkill added game birds to the venison, hare and other usual fare. After all, the Green Man Inn was far away from any likely visit by the de Lacy ladies, and that rough hostelry was the place of exchange to provide much of the variety.

If Alesia and Margaret felt inclined to enquire from where extras may have come, which they did, it was as much out of interest as a question about propriety. Any stealing of the King's wild animals would doubtless be forgiven to them in due course, but it was best not to take it all too far, nor to be blatant about it. With all the inflexion in an unrepeatable tone of voice, it was explained by entertainer Lesso de Vacary that an excellent meal was obtained with the bow. No arrow being mentioned, Peter the Chaplain gave somewhat of a start, having what he thought was a realistic view of human activity. He also knew that within the state there were sub-organizations of lesser folk, in all occupations, which were not only uncontrollable, but without which England could not operate. Alesia glanced quickly at her mother, who apparently thought better to reveal no knowledge of such sealing of minor transactions with a bow, in its other meaning of a small lean of the torso. Doubtless it was one of those many things that authority had to ignore, yet knowing of them, and not daring to laugh at its own weaknesses. It had been part of the humour of that evening, like the in jokes of a garrison.

John, the senior of the two huntsmen, had been several times pleased with the day's work. There was plenty for the catching. The household was smaller than usual, with the lord being away with many of the men. And an early finish on a good day meant a visit to an inn. There were a good number of them, but none so useful as the Green Man. In this one the host was a man called Ingar. A rough man, too. Perhaps a good soul, but he never indulged in thought. A clever man could trap him, but he was rarely communicative enough to be trapped. His intellect was inscrutable and yet not aggressive, rather as that of a stallion. He had his fixed unwritten formula for his ale, he had the licence after his wife had died, and to consummate those attributes had been the culmination of his wits. When John the Huntsman came through the rough planked door Ingar was ready to do no more than to pour an ale and to receive a coin.

That having been transacted, John generally looked round to see who was there for conversation. Torkill and the hunt assistants also came in, except the pair who stood by the horses and the kill. It was no different from any other infrequent passer-by, except for a tension in the air, for John had the look of one who had something to say, and yet knew not to whom to say it. There was a vacuum to be filled. More often than not there was someone there to fill it.

"Whose huntsman he?"
"The Lord of Lincoln."
"Ah.Thought so."

John, as usual, waited. This had gone only halfway. Sometimes he wanted to laugh. The system always worked. Once, that is, it was shown that the risk was minimal. In the meantime any three or four other locals would look anywhere but at John. There would be a covert movement to check outside to see if he might not be what he said he was. Then there would be a scratch or two of some offensive insect living in a rough garment.

"A good day, then?"
"Aye."
"Ah."

John would tell by the eyes who would come forward. Ingar, dissociated from any interest other than the rough calculation of his selling gallonage, provided an ale or two.

"You've got some nice venison."

"Aye."

"Ah."

If it was against the Forest law to do any transaction at all, which was true, it was not just that which made communication so taciturn. Any bargain was suspect for perhaps being done down; any change in one's possessions had to be, or at least appear to be, for the better. A compression of the lips accompanied by a slow murmur of contemplation was the nearest any peasant could get to giving out an appearance of wise decision. Facts had to look as if they were being weighed.

They were - the risk to one's self esteem in a bargain - fear of change - and whether attendance at the Forest court would be the end result. John himself usually finished relaxed, with a blank expression. It seemed to affect disinterest. It was not intended to do so, but often dismayed the other party into thinking that John was going to say no more, and that the deal was off.

A leg of deer, half a carcase, a few hares, they had an unofficial value for pheasant, partridge, woodcock, which could be too elusive for the huntsman with too little time. There was a grading of the risk as well.

In the Green Man Inn it was not concluded by shaking hands. By exchange the birds became John's with a light bow. Afterwards it was as though nothing had been discussed except a little extra news.

For the household in London did have the advantage of receiving news and gossip from the events of state earlier than anywhere. Couriers might leave a half-message or two on the way from the coast. The disputes and the jockeying of King, lords, ambassadors, bishops, chancellors and anyone in authority who had anything to propagate, all that was reflected in London talk, much of it before it was sewn into a more coloured weave. The last thing that was allowed as truth was routine. People had plenty of that already in life's struggle for food, health and shelter.

The patrons of the Green Man would rather receive their penny a day and do a bit of poaching.

"John! I wish to meet these people."

Alesia thought there was an interest here which she was missing. It was evening. The hunt had returned. Servants had fallen on the deer, which had been much exposed to the hot sun. It was cut and dissected without delay. John was slightly shocked at this request, if it was not an order. He achieved a moment's delay in answering by an unnecessary correction of a young butcher's cut.

"Lady Alesia?" he enquired then, as though for further instruction.

"I wish to meet these people," she repeated. "The ones you meet."

"Would the Countess be coming too, lady Alesia?" He was really groping for his answer to her; even more for preparing her for a negative one if he could manage it.

"No. My mother does not always come hunting when I do. Very well. What is the problem?"

"Milady, of course your huntsmen will be most pleased to have your presence with them..."

"Yes, yes...I know... Unless I come in disguise it will just be out and hunt and back again."

It was an occasion when both must understand the differences in their lives which had to remain unexpressed in words.

"Further than that ma'am, I do not think that you would understand the people in Essex whom we meet. There is of course" John added hastily "more hobnobbing when we are on, shall I say, on our own, with a rougher attitude."

Alesia looked displeased in that there was something from which she was being shut out.

"What I mean, milady Alesia, is that you would not follow the tongue they speak."

"I understand several tongues, from Dorset to Lancashire, I would have you know. What you are trying to say, John, is that my presence would stop the very thing I want to join in."

In a fatherly way for a young man, John nodded.

"Lady Alesia. The common folk we talk to, if we have time that is, in the inns or fields - they would stay silent in your presence. In the household we do not, I suppose because we ... well, I cannot say."

John had arrived at the limit of his capacity for expression.

Alesia, as she grew older, felt a little more each year that her commonality with folk was being decreased. It was becoming more of an exercise rather than childish freedom to communicate. She realised unhappily that she was entering an upper constricted circle.

"I rather liked my idea of disguise.." She smiled wanly.

"Perhaps one day, lady Alesia" agreed John.

They had got very near to the flyting game of interpersonal disputing, except that they had not sat opposite each other, knees to knees. It was as near as they were able to express in mutual liking. That firm separation enabled close communication with neither ever venturing too far into the Tom Tiddler's ground between.

Mabota stood quietly by, with the detachment of a servant negating personality so that she would not obtrude. On their return to Alesia's chamber she asked, after the diffidence of asking if she may ask, if her mistress knew of John's antecedents.

"Not really, Mabby, except that he's of Saxon stock, I believe. Why?"

"There was a priest in the family once, and I sometimes think he's prone to the same manner now."

"When was that?"

"Oh, many years ago, ma'am. It is said there was Saxon John the parson, a married priest, who was dispossessed like many by Remigius, who was Norman King William's new Bishop of Lincoln."

"Our new bishop? Mabby, that was generations ago."

"It's still fresh to them, lady Alesia. John is a good man, though. But he keeps himself to his business."

Alesia just thought that that seemed to apply to most folk, when a servant came up to inform her of the lord Thomas's arrival. During the shortening of the period to their marriage it seemed that his affection for her was growing. His visits were becoming more frequent, his talk more confiding, even if on his own affairs. This meant for the most part his work at the Savoy.

"That will be safe and strong. It will also be comfortable. A palace, not a castle. I trust father will approve on his return. Its mostly his plan, in any case."

There was not much scope for Alesia to talk about her dresses being prepared. Thomas was on about something which he wondered whether they had heard. "A fight was arranged between the French and English fishermen, to be in the middle of the channel. That was how the decision was to be reached. A marker boat gave the position, the fight took place. The English won and nobody now believes anything to be decided at all." With a gleam in his eyes he added "No writ can stop a fight for fish."

Thomas had found it all exciting. He fell silent, but gave no hint of the reason, his frustration at not having yet authority to bring such muddles into order. Before Alesia could bring him to a new line of thought, it had already changed. She was close to him, and he took her between his hands, pulled her forward, and kissed her on the forehead, firmly.

"We'll do our job properly" he propounded, and Alesia agreed, supportively, and continued with desultory chatter.

"I suppose I must return to guide some of the masons who don't seem to know how to arrange a defensive stair." And as he excused himself to depart, with an awkwardness he added, as if from a cool detached examination: "You're beautiful."

It was the first compliment that she had received from Thomas that appeared to be other than polite conversation.

"Lady, it will not be long now before we journey to Oxfordshire. I mean for your day...our day. Dresses, food, orders, wagons, everything is proceeding. It will be lovely, I'm sure."

"Good Mabby, yes, it's fun to move, and especially for such a reason. Thank you. I hope it is a lovely day. But if it hadn't been a bad summer so far we would have been off to Canford. As it is, we're staying in London. The plague has stayed away, so we're staying here. Do you know what Lord Thomas said to me?"

"No, lady Alesia, I do not."

"I haven't told you then? A day or two ago he marched in straight off Danger, that's his favourite horse..." Mabota brightened up with hope of a romantic note, perhaps a quotation about love. Noticing, but with no more than a slight raising of the eyebrows, Alesia continued. She did, however, feel slightly that something that should have been was missing.

"...the Lord Thomas demanded that my journey to Everswell for our wedding should be in a litter. He seemed to want a better show than that given by a horse-riding wife. He also wanted a larger, better escort, but I didn't think that was possible - yet. That's up to him I thought, not us, and when he can. He wasn't all that pleased, but he understood, I think. He certainly wants to make an effect. What do you believe about that, Mabby?"

Mabota hesitated but had to relapse into the confidence of saying what she did think, instead of the more wary way of trying just to please.

"Ma'am" she spoke, slowly "the Lord Thomas is perhaps not so modest as the de Lacys; and he wishes the people to look up to the King's family. So he wants to show you off."

This last sentence was an extra, with which Mabota was rather pleased. She felt it brought the whole thing together, and would be something which she herself would like to see.

"You like the idea? asked Alesia.

"Yes, milady. The King has to look and be better than us - we, I mean - the people, that is."

"Lord Thomas is not the ... but, yes, as his nephew, it does apply."

Alesia would have to grow into a life more surrounded by other parties and considerations.

"The trouble is, Mabota, that from a litter you cannot pick the blackberries as you pass."

Mabota gave a hint of a curtsey, which was not called for in the situation of the moment. It was to deflect from the expression she felt had come to her. A remark was about to have burst out. The slightly bemused look of Alesia did, however, make her feel that after all they were close enough for personal remarks. With friendly affection Mabota thus remarked:

"You would have been such an imp as a free young child."

This was enough for Alesia to ponder on.

"I did scrape around a good bit, you know, Mabota..." she expressed the name in full unconsciously to her elder "... am I restrained? Perhaps I shall realise it one day. Perhaps," she added, with a jaunty look "I shall put that right."

The wedding was to be attended by come who may, by come who could, and come who were going to be already there with the Court. The date was to be two or three days after the King turned up at

Woodstock. The legal work of transferring manors and appurtenances from the de Lacys to Thomas of Lancaster would be confirmed. It had already been agreed, and some concluded. Not a soul suggested that such promises would not be effected, but there were voices which deplored the continual return of great estates to the royal family. Some of the voices were subdued - those of barons who feared the increasing power of the King as against their own. The expressions which were well heard were those of the Holy Father in his objections that the recent Statute of Mortmain stopped any further gifts of land to religious holdings without the permission of the King in Council, who thought that they already had too much for secular revenues to be maintained.

Alesia's marriage was to be a reorganization of power, and there was more than one who considered his own son's standing should have been improved, so damn Lincoln for being forever tied to the Crown. Alesia had thoroughly absorbed by her environment the source of their family's maintenance, from the fundamental value of crops in the soil, of organization of men to keep affairs in order, and the command of their position as also expressed in culture, and mostly comfort. She admired the King and she admired her father in their confidence in steering affairs to keep them as they had been. They displayed an urbanity in their power, as though there was no disturbance that could upset the present and future of the King's inheritance.

Henry was amused when he heard of Thomas's demand about the litter, treating it as a request for more dignity from his daughter.

"It will be a better show, won't it? Well, he's some rights in the matter now. You are to be his. I am sure you can play the part - so far as you approve it."

They agreed that perhaps it was a time to appear like a state occasion. Alesia herself felt a delighted sense of pride at the notice being taken, the clear desire of Thomas of Lancaster to see her as someone important. That serious attitude towards what had been mild pleasure in her own appearance had in one stroke made her cease to look back.

"Mabota, I wish to inspect all my dresses and all my jewellery, and all my possessions. I shall need some new things. I am tired of being served up everything by somebody else."

Mabota thought it was late for this review, but saw no reserve twinkle in Alesia's eye. She summoned help at once and maids displayed it all, item by item.

"That can go. The ribbons are childish now."

Alesia disposed of the garments of innocence.

"Mabota, come with me to the stables." The challenge of Thomas's demand was to be met. There was to be no doubt that she was to be a credit to the family. So, within the compound of Lord Lincoln's Inn, to the north end, they repaired. A different tone spread at once through the ostlers and farriers, on noticing Alesia's approach.

Curiosity and quiet behaviour overtook their general mood of noisy work and unbridled language. After all, the lady Alesia might comprehend too well. Their usual guarded attitude with the family in residence swelled into alert attention with a member of the family in the stable yard. Their task was then clear enough, to carry on with shoeing, feeding, cleaning, or appearing to be so occupied, and to speak when spoken to.

Richard Revel, the man in charge, was not there, and Robert de Tracy approached Alesia. As master of the horse he was the deputy, and competent enough to show that all was well. He was a man of easy attitude to others, one who seemed not to push himself. No-one could complain about his general air, not exactly ambitious, but always expecting more. People mostly wanted to do things for him; he had that sort of air that brought others to help him. His temperament was at least outwardly comfortable and confident.

"Lady Alesia?" was to Robert enough of a respectful enquiry, for he steered his life upon what others had to offer.

"Inspection, ma'am, yes, of course. Possibly no decision has been made, though. May I show you my suggestions?"

Which Alesia agreed to, and with but a pause to glimpse the fascinating hammering and shaping of red hot iron, she and Mabota were led into the middle stable.

"I would suggest two of these cobs, lady Alesia."

There were some twenty of them, and many more empty stalls. The others were either in use, out exercising, or hunting.

Alesia could really see nothing amiss, but communication of a sort was necessary if she was to have authority. She fell into the usual talk about horses.

"Surely, master Robert, not every single one of these horses, and mares, is fit and well to undertake a journey to Woodstock, all patient and calm in a litter's shafts."

She was regretting this litter affair, the idea seemed so staid.

"They do appear to me to be so, lady Alesia, at present. We remove sick horses to the far stable. In a week or two, when I understand the journey may be, there could be a change. The work of the coming and going of disease is in the hands of God. But at present, yes, these are fit."

Robert de Tracy asked if the lady's travelling was in future to be much by litter, because if so that would enlarge his need for providing trained horses. Alesia had not thought how far this dignity was to be forced upon her, so she had to be non-committal.

## CHAPTER 13

From wherever the Court had to be in its constant circulation in the realm, foreign policy and domestic decisions emanated. In a more or less suitable week it would sojourn near the centre of England. Everswell, near Oxford, to the north, was a comfortable place for the family to stay. The family - now just Alesia and her parents. After all the antecedents, connections by the score, there was less than a handful of older close relatives, of young ones, none. The de Lacys of Ulster, had died, childless. Henry's brother and sister remained unmarried. Any descendant would not be named a de Lacy.

For their restoration after a journey damp overhead and underfoot they needed the amenities of Everswell to recover their wellbeing. There they would await the Court, and the convenience of the King's family to fit in the wedding of his nephew. The associations of Everswell itself were more fitting for the de Lacys and Alesia than for any, apart from the King. Or, by contrast, some could think that the de Lacys should have been allocated another place. No reason had been given in the general planning, and no-one knew if the Clerk of the Household had managed it with tongue in cheek and a sly smile.

Everswell had been designed and built as the surroundings of Fair Rosamund. It was over one hundred years previously that she had died, in 1176, but she still influenced the social base of who was who and what lands and privileges the family deserved. Over-privilege in one instance, for Rosamund herself, by order of King Henry, had been interred in front of the High Altar in Godstow nunnery nearby. It was more than the saintly Hugh, Bishop of Lincoln, could countenance in his diocese, and he took his earliest opportunity fifteen years later to have her mortal remains removed from the holy place and re-interred in the Chapter house.

Rosamund's nephew de Clifford had fought for Simon de Montfort, but had changed to the King's side - his grandson was now nineteen, firmly for King Edward. He would be at the wedding, with relief perhaps that he was now on the right side.

Everswell was not large; it was in Woodstock park; its garden was enclosed. In Woodstock itself there were cloistered walks, a spring which enlivened three rectangular pools, an enclosed garden with rooms and waterways - the structure had grown into a tall irregular rambling block of a structure, buttressed by added chapels and half-towers. Enormous sums had been lavished upon the place by King Henry, with no visual coordination. The building had become romantically overblown with stonework, not excepting the first ornamental battlements in England, with heraldic decorations. The love between Henry and Rosamund had been linked in their time as that of Tristan and Isolde.

Alesia was to be received in the Great Chapel. The King's Chapel was too small, as were the Queen's, the Round, St. John of

Walsingham's, and St. Edward's. The late King Henry's three times a day at Mass had indeed been well accommodated. She was escorted round with her parents, and took part in a brief rehearsal, with a clerk playing the part of Thomas, nervous in his self-consciousness at standing by her side. Descending the stair by the great oriel window, other arrivals could be glimpsed settling their tents and their horse and wagon lines where Henry had formed a zoological garden - removed by his son to the Tower of London. Rambling and incoherent, Woodstock was a lesson in how not to lavish resources onto a dwelling. Halls, chapels, chambers, more and greater halls, all with piers and carvings of changing styles, Alesia thought it was a strange place to love, except for some of the gold inwoven tapestry.

Now the murmur and noise of camp increased. Soon Lincoln's men would be met with King's men, and with the men of three bishops and the men of eight earls, and their esquires and their pages, and with those who attended them, and with men who looked after them. There would be conglomerate living and sleeping in corners and corridors, in kitchen and halls. By group and status and task each was pecked into their correct days work.

The hubbub was already compounded by cattle arriving on the hoof to be slaughtered, by goose-girls and their geese, the hens by cart. Alesia and Thomas at their nuptials would lend an hour of interest, and a feast, to the ordinary work of the King's court. It raised the tenor of those few days - the State was thought to have become more secure, there was confidence in the future - a hopeful time for the procreation of legitimate offspring - and yet it would all be deferred until the two partners in marriage became of age. These nuptials were all preliminary, to attain the correct legal state of what they represented.

Thomas and Alesia had to join in merriment at the breakfast - she being presented with ceremony with the egg of a swan - hopefully boiled to correctness for eating - a symbol of beauty, from the kitchen. The great thing in its wooden cup - turned for the occasion - resisted all but Thomas's dagger before it yielded its strong tasty yolk and white.

At the door of the Great Chapel the marriage was solemnized.

"Here I take thee to my handfast wife to hold and to have at bed and at board for faver for lather for better or worse in sickness and health to death do us part if holy church it will ordain and thereto I plight thee my troth."

They moved, then, into their places to join those assembled for masses and prayers.

So Alesia was thus in front of witnesses set to life with the future Earl Thomas. The strength of his assertive voice cheered her mother and father. His own pride and the weakness of his cousin, the prince Edward, would, however, bring him to rebellion. He would be beheaded in front of that cousin who now stood nearby. That cousin's son would reinstate his spirit by the astounding act of bringing about his sanctification. Yet this day that young man, of fourteen years, to Alesia stood as a strength to assist her.

"Well!" demanded Maud Picker, with her large strong arms at last able to rest on her hips, as she stood behind the bench of bowls and platters in the Great Kitchen: "It's time we were told something!"

Her assistants and the scullions looked up towards the servers with hope in the interest of gossip.

"What, for example?" asked the server Matt, unimaginative, and thinly imbued with a belief that the utterances of his superiors were confidential. Maud dismissed him as no good, and chose a more likely fellow, Walwan the messenger, who was working between kitchen and reception. As the pressure faded, so the received eavesdropping developed.

Walwan was not married.

"I'm never in the same place for long. It's not that I wouldn't mind."

"You've never thought much of laws have you, and marriage law is no different" taunted Maud.

"Church law allows a man to beat his wife" was the rejoinder, scarcely finished before a quick dodging of Maud's right arm.

"I'll tell you what's been said" began Robert Wandad, janitor, who had come in for food, "I hear it all as they pass in and out. There's some as don't like this marriage, and why? All that power back to the King's family, that's why. About half all the great Lords' power is now back to the King. And there's some who don't like it."

"It'll help the Lord Edward to control them, and he's learnt that lesson. You can't stop the Lord Lincoln helping the King. It's the de Lacys through and through."

"I think the lady Alesia was very pretty" interpolated milkmaid Mary Mauveisin, bringing the conversation to matters of importance to her. "She seemed to glide past, she was so shapely in a long white gown, and unveiled herself to smile at us."

"The veil was from Italy, from the old Countess of Saluzzo" Walwan informed the throng. This imbued it with an ethereal air, for being from such a nebulous and thus perfect place, the land of the holy church itself, though it was but from Henry's maternal grandmother.

"And she wore ears of wheat, like any other bride - bread for life and pudding for ever."

"She'll have that alright, she'll not starve. Not like my bidding wedding."

It was hard to tell whether that kitchen woman minded about the difference, perhaps because everyone she knew was in the same state. She continued:

"As we went round Thorpe in squire's wain to collect such gifts as came it poured with rain. All we got was wet furniture and I don't reckon it's dried out these thirty years."

She picked up a chicken leg from a table, which would help to maintain her now well upholstered figure, and produced further information:

"My kids have got it. It's all lasted, I'll say that. I move round all the time. I decided there and then that a kitchen in a household was better than my own."

Her husband, Robert, an ostler, was just listening and not expecting to have to utter, being perfectly content, so long as he was shortly to get back to his horses. But they were all looking at him, since his wife had joined in he was apparently expected to do the same.

He did have something to say, when pressed.

"They'd all cause chaos if it weren't for the King and Lord Lincoln, and it's a tragedy about his boys. I only hope the lady Alesia has the same abilities, but it's not the same."

"So what's not the same?" was demanded by his wife, amid merriment. The apparent position in his status was that his wife had the power. She was however suitably far away from him, and he took a large sip of ale, before he spoke further:

"Well, Surrey creates about his rights to his land being his own affair, but the King makes the rules, and he submits in the end. The church demands more and more land and the King stops that, and they have to submit. The way they talk when they're out and about is what I hear, and Bishops are full of complaint about what they haven't got hold of for the Holy Father."

Any continuance was interrupted:

"Now Robert ostler you remember the Holy Father is behind your marriage to me and thats fixed in your life, so less of..."

Robert grinned with the rest of them, and finished the ale. It was pleasing to him at least that a plump wench refilled his leather mug.

They all soon ceased their cheer - partly because there was work to do before nightfall to be ready for the morn - but there was some more news to assess. It came from a server, the last one to come in.

"Edmund of Lancaster - I heard him - said that if there were war with France, then he would renounce his homage to the French King."

How could these lords discuss such things on the lady Alesia's wedding day? It was thought strange by only one kitchen girl that no-one had said much of Thomas. It would be a few years yet before their loyalties would have to change.

Alesia herself had, with Thomas, been with all the company of nobles, ladies, bishops, priests and their attendants down the line. They had been shown off and had spoken and they had listened.

Thomas and she would move among the camping throng of escorts next day. Alesia would look to the household staff alone if Thomas could not be persuaded to join her. And when the next day dawned no morning had seemed clearer, brighter and full of the future, except that the King in council continued his usual affairs - Master David Martin was restored temporarily to his bishopric of St. David's - Walter son of Giles de Northfolck was pardoned of outlawry for the murder of Robert le Pestin of Bruges if he surrender in forty days - there were two more pardons for the death of Adam le Tawyer who had resisted arrest in the New Forest by night - and an outlawry ordered in Stafford after the last eyre was nullified because Geoffrey de Wodehamcote was in Worcester gone.

The morning after it shone mistily with thin October sunshine, and in hope Alesia looked to feel different, charged with import. Married, yes, yet nothing one could touch or hold or feel. Looking round in the earlier hours in the secluded gardens of Everswell, away from the hubbub and drama as after the iumpact of a struck cymbal, there was nothing of wonder to relate to, except for nature itself. The dripping dew on the leaf and blade was all that moved, gracious and bright in the sun and mist and earth that brought it about. A close fixation of her eyes upon them made her bite her lower lip in thought; a hand strayed to run her fingers gently along a plant - for none but God could create these. Without Him all life was impossible. Looking up in wonder to the whole surround, to plants and trees, hedges, and through to the pleasance, the wisp of proximity to nature overwhelmed, to be swamped with clear reality.

On her return her father called for her presence, with Thomas, and confirmed what he was going to do. His lands in Cheshire and Lancashire had been settled in law on Thomas, but it would not take effect until Henry himself died. It was no more than had been leaked already. As he concluded the talk he rephrased the main purport, having felt the lack of responsive feeling from Thomas.

"When I die, Thomas, these lands are for you. Perhaps much else. It is but a start to handing over the reins."

"I had not meant, sir" Thomas gained his mind on the matter "to doubt in any way. Nor to be doubted. I wish to join you."

"Good, so you will come along to Gascony in a week or two. That's early, isn't it, at fourteen years!"

Without waiting for an answer, which he had assumed, Henry left them together.

"You're in a hurry, Thomas" put forward Alesia, with a pleasant smiling tone.

"I suppose I am impatient. I am sorry if you find I am sharp with you, but I would like to say I am proud to have you as wife. And I think you'll be a good counsellor from what I've heard from you so far."

"You have not been so brusque with me as you suggest. But patience, patience. Lancashire, Clitheroe particularly, will support a good household, when that year comes. And your father has over six hundred manors, which will come to you. In the meantime we get paid anyway from our parents."

"Aye, Alesia. I view the prospect not so much about that, as..." he hesitated..."no, you are my wife - as that weak son of Edward, and I can't exclude the state of these manors under my indebted father. But, to Gascony! I look forward to that, except that here we are, joined with ceremony, and as soon parted."

"I feel that as much or more, but at least you will be active, and in new places. What do I have to do? Ladylike pursuits! I will want to come with you. Meanwhile I will watch and wait."

Whatever practical application Alesia's last statement might have, the sentiment was a valuable one to a man of position such as Thomas. Information and its interpretation was a vital ingredient of life and protection. Alesia had already seen the need for wives to be as a general's aide-de-camp, and had noticed the family conflicts or the opposite - greater closeness - which could result. The greater the lord, the more the hazards of others' envy, disloyalty, demands of preferment, sycophancy and downright deceit.

An opportunity came within the day, as King Edward requested Alesia to sit by his side at the meal before his imminent departure. On his right thus was Alesia, then Edmund Earl of Lancaster, the Countess of Surrey, and bishops interspersed with Margaret and other ladies, firstly Margaret Countess of Lincoln. To the King's left was Blanche Countess of Lancaster, the Earl of Surrey, Mary the young daughter of the King, then Thomas, and the long table, sideways on to the length of the King's Hall, included Henry, and the young lord Edward. It was all to a balance of status, in accordance with the King's desire to show acceptance of his new niece.

Dining was in the presence of several dozen others, on this occasion not going lower than knights, except for esquires of direct assistance to them. The new Bishop of Bath gave a ponderous grace, as a man speaking to influence others.

"I hope" the King began in the first course, "Alesia, that you will enjoy the entertainment that we shall have. Tumblers mostly I believe. It amazes me how they throw themselves about so. It seems a dangerous way to gain one's daily bread. I have often tried to think of a military use for their agility."

Alesia had been considering how to conduct her evening next to King Edward. It was the first time he had given her his full attention, other than the many previous times of casual passing words. It all depended on his mood. She knew that he had grown irascible since the death of his Queen Eleanor, and Burnell.

"Indeed I expect I shall enjoy the evening very much" was all she managed before Edward spoke again.

"It has been a perfect few days, without too much happening - and you yourself must be cheered by your future being settled."

"Even without Thomas, sir, there have been pleasant occasions in your presence. Now, it is even more, for me, of a family gathering."

The King smiled towards her.

"Thomas needs tactful moderation. I am sure you can manage that. He's headstrong, and indeed, sometimes one has to be. But with you..."

In some surprise Alesia asked:

"With me, particularly, sir?"

She had been so organized into the connection that she was by no means sure that any personal quality was involved.

"You, Alesia, I know you will cope with him. That is your nature. And you sit here with a mix of blood from before Norman William, from poor Llywellyn, from my grandfather John, and from many sturdy aides of England."

Edward gave a quizzical smile and leant towards her slightly. Alesia looked into his face, responding with equal expression.

She returned a daring comment:

"Ah yes, and from that fair lady."

So they laughed together, and all in the great hall set themselves for a cheerful repast.

The King was lively, confident, urbane, and with little appearance of weariness in his life of adventure. After being sorely wounded in the Holy Land and saved by Queen Eleanor, after lightning in Westminster striking those beside them, and at one time he took up arms with de Montfort against his own father. Yet here was affability itself with the young wife of his nephew who was to inherit the forfeited de Montfort estates, which had been granted to Thomas's grandfather.

So politics had to come into it.

"It about matches the turbulence caused by one of your forebears against John. I was pardoned; so was he. One has to be practical, though these issues do bring out feelings." Edward chatted and looked closely at Alesia all the time, and she attempted insignificant answers.

"All that, surely is over, now that succession is getting more certain, isn't it?"

"Not a bit of it. There has to be a constant assessment of who may do what."

Alesia thought she was in no real state for serious and thoughtful political statements. This was partly because her knowledge of these matters was no more than a catalogue of happenings. But there was another reason for slight confusion in her mind, in that Edward at forty four years old was in his prime of vigour, and never before had Alesia seen a man say so much of one subject and obviously think so much of another. Clearly flirtatious phrases were on his lips and the expressions in his eyes, and restraint in the forefront of his mind. The King found his refuge in narrating his own actions. The church had collected much money for a further Crusade, but Crusades were quite useless and would achieve nothing. So that was why he had taken the money from them. There were warlike costs in England.

"How difficult it is, though. One has to make plan after plan" expressed Alesia "before one takes proper root. Poor little Margaret of Norway. Prince Edward lost in that ship his future wife, and we lost alliance with Scotland."

"I shall not lose Scotland though; Baliol can maintain himself there."

This was spoken with some bitterness in the tone; Edward himself unmoderated. Alesia did not dare to voice the gossip that he was always harrying Baliol to do more for him than Edward himself would do for the King of France. In a short silence, she was trying to frame some question in the manner of smooth comment, when Edward softened.

"About time we had those minstrels! I do not wish to get sharp. By God, Alesia dear, you'll have to tone down our Thomas too. It's in the family. Except perhaps my son, who is quieter than me. Alternates in generations."

The King grew contemplative.

"With capricious nature, and mysterious Acts of God upon us, Alesia, there's not much between Thomas and my position."

The talk from her other neighbour contrasted in its coolness. Lord Surrey was for maintenance of his prominence in the state, against the background of historical reasons, which to him were proof enough. He was firmly lodged in his lands in England. Every Crusade had been a disaster for over two hundred years, and had led to the rise of lesser men. Lords had raised their funds from them, only to return to find they had no authority and fewer resources. Thousands of foolish ignorant people had got lost on the way to the East, been bamboozled either by false guides from Constantinople, the Venetians, or the French. Many had fallen easy prey to the Turks, or to others when they had got only partway to the Holy Land, while waiting for divine guidance, not knowing where they were. Richard bankrupted England for his crusading and we have not yet recovered.

"There is certainly plenty to do for England" ventured Alesia, with a non-commital remark, knowing Surrey well, and from family talk the de Lacy position relative to him very well indeed. "My main hope is that I do not myself get too close to all this politicking."

Surrey smiled, at the genuine remark, feeling at least she might not be urging too much competition from Thomas.

"You have a family between you and the decisions. It's better." He spoke so as not to be overheard. "I am thinking of Philippa of Flanders, detained by Philip the Fair to prevent her marrying our young Edward there. Talk about Edmund being tricked: Philip invited Flanders, his Countess and Philippa to Paris and put them straight in prison."

"I am afraid I do not understand why. It has been said that the people of Flanders want to join France."

"Some of them, yes, but the Count does not agree. That's the sort of politics to be avoided."

Surrey did not go on. He would have revealed too much of his belief that the Channel should be the boundary of Royal ambition, marriages, inheritances, and rights. So he veered slightly.

"A mixture of honour and revenue keeps men going on these things, my dear. They think it is better to follow that, than to be at peace."

When Alesia had assessed and eaten most of her venison course, and it was the turn to resume conversation with Lord Surrey, she looked to him, and noted his weatherbeaten complexion; she saw his greying hair, and beard thinning and tidy; to her he appeared rock-like in his air of security and confidence. It seemed enviable to her that he could seem so sure - perhaps it came with age. With relaxed but strong expression Surrey looked again at Alesia. Perhaps he was wondering if the children would fight each other as had their fathers. She would try him with the question she had asked Mabota:

"Lord Surrey, your life must have been adventurous. I have often wondered if there is a moment when it all seems right, a drama to focus it, or proof at a moment that it is - as one might say - ..."

She was unsure how to complete her youthful enquiry. Lord Surrey was no philosopher but regarded the matter seriously. A girl was asking him for advice, which he could scarcely recall happening before.

"No, no" he replied, groping, "it just goes on. Yes, life just goes on. Things to do, so you do what you can." He could not think further, though to himself he felt there was a more helpful answer. Failing, there the matter was left, Alesia hoping it could not entirely be so. Maybe light dalliance would have been better.

As wine developed joviality, group coherence of all in the hall grew. In the entertainment was something for everybody, even for the irresponsible who considered the barking of the dogs at crucial moments added to the fun.

At its finish Thomas moved along to speak with Alesia, to be greeted with:

"Thomas dear, I shall need the ride tomorrow to clear my head."

It was a way of getting the point across that the journey to Dorset was to be on horseback. Thomas made no reply to that, for he had only pleasantries in his mind.

That day they trotted across the pasture to Woodstock. The smart turnout of her mount, and the crisp look of Alesia in charge of it attracted Thomas's pride. Having all paid respect to the King's group on his leaving for the East of England, by recognition of banners and hearsay down the line the retainers of other lords positioned themselves in attendance. Some had renewed acquaintance, many would never meet again. Such a possibility, even if they wanted it, was not in their own control. It was easier for the Lords and Ladies in the Royal social round, but they too made their farewells. Surrey and his elder son rode towards Alesia and Thomas, and with their faces clear in the morning sun it seemed a genuine pleasure at having gained greater acquaintance with them. No-one was foreseeing the next reign, when that elder son would be their enemy, and have Alesia abducted, imprisoned and brought before a court.

Oxford, to Marlborough, to Salisbury, to Canford was the route the de Lacys and Thomas were to take. The baggage train and the men assembling for the expedition would plod their way southwards to Reading, and through Berkshire and Hampshire on the more usual route. It was better suited to heavy loads, with closer towns available for victualling so many. They were also properly placed for change of carters and the transfers of goods to fresh wagons for traversing each succeeding county. With this number it was at a slower pace than any lord could tolerate for his own movement.

The route to the coastal assembly points was not the only one. In Salisbury itself there passed a constant stream of those summoned from many manors of the western shires. The Bishop of Salisbury noted such large numbers at masses that doubtless some were blessed in their enterprise on more than one occasion. Although his message was the same each time he comforted himself that should some receive it twice, then it might well cheer them more. At his great age, with his patriarchal appearance, it appeared to the simple throngs as patronage from a living saint.

"A great red dragon with seven heads and horns appeared in heaven. It was as a great portent; with his tail he swept stars down to earth, and stood in front of God on his throne. Then Michael and the Angels waged war upon the dragon, and threw him down to earth. So to heaven Christ has gone up, and the devil has come down. The battle has already been settled in heaven. Let not the devil trip you, the supporters of Christ, for he wages war on those who maintain their testimony to Jesus."

And it was also about Michael that Longepee concluded his address, booming with enthusiasm to the vast throng in the nave: "So let it be especially St. Michael the Archangel, the great warrior, to whom you shall give your devotion. This day is Tuesday, the votive mass is assigned in his honour."

Afterwards the de Lacys and Thomas walked with Bishop Longepee, so that he could show them his new cloisters.

"We continue the work of our - I was to say forefathers, but it is only so long ago as our grandfathers that this house for the work of God was finished. In its main stage, that is," he corrected himself: "A marvellous time that - the surge towards great public places of assembly for the conciliation of God. Now we are trying to add to it all - we cannot improve. But not much more will be possible in my lifetime."

"More lord Bishop?" asked Alesia. "It is already splendid."

Longepee smiled. "A little more, perhaps then. Some feel the need for a greater tower, and a soaring spire to the heavens. It would save that extra toil for inspiration."

On a practical note the bishop went on, not wishing to lose the opportunity of seeking a contribution:

"Indeed there has already been so much from us Salisburys."

Henry and Margaret would no doubt have to make payments in time, but for this moment purely made amiable remarks on the matter. Then Thomas broke in:

"Sir, I wish I could project my voice to more than a thousand folk as you can. It could be heard throughout the whole building."

"Thomas, my son, it is of course what I practice to do, but you noticed the podium is in the middle of the building. It helps a great deal. Not so much my doing though, it was the method at Old Sarum, before the holy father allowed this new place here. Although," the bishop grinned impishly at his daring, "I did have it moved a space, to stop an echo."

"Of course," he continued, on another train of thought "if we could have the bones of Osmund from Sarum we would have much more prestige. As it is, so many pilgrims still go to the old place. It would certainly help with the spire. Now, what about that?" He turned to Henry, and then to Margaret, because the Earl's face gave no sign of being influenced. Margaret hesitated, and in the end Henry just made a temporising non-commital remark. But he felt he must give some explanation to this dear old man, one bishop who regarded religious work as the basis of his appointment.

"No, William, it is not that the expression of piety in your proposal does not commend itself to us, and we will arrange for support." Henry placed his hand affectionately on the bishop's shoulder: "When I am forgiven at the exchequer for the costs of paying this crowd of your pilgrims for going to France; let us think of it then."

"Bad as that, is it? Yes, I suppose it is. Well, it can wait. There is no fading in my hope and exertion for such endeavour."

In contemplation the bishop walked to his palace, and they along with him. On the way there were many to cross themselves and make obeisance as they passed by.

"I enjoy these people being here. I am afraid Roger, the dean, you know, thinks I speak in his place too much. I just tell him I am old fashioned, and will carry on in the manner it used to be."

There were regrets at leaving a couple of days later. It was rare to find relaxed hospitality, and a host so detached and unreal, secure in heavenly proofs. He gave his words of farewell:

"Henry, in a storm, remember, break bread, give thanks to God, and eat it. Inspire the others to courage that way. It has been proved by Paul."

"I am aware, William, of the chapter if not the verse."

Then they trotted southwards.

# CHAPTER 14

Between Canford and the sea the heath shone aglow as it received the autumn sun. The damp warm air stirred as it lightly evaporated the rain of the previous day. Resting sprawled by a clump of elder and hawthorn scrub were half a dozen young men. They were on the journey to Poole harbour to join the expedition to France. It was Robert, Llew, and dai Cerrig who were talking, and it demonstrated that all the party were Welsh, for the other three could understand.

"We'll get there today, and that's as soon as we've been told."

Llew was reassuring enough. They were not the last on the journey, nor the only ones to spend the previous night in the shadow of Wimborne Minster.

"They say it's just over this heath."

"And they don't say how big this heath is." Robert had his feet relaxing upward on a hummock.

They soon prepared to walk on, for the sun had just noticeably dropped from its zenith, and they had eaten the bread and the beans they had been carrying. Llew crossed himself and was ready.

"What's the matter with you, Llew?" dai Cerrig asked, taunting, "impressed by the bishop?"

The gesture had made Llew more at ease in this bleak place. He had in fact found uplift in the splendour of the colour and the ceremony of the Cathedral in Salisbury.

"You, dai, have been along here before. I haven't."

It was sufficient explanation, now in an unfamiliar foreign place.

"Not quite, Llew, last trip we took ship from elsewhere."

They now all walked on, along the wide sandy path between heather. Behind them there were others, doubtless on the same errand. In front, a party of riders cantered towards them, for whom they had soon to stand aside. There was some relief that the jingles and snorts of a dozen horses in one group did not seem to presage any authoritative move over them, for the riders gave no sign of halting. Indeed they passed by, troopers in front, two clerics and troopers at the rear, and in between, a lady and her maid. It was a lady who was suddenly recognised by both Dai and Llew, but who were unable to speak in their brief surprised pleasure.

"Halt!" If Alesia had not raised her arm as well as reined in her mount, and if her shout had not been imperious in tone, then the unexpected command would have had no effect. So it was some yards past that they did halt. Alesia turned at once, to trot back to that group of young Welshmen. In a different but nearly as loud a tone in fear Mabota cried "Ma'am!" The chaplains gave more lengthy warning, but Alesia took no notice. When the troopers comprehended what Alesia was about, they formed a line in the heather, alert, a respectful distance away.

Alesia walked her horse forward. Through an expansive smile she spoke on a note of warmth and surprise. It was also in juvenile North Welsh acquired in Denbigh. Her voice rose and fell in feeling.

"Dai, Dai, Dai Cerrig. And Llew. Your friends. It's Robert isn't it? The others?"

They mentioned Ifan, Ifan ap Ifan, and David of Ewloe.

"What a pleasure to see you. It's a far cry from home and the hills. You're going to Gascony, I suppose. I wish I could. What's the news from Denbigh?"

Alesia had jumped down to converse the better with these very young men with whom she had played and chased in childish days. Dai was the talkative one, and asked about Lord Lincoln. Yes, he was well, and the Countess was with him at the ships. And the Lord Thomas.

"They've reserved us a place, I presume?" was a question which brought laughter, and cautious smirks from the three who had not met Alesia before.

"How do you feel about going?"

"Why not, they say the weather's better in France. I'll go along with that." It was Ifan who spoke. He tended to stare, never before having been so close to an aristocratic lady.

"Whether there's danger or not, I don't know. Wales is not exactly quiet now." Ifan's tone was entirely conversational right through, but his eyes flicked significance into this last sentence.

The hope and success they wished each other seemed small before their great commitment to travel and war. With permission, dai Cerrig held her stirrup for mounting. Alesia's party re-formed in silence; her clear farewell had no detraction.

"Oh, I pray, God be with you."

Those who had been at a distance had by now caught up. These were from the borders of Wales and at home were under threat from Welsh marauders.

"Who might she be? The captain's daughter?"

"In a sense," said Dai, adopting a median border English, "and her dad's waiting for you." He did not feel like a fight at that moment.

It was to be the next day when Margaret returned to Canford. She was to wait with Alesia and maintain the de Lacy presence in England. Reports and revenues would come from their manor courts and manor houses; petitions would arrive from their priories and priests. The work for the expedition would reduce, but still all information from it would arrive first at Poole Harbour and Canford from France. So Margaret duly arrived after having watched the widespread flotilla thin out over the water to fade slowly into the morning mist. Matilde, wife of the thatcher Gvas de Rotington, was nearby as she dismounted, which upset her equanimity. Most times Matilde could do that just by her acidic manner of depreciating everything of which she spoke. Margaret thought that her name gave a pleasanter image than her nature. This time Matilde had news to relate. It was bad news from someone who within herself enjoyed announcing it.

"Lady Margaret, I think you should have been sent for. The Lady Alesia is in pain..."

An instant glance by Margaret at the unfailing curve of bitter pleasure that Matilde could not clear from her lips convinced her at once that she need hear no more. To the low-roofed chamber at the south of the manor she ran. Alesia lay there, quiet in a bed, eyes open in welcome. Above all, to Margaret, alive.

"Mother, mother, really. Not much. I fell off because of a hidden hole in the ground. Just outside the fence."

"Matilde said you were in pain."

"Matilde will say anything, but yes, there was some. There still is if I move - much."

Margaret, sitting by now to hold Alesia by the hand, was both distressed at not being forewarned, and fearful of what may be the consequences of what could be portended by a dreadful bruise and the clearly agonising sharp pain from any exertion.

"Mother, I stopped any message to you myself. It would have been late yesterday, and it would have distressed father all the time he was away."

Margaret nodded at that.

"It was not the fault of Rad; I was only cantering the last stage home, and there was a rabbit hole under some grass, all hidden. So I came off. Even that would not have mattered much. There's time to think as one comes down, as you know. I was expecting to be perfectly alright, but there were two big stones and I hit them on the edges. I just think I've twisted something."

Margaret was not so easily calmed. There would have to be further information and knowledge.

"There is Magister Gibb Cywe, who knows of these matters. I will have him sent for."

For herself, Alesia did not feel that it was for him. There was only a wide bruise to show. It would relax her mother, perhaps, but for herself she was going to keep her anxieties unspoken. She turned her head to ease it, and in a way to avoid further examination. It confirmed her mother in her worry that there was indeed more to discover.

She fell silent with helplessness. She could guess from Alesia's reactions that something internal was amiss. Alesia was arranging herself to be as comfortable as she could be.

"It will pass, dear mother." Alesia spoke kindly, at the same time wondering how it came that the invalid should try and comfort the healthy.

Magister Gibb Cywe arrived two days later from Wimborne soon after the sun had passed its noon. He looked towards it, and glimpsed round the shadows of the manor and its buildings, to gain inspiration in the ambience of the place. Frowning, he found no responsive feeling on which to relate his attitude. His plentiful beard obscured most of his expression of groping thought. A large man, he preferred medicine to the Ministry in which he had first been trained. He had discovered that his personality gave confidence to the sick, and to their relatives. To foster that he was not above contriving an expression suitable to demonstrate an air of special wisdom, or such other as he considered necessary. In those cases his beard was moved aside by a contemplative stroke. Its usefulness was that his face looked weak without it. He had been to Canford many times, but the Lady Alesia would be a special test of his reputation. As to his knowledge of his profession, he could recall with assurance the effects of earthly and heavenly remedies. The educated accepted them in that order; the poor would listen to little but words from heaven. Well placed in his dual studies, he was aware he was ahead of those who sought his advice.

On entering the chamber Gibb Cywe assessed in a glance Alesia as pale and ill, but not treating her injury seriously; Mabota who sat by her looked equable and kind, but her lips just too tight for relaxation showed that she did not want to say too much; the Lady Margaret was in a fit of worry - which he put down to her imagining the worst that could be.

"In the name of God, Amen."

After a few welcoming words, and the story of what had happened, Cywe spoke directly with Alesia, getting her to press several places firmly with a thumb, and to report the reaction. His calling was allowed no visual inspection, but that there was surface damage around the pelvis was clarified.

Mabota's expressions as it proceeded confirmed to him that he had not been told all.

It was enough to indicate that Mabota at least was holding on to some secret. It could only be that there was worse to hear, but not in the presence of the Lady Margaret. As best he could he assessed the liver and the heart, the veins, the arteries and the nerves. To check the brain Cywe spoke to Alesia, coming close to her face to watch it more closely and to prevent her mother from answering.

"Have you had convulsions?" She had not. "Have you eaten satisfactorily?" She had eaten less but there had been no trouble.

In this situation this was a mercy but worried him about an inner problem unknown. Cywe in present company had to postpone further discussion. He then gave his conclusion to the three of them:

"The wound appears to be superficial. Keep that part of the body especially wrapped up and warm. I will return the day after tomorrow."

Observing Margaret's attempt to raise a question, he continued with calming explanation:

"Those which we call the Spirits - natural, vital and animal - they have taken no traceable harm, milady. The pain is reactive in an inner place which is not related to basic life and health. It has to be given time to progress for further diagnosis."

Cywe could not stake his reputation on any promise, and he was confident enough of others' belief in him to omit any prophesy of immediate cure.

"Treat the lady Alesia normally, except for avoiding the movement which causes pain. Fasting? No, no need at all in such youth. Just bathing, rest, and such food as the lady Alesia wishes. Nothing difficult such as bleeding."

He asked for her birth date. He might give his reasons later, so did not enlarge upon that. He would be examining the written authorities for such portent the date may hold. Then Magister Gibb Cywe stood in an attitude of prayer; Margaret and Mabota knelt, the first at the end, the second at the side of the bed. After explaining that health and holiness were both linked in derivation, he led prayers for Alesia's restoration to her former state, and that any worse development may be cast aside, in the name of St. Nicholas.

He then informed them that he would not be expecting any digestive trouble but he would bring a suitable herbal drink in case. He felt that he had uttered enough to give hope, to enable them through prayer to help; and he himself was satisfied that he had put most of it in a different way from that which they might have tried to explain before. He was secretly worried about his ineffectiveness if anything more deep was amiss. This was compounded by Mabota when escorting him to his horse.

"Well?" he demanded of her. "Tell me the rest," he urged again with authority.

Mabota was uncertain between being cause for distress for the Lady Margaret and doing her best for her Alesia. Her peasant belief was ingrained that these matters were not the perquisite of man to meddle with. But Cywe was in holy orders. With hesitation and half-retreat she whispered:

"Blood....much, sir."

"I thought so," replied Cywe. He strode at once to his horse and rode away. His reply was as much to indicate authority as to disguise his lack of knowledge of the inner mysteries of the anatomy. As he rode on he considered that there was little to choose between the herbs Chervil, Magwort, and Hyssop as a remedy for the bruises. His active mind enjoyed pondering on which he would apply first. It was well to have some tactic in reserve. Before he dismounted at his stable he paused with his hands in the attitude of prayer. He had harked back to his medical studies but as ever could recall nothing practical on anatomy. There had been only declamation of ancient writings. So very much would depend on the approach to St. Nicholas.

Two further visits showed Alesia to be improving of herself. At least de Cywe's reputation for infallibility would not be spoiled. The herbals must have been effective, though he could not obtain the foreign ones which could add an extra effect. He had felt Alesia at this season and in her health would not have evil humours waxing in her blood. Only prayer, repetitions of Psalm LI and Paternosters while the medicine was being prepared seemed necessary. The doses were to be drunk from the small church bell. He was nevertheless anxious on his own behalf that inside Alesia's body there may be some malformation that might have caused pressure for that bruise. His thought could not be forwarded. It was, in any case, all having a successful conclusion. He had the confidence of the de Lacys over the years, and they had never seen cause to test him with counterfeit evidence for his diagnoses.

The Lady Margaret suspected little that she could put her finger on. She noted certainly with interest that Alesia was calmly and quietly well behaved. The reason could surely only be the modest accession to a more mature life, and one in which she could represent rather than have to act.

The behaviour was however based only on Alesia's having to move slowly, or to sit still, to mitigate the pain while her injury was healing. To wince would have revealed more than she wished, and would have induced more comment than she was prepared to endure. Alesia did not find it difficult to act the part, though she was surprised at its success. Of course the pain would go away in weeks, had said Magister Gibb Cywe, and its extent was not revealed to anyone. So, expected to be a lady of gentle habits, attended for her wants, the outward appearance was not hard to achieve.

In early winter she began walks round the village of Canford, first to the church to show thanks for her recovery, as she told Peter the Chaplain one day out in the street.

"Maybe you have not so much to occupy you now, Lady Alesia," he counselled. His prayers by her bedside and alone in the chapel must have assisted.

This she took as meaning that he doubted her full recovery, and a hint that in time she would be perfectly well. Perhaps showing his background fear that the future would not be so easy as now - in that her anticipated litter of children would be a strain to acquire. His expression seemed based on keenness to welcome them, baptise them and to strengthen thus the church. His selfish thought caused Alesia to distance herself from him. Her desire to be the principal of the Lincoln and the Salisbury lines was not to be. Apparently now he regarded her just as a Lancaster attachment.

Alesia responded, to divert any distress, in a mixture of English and Latin:

"Vacta est alea. And if the die is thus cast, I hope also I have more in my future than child after child after child.."

"Lady Alesia, of course, but cuculus non facit monachum - if a monk's holy mind is not made by the cowl, I suggest you will find that a woman's maturity comes from the experience of children. It is part of pride and self-assessment on this earth."

"Quocunque trahunt fata, let us follow." Alesia replied, with an instinctive caution in preempting the future.

"Indeed, but may the Fates direct you happily. Ah, here comes your Magister Cywe, milady."

On riding through the village the doctor reined in by them, expressed his pleasure that at a glance he could see that Alesia had improved. Nearer to Alesia than the others, he dismounted and turned to her:

"Are you riding yet?"

"Shortly" she quietly replied "in truth."

Cywe silently thanked the Lord his God that whatever the disruption may be the pain was fading, and the physical impediment could disappear. Only one or two more prayers were called for. It was necessary to conciliate unknown forces, and to seal the mind against fears.

Cywe had also to visit the house of the reeve de Sextenby, with an illness preventing him from representing the peasants at the division of the harvest. Mary de Sextenby had seen Alesia in the village, with attendant gazing children, so an invitation was extended to enter her abode. Alesia, Mabota, Peter and Cywe did so, the escort of three soldiers stayed outside. There was no need for them to enter, indeed little space. Meat was being cut and salted, fish and vegetables were being stored, cider was being pressed. In the second room clothes-mending was temporarily put aside; the young children were popped out into the village street. The ladies young and older stood for the doctor and curtseyed for the lady Alesia, all glad enough to divert from weaving, spinning, sweeping and mixing a cauldron of soup.

de Sextenby was wheezing in his breath, and sweating as he lay on a settle, scarcely separated from all the domestic activity. With the shutter by him closed, his corner was by no means light. Through a gap a touch of reflection glinted for a second on the crucifix which was hung there.

If de Cywe had hoped to further his reputation, or at least his show of knowledge and power, he was about to fail. de Sextenby would not be bled.

"It is the source of your unease, de Sextenby. The time for bleeding is good enough. The moon is not in Taurus, and it's not in Pisces. Not too late before the winter, though Lent is best."

"I get this every winter."

"Quite. One day it will be too much, unless you release the cause de Sextenby," continued de Cywe, with a sad petulance in his tone, "with no new moon, no conjunction, no proximity of Mercury or Saturn, nothing can be more persuasive."

"It will go. It always has."

"Why did you send for me?"

"I didn't. Father Roger did. He wants to make sure he gets his tithes."

de Sextenby then noticed Peter the Chaplain, and begged pardon.

Peter was able to smile encouragingly, not being involved in tithes. Mary de Sextenby apologised to Magister Cywe for her husband's obstinacy, in a fluster as to what reports would be made about her household. But the freedom of de Sextenby to speak further had been spoiled by his now knowing who was there, and de Cywe had to regain the initiative. Therefore he placed his hand upon de Sextenby's brow and sonorously uttered a statement which could not be understood by the patient.

"Magna est veritas, et praevalebit. I will pray further for you."

It was harmless enough, thought Alesia; of course truth was powerful, and it would prevail. She considered also that de Sextenby would get by, with his wife's herbs. de Cywe had started with an unacceptable proposal, but then he knew of Mary's herb concoctions and their unassailable reputation. They left through a gawping group of urchins in ragged cloth that crowded by the doorway. The colours of Alesia's dress alone were a special sight in a drab and muddy life. There was, always hope of a coin for holding a horse, but on this occasion there were only those of the priest-doctor and his servant.

It seemed appropriate to Alesia to speak to a child or two, and ask about their doings. Of she who had replied that her name was Emma it was also found that she was still too small to help much with all that was going on.

"I never hit the corn in the right place" was how she enlarged upon the subject.

Then there was the solid faced boy who Alesia thought should be approached in that he looked resentful at being left out. He was Warin le Gardin.

"My father says that with all who's been around here we'll not eat through the winter" was his contribution, which made Alesia cease any engagement. After a hundred yards of the walk returning to the manor house the urchins realised that no more of interest would ensue, so they turned away to redirect their idle curiosity.

"The length of winter will pass with more entertainment than we usually achieve," was Margaret's cheering remark that evening. She continued:

"For when these fields have been ploughed and sown we'll have entertainers. There always seem to be more of them on a greater circuit down here. But there is one point you may not take to, Alesia..." and Margaret had changed the line of her talk "...since John and Edmund died you have had much privacy. But Nicholas and Eustacia Cantelupe are to arrive sometime, and in this manor they will have to have your chamber, so you will be back with me. I think often anyway that you have been too much alone. Then there will be others, but in this manor we always have to crowd in as we can."

"I can see that, mother. Every doorway has an esquire or a clerk asleep at night. As for the barns, either folk will sleep on the hay or be suffocated by it being tipped on top of them."

"It will thin off soon. Your father is to return by Portsmouth. Why, I do not know the obscure reason for that decision. Or perhaps you would prefer to share with Nicholas and Eustacia?"

"With you, mother, and the reason is not that I find him rather coarse."

"He's an old friend and looks after our interests in Nottinghamshire. I can only say he must be very coarse to stand out from the rest. They will move on in a few days to their other lands in Gloucestershire."

The de Cantelupe entourage infiltrated such corners as had been left by others. Esquire by esquire, chaplain by chaplain, down to ostler by ostler, all of them flocked by those of their own feather. Nicholas himself, tall, a greying beard without care, had the capability of brashness. He knew the system to achieve revenues, beyond which his mind produced little except knowledge of the earthier aspects of animal life.

"Horse breeding, Alesia, done any? Vital. Oxen too slow. Horses have got to replace them. Plenty of mares don't get the chance because people can't see beyond the cost of extra food. And you can't eat 'em like that ox roasting in the courtyard. Me, knowledgeable? Not me. All I know is that it happens, and that the longer the horse and the mare are together the more contented the mare."

He glanced at Alesia. He had been talking long enough for her to get the drift and to compose her expression into unemotional attention.

"You seem to need fewer men at work down here. Lighter soil, I suppose. One farm we have, three hundred acres, heavy land, needs over sixty men at work from harvest to ploughtime. Carts, harrows, draught animals and all."

In the courtyard Alesia could see and hear his qualities - the common touch with all the orders below him, steward, bailiff, reeve, cook, villein, poultry-woman, down to boys and certainly with girls. The shallowness of his booming outgivings were not theirs to analyse. He had something to say, which communicated. No reply was expected, nor would have been absorbed by de Cantelupe, but this audience was not in the habit of taking initiative with replies.

Slight rain did not dampen the eagerness for that roasting ox to be distributed, the hearty tasting by Nicholas adding to the anticipated enjoyment. Eustacia was used to this, but Margaret had a different appreciation of best behaviour. She urged them to the hall for their proper repast. Sir Nicholas gave his latest political thought:

"The Templars are trying to continue the struggle in Palestine, but England has virtually given it up. Rightly, I think. After such carnage, slaughter and blood shedding silence may fall, but not a Christian peace. The Templars in their own vast estates have become predators on their people. Piety and charity have ceased. I am no saint, but pillage, slavery and murder cannot be in the name of God."

"I view with horror the idea of fighting for Christ's birthplace, though the Pope presses for it."

"He will be losing his grip on England if he goes much further. He should restrict himself to higher things."

Nicholas looked towards the far end of the hall, from where food had begun to be carried in. The servants held the dishes high as they passed the lower tables. Dogs jumped up by them, instinctively alive to the smell of food. There was skill in the servants' manoeuvres to avoid calamity. It was always an intriguing enough spectacle to see if one day some dog would manage to snap a meal. The minor contest always amused Sir Nicholas; even so, by the time the dancers arrived he himself had begun to believe he had talked enough.

Having travelled across half of England he was however thought to have something extra to relate, but no.

"It's much the same," he stated, not really having made any special observations in his travelling. Eustacia was unable to produce more than a stumbling horse, so in the atmosphere of a real need for entertainment the first dancer was hailed.

He was preceded by a youth, who, with extravagant obeisance and indications with an arm towards the door, showed that he himself was but the assistant. There was a faint rumble of surprise that in this unsophisticated rural area he should appear clothed with only a strip of cloth. The entertainer himself entered likewise, tall, lean and dark, with a robust mien. Each carried a light metal sword, a realistic dummy, which they placed crossed on the floor. This appeared to be symbolic, for they at once retrieved them, walked towards the head table and bowed.

"Hugh de Drois, Roger de Mohant, my lady."

A sudden sharp leap by Hugh, a clash of the swords, and a swirling dance towards the far end of the room brought all to anticipation of lively movement. It came. The idea appeared to be the vigour of Hugh in a charge towards the top table in a mock attack. Roger failed to stem this and they moved nearer and nearer, towards one end. With sword beat in rhythm, and backing from minstrel twanging in time, the dancing duel took a tense form of the movement of limbs, starting in front of the chaplains.

The company tried to appreciate the finer points of the encounter, liking the rumbustious bits the more. Each important person was meant to be attacked by Hugh, and protected by Roger. The timings of the mock duel never missed the beat. The two participants moment by moment and strike by strike warmed with their vigour. Hugh at the end appropriately tripped, rolled on the floor away, and leaped round and round again to the far door.

All in hall had been building up to their loud cheer of appreciation at the act.

Sir Nicholas turned to Alesia:

"They say the ancient Greeks fought more or less dressed like this, but it was warmer there I imagine."

"There is not much to imagine, Nicholas."

She wondered if Joan of Hinton, who next gave her turn, would reveal as much, but she only sang.

Eustacia leant towards Alesia:

"What a shame. Nicholas's idea of entertainment relates to Salome."

A Sergeant-at-law conversing with a Doctor of Medicine.

# CHAPTER 15

Such events of interest as there were each day came only from the variable weather, the sun, rain, wind, cloud changes being the unremitting element in deciding what best to perform to maintain life and as much comfort as possible. Work was arranged and rearranged, all to the end of being able to feed as many animals as maybe through the winter, and for a harvest next year. Anticipation of excitement rose at the arrival of every horseman who came by. Hard news was spun out from parish to parish by added invention. Gossip and superstition helped to occupy minds that had no other impressions.

Mary de Munficher knew perfectly well that Lord Lincoln was going to arrive with startling unexpectancy. She had dreamt of his landing and soldiers drinking the water in her well, until disturbed by a horse which could only have been Henry de Lacy's. That was her explanation of it, and it was previous to a messenger having ridden through a downpour to announce it at the manor.

Henry's arrival was indeed a fact. There was a lull in Gascony. Further discussion and instructions were required as to the army's objectives. Thomas came with him; after a week he was recalled to Portsmouth to join his father, Edmund.

Lord Lincoln had made considerable diversion from important work to spend time with them. He would soon have to leave for his return to France across the narrow seas. Savouring a further few days of family company in the extra heaven-sent delay of contrary winds, there came one morning early a fine but exhausted horseman.

"Your proofs are not needed, Nigel, I know you," was Henry's greeting.

"I come from the King, Lord Lincoln. It is Wales again. You are summoned to meet with others he has ordered to Shrewsbury."

"And proceed from there as required?"

"Yes, my Lord. The King has sent orders to the north-west in your name to save time."

"Will King Edward be at Shrewsbury?"

"No, my Lord. It is for your command."

"Is this more important than Gascony?"

"One must suppose thus, my Lord, for you have recently reported to him. He has that information therefore."

"Yes, of course. Is there any more? As if one large surprise is not enough. How great is the revolt?"

"It is only speculation now, but ten days ago it was said to be determined, if not great."

Henry had men from the ships assembled, and sent confirmation to Edward. It all went well, so he moved north. Margaret and Alesia would travel to London.

"Marriage" commented Alesia "would indeed appear to be for the procreation of children, a hello and a goodbye."

Some of the preliminary information had been wrong. It was rebellion in south west Wales, in Glamorgan, as well as in Gwynedd at the north. There it was by Madog ap Llywellyn. The second rebellion since Edward spread his castles round Snowdonia, mused Henry. Once again the Welsh would doubtless be defeated. Perhaps Edward would ease the harshness of his representatives in Wales, but it was only perhaps. It was obscure as to what sort of situation he was entering. Henry discounted all the intelligence he received en route. He would use the strength available to drive the worst mobs before him. They had taken the opportunity of being full of harvest. It could not last long. Wales could never unite; the mountains were too much of a barrier. It could not be absorbed into England because of the independent attitude of the Marcher Lords.

While no strategic decision could be taken almost until he could see the opposition, at least he could consider his own organisation. It was something to think about on the ride. How to distinguish the loyal from the disloyal in his own men would be his major concern. Away from Wales in France all was well because the surface loyalty was not scratched. There was also some hereditary legality for the presence of the King's forces. Employing Gascons in Wales achieved the useful effect of giving them opportunity to exert some of their own suppressed feelings, without relation to the destructive outcome. This time, however, Henry had with him mostly his own Welsh from Denbighshire, commanded by Anglo-Normans. Not a sound unit for a punitive expedition in Wales itself, but it had to be risked.

They reached the River Dee, half scrabbling down the steep bank to ford it, then to move along its northern side, having camped two nights at Chirk. To this place came the necessary intelligence from which strategic decisions had to be made. Sporadic disaffection in small gangs showed absence of disciplined leadership, except towards the south west of Gwynedd. It was spread generally, but with that one attempt at grouping in the area of the significant Welsh mountain Cadair Idris.

Henry considered it necessary to get the Welsh to concentrate more, and if he moved towards Dolgellau then he would divine a reason to charge. He chose to inform the garrisons by messengers that his force was taking that action. To Harlech and Castell-y-Bere castles were sent additional orders to block the valleys of escape from his advance. All very tidy, he thought, and warned his messengers of the grave difficulties of reaching those castles. He had sent only Anglo-Normans, which point may not have been lost on his troops.

Lieutenant of horse de Puy gave one more report, which compounded all the others which Henry had received. There had been desertions, there was spiritless caution among the Welsh archers and the baggage train. It was better to hear from de Puy and officers like him rather than from those who would not recognise that Henry wanted facts not covered up fear. He knew already that the further muster from his own Denbighshire had been a failure, though he had been told only of the numbers who had responded. The thoughtless confidence of some revealed them as uncomprehending persons, Henry considered, as did the exaggerated fears of others. His own quiet attitude came partly from the simple need to show it in front of the others, and as much from the inconceivable idea that he would fail.

"My lord," de Puy spoke "such as I who are near the men, see doubt in them as to where their loyalties lie."

Henry was pleased at the same time with the calm attitude of de Puy, completely unexpressed, but showing clearly.

"There must be some way," continued de Puy, "to have a test. Even as Gideon was told by God to take his men to drink and to choose those who lapped the water from their hands, because they kept thus their eyes upon the enemy."

His voice faded as a glazed look spread over Lord Lincoln's expression.

"de Puy, that has been going through my mind since we crossed the Severn at Shrewsbury. I would possibly use the strategy sometime if three hundred men could spread confusion as did those of Gideon. There is, however, in our circumstances a prime difference from his adventures."

"Of course, my lord. There it was the Israelites against the Midians."

"Yes, and here we have Midians against Midians. I regret I know no test for that. We will go forward. Let the disaffected leave."

Within days the Vale of Edeyrnion was traversed and the foot of the pass below Foel Ddu was just ahead. Nothing but sullen stares had been met. Where any Welsh at all were not hiding, they were perhaps more dour than usual. Avoiding Dolgellau, they reached the waters of Tal y Llyn where Henry camped to await information from Castell-y-Bere, round the next valley. He ordered the archers to the front, a move he had learnt from Guy of Warwick. They were better than horsemen at reducing the enemy, and more manoeuvrable in these rough valleys. Using the lightest armour for horsemen, Laurence was to manoeuvre to protect the rear by manning the narrow defiles each side of the water behind them.

There was no attack from the Welsh, and no messages from either Harlech or Castell-y-Bere, the latter so near over the southern foothills of Cadair Idris, but some five miles round the valleys. On the alert in the extreme quiet, remote bare country, surrounded by dramatic mountain, the tension seemed purposeless. Yet it was felt by all. The interweaving clouds above obscured and revealed in turn a nothingness which mocked.

"Lauder, get up to that col and reconnoitre the castle from the top. Wave a flag if it's right for us to move round the valley; we will be getting ready to do so; you'll have to lighten your armour even more."

Henry had chosen Lauder as an indirect way of getting him to realise he was at war, and in mountainous craggy land. Lauder moved off, with a few men. There were many who cast eyes up the hillside as they rode on, as the companies regained their marching order. There seemed to be another person way up on the mountainside, and it was by her red garment a woman, coming down. She must have come from near Castell-y-Bere, over the top. It was enough for the troops to watch idly as Lauder and she closed on their course. In an instant Henry's own suspicions were confirmed. Lauder struck her down. Spying upon them she may well have been, as Lauder rode higher; Henry suddenly knew of his own danger.

There had been scarcely a man in his army who had not had instantly to decide whether he was for Lord Lincoln or for his countrymen. The noisy murmur developed.

"My lord, we held our men in loyalty till then."

"de Puy, order the advance to Castell-y-Bere."

There was no point in wondering what, if not that incident, might have had the same effect. There had been tensions for days. There had never been a message from the castle. Remarkably his force began to move.

"Lord Lincoln, with respect, lord, should we not lead with the horsemen and not the Welsh archers. I beg your pardon for..."

"I know what you mean, Montaigne de Soire. This has the balance of advantage."

At least they would not be between two masses of Welshmen when they arrived at the castle, but the Welshmen could easily combine against them. Montaigne's expression showed his shock: so Lord Lincoln had retreating in mind if anything went wrong. It was his duty to attack the rebels, but there was no sideways retreat from these deep ravines.

"Yes, Montaigne" said Henry, quietly.

He had seen smoke mingling its colour in the mist from the valley beyond. He called for his captains.

"Well, de Puy," began Henry "Gideon reduced his force by heavenly command; we reduce ours by mob emotion. With a few month's notice we would have brought Gascons for this job."

To the group itself Henry turned, sitting motionless and upright in the saddle, the better to depersonalise his authority.

"Firstly it is our duty to get round that valley to help those in Castell-y-Bere, if it is not too late. We must then regroup."

After questions of news from there, of how it may be done, of the position of supplies, and no ideas forthcoming, Henry continued. He answered with commands.

"Tell your men that we attack the brigands who assail Castell-y-Bere. Tell them also that failing assembly in the castle, we join together back at Tal-y-Llyn by nightfall."

Henry hoped thus that the hysteria of the rebellious men would be fully occupied in tearing up the castle, and the true soldiers would come back with their officers. So, the order to advance round the hill was given. It was at once obeyed. Some had already gone. All, for one of two reasons, as friend or enemy, desired to march that way. To his further orders, with some persuasion, two detachments had been formed, to guard the baggage, and the rearward valleys.

This was the day that the quiet lonely castle centred a cacophony of vicious life and began its everlasting silent death. Pale mist which embraced the upper valley sides was down here obscured by the clouded smoke. The entry to the castle having been effected the infectious success of the oppressed against authority brought each to seek something more to burn, another to kill, anything to destroy. And this castle, taken over by King Edward some ten years before, had been a Welsh one. Its associations with the homeland had been contaminated.

It was not as though most of the Anglo-Normans had not seen such an event before. But this time no-one could tell who was for or who against. No rallying cry reached any heart, or, if it did, the one who heard had of necessity to shrug it away.

Lord Lincoln was slightly up the slope of the southern hill. He must keep what force under his control that he could. Chaplain de Kyghon approached him.

"This is beyond my simple teaching, Lord Henry. This wild spirit is not your fault; they try to find themselves by destroying all that is not theirs."

Henry looked at him. It was his error he felt to believe that his own men returned to him his own paternal thoughts for them. Only in proper circumstances, he now knew.

"de Kyghon, I am obliged by your kindness. It is, however, my failure at this time."

He turned to order the move back, and for those who would come, to be extracted. Of this last he felt the fewer the better. The battle more than lost, but the kingdom would survive. It was still loyal Welshmen that he wanted with him.

There had not been a force for him to fight; the garrison had been overwhelmed by Welshbefore he had arrived. His own army was out of control. The commanding group of horsemen turned, gained some sort of order, and moved a hundred yards down the Dyssini Valley.

Most of these Welshmen were archers. Henry looked intently to see if any were grouping with his side. He observed some esquires urging as many as they could to do so. A mistake, because it would alert everyone to his weak position. It had to be done, both as a last chance to re-form, but also to back up whatever loyalty some men might still feel. Enough to make a company straggled in. They had not got up to the castle themselves. They had seen fighting around there, and a lot of it had been over the loot.

Dispirited, untidy, bedraggled as they were, what was now left, which was just those prepared to acknowledge discipline and to retreat, set out to go back round the hill again. Henry led. His inner spirit was not as it appeared to the eye. His controlled voice gave an order. In an hour or so they reached the rearguard parties.

There was still a certain element of hesitation in the men obeying. At last Henry read their minds more clearly. It was not appropriate to their feeling to form up again to face any of their own countrymen. Henry rode among them, to speak with them.

Robert ap Howell, one of the Welsh, was nearer than the rest as he passed by.

"Look up, lord. They come over that path from Llanfihangel."

Groping down the hillside were moving shapes constantly taking cover, now beginning their descent.

"Go, lord, go."

A quick glance exchanged with Robert made Henry accept the honesty of this advice. He shouted to them all:

"The baggage train stays. Each man gather several days rations. Follow the direction of the rising sun. Make then down the river to Ruthin or Denbigh." He deputed Robert to pass it on in Welsh.

To the horsemen he called out, in the sort of English that Anglo-Norman had become  that they themselves would do that now."

It accorded with the Welshmen wishing again to loose themselves from their rulers. Arrows fell from the hillside. Two esquires with wounds clung on. There were only two hundred horse to move north east away from the disintegrated army. Even that force was vulnerable from the hills, for they had no means of patrolling the upper parts of the valley sides. Dark was falling, which gave some hope of rest.

Yet when they reached the small area of level ground by Talyllyn, where they had camped, a cry echoed all round.

The brushwood was alive with archers, shooting for havoc in their ranks. One squadron charged over the short rough ground. The archers were scarce visible in the brushwood, and too far up the hillsides for horses to tread. Horses, injured, reared; men injured, fell. Arrows began to reach the main company.

There was no prospect of a gallop along the lakeside, going back down the valley would serve only to meet again the other Welshmen who followed them. Swords were no answer to archers who could not be reached. Except that is if the swordsmen were on foot; so they took cover in the rocks and trees, hoping the enemy might come forward. The shades of·the night, now darkened, just forestalling the order to save themselves by immediate flight.

"Not quite a sauve qui peut, Messieurs" stated Henry to his nearest esquires.

Now he shouted loudly to establish a focus of command, to try and hold his authority. An order was to be passed down the line. In the usual tongue it was as good as code.

"Far end of the lake, take the valley southwards. Down the river, along the coast south to Aberystwyth castle. de Puy, Fontaine, Giscard, your squadrons go with mine, on foot. The others, bring the horses. Keep well apart."

It was as good as he could devise. It would get them out of Gwynedd. He had no news from Aberystwyth, but failing success they would turn inland again. There would be ships to be had there. At least the rebellious population in the north would be avoided. Some gathered round him in the dusk. He assumed his orders would be obeyed. The excitement of the hunt came upon him. He looked for the shadows of the rebels as his group made their way along the southern slopes.

"The devil, as a raging lion, walketh about..." Henry felt comforted "...seeking whom he may devour, whom resist, steadfast in the faith."

Steadfast in the faith his enemies were not, and he looked to teach them with their blood. Hopefully pursuit would be delayed by their raiding the abandoned rations.

More horses than men had been hit. There came some relief when away from the lake, for its light grey surface had silhouetted the targets.

It was a slow and stumbling walk to that next valley. When it seemed that they were on its brink, Ronald, an esquire, urged sleep for his lord. By dawn they had managed some for each. They had turned to the south but had managed very few miles. Devouring their rations seemed as a welcome picnic in the thin rays of the sun, which held some warmth. At first the valley was empty, but soon a platoon of men and horses appeared, and then another. Then, well below them, others who had walked that night's journey. They must move on quickly. What they could do the Welsh could do more swiftly, or even cut them off if they realised where they were heading.

Down below the last of the horses remaining alive or uncaptured after the fighting of the night were picking their way along the rough track that served as communication here. Not one of the men escorting them seemed to look up to the hills where Henry was, yet where could have been their enemy. It was disappointing. It was careless. If what had happened last night to the horse party was as Henry guessed, then the Welsh remembered their training better than his Anglo-Normans.

It was an apprehensive group gathered now by the river in mid morning. They were to refresh themselves as much as possible.

"A banner?"

"None, Lord Lincoln."

Henry was to have ordered that it be hidden. Their situation was indefensible except by flight, if they were attacked. The Welsh could be behind rocks or trees, and at a range which they could vary by scampering up among hillside cover.

"Perhaps, Lord Lincoln, we should avoid Machynlleth, and make inland for Powys?"

Henry gave a short sigh. His own horse lost, he was astride that of a missing officer. The short sigh was because he was not sure of a welcome there. Marcher Lords made their own rules.

"We will assess the situation when we get near there."

They passed disaffected Welsh, but snarling folk just were not worth killing, even if the spirit to do so was still there. The horses and men now watered, a formal line-up stirred a little morale, chaplain Philip of Haksi praying for their souls and for those of the dead and wounded; praying for safe passage; praying that they should be deserving.

Henry beckoned de Puy:

"I thank God you are still with us. This is a different order. We go up river. Then southeast along a valley, and over the hills. Then down eastwards along a river that gets ever larger, and in three days we shall be at Shrewsbury. Pray order the company to keep their damned eyes open. Not one of them has looked upwards this day."

Calm would descend from prayer in the peace of a wooded glade. Something must be offered to God in propitiation; his conscience had to be assuaged.

Yet to outward appearance it was the former fresh and patiently authoritative Earl who ultimately arrived back at Denbigh. Caernarvon had taken a breaching but survived, though the town was wrecked. Henry de Elreton of Conway informed him straightforwardly that the French Wars were nothing to do with these people, and as the King takes their meagre money for his wars then he should expect this sort of thing. They had held out, however, but were hungry.

The next year, 1295, showed no retreat when, on the 24th of June, Henry left Wales. All was calm and his summons to a Parliament in London had been received with equanimity. It was to be a summer on the move, for by August the family were at Pontefract castle.

"By December I will have gone once again to Gascony. Edmund and Thomas should be back in London by now, and once more we shall all be returning."

"Thomas, again?" echoed Alesia.

It produced an indulgent smile from her father.

"Yes, darling. From Plymouth."

"Dashing about from port to port. Good heavens, that's two weeks from here," echoed Margaret.

Alesia was amazed that her mother even knew where it was. Nevertheless, the organisation had already begun, and it was the turn of the south west to provide the ships.

Henry confirmed the transfer of Hebburn and the monks of Stanlaw to better and drier lands at Worley. It was some conciliation for past and future dangers. He would bear in mind that he should do more. It was more immediate to get the Shire representatives and the lesser clergy to agree in Parliament to providing funds.

# CHAPTER 16

"And now it seems so sudden" - Alesia spoke to Thomas. They were at the Savoy palace. Her move there had been with due ceremony, and cheer mixed with the curiosity of hundreds. Alesia had been delivered to her husband.

Three years had turned into the past. A time of events; but now Alesia, just seventeen, was produced to her future household, at the end of the year, almost like a Christmas present.

Thomas's father Edmund had died in Gascony. He was worn out by the trickery of the French, the burden of defending his brother's inheritance of Aquitaine, and by their unfulfilled promise to return Guienne. Earl of Lancaster, Leicester, Derby and Ferrers, his first wife Aveline, daughter and heiress of the Earl of Albemarle, had died in 1273. Thomas's mother was Edmund's second wife, Blanche, daughter of Robert of Artois. Edmund's father had been the second surviving son of Henry III.

Edmund was to be buried beside his first wife; dower income to be provided for Blanche. A fitting tomb and memorial was planned for him in the Abbey of Westminster.

"From Holborn to the Savoy palace is about the shortest journey I have ever done, but its implications are the greatest of all" expressed Alesia. "Far from just listening to what I am told is happening, I hope now, Thomas, to give my opinions to you."

"It might well be valuable," answered her husband. He had a straightforward approach to state affairs, to which honour, the baronial inheritance, and the status quo were the foundation. Other than those solid rules there was little. He accepted Alesia's statement equably, in the wondering knowledge that much had happened recently, and those had been events which moved the social scene away from his inbuilt beliefs.

Edward had set about his neighbours. Apart from the Welsh, a victory at Falkirk, and a journey to Flanders to urge help against the French. It led to levies and taxation to fit. Archbishop Winchelsea quoted Pope Boniface's laws for clerics and refused to allow the Church to pay any taxes. Edward quarrelled, restricted their liberties, and outlawed the Archbishop and the clergy. More estates fell to the crown. Baliol died, and Edward refused to agree to a successor. He was determined beyond all restraint to maintain the throne, and power, and the overseas inheritances. He did not accept his limitations. The barons would not follow. They refused to attack Gascony.

"There is no feeling for this remit" stated Henry.

In the Savoy Palace were Alesia and Thomas, his mother Blanche, Henry and Margaret.

Alesia was astounded to hear this remark from her father:

"Since Edmund's death the feeling has spread. It is not thought part of feudal duties. I don't mean for myself, I do not mind. But this country cannot stand the strain of war north and south. It has all been going on far too long. It is quite easy to live in this island and defend it. In fact it is enough, and the exchequer would recover."

"Remembering my so-called Provence inheritance, it seems to me that Philip of France agrees only with what expands his own dominions." Thomas sounded deeply bitter.

Henry eased the atmosphere.

"I do not believe that any longer one can have dual loyalties. If the land is in France, then Philip will have his say. To stop that, one must live in France, and be French. That is, I hope, realistic, however much one does not like it."

"Then the French would be back in England again, surely?" Alesia put that forward, and proceeded with a demure smile.

"I feel that if a territory is acquired by marriage, then..." and there was no need to complete the sentence.

"There is also conquest to consider" replied Thomas, with a cool air which could not be interpreted either as dry humour or a contribution to their discussion. It was Margaret who summarised the matter, which to her had gone far enough.

"Thomas, you have now been given much. Edward accepted that your tenants should give homage to you even when you were a minor. Now you have succeeded to your father's lands totally, and all that in a couple of years. You owe much to the King, for that, and Henry - you sound sometimes as if you are urging Thomas to be disaffected. Let me tell you, and it amazes me to have to do so, that Edward is on top of the world. Particularly after Falkirk six months ago. And more, so he takes more and more power. True. He needs it."

Blanche was feeling most equable, warmed by the fire -

"With you men, I echo, he needs it. What would you do Henry, Thomas, if you needed support? The Church refuses, it has grown to be even more alien. Every baron I know seems to need individual persuasion, which is impossible. So men from the shires are called to Parliament. Who, then, is to blame?"

Contemplation in silence by the two men was the only reply. It allowed the ladies to turn to the preferable domestic matters.

Thomas and Alesia were host and hostess these days, becoming settled at the Savoy. Shortly before they had taken full possession, and had entered to the adult life of Earl and Countess, Thomas was already an adviser within the King's Counsels, and Alesia's opinions had more force by coming now from the Countess of Lancaster.

Their pre-nuptial dinner for over a hundred guests at the Savoy was her first grand entertainment. She was expected to be nervous and shy.

"Seems an old hand at this" murmured Surrey, with grudging admiration.

Prince Edward was most jocular:

"This is a fine turn of display, Alesia. Without you, though, there wouldn't be a proper focus to the picture."

He always seemed detached; Alesia's female feelings never met human response.

Blanche was prepared to give advice, or reminisce to Alesia to keep up her confidence. She was not given the opportunity.

"She is the least apprehensive new wife I've come across."

There was a reason.

The pre-nuptial dinner was somewhat late. The young couple frequently grinned towards each other. Maybe some suspected, and some wished to suspect. Only two actually knew of that previous episode.

It was when the palace was not finished. Alesia was being shown round by Thomas. Nothing of the whole building, from kitchens to chapel, from halls to stables, rooms for exchequer and clerks was omitted.

Alesia's energy would not run out until every corner had been seen, and they rambled further and higher in the rambling structure. She did not know whether she urged this privacy on purpose, but the action went with the look in her eye and the shape of the red dress.

Through the small low window was the sun upon the meadows beyond the Thames. Enough straw was waiting for some usage in that small room to give some comfort. At least it allowed some semblance of preparation of a domestic scene, for as much was in their minds. Rational thought was suspended; each sought nothing but the physical touch and feeling of the other. To Alesia it was an awakening by unsubtle strength, by submission, by hope, with curiosity of the relaxation of being commanded.

She wondered if she would feel regret, but it gave her only cheerful hope. If there was pain, it was lost in joining in his strength. It was the future of her body, and it showed promise. It was a secret between Thomas and her.

Thomas's lips had showed that caution prevented a beaming smile.

"I'm glad" had been Alesia's response. "At least you have stripped me of one of my possessions. I began to think you would achieve the others first."

"For myself, I think that with you as well I shall never get through the eye of the needle."

Some guessed by the carelessness of her head of hair. They kept the knowledge they presumed upon for their own amusement.

Waiting the further time before cohabitation was due to the force of circumstances.

"Established as we now are, Thomas, it is as though the past has built towards it."

"Yes, indeed. Darling Alesia, you really are on my side. That is what I wanted."

"Of course it shall be. Is it to be the same life as our parents had, or have you - we - ways to improve matters?"

"Live more together, instead of forever to Scotland or France I think you mean."

"That's part of it, if not the most. For example, father's now off to Rome - always on his own."

"With a couple of hundred others, actually!"

"You know what I mean. Are you going to be sent everywhere?"

"I suppose so. I can say, however, I consider that expeditions to France are useless. We are being bankrupted by them, even the revenues in France have run out. We have never gained anything by going over there. There was honour at one time. Now it's negotiations that can't be trusted. It all killed my father."

"Perhaps the Pope can establish peace between these Kings."

"Yes, yes. But he's another politician..."

Alesia gasped.

"...in these terms. As Henry's going for a year it looks like a difficult job. Anyway, that's a year or more ahead. In the meantime, we'll be dragged to Scotland. It is simply not possible to continue like this. Ever since the Crusades, and with a demand for another, there is no money left. It is all borrowed. It ruins the ordinary life of this country."

"We have at last won fully and properly in Wales. Perhaps Ireland, but not in Scotland."

"Exactly, and we can't win in France because it would mean full defeat for them, and it's too big. So Edward tries to marry it into the family. He will continue to do so, I suppose."

"It's as good an idea as any, to keep up the possibility of getting it."

"Anyway, it is not my responsibility. In the meantime I have to check on my own affairs. I am going back to what de Montfort received."

Next day Alesia and Thomas visited Lincoln's Inn. Even before any hospitality was dispensed towards them it was obvious that excitement pervaded the air. Henry was to preside in place of the King in a court, on an alleged proposal to poison King Edward and Prince Edward by Aldebrandus Malagaile and Berimus Mayamund, merchants of Lucca. They were further charged with counterfeiting the King's Great and Privy Seal and the Seal of Prince Edward.

"Surely they couldn't expect to get away with that?" queried Alesia. "There's far more to transactions than just a seal, surely? As for poisoning the King and Prince, what use their seals if they do that?"

"It will be interesting to see if those questions are asked," was Henry's response. "I am only in effect judging the proceedings. It is astounding what people will do and expect that they won't be found out. Just like those who besieged my manor of Clonlyg in Suffolk with cover horse and took goods and timber. Robert de Retford and William de Bereford dealt with them."

"There is, however, too much disappearing by default" rejoined Thomas. "Everything has to be guarded these days."

In the afternoon Thomas de Fissheburn and Robert de Hephale arrived, known for some years to all.

"If this next journey to the Court of Rome gets under way," stated Henry, "then you two are my nominees for my affairs in England. I shall be consulting Amadeus, Count of Savoy, Sir Otto de Grandison, Sir Hugh le de Spenser, Amaneus, Lord of Lebret, Canon John de Berwico in addition to Sir Benedict Gaytanus. There must be a peace arranged between England and France."

Thomas brashly interpolated - "I hope Henry that the long bow is not forgotten, and its effect at Falkirk."

It was not contradicted, so he continued.

"It avenged Stirling Bridge, where trying to save money on the forces led to our weakness."

"Also, it is said," added Alesia quietly, "that Lord Surrey overslept."

As always when Surrey was shown in a poor light, the de Lacys felt satisfaction.

"I really wonder, I really do," asked Blanche, with Alesia in mind, "if you men realise what effect all these wars, or battles, or fights, call them what you will - do you realise what effect it has on we ladies left behind? You know you're safe, perhaps. Maybe sometimes you know you are not. We know nothing, we have no power over anything where you are. Then suddenly..." she managed to keep up her tone of voice against her deep feelings of her recent sorrow - "we get bones brought in to bury and sanctify. To build a monument over. Thomas, you talk glibly of all this. Exciting it may be to you. It has only one excitement for us. That you come back."

The men began to answer at the instant.

"Come, we think of you. But surely it is not our, certainly not Thomas's fault that Welsh, Scots and French are for ever marauding."

"Don't the English - us at least as in this country - don't we ever 'maraud'?"

"Do you know," responded Henry, I am not sure that we do. I..."

In an interruption Thomas interpolated:

"If we did not push these people out, I think you would blame us more."

"Dear Thomas" it was Alesia who spoke, "I have these feelings, of course. I put my trust in my Creator, for you and for me. Observing the laws of God will mean success."

The tact of her elders was expressed by letting that observation pass. Had so many not 'observed the laws of God?' Henry knew that secular organisation by him achieved better effect than the Scots habit of consulting holy portents before deciding on action in war.

The 1299 expedition against the Scots was cancelled. There was a summons to York for the twelfth of November. What was in the King's mind this time? Not another review of all the nobility surely, as at Salisbury a couple of years ago? Perhaps, because Lords had refused to act except following the King in person. Either Edward had calmed down, or he had other ideas. They decided to make it a leisurely journey.

Alesia noticed continually that more interest was being taken in her. Not just by her relatives, but by her friends, and not least by all those in the household. She fully comprehended that to burst in to a meeting of the Council of Lancaster would result in a silence, respectful, or otherwise, waiting for a lead from their lord Thomas. The more the glazed look behind most people's eyes when she was conversing with them seemed to indicate that what she was actually saying was of scant import.

"It is as though I am not allowed a direct interest in my household affairs. I do not propose to be just an ornament."

Thus Alesia spoke to Mabota, and enlarged upon it:

"I know Thomas is not satisfied with the way his estates are run. Officials die or leave and then debts are found. Some bailiffs and keepers of the fees are not supervised by our central officials. Thomas is trying to check the work of his receiver-general, and it doesn't improve his temper."

"Oh, my lady Alesia, these things are not for you, surely, Lord Thomas will cure the trouble we can be sure."

"Well, they don't seem to want my help, anyway."

"Ma'am, surely you must know their real desire and hope? And ours? And mine?"

Alesia recoiled.

"Not at once, yet, surely. Do you mean they've nothing else in their minds but that. It's only been a few months. Really! Mabota..."

Alesia faded out a sentence. She was dieing to mention the amusement Thomas and she got from their pre-marital adventure. Nor could she mention the relief they both felt when she was not pregnant on their official nuptial night. Nor was she pregnant yet. So she changed her line.

"There are other things to think about, Mabota. As if I would tell them."

So she was not. To Mabota they were all looking for the bloom on her lady's cheeks. They were assessing whether her mistress was a-blossom with pregnancy.

"It is important to many, dear Alesia."

"It is important also for gossips."

Mabota was upset to leave it in this tone. To her the need for continuance of her charge's family was deep-felt, part of her strength and pride. As if she had felt an instant of doubt, but quite unconsciously, Mabota rejoined:

"It will be. It will be."

That it was pressed no further left Alesia with a silent thought, which she was half-prepared to utter. At least the Lord Thomas appeared to enjoy himself; he made no complaints, and asked no questions. She was apparently enough for him. Doubtless she herself would catch up.

Thomas was in amiable mood. The reason was unaffected by any doubts over his wife. It was the longbow which cheered the York gathering.

"An arrow every few seconds. At least a furlong."

The great Durham Bishop Anthony Bek agreed - he had been with Edward and the Earls that twenty-second of July at Falkirk. Wallace, betrayed, was for a pinnacle at Smithfield.

Alesia was pleased enough to smile. In her own heart she was, however, troubled. There was but one thought, that now did beat rhythmically on her mind.

'Bathsheba, wife of Uriah the Hittite, slept one night with David and bore him a son.'

'Bathsheba, wife of...'

Child bearing was prized highly in the Lazards of these times, the accidents at birth, the childbed fever, the early deaths.

It was no use trying to talk to Thomas of this, their relationship was too fresh. Any doubt or worry must not get across to him, nor even be uttered so that anyone might divine her secret anxiety. Perhaps it was just a little strange, that was all. But she never had the feeling of inner hope. It must happen sometime, surely. There were so often surprises when one least expected it. She closed her eyes to brush away a vision of Abraham about to stab his son Isaac to make of him a burnt offering. It was indeed suggested by God himself - at the last moment providing a ram caught in a thicket to be the real sacrifice He had intended. 'God will provide' called out Abraham. Till now she had hardly related her own physique to those of the lesser folk, and the ribaldry on pregnancy so often heard. 'God will provide' mused Alesia. She swallowed deeply. Surely it was early to be worried. But with the uttermost secrecy she would feel calmer with a consultation. Not with the One whom her father had consulted. But they were now in York, where there were plenty of others. Calmly she would send Mabota for an afternoon walk in the market place, to seek out whom she could.

"To find, Mabota, an anchoress who will come here to have a quiet meeting in the garden. Do not bring her first. Tell me of your feelings. She must not be well-known. She would have to come here in the guise of applying for service with me."

Alesia regained hope, that Mabota's judgment and honesty and innocence would from the melee in the surrounding city produce an advisor compatible with her, and knowledgeable in mystery.

It was not often that Mabota was ever away from her mistress, and rarely was she alone. Moving in the city streets, she felt kinship with the crowds in the memories of her humble origins. She spent far too long fascinated by the cheapjack vendor of physick. His words and expression were such as to prove it as an elixir.

"And I take it myself, I tell all of you. Am I not strong, do I not look so?" Ribald replies from a crone or two agreed. "I will drink some now, and I will guarantee to be back in this market week by week for many years to an old age." As someone purchased a phial, he continued without stopping. "Not all can make that prophecy, and for my sons - thank you madam - and you know I have been treating myself with this medicine for..."

There were some who thought that he could do that because he never had to pay for it. Mabota, however, noticed that however often he took the vessel to his lips he never touched a drop. But that was not the sort of talk she was looking for. She pushed through the rows behind her, to the vendor's evident disappointment, for her attention had seemed promising.

Mabota had only one starting point. Every ordinary type of acquaintance would produce the wrong answer. She had to find someone who would give confidence to Alesia, all with an air of it coming from high authority. To Mabota her memory of pregnancies in her family was the worry that another one would start, rather than urging them on through the occult. She knew her goal was near the river, some yards along from the civil landing stage. She had gleaned that in gossip the last time she was in York, without trying to store detailed information for future use. Then it was 'up the bank a bit and behind the drapers, if you ever want one'. Thus, cautiously, Mabota stepped along the gravelly mud amongst the tangle of the ropes of market boats, and turned into a defile made dark by the upper storeys nearly closing together above. When she saw the draper's shop she became apprehensive rather than relieved. While this was her job it was not her world. For others, maybe, and certainly the lords and ladies could get away with it, or afford it. For Mabota the church held enough for guidance and further probing could only be dangerous. For an instant she faltered at her task, which might well be beyond her. Fear or not, however, she had to continue seeking.

She now had to ask in as roundabout way as possible upon which door she should knock. Just at the corner the alley joined another, and lit by a thin shaft of sun there sat two old ladies spinning wool. Their rhythmic movements of pull, twist and wind were not interrupted one whit by their talking with each other. They looked towards Mabota, who hesitated to move forward. They seemed to feel it was not their business, so they just carried on. Mabota made to walk past, but had to draw back for lack of knowledge, and stood near them. In the manner of what she had observed she began conversation obliquely.

"That's good local wool, I imagine. I was brought up to spin, but I could never get an even tension."

"Perhaps you thought about it too much, dearie. It's just routine, and it's alright when the air is damp. Are you lost? The Market's up that way. Or if you're looking for your boat it's this way."

Two nods, one back, one sideways showed some helpfulness. Mabota explained that she was not really lost, but... was on an errand. This confirmed what the women had already guessed.

"I suppose a fortune teller, yes, but someone with a little more. I know no more than that. Not for myself."

Mabota was regretful to admit the last point. To the women it became clear at once that there was money about. Three or four names were mentioned.

"She must not be famous. She must come to my mistress. She cannot come here."

Mabota closed her eyes, hoping to God that no-one would guess who her mistress was.

"It is strange that a high lady might not want the best. Secrecy of course we understand. That's why these folk are near the river, for unseen access. But we do see all sorts come a visiting."

The two grinned at each other.

"Tried a bit of it myself, for a while" chortled one.

Nothing more was needed to strengthen Mabota's opinion that these sessions were useless. Perhaps, therefore, at least harmless.

"Just past that tavern; on the right. There's a door in a garden wall. Try Mary."

The other one agreed.

"She's youngish. Polite. Friendlier than the rest. Less of the stars about her. More of the animals."

Mabota bobbed slightly as thanks, and walked along quickly. Perhaps Mary would reward them for the introduction, she thought. For herself, she carried no money, and as the women did not call after her she was sure. They must be used to it, it must have been their pitch; and neither of them had stopped spinning.

To get through that door in the wall was of itself a relief - from those who had drunk too much in that tavern. The tiny yard inside was the home of several hens, a cockerel, some rabbits, and out of their way on a ledge, a couple of boxes of assorted growing herbs. In the one-room dwelling Mary was tidying round, visible through the doorway.

"The door is always open ma'am, when I am not occupied. I will now fasten it, and we can talk."

Mabota entered the hovel. From her words and now Mabota was no longer a silhouette against the light, Mary gave a slight start of surprise, to see in front of her no lady.

"I seek someone for my mistress."

"If you will explain the problem, an arrangement can be made. There are many lords in York, and the King himself, so from whom are you?"

"At present I cannot say. No word of this must get to any other person. My mistress is young. She wants comfort. I have to choose who shall speak with her. She cannot come here. You would have to go to her."

"Surely then I would be seen?"

"You could be in the guise of seeking an appointment, perhaps."

"Again I am known in high places. I am not objecting. I am trying to show the caution you are seeking. My name is Mary Clemens, by the way. I was once a nun, but I fled. What does your mistress want?"

Mabota had been talking to this younger woman, who had the air of having set up as a personal counsellor. A failed nun, however... well, Alesia need not know. She could not help but cross herself, to the amiable amusement of Mary Clemens.

"Your name is suitable. Or the one you have chosen. Perhaps your experience and manner are appropriate."

"I should not let you down, oh servant..."

"Mabota..." and to keep her end up, she added - "..de Puteo."

"Right. Clemens is my name, my real one, which is perhaps unusual. Before I finally decide I want to know the problem and her date of birth if known."

"Do you ever wish to know her name?"

"It is not important to me."

"Very well. She is worried about barrenness, and she was born upon a Christmas day."

"Anxious already?"

"I agree, but nevertheless she is."

Mabota's jaw then opened to show her astonishment. This woman Mary had guessed for whom she was there, and by her quiet calmness had disarmed her caution. Now Mabota had to suppose that Mary was the suitable person upon whom Alesia could unburden such a notion. It would be all over the town otherwise.

They agreed that the castle garden was far too obvious as a meeting place. The Cathedral was too public. The river path by St. Mary's Abbey was too risky for both sides. With some mutual excitement in planning a drama, they decided on the southern riverbank, where it was open; a meeting apparently by accident. Mary said yes, it was more expensive, but ladies were always difficult to arrange. Cash.

As Mabota decided to leave, Mary called her back. Mabota turned, to see Mary sweeping a hen off the table with a swift left arm. She wondered if an omen had occurred, for Mary tasted the crust the bird had pecked at.

"You are Mabota, I understand, servant of the Lady Lancaster. Do not worry about that knowledge - the town is full of talk of who is here and what they think they're doing. Perhaps the lady will not agree to ride out as we have discussed: perhaps it would be easier if I did dress as a poor girl, as though asking for work? I could meet you at the field door in the castle wall?"

Mabota hesitated, wondering at this concession, and retraction of authority.

"It would be simpler, if you can do and say what you wish to do in that guise. A quiet corner could be found, and that's what my lady said."

She still did not admit in words who was her mistress; this young woman was not showing enough of the mystery that was expected: for herself, however, she was not prepared to worry about that. Mary understood, had a compromise, suggesting that they would meet that way, and if the riverside was better, then Mabota would come out to tell her that.

Worked out with the desperation of a lovers' tryst, it was not to be the next day nor the one after that. The meeting did take place, through the persistence of Mary's constant watch upon the movements of all the great people then in York.

"I am Mary."

It was all she said to the lady on horseback, who was nearly alone one hunting day. So Alesia and Mabota drew in. It was a great relief to them both. Mary's rural disguise had even deceived Mabota.

"At last. It would have been easier if I had not wished for secrecy."

The escorts and Mabota settled at the field side.

"Some of the plan and some chance and fate, Lady Alesia. I know... your... question."

Fortunately until this moment, Mary had hardly looked at her client. As she did, her last two words were hard to utter. Then could Mary say no more. She put out her hand and arm to touch Alesia, but could not move it as far. Her eyes dropped, and then her head, and she remained in silence. In her mind was no more than Alesia's cool calm eyes, her face framed in waving black hair. In Mary's eyes were tears. In her throat a phrase that would not come. Mary knew there was nothing there except her own reactions, as such reactions she had had once or twice before. And what they meant was that she was in the presence of the coursing inevitability of disaster. Mary managed to look again at Alesia, with a quick turn of the head for reassurance in her shock. She never got to, nor needed, any outside omen, nor indication from the behaviour of nature around them. She saw nothing as an aura around Alesia. She perceived no more than showed above on a starless night. She could not express hope, even in this meeting which at first she had not even treated seriously. She was shaking slightly in herself at the strength of the manifestation that the power within her had deep and real meaning.

In silence still she walked away in contemplation, towards the nearby river, to gain relaxation from the tension of the experience. This would not do, Mabota thought, and made to follow. She feared herself that she had found a useless soothsayer for her mistress, but Alesia called her away. It was apparent to her that by being afraid, it seemed, to say anything, Mary had said much. For she had seen her expression so deeply affected. Some ragged urchins coming along the bank emphasised the hollow feeling she experienced with fear in mind and body.

Mabota was duly sent to Mary the next morning, with money and a request for words.

"My mistress feels she understands at least your message, silent though it was. I might add that I myself do not."

Mary had had time to think upon the matter. In the background she considered her own position, her own reputation. Some recommendations would be useful. She would like the lady Alesia to return. It had not been an interview, however, in which she could have produced temporising half-truths to maintain curiosity as well as the hope which all clients needed. So Mary temporised.

"Messages miscarry."

"Make it short, then. Or write it down."

"Not the second. I will follow your first. In the meantime, I know that your own heart is not in your errand. So you might yourself advise lady Alesia to go to her priests. They have a large number of them. I have seen all this from the inside of a nunnery. Nor was it a choice of mine. I was pushed in. Perhaps I know the certainties of God and nature better than you do. I have examined all the standard usages of my calling, and I am confirmed in my first deep impression. That is, I am not disconfirmed."

"The message."

"Ah, yes. Repeat then this to me, so that I have the knowledge that it will carry true. Do not add one word. You will be questioned, of course. You know no more than this..."

"Very well. About any possible pregnancy then."

"Yes, Mabota. Just this: 'Mary cannot see one.'"

Mabota caught her breath.

"Ever?"

"Mary cannot see one."

"Could someone else?"

"I have spoken."

Mabota did not like this turn towards Bible phrases in these surroundings. Perhaps that was why Mary had uttered them. Mabota was doubtful as to her next move. It seemed so brief an examination, from what she had heard of others. Mary brought her out of her hesitation.

"You seem surprised at the hens and the cockerel. No. I am not a witch who needs cats and toads. Cockcrow cleanses the day from the spirits. You are still cautious, Mabota servant. Get the witch ideas out of your head."

"But pregnancy. All right, I'll ask you. Did you recoil from Lady Alesia because she was, is pregnant?"

"You're on about witches again. Although I tell these things I am more than a fortune teller. I say to you that if Lady Lancaster were ever to be pregnant then I would not have left her straightway. Loyal as you must indeed be to her, say no more than my message. She must herself believe it gradually. You must watch that, over whatever time it takes. That is why my message can be doubly interpreted. Be kind."

"I will go, and I will see if the Lady Alesia will wish to see you again."

"Very well. There are other subjects. But delay you any other. My answer will always on this matter be the same."

"You cannot see one."

"I think I have been too precise."

Mabota noted that Mary was not going to comment on the money she had been given, so she droned the message once again and left the little yard at once. If the implication was true that this statement was as near Mary dare go to a prophecy, it was only reinforced by the strange silence and stillness of the hens in Mary's abode. The labyrinthine lanes, too, appeared hushed as she groped for her return route.

It had all seemed clear when Mary had given her judgment. Yet was it a statement which only sounded wise? Mabota received the same question from Alesia as she had herself demanded.

"Cannot see one - now? I know that. Or in the future, did Mary mean that?"

Mabota had no wish to answer. She did not want to confirm it, and for herself hardly considered it to be a possible prediction.

"She was quite clear that those were her words, lady Alesia. And no others. I was not able to discuss."

There was no point in taxing Mabota further. This Alesia knew. She also feared that it meant - ever. At least a prophecy of certainty meant that Mary was not playing along for more meetings and more money. Mabota then uttered with a quiet deliberation emanating from her own need of hope, but Alesia had to turn away from the tears which she saw forming in her servant's eyes.

"Mary cannot definitely know, ma'am, what the future holds, not too far ahead. If she works on planets influencing you, I don't think she can foresee all what may be."

"She had a very strong reaction, Mabota."

And Alesia's tone was that she could not talk about it in an abstract manner. And Mary could not have known about her accident in Dorset. She did not want to hear any more. The silence would have been of great length, but Thomas entered. He looked brisk and purposeful, so Mabota left.

The prepared answer about the unsuitability of the possible new member of Alesia's staff was not needed. He did not ask. He did not notice any perplexed mood that might have given Alesia's feelings away, for her embrace was stronger and warmer in her need for comforting. There had to be hurry; they were to leave York the next morning. The preparations for departure were a help as a diversion. Alesia's fear was strong in the thought that Mary would be right. The dawn glowed bright with the beams of the sun. In three days they would be in Lincoln.

Woodstock, Oxfordshire.

# CHAPTER 17

"In at least one matter, Alesia, you have defeated me" called out Thomas as they rode together the last few miles to Lincoln. His tone showed a marital taunt and no kind of objection.

"If it should be a cheering thought, then tell me what."

"It is clear that I shall never again achieve your journeying in a litter."

Alesia was for a second wondering if there was more in this than the simple point. Her mind was more full of the January drizzle than of banter.

"Lying down like a dead doe being carted is not for me. I just can't. Even though it might be more comfortable in all these sloshy miles. I hope it will be drier on Lincoln's hill. Strange how we always nest high up on some eminence, as do guinea fowl."

Thomas gave a light laugh; and avoidance of some greater muddy stretches drew them apart.

The King himself would arrive next day and stay first at the Bishop's Manor house at Nettleham, just north-east of the city. The Prince Edward was to lodge at Somerton Castle, a few miles to the south. No guinea-fowl roost there, but defended by double moats on the plain of Trent. In due course that Prince would have Alesia's husband executed, and his son would order her detention in that very castle. Every roof would shelter more souls than ever before. The Earl Marshal, Roger le Bigod, Earl of Norfolk was comfortable at the house of St. Katherine's outside the southern gate. Robert, Earl of Carrick, the Bruce, father of the Scottish King, was nearer in, at the Grey Friars at the bottom of the hill. Also at these places, and overfilling every other, were two Archbishops, eighteen bishops, eighty abbots, the Prior of St. John of Jerusalem, and the masters of Sempringham and the Temple. Those who had any connection with the trading fraternity used that influence for accommodation. Corners, corridors and rooms turned into dormitories for the others, which came to eighty-nine barons and knights, seventy-two county representatives, sixteen masters of the law, twenty-two masters of the Council, the Chancellors of Oxford, and of Cambridge, and some others skilled in law.

These all, for a Parliament of three hundred, several times that number to look after them; their horses and men to serve them. Amongst them were those who preferred work with horses, because their needs were obvious and there were no complaints; those to whom personal service gave periods of idleness and the importance of association with their betters; those who preferred the cookhouse because of the security of food and the warmth on a winter's night for sleep in a corner.

It looked as if it would be a stay of a few weeks. At the end of it there were more young women of Lincoln married, and a further number who should have been.

"I enjoy talking with all these people who visit our halls and chambers in this castle" stated Alesia to Thomas, when most of those required had gathered in Lincoln.

"I would, however, also like to know what is going on where I am not allowed."

Thomas laughed. "Alesia, I imagine that you know more than I do..."

"You ride to Nettleham Manor daily."

"Certainly, darling, but I wait upon Edward, with Henry, young Edward, Surrey, Carlisle, Berkeley, Warwick, Hereford and a few others. Master Geoffrey de Vecano stands about hoping for titbits to send to Pope Boniface his master. Thus we have to say as little as possible, except to Edward in Council."

With Alesia showing some disbelief, Thomas pursued the matter.

"You are nearer, I expect, to what people actually believe. You're on your home ground. What do you gather?"

"I have only to walk through the bailey and I am made privy to what are said to be the King's private considerations."

"Sounds useful, and what are they suspected, shall I say, to be?"

"Well, Thomas, you know the last session in York was suspended because of the Welsh wars."

"Of course" Thomas stated patiently.

"Did you know that many of the prisoners who were left untried died of hunger? Even those in for debt were fed by their creditors with bread and water."

Thomas was silent, wondering how deep his feelings might be, and if it were even possible to prevent such happenings, especially if those on the spot could or would effect nothing. 'Alms to prisoners', he mused half aloud as though he was groping for a sound basis for such expenditure. 'Keeping them alive because dead men do not pay debts' he decided not to utter.

"It will be agreed, I expect that I myself will be given leave to have a gaol at Leicester, instead of prisoners having to be taken to Warwick."

He spoke in a tone of caution, anticipating a chiding reaction. So he added:

"I know what you are going to say."

Alesia said it, and concluded:

"Any such mishaps would affect your, our, standing and reputation."

Before Thomas had fully absorbed that into his being, Alesia was talking again.

"I am pleased and proud to hear another item about you, dear Thomas. You are making your way by yourself. Is it not true that you will be asked to add your seal to a letter to the Holy Father in Rome. Is that not so?"

"Who told you that? You do know at least as much as I - it has not yet been broached - officially. It is a start. Yes, a step I like. But who?"

"After deep thought, and anticipating your question, I humbly suggest that if I tell you who tells me what, then they would be prejudiced. My usefulness to you would be destroyed."

"Drastic, I know, so I'll leave it. There is another matter."

"Which is? No, let me guess."

"Very well. I'll wager you don't guess this one, though."

"There is so much being bandied about. I will try on the half of it which I believe."

"Well, then?"

"Is it that Ferrers is suing you..."

"Over the Ferrers estates? In part, I suppose. He won't get anywhere. But it's a damn nuisance. It makes money in those manors harder to collect. It is only because he was hoping to get his father's lands back, but they were confiscated. While they were with the Crown he had hope, but they were granted to me."

Alesia's immediate thought stayed unexpressed - an enemy had been created.

"On the other things - oh, is it about young Edward?"

"No. It is not that, in fact."

"I mean the entitling of him to be the Prince of Wales, and Earl of Chester and to receive Welsh lands."

"Alesia, I am astounded. All this must come from clerks, or who? Does everybody talk every day, every evening?"

"They do. Has anyone told them not to?"

"Well, no, but... anyway, you have not guessed right yet. You can't really - I've only agreed something personally with Hereford."

"Thomas, that's not fair."

"We told Edward, and asked for his confirmation - perhaps he has not spoken to you yet."

"No," returned Alesia, in her eagerness to know. She had to ignore the teasing in the last few words - "What, then?"

"Hereford and I are to hold a Great Tournament in a year or two. At Fulham, we thought."

He drew Alesia further away from any possible earshot. Thomas continued:

"I am no philosopher. Hereford suggests we have a show of power. Keeps the organization in trim."

"What organization?"

"Barons. There are too many men of the shires getting forward. Even two knights and six burgesses from Lincolnshire in parliament now and foreigners in power continually increase in number. Hereford says we have to show our initiative. There are more others than barons at this Parliament."

"And Edward? He's been against tournaments."

"He needs the skills that come out; and he made no adverse comment. Life is not all like Sir Yvain chasing enemies who run away."

"Yet like any woman I wonder at my own knight in armour looking to all that so soon. But I look forward to being proud of you, and I will help."

"A lot will devolve on you, Alesia. The hostess. A great occasion."

"Just this - dear Thomas - if an enemy does run before you and you are caught in his castle, you keep off the beautiful young maiden who helps you to escape."

With an extravagant bow Thomas urged that indeed such a rescuer must be herself. As the news of the tournament spread in the family Henry de Lacy was quite direct in asking Hereford what was in his mind. It was strength. Henry pondered as to the strength of what. The conversation did not develop. Already the obvious effete weakness of Prince Edward was apparent, emphasized by his affection for his young companion Gaveston. There was a vacuum to be filled, and with unconsidered feeling Thomas and Hereford were being drawn into it. He concluded that a tournament was sufficient justification in itself, and it should be a superb day.

"Week" stated Hereford.

And on it will go, and on for ever, thought Margaret as she thought of her father, whom she only just remembered. Perhaps his death in the jousting would be enough propitiation. Surely it would not happen twice, and her daughter's husband would be safe. She was glad that this had apparently not entered Alesia's mind, who looked as if she was pleasurably excited. Later, in passing, Margaret conversed with her - and yet left unspoken the very thought that she feared - that a granddaughter might sometime be similarly orphaned as she had been. In a flow of confidences she did say -

"If only I could have cheered your father with a further child! He seems now so bereft of human response. He is there with me, and yet that affectionate tone has never come back. He tries, of course, to pull himself forward on his hopes for you."

After a pause in which clearly she would not perceive any reply, Margaret added:

"Henry, with all his apparent logicality, placed his belief on transient life. I do not really suppose any further children which we might have had would have caused much more than fear in his heart, though."

Alesia could respond only by smothering her own doubts and worries. She just expressed doubt that she had influenced Thomas very much.

"Yet," prompted her mother. Then they were joined by their menfolk, straight from their council meeting at Nettleham.

"Edward is moving into the city in a few days. He has got all ready

- in his mind anyway. Everybody has arrived and so we can hunt while the scriveners prepare for the parliament."

"Are we invited?" was the query which promptly sprang from Alesia's lips. "I trust mother and I are allowed a seat - to watch of course."

The silence which followed was compounded of shocked surprise and a mental search for precedents. Thomas had no experience of such, but surely there was no reason why not. Her father therefore took up the subject.

"Unofficially there are always folk milling around, unless there are objections. Edward does, however, want full support, and information to spread. Doubtless the informal could become formal on this occasion."

"Much of it is routine," he continued, "but it might be interesting a time or two. I will have you found a space at the edge of the choir, where you may observe."

He was as good as his word for the ladies, indeed early on the day they traversed the Cathedral, seeing the office which had been set up in the chapter house; praying by the shrine of Queen Eleanor, encased as was her image now in gold and pearls; then they were settled by the southern steps, not far from the altar. Attendance on her mistress at such as this occasion was what Mabota appreciated, though it caused her puzzlement. Alesia pressed her to reveal why she revealed such a look of doubt.

"Here we are, Lady Alesia, to witness protests against the Holy Father..." and she faded away at that.

"In his own choir, you mean?"

Mabota was forced against her will to make reply, which she had to utter in a whisper.

"Yes. Strange, but I do see that he cannot be both Pope and Caesar."

No more was needed to be said and the assembly grew, with increasing attendant murmur. The three hundred participants represented the capacity of the choir.

A hush enveloped the throng, spreading from the great west door, demonstrating that Edward the King had entered the building in procession. His family were directed to the north side of the choir, opposite the de Lacys. King Edward, with his nephew Thomas, Henry, the Bishops of Lincoln and Carlisle in attendance were escorted to their places.

The first business was straightforward enough, given the feeling of all classes of English present, namely that the bull of Pope Boniface III, the Clericus Laicos of some five years previous, should be repudiated. It was not acceptable that clergy should pay no taxes.

Edward had wanted a large and diverse representation, and its support, and he achieved it. "Clergy must not be completely immune from taxes by the state, though immunity is written in decree from

Rome," explained Henry to the assembly in a loud, slow, and clear tone. It was appropriate to do so, because prejudice and decision were arising out of hearsay. It would be as well for all to know what the Pope had stated: "...that these burdens are without licence from the Apostolic See. Therefore all who pay such taxes without Papal permission, and all Emperors, Kings, Dukes, Earls and whosoever would exact or receive them without our authority shall incur the sentence of excommunication and interdict until death."

Maybe every vote was not individually noted, but it was certainly carried by shout of acclamation, heard outside in the Cathedral close. The clerks crowding by the doorway to the cloisters added their modest but well-felt rumble of approval. Satisfaction at this anticipated result showed in public reaction in the crowd in the nave. Something offensive would be stopped. The better folk were taking the greater risk against the Holy Father's spiritual power. Taxes might well go down, or at least not up.

While the clerks were applying their barons' seals to the letter to the Pope, word of mouth spread the news as fast as Edward would have wished. Some of the higher clergy were indeed antagonistic to this parliament's business, but they were not there. They were without effective organisation, for although they were many, they were scattered. It was popular to decide in accordance with the bitterness of the people. It matched the need to tax the money of the Church, which had the country's greatest share of resources.

As the three weeks of this vast conglomeration ran on, the seriousness faded as the tensions evaporated as decisions were made. The clerks and lawyers took them up and for days the city was spattered by the hooves of fast horses. Reception after reception by King, Bishops, and Earls added to the hubbub. News, review and opinion of the proceedings was immediate, with much added, and little expressed doubt of the correctness of the action taken. The whole gathering was reassured. Strength had been gained from rumours of King Charles of France repudiating Boniface's appointment of one of his own family to a post, and his repudiation of the Pope's counter threats.

For Thomas, however, there was something underlying the whole trend of events. To his opening about how cold the Cathedral could be, Alesia demurely stated that by arranging herself as a tent about her stool, then even her feet had been cosy enough. Thomas was finding her comments on events of interest.

Thomas cynically remarked: "Here we support Edward, tomorrow he reduces us."

"Thomas" spoke Alesia "I really think you see things that are not there. No, that's too strong. The King increases his power and scope, yes. Sheriffs now to be elected, and regulation after regulation. But why does that bother you, ...us, we're meant to be close to the State in all things, including relationship."

"It makes all barons little better than the men with no duties, and no responsibility. And indeed, your father agrees with me, even though he sees it through. He is even stronger about the matter."

Also, for a century, the assertions of the Popes had been a major dispute with Rome. Even the great Bishop Grossteste had complained, supported by the clergy - more particularly about mere infants being inducted to church livings. The Pope had threatened vengeance. England responded that "it was not desired to raise a tumult in the church and precipitate a revolt, for separation which must one day take place."

By now the Papal declaration of Scotland as a fief of Rome showed his power to have over-reached acceptance. It was going too far; independence in England and Wales on temporal matters was asserted by Parliament, perhaps more meaningful for its moderation. They felt better for asserting command of their own.

Alesia joined in the great surge of feeling which derived from their unity. She had, however, troubled thoughts of her own which seemed to show little sign of resolving. Now nineteen years of age, yet there had been no pregnancy.

It was for herself to weep alone. It was the only protection for her morale against so many questions indicated by looks, overt examinations of her body, eyebrows raised above concentrating eyes which as quickly reverted to normal when she noticed.

No fulfilment joy for Alesia. It must have been that accident at Canford. No alchemy or magic could overcome that. What was within her was proved to her by feelings, yet hope had to strive to overlay them.

A tournament.

# CHAPTER 18

The summer fields of Fulham were alive in the sunshine with colour. Caparisoned war horses vied with applied fabrics for attention against the designs of escutcheons and crests and tunics of the warriors.

"Tournaments" said Alesia to Prince Edward, "are alright, I do not doubt. I am sure they have tremendous value in keeping horses and knights in good form."

Prince Edward noted a tone in her voice, which made him wait for a follow-up, which soon came:

"...fine, in fact, if the participant is not one's husband."

Edward sympathetically assumed that Alesia was thinking of her maternal grandfather's death in jousting at Bawtry.

"Not at that moment," replied Alesia, "also, I never feel like sitting in a row of ladies in a grandstand. I would rather be among the horses..."

"...and the men who look after them."

At this interpolation by Edward both Alesia and Gaveston grinned amusement at their mutual interest in the male sex, though different types they would be.

"Do you mind when I take part in a joust myself?" asked Gaveston, with minor mischief in his eyes. Alesia's immediate reply flashed into her mind:

"On behalf of Edward, of course I do," she returned, to their understanding amusement. Because of Gaveston's remark she wondered - had they watched her yesterday? If they had they had taken the right attitude. It had been amusing, it had fitted her present situation, her temperament, and if they had seen her it seemed also to have fitted theirs.

What had happened was that in late afternoon there had been much imbibing and eating and talking in the packed crowd of lords and ladies. There were those who moved round to mix with one after another, and there were others, much less numerous, who received their friends by standing in one place. These last were the more important, or those of a mind so to appear. Alesia, by rank among the highest of ladies in the land, and greatest after Royalty, was perfectly poised in her single position, chatting happily in her changing small group. Similarly there were other knots of folk all over, and much movement. Used to the minor buffets of such affairs in passing, there did occur one or two gentle pushes in her back. Seemed nice. Seemed nice again. A squint at the shoulder showed the person to be a man, so did the feelings. Apparently stimulated by this accidental approach he did not move away. What effect this subtle contact back to back would have upon his conversation with his friends became Alesia's interesting speculation. She was unaware for herself of little such change other than their mutual slight deliberate moves of communication through contact. Amazing, she thought, how many beautiful nudges could be effected in that position while apparently standing still. Her unawareness of any effect upon herself was only due to her feeling this diversion in continued concentration. It was so, but it was not on the subjects in hand. Before long all the meetings were nearly over, formalities were taking the place of conversation, folk were drifting away, and the suspicion of the mystery of Alesia's expression became forgotten and unsolved as it all broke up. Except for one person. The man broke contact, and Alesia dared not look, and maybe nor did he. Someone did, a lady she thought from just that shadow which impinged so slightly on her side vision. It was as they departed, to see what if anything was going on. Remaining standing still by no decision other than the tension which prevented her moving, Alesia even smiled as Thomas came across the grass to join her.

Thomas smiled in return. While his rank had thrust upon him the exercise of power, his only quarrel with Alesia was the interpretation of what should be done with it. His opinion was that his acts were forced upon him, and Alesia's recommendations to do nothing except support the King could not be tolerated. Regrettably he was strengthened by his need also to appear to be acting as prominently as others thought he should, straining his innate abilities. With all this, however, underneath the image was the man, needing genuine communication with his wife. So latent warmth shone forth.

The pleasure in Alesia's mood, grown from reasons unrelated to Thomas, showed satisfactory on the surface; the amiability of joining with Thomas in relaxed companionship allowed her to bury the twinge of deceit. The incident that afternoon had, however, begun to make her realise that she could not for ever play a part in life devoid of feminine feeling. Suddenly she visualised her friends; a picture came into her mind. There they were, even as individuals, alone each one, scattered upon a wide landscape of fields and trees and a stream or two. They stood motionless, statues placed in an overall composition. It seemed that they were pieces on a surface meant to be alive in nature, yet their souls were not expressed. Thus caught in a power beyond their desires, attached to a patch of ground which was allocated with them included, Alesia saw the poor chance their ideals of a love-decided marriage would have to flourish.

It would explain the antics of some of her friends as they let themselves look round with open eyes for any fulfilling adventure. Apart from women friends who acted thus after difficulty in achieving self expression there was her own infertility. She felt incomplete. Sometimes not so much that she minded for herself, but because of the reactions of others. Her mother was clearly disappointed, if not worried. She blamed everything from herself to lack of prayer. Some ladies based their own superiority on the numbers of their young, and with no better reason showed it. Thomas was enigmatic on the subject, and perhaps really did not mind too much. Alesia at least could be uncertain whether the fault, if so it were, was with him or with herself. Until Joan Ploucoun, that is. Alesia forgave, understanding. It was usual with men, but Thomas would have had deep reasons just like those female friends of hers who had to hold up their own morale to themselves.

Thomas had halted at Clitheroe on a journey north, and when he dwelt in that small castle with his overflowing retinue he took on an air that for the place itself seemed too great. It was just that the surrounds themselves were too cramped to encompass his status. Aware of little but restlessness, he went across the enclosure to where his clerks were working. There must be some questions that needed answering, and at least it should relieve his aloneness. It brought some calm, Thomas astonishing some by his affability. The clerks appeared to have no worries other than those induced by him, he thought. They seemed also sedentary and comfortable, and served with plenty of refreshment.

This last came from the ladies and camp followers, distributed as they themselves decided was convenient. How sluggish was all this organisation of movement. An army was a snail, complete with house. Yet he accepted a taste of hot soup from the wife of a tenant mason. How strange that none of them would be here, except for him, for his ambitions; more, for his duty as he reflected it. He was their leader and their purpose.

While talk was respectful, yet easy, all being committed to life in the one lord's household, there came up to them a friend of one of the women, whose name he overheard as Jane Ploucoun. While as covered as the other women by her clothes, Jane's followed her shape with accuracy, to provocation in demonstrating that she was female. Yet by her face she had no fatalistic attraction. It was plump, slightly pointed, with not much chin, all of a decent motherly type. Yet her air, undeserved by her basic personality, gave a glow of outgoing hope and eagerness.

Thomas engaged with his eyes, and spoke to her with enquiries of her place in the scheme of things and what she did. The short conversation was no more than the contact and expression of affirmation of mutual stimulus, the words themselves unimportant, lost on the air as soon as they were uttered. If this dual communication was noticed by the others present, then it was only because of their own same experience. Yet Thomas, after a few moments of human delight, moved off to return to the keep.

This is the way, he thought in general terms, how nature urges the continuation of the species, as it urges through the desires of men and women. And yet, with himself where was nature in doubt or fault?

To Jane it had been a harmonious exchange, arousing feeling. Her young husband had been drowned in a flooding river, and she was back with her parents in the village, so she was suffering a certain deprivation with no apparent future. Nor was she considering that the great lord Thomas had any place in it. But not long after Thomas was descending the outer steps Jane appeared at their foot, on her way up with a basket of fruit. Thomas's mind was in its usual state by now of self-doubt and wondering what he should next do. Jane smiled, with obvious pleasure, to revive and reassure Thomas, his company having received her approval. She almost ran up the steps, and Thomas turned, with an unspoken enquiry.

"To the seneschal's chamber, Lord Thomas, is this order."

"That is where I am. Perhaps they are for me?"

"In which case I shall arrange them for you, lord, and..."

Neither Thomas nor she felt that further talk would clarify any matter whatsoever. Jane wanted to add that she would arrange herself as well. Her second thought was that that was too forward, so she tried to express her willingness to wait; and next hoped to be told. So her voice had tailed into silence, and Thomas had nodded. Thus with no audible expression of what was their true state of mind they had achieved full understanding, yet taken literally it could have been for either party the opposite of the interpretations. As evening darkness clasped the castle both were embraced in the deepest comfort. There had been no deliberate decision of either of them, nor was there haste.

Having reached the privacy of Thomas's high chamber, with mostly a private journey, through the avoidance by all others, there had been communication without conversation. It must have been the dual nature of Joan's attraction. For a long pleasurable time tomboy wrestling ensued. If it was sensuous it was mildly so; if it was physical stimulus it was of a patient and confident kind; that it held the two in enthralled gripping movement and feeling of each other's willing bodies was certain. Reactions were felt beneath and within their clothing which inevitably one by one became loosened and removed, for friction until unbreakable contact. In good and equal spirits the beautifully postponed conclusion made at least Thomas think that perhaps he was in life too brusque, that leisured communication made for more enjoyable rapprochement.

The few days subsequent beheld this private scene of joy of feelings in woods and on the moors.

Thomas would return, he said. He wanted to. He would rather that this private person seduce him from any duty. At least, some part of him was encouraged by the human but plain personality of which Joan was a prime example. On the unavoidable break, for the march further north, he experienced a solid belief in having felt genuine concern for another person. Before all the column of his men had wound away beyond the river, she was weeping, hidden away for secrecy.

Alesia quarrelled that the child was designated "... of Lancaster." That such may never be her lot brought her the fury of more despair. Mabota paid little heed to poor Alesia's later explanations, because the true basis had not been uttered. Mabota, maid servant for many years, had suppressed her own human feelings for much longer. By her silence the possibility dawned upon Alesia, and it brought her back to kindness.

"Different reasons, my lady" answered Mabota, when she had been asked about her feelings. "Even so, I have never challenged the possibility by getting married, so I am still unknowing. Besides, I have never had much time to think about it, certainly not to worry on the subject."

Looking at her, Alesia felt a twinge of conscience in that she herself was the cause of Mabota being trapped into a celibate life, in that it had not been feasible for her to escape from the de Lacy family. Yet she must have met hundreds of people, superficially maybe, but occasions from which romance could have developed. There had been no conscious effort to hold her into the single state.

"No, my lady, I am quite happy. I have a life that satisfies me." Mabota spoke as if she had read Alesia's thoughts.

Alesia looked closely at her; there seemed to be no reason to continue the conversation nor to comfort Mabota in any way. While Alesia herself must climb above her own situation, their long acquaintance had constantly helped them both; they softened instinctively each other's tensions. Now, however, Mabota seemed detached in manner. It was not so much attitude or voice, just that she was not so bonny nor so outgiving. It was the first time ever that there had been any change in her. Alesia would just watch for a few days. Mabota had noticed the extra intentness and focus of Alesia's eyes. She, too, was not prepared to speak on the matter now. She was only getting a little forgetful now and again, nothing particular was wrong about her general health.

It was a year or two later when Alesia had to realise that her maidservant may not have the stolid energy that she had always demonstrated without any sign of flagging. They were to leave London for the 1307 Parliament at Lincoln. Sir Ebulo le Strange was discussing the arrangements for transport of Alesia and her household. He read the order out loud, and added just that the lord Thomas had told him that afterwards he would be responsible more often for her safety and travels wherever required. It was to do with Thomas's increasing duties, for the present to do with the possible marriage of the young Prince Edward with the French Princess, Isabella, daughter of Philip le Bel.

"She is, it is rumoured, beautiful; some say the most beautiful in the world," stated Alesia, accompanying this with a hint of jealousy for such praise, and adding "it must also explain why the location of this Parliament is referred to in French as 'Nicole'."

Not having ever seen the Princess, Ebulo le Strange could not express an opinion. He was too reticent to suggest that the praise may well be biased by sycophants, or by others who had not come across enough young ladies to effect a balanced judgment. His only communication was a faint wondering smile of contemplation. Alesia responded to that.

"I also," she said, "wonder what she will make of relationship with Edward. Shall we only hope that it will be as close as his love with Gaveston?"

They both then agreed that the French name was a throw-back to their invasion and battle in Lincoln of four generations ago. They hoped that it portended nothing. What mainly occured in the exchange was the growth of feeling between Alesia and Ebulo. They felt simply that they were at ease together.

"Usually not much happens on these journeys," said Alesia drily, "so is this a sideshow you have organised?"

Ebulo laughed. He had been wondering with a little anxiety how Alesia would react to what they had just witnessed, in a market place about halfway on their travels. Pillories were not unusual. Nor were stocks. The degradation of poverty was constantly visible on the surface by the groups of ragged urchins running about. It was not helpful to delve beneath the surface to find the insecurity and hunger and misery which was its result, and about which nothing human could be done. So good feeling could come only from pecking those below. Coupled with idle hands and irresponsible mischief people in the pillory provided the material for exercising self assertion. Cecily Smertblod was in it again, firmly held by neckhole and wrist holes. The difference this time was that Aundrina the widow, who used to feed her, had died; and she had only the drink from Sara. With a kindness which went awry she also over-supplied the receptive old guard Bogo son of John son of John of Newton.

From horseback it was easy enough to discern the pantomime. Cecily Smertblod did discern in foggy measure what was afoot; Bogo was, however, right out. Cecily may not have minded too much, but Bogo was meant to be on watch duty. This he could not do while blotto. It was a matter of laughter for the crowd that gathered. Some gentlemen would have stopped the proceedings, but Ebulo regarded the whole as either suitable compounded punishment for the criminal, or public entertainment for miserable lives. It was milder, thought Alesia, than what our class does to each other. There was sensuous pleasure in this.

The long and dirty clothes, first dragged up and over her head by youths, had soon been torn away by opportunist women who were short of cloth. There was plenty of mud around, and shortly plenty adhering to Cecily. She had ample dimensions, yet nothing like enough to accommodate all those willing to throw, place or massage in vital places all for their amusement. To some extent it began to sober Cecily, whose only response could be one vague thrash with one leg at a time. Rain slowed it all, but mainly because Cecily was able to shout, and in the drenched Bogo sobriety began to stir. It was interesting, but not so entertaining, to turn to watch the aristocrat group pass by.

Undercurrent of passions had given way to whatever was in their grasp. Alesia had thought that the prejudices of their betters controlled more power, more harmful intent, with worse actions resulting.

In due course the contrast was exemplified in the splendour of the marriage of Isabella and Edward in Boulogne. It demonstrated that power, by including four Kings and three Queens present. Edward, having left Gaveston behind in England as Earl of Cornwall and Regent of the Kingdom, showed his passion to him as he returned to England by his hugs and kisses. That was the subsurface reality. Lords and people would not refer to the new Earl as other than Piers Gaveston, to his great complaint to Edward. Isabella herself did receive a tremendous welcome in England, which in his personality her husband was unable to join wholeheartedly, having already his male lover. The effect came to be a dissolute Court, enmity between wife and husband, which struggle the wife ultimately won by trickery. Banished, recalled, captured, murdered - this was the future for Gaveston, brilliant, strong and clever. He had one friend, and was unseeing in making enemies and thus not adding to that number.

Counselling peace to Thomas, Alesia did not perceive the weight of prejudice amongst those urging him to action - barons had always been the controllers of the realm. They were offended enough by the King's deviant public habits. Insult by his constantly turning to shire men for support provided their further discontent, though it was caused mostly by their own lack of co-operation. Now Queen Isabella was bringing in French for preferment, many of them ladies for marriages. The foreignness of church and state was growing compounded.

There was little more that Alesia could do, nor wished to do, than to support her husband. Her father Henry was as often away - to Scotland, to Parliament - when he returned from Lyons after a four-month absence to congratulate the new Pope Clement the Fifth on his election, there was a public welcome by the Lord Mayor of London - to councils, for the knighting of Prince Edward at which he assisted with the Earl of Hereford. Visiting Denbigh again, to Scotland in charge of the Prince, to Parliament again, which he opened, and northwards once more, being then with King Edward the First at Burgh le Sands on 8th July 1307 at his death.

At present friendly to Gaveston, Henry promoted him as Earl of Cornwall. A few months later he joined the party against him, yet early the next year he bore one of the swords of state at Edward's coronation. Gradually won over to Gaveston again, insult rekindled their enmity. In all this dispiriting atmosphere he abandoned his desire to establish a college at Oxford. He joined with Thomas in refusing to attend the Parliament at York if Gaveston were to be present.

This was a great fillip for the factions round Thomas in their urgings for the new King to be brought to heel, Thomas being committed to this aim and was thus never brought in to state affairs. He was pardoned for his and his father's debts because of what they had done in Scotland. While having witnessed Gaveston's charter as Earl of Cornwall, he soon became active in securing his further banishment. While he carried a sword at Edward's coronation and acted as steward of the subsequent feast, he was later sworn in the Painted Chamber at Westminster as one of the chief Ordainers to control his cousin the King. To orders for military assistance more than once he offered knights and servants and horses only in single figures. For this he was pardoned as not providing support fitting from an Earl. The practical matters achieved by Thomas amounted to getting reports upon many manors, down to the inspection of the book called Domesday about his tenure of Wilton in Yorkshire. For anniversaries for his father Edmund on the 4th June, for Blanche his mother on the 4th of May in each year he gave a property in St. Mary le Strand to the Bishop of Worcester; also for himself after his death, to be celebrated in the cathedral church of Worcester.

Alesia contrasted the attitude of her father with that of her husband, but received only temporising answers to any questions:

"My dear Alesia, Thomas must show that what Edward does is not acceptable, and that he omits to take action which he should... under every possible heading. Edward needs pushing, and will only get away from his way of life if he has to."

"Yes, father, but - of course there's a 'but' in it; what is Thomas's position in this? He has no power to carry out a national requirement and never will have."

"If you are anxious about Thomnas, Alesia, do please rest your mind. He will not do anything foolish."

Alesia pondered for a moment on that. Her father sounded as though he himself had no anxieties on that score. He did not sound to be all that committed.

"But father, Edward takes no notice. You know he resists all that is urged upon him. It has to get really unpleasant until anything is done, and Thomas does not have all that patience."

"Yes. I am in Edward's council, however, and..."

"You're always away..."

With some irritation at the beginnings of a probing conversation Henry almost snapped back his reply:

"More so since your mother died..."

"I am so sorry, father. I understand."

It had to be left in that setting. It always was. Alesia hoped constantly to discover some of the future if not firm conclusions. Her anxiety for the present stemmed always from the situation pressed upon Thomas, and his acceptance of it. His brusque personality and the ordinary inability and resentment at being under the command of a weaker man could only result in the forthright derogatory attitude he took towards Edward.

That King was certainly persuaded to give way to allowing the Ordainers' shadow government by the possibility of another Battle of

Lewes which had been occasioned by a former Earl of Leicester, Simon de Montfort. In Edward's case it was diverted into a contest between the intelligence of his own evasions and the strong arms of the opposition.

To achieve some calming influence upon her husband Alesia tried a week or two later to open the subject with him.

"You appear, Thomas, as though you are coming to some fresh decision, but I thought that it had all been organised now. Are you not finally decided with..." she hesitated over which descriptive word to use, and decided on neutrality "the others that you are going to control the state and Edward's household? Surely it's all agreed with your Ordainers?"

Thomas did not reply for a long moment, but his response was civil:

"Alesia, that is correct. That seems clear, and I can see that through, particularly now that Gloucester and your father have joined us."

Alesia, however, was not so sure. Only Hereford and Warwick of the greater Barons were giving real support to Thomas. There were the many others who offered only their own feelings. Even so, with Thomas now sworn as one of the Ordainers, in reality the leader, he should have been more cheerful.

"It is a very great pity," continued Alesia, "that one man, Gaveston, should so disrupt this whole land, and cause such enmity. Why not just ignore him? It is not as though you live and fight for him. There is a country greater than he to be considered."

"Yes, Alesia, but there is no way to do things, other than influencing Edward, and that means his lover."

The contempt in the tone of that last word could never be compromised.

Since Thomas had known all that for years, and since by nbow much opinion if not action was moving in his direction, it seemed strange that he did not exude confidence in the future.

"So my father has joined you at last."

"Yes. He has had enough insults from Gaveston, and to be addressed as 'burstbelly' is more than he will tolerate."

"He calls you 'the play actor'."

"I know that well enough, but I have been convinced of the rottenness of that couple for a long time. Your father, and all of us, have been provoked further by lovers' giggling over great matters."

"It is indeed all very sad, that such a father should have such a son."

"Then..."

"Of course someone has to rule properly, but..."

"But...?"

"One can only say be careful not to go too far, which is what I fear."

There still seemed to be something gnawing at Thomas's mind. What should have been in him an attitude of future success had some shadow cast upon it. After some more moments he still spoke with hesitancy. He looked towards Alesia long enough to worry her about what he might say. His gaze was trying to achieve reaction to his latest information.

"I have just come from your father."

This Alesia knew, but the purport of Thomas's statement meant nothing. It spurred her anxiety, but still no thought could she form to express.

Thomas spoke again:

"You don't know, then?"

With haste and deep concern Alesia had to demand what did she not know, what ill became her father?

"No, no, he's well enough. Apparently even you had not heard. Not an inkling? I am surprised he told us first, as tell you he must, of course..."

"What, whatever..?"

"He states that he is to marry again, a ..."

"Marry?"

"That is what he said."

"No, I did not know." Her thoughts and impressions raced. Was it true? Supposedly. Who might it be? There were a good number of widows who would be interested candidates, some who had made it obvious. So? Well, let her father get happier, for death had parted Margaret from him. The secrecy, if that is what it was, hurt her a little, but perhaps this was obliquely a message, for they had not seen each other recently. Yes, alright, good for him. All she at this instant was able to utter was a single syllable:

"Oh."

Its tone came from surprise, from instinctive pleasure at her father's future, but the tone of that briefest sound incorporated the discord of noting Thomas's displeasure. Why had he spoken of it with that attitude? Alesia was suddenly glad she had not heard of it first, because when she told Thomas he would have been taken aback, and she would not have had a chance to recover her balance without him noticing. What threat was it to Thomas? With an inspired avoidance of direct challenge, she asked:

"To whom? He's kept it all to himself."

"Joan, daughter of Lord Martin."

Heavens, she was young. Lady Martin herself was about the right age. Alesia could neither laugh nor cry. It must have been quickly arranged. Oh, God, was that the trouble? Her father was sixty, well... Trouble was that with arranged affairs these matters had little shadow to cast before them. And to cry. That was the greatest possibility for her. So she had to guess that it was about inheritance. The Lincoln estates, that must have been what Thomnas was so anxious about. She was already allowing most of the revenues of the Salisbury estates to him, which she had received from her mother. Was more really necessary to support his profligacy? Might there not at this late time in Henry's life be a new heir?

Alesia sympathised with her father, though not so young in spirit, still aggrieved by his male heirs having to lie in their graves instead of being the greater men that they would have been. His unfulfilled family future and hope may well chance now into something.

To her chagrin she realised that she had analysed Thomas's attitude. What else could it be, when he should have accorded the news as pleasurable, that for him it was a personal assault? So it was as deep as that for him, seemingly an unconscious admission that he himself, having no heir, may be depreciated in reputation and in the power of resources.

Poor Thomas. That was Alesia's other thought. Or was he like all men who pushed forward with material power and expression, and never lived by the humanities? But as much as any other impression in her mind, she felt Poor Alesia for herself. She could find no traceable use for her mind, for her body, for her own persona, just and only had she value for the derivation of her name and its attachments. She felt danger in that unhappiness, for there must be love to give, and she must be loved.

Whatever was represented in the relationship between Henry and Joan, their marriage did bring a new air of stability to the scene. Edward arranged further grants of revenues to them both and arrears from Lincolnshire dues were paid to Henry at last by the Sheriffs. It was partly connected with Henry's appointment as Guardian of the Realm while the King was in Scotland, a separation of Henry and Thomas in judgment and trust. Further, Edward had acted in concert with the French, and thus his wife, to dissolve and arraign the Knights Templars. He acquired their properties. He had found Thomas was ineffective, and was thus an attacker he could absorb, Isabella, however, gave no help to the increasing patriotic English feelings of the nobles.

After seven months of Henry's newly married life, his last winter had come. In early February, 1311, he sent for Alesia. He received her in his bedchamber; though apparently well, and sitting alert, she feared as soon as she glanced at the dwindled comprehension in is eyes.

"Young Edward does not recognise how old I have become. Even as one treats long-familiar people as still young, I did not know that young people did the same of their elders. That last appointment as Guardian is not three months ago. Fortunately little action was required."

Henry smiled wryly, and waved away Alesia's commiseration and thoughts of hope.

"No, darling Alesia. Just let me touch you. Do not make me weep. I am not in pain ...yet. I have at last run down. And out, before long.

Breathing mostly gone, and this weather does not help. I think I could have done more in life, but it has not been simple."

"Father - my dear father, how untrue that sounds. It is one of the things you must not say - nor think about. Above all I give you my love."

With Henry nearly prone, Alesia sat at his side; they holding hands in silence. It was comforting in the fire-lit chamber, the last of the de Lacys secure in feeling together.

Shortly Joan entered, and refreshment was brought. Alesia was to stay at Holborn until Thomas's return from Berwick-on-Tweed.

Henry wished to see him as soon as he reached London. Alesia and Joan exchanged a glance, showing that there must be peace between them. A simmering step-daughter and step-mother relationship would now never develop. Indeed, Alesia would never have thought it to be a tense situation at all if Thomas had not become bad tempered about the possibility of money and manors disappearing on Henry's decease.

Some days after, at the Savoy palace, Alesia tried to calm him:

"It depends on father's will. I mean also what his own desires are. I am sure that whatever it is, Joan will be reasonable. Besides, nearly everything is already for you."

The trouble was that recently Henrty had been given more lands and revenues, and Thomas had had a hard time with Edward at Berwick. Harder again to dissimulate the idea that there could be any respect for the KIng.

"There will be dower, probably half of everything. Edward will give me nothing, so there is nothing else to work with."

It was not the time, as they both knew, to quarrel on this with the King. Of course Edward would not pass extra power to Thomas. Not only was the tension between them growing, but no normal baron could possibly need any more than five earldoms. Thomas would, however, not be satisfied with the forthcoming Earldom of Lincoln without all its material power.

"Let us see what father may say."

So, back to Holborn, to be received by a weak and not very comfortable Henry. Yet greeted with affection, Thomas included. Some way through slow conversation about the Scots, the French, the Welsh, and where else there was need of such constant effort - Henry managed to beckon Thomas to rise and to come nearer. He raised his arms to hold him firmly as best he could, and spoke with some clarity:

"This Harry approaches his end. I pray that your time may be long. Stand with the right of the realm. Resist the King. Be governed by the counsel of Guy of Warwick."

Soon Henry fell back, and seemed in a peaceful sleep. There had not been a moment to do other than to nod, to place a hand upon his shoulder, and to utter that it would be done. Henry may or may not have heard the response. It was his chaplain who met Alesia and Thomas next morning, to tell them that Henry's soul had now left him, on the feast day of St. Agatha the Virgin.

The Earl of Lincoln was buried in St. Paul's on the 28th February, 1311. The Cathedral was packed with all classes from King Edward the Second down to commoners of every station, with lawyers prominent amongst them. His stone effigy lay clad in chain mail and tunic, cross-legged, with hands clasped as in prayer. His head rested upon a cushion flanked by angels, his feet rested upon a small curly haired dog. The base of the tomb was edged by twenty four figures of monks and nuns. Thus it stood for three hundred and fifty five years, when it was engulfed by fire. For lack of reliance on the safety of any wall or structure of the Cathedral afterwards all that remained of the building and contents was demolished and razed to the ground, for the new St. Paul's to be built.

Being the principal mourners Alesia shared the lead with Joan, as the procession moved to interment in the tomb monument. Grief mingled with fear of the change to an unsettled life for Joan, but with memories for Alesia. Guided through the routine movements it is doubtful if she could notice or wish to notice anything through her tears. There was the throng, the press of people, as such a measure of her father's importance, now cancelled by death. To Alesia vivid impressions going back to Daddy as the background of life. She could not be the future of the de Lacy family; that also was dying. There were those present who felt that she should not be disturbed by casual conversation, for that was all that could be made at this time. When Alesia was away from Thomas and Joan it was Edward who spoke with her.

"Alesia, cousin, may I say I feel a light has gone out in this land. I much admired your father. He has left a great legacy for proper regulation by laws."

There was not much more, it was a matter of rapprochement, based on genuine expression. How strange, thought Alesia, that a man with so many antagonists could converse so evenly. Having known him for all of his life she was brought to respond in friendliness. As he spoke of his appreciation of her father's loyalty and support she shook her head lightly in a movement of pleased communication. She was looking closely at Edward and towards Gaveston, basically wondering how these men of their persuasion seemed more cultured and intelligent than others.

# CHAPTER 19

The young woman called Frathesancia stood among the staff at the Savoy Palace awaiting Thomas and Alesia's return. The implication was clear, without the asking. Mabota had deteriorated in health too far. It had coincided with the anxiety in the household about Henry and all the increased work involved, so in part the cause of her exhaustion had not been difficult to analyse. One look by Alesia when she had reached Mabota showed that she was thinner and wasting slowly; unlikely ever to be her real self again. Sorrow and sympathy were not correct.

"Dear Mabota. We're not expecting to leave London for a while, so you can easily get better."

Mabota put a good face on it all. Either they were humouring each other; or maybe Lady Alesia would know.

"I cannot see improvement yet, my lady. It's all been happening so slowly, for so long, but at last it has been sudden. I wish you could rely on me, but please, I beg, think of me of being so regretfully a weak vessel."

There was a long silence. In a sense it was full of thought. Of the past, the links between them as long as either of them could remember. And more than thought, they both knew that the type of life which had made them constant companions must itself continue. That meant Alesia, and Alesia without Mabota. It also meant that Alesia would have to be with someone else, and neither of them wished to broach that subject.

It was done for them. Frathesancia came in with a request from Thomas for Alesia's presence, and as soon left the chamber. Mabota managed a smile.

"She's brighter than me, ma'am. She's more cheerful I think, than I...er...was...I'm only suggesting, of course. I know her mother well. With the allowance I bought herbage from her for the ponies - until I was granted that plot. She - her mother - knows a good few remedies."

"I do wonder if she's not too young for me, but..."

"Ma'am, let me say that you'll sparkle together for a long time - should of course you agree. I am so anxious that you be looked after."

In spite of what Alesia had heard about future movement through the country there was to be a journey North to Pontefract. It was fortunate for planning that the date had not been set. There was much to arrange and much to correct, and much to set in motion.

King Edward borrowed 4000 marks from Henry's executors Nicholas de Reding and Robert de Silkestone, who did not trouble to regard the money as a loan.

While the will was proved in three months by the King's Treasurer, John de Sandale, and Sir Henry le Scroop, the King's clerks trembled at Thomas's fury at their omission of Denbigh Castle and the land of the Cantred from their transfers to the House of Lancaster. No matter that it might have been at the King's instruction. If it was all being reserved for Gaveston, then enough was being said to frighten the King off that. It was tidied up by the autumn.

In a voice that sounded as cold as it did authoritative Alesia informed de Silkestone that the clerks were taking her manors away in addition to those of her father. She had to blame anonymous administration because she could not be certain whose was the error. It became clarified by de Silkestone hesitating.

"Well, ma'am. Your mother's lands.... did they not devolve upon your father, and..."

It was enough.

"You will hear from King Edward."

de Silkestone did. The King's order was that he was not to meddle with Alesia's mother's manors. They were of her personal inheritance.

"I suppose," said Thomas with a sense of doubtful wonder, "I shall have to go through the ceremony of fealty for your father's possessions."

"You will do it very well." With that sentence Alesia was mindful of Gaveston's nickname for him - the play-actor. She was dying to say so, but smothered the doubtful humour.

Thomas cast her a quick glance. He remembered more of her father's last words to him. It was about his three earldoms from his own father and two more from Alesia. That was his great power. So wherefore his trouble? With no preliminary introduction of the subject and no explanation of the build-up in his mind he said:

"Oh, Alesia, we are able and we have to do great things together."

There was no one moment apparent that decided the pattern of life of Thomas and Alesia. It was not a steady one, but which with variations proceeded to disaster for Thomas, calm and buffetings alternating for Alesia. Thomas's influence was increasing; Edward could neither contain nor conclude it until he had built his forces and waited with patient strategy from the strength of his anointed kingship.

A Sunday service included the Song of the Ass, during which a young girl representing the Virgin, with a child in her arms, rode an ass into the Cathedral up to the altar. To Alesia her own barrenness was symbolised, and prayer and prayer and prayer had not defeated it. The Palace minstrels played "C'est la Fin." No-one would guess the bitter aptness of its theme applied to Alesia. 'It is the End. No matter what is said. I must love.'

Just look at Joan, thought Alesia, my stepmother of only a few months, with about my years, already looking all the time as if it was Audley she had wanted to marry. Thomas would be demanding her dower back.

And as to Thomas, there must be hope for success between them. Was she not becoming? There could be no fault there. It was just that love did not seem to thrive. There was so precious little that she could do for him. Where she could be a friend and counsellor her opinion was rejected. His course he had chosen. He did say that he had to take the position which he had done. He had now been formally elected to the office of the Head of the Ordainers, in the symbolic location of the Painted Chamber at Westminster.

While Alesia feared for the future, there could be success in what the Ordainers wished to achieve. She had been rejected when she pointed out that he could equally have chosen to support the King, that the personality of the holder of the Crown was of less importance than the principle. He had the choice, he need not be diverted from it. He could resist the other pressures. He accepted none of this.

All that remained was the routine of household organisation with herself remonstrating against extravagance: against the thousands of pounds spent on entertainment; that this brought no loyalty to him; nor to his cause; nor could it go on without more and more debts.

Odd it was that outwardly, in the minds of others, this all passed for success of marriage and importance, certainly to those classes who could have no hope of emulating the smallest part of it.

At first Frathesancia was one such, with brilliant skill in dressing Alesia's hair to elegance, and living the vicarious pleasure. She ordered the latest headdresses of simple bands, and silken bandages for under the chin. Her Lady Lancaster was the first to wear richly embroidered aprons, completing the youthful fashion.

Thomas was impressed, and seemed thus approachable. Alesia's unobtrusive gentle kneading of his fingers drew his attention to intimacy. There was hope again of consummation of love. It only needed Gaveston adding a nickname to Thomas to bring her to cease her criticisms of Thomas's dangerous course. She put it the other way, however:

"I like the 'Old Hog' better than the other one, dear Thomas."

It had, however, lodged in fury in Thomas's mind. Follow the counsel of Guy of Warwick, yes, Gaveston's 'Black Dog of Arden'. There had been by now Guy's oath sworn to avenge himself.

The Ordainers' influence surely must prevail, Alesia had to think. These proud men cannot forgive; but let us pray.

"One last word, Thomas. Gaveston is not the trouble, he is just the symptom. The King is the cause, and cannot be changed."

Thomas was silent for some time. It was not possible to tell if his thoughts raced through plans to deal with Edward, or whether he was assembling his arguments that the King would have to bow to them. It seemed the latter.

"Alesia, we will prevent Edward having that symptom by sending that man out of the country again. This time for ever. We are considering de Spenser to be put into that office, and Edward will have to accept his administration."

A man of the Lancaster entourage, a distant poor relation. That should be satisfactory.

All seemed well for domestic security as far as Alesia was concerned. Frathesancia arranged for better soaps, from olive oil instead of fat, she prepared much smoother remedies of skin from beet, lettuce and herbs for the winter ills, and ointment from lily of the valley, lard and old wine. She rejuvenated Alesia into the next generation.

Thomas and the Ordainers were moving forward to their goal. Gaveston was exiled. Surrey had come over to the cause. Edward had been coerced to accept the Ordinances. Thomas's homage for his newly inherited lands had gone quite well, in the Convent of the Preaching Friars.

Edward continued confident that his problems had at least been diverted. He showed his unconcern by continuing as though nothing had happened.

Within months it was disaster, for the one reason that Piers Gaveston returned from banishment: Insurrection began, which would continue for ten years. There was intermittent peace from intermittent weakness. Thomas gathered his forces, followed Edward, his Queen Isabella, and Gaveston northwards. He occupied Newcastle-on-Tyne, while they were at Tynemouth. He seized their provisions and treasure and Gaveston's horses and arms. The Royal Party were left alone, but Gaveston fled by sea to Scarborough Castle. He was captured. He was promised immunity by Pembroke and Warrenne, and taken South. At Warwick's orders and in Thomas's presence he was beheaded on Blacklow Hill. His pleas for pity were ignored. The dishonour of the action lost Thomas the support of many earls.

Sir Ebulo le Strange arrived at the Savoy Palace.

"Sir Ebulo?" asked Alesia, with such anxiety that he was for a moment unable to begin. His first suspicion was whether Alesia would have minded about any bad news of Thomas.

"Ma'am" he began formally, not in fact being sure of how closely he should address her, "the lord Thomas has sent me to you. I am to escort you up North."

"That does not sound like all there is to say."

"No, no, it is not." He hesitated at some length. "I can say that Gaveston is dead."

"Good God! I suppose you are saying murdered! Not, oh not, I beg, not by Thomas!"

"No, no, no ma'am. Captured at Scarborough..."

"That had come through to London."

"...at Warwick's orders beheaded. I am sorry, my lady."

"Sorry? Sorry? Why you, sorry? I suppose you mean for what will follow? For Edward's reaction. Is this to be the cause of a final battle? So Thomas wants me out of London? Very well. In haste? This very afternoon? Tomorrow? How long have I?"

Shock at the sudden and unexplained basis of this disturbance began to smother curiosity. Obviously Thomas must carry some responsibility for this happening. And Ebulo himself?

"Ma'am. The lord Thomas, I think I must say to you, and of course to you alone, is preparing to march on London. I am ready now, at least to get half a day's ride North out of London, today, but first light tomorrow would be more seemly. But no later," he added.

"God save us from these follies" muttered Alesia, and crossed herself. "God save us," she repeated out loud.

"The lord Thomas, my lady, is well..."

Alesia questioned with her eyebrows.

"...but he is indeed determined with fury."

With the Devil within him, how could he be well? Alesia was seared with the thought.

"Very well, Sir Ebulo. I must hear more when preparations are made...for the morning. There is no moment to lose now..." she turned to Frathesancia, who at once bobbed and without instruction scurried off. She was aware of whom to fetch, in fact better than her mistress did, because she knew who was left after the constant demands of the Earl upon the staff resources.

"Who else?" asked Alesia of Ebulo at supper. "There are others in London who may like to leave. The lady Joan, for example, - Audley as she now is. Nevertheless she is connected in a way.

"My lady, I have no order for that, but let it be so, if you wish. I can send two or three men, but there is the question of secrecy."

"Yes. Leave it alone. Audley is implicated enough already. No. I've changed my mind. I will send a clerk confidentially. And so..." she added with almost jaunty relief "...to...where, after all?"

"To Pontefract, lady Alesia."

It was but few minutes after dawn that they set off, a party in all of a few dozen, not to be too obtrusive. London declared for the King, closed the gates, and frustrated the attempted takeover.

By December Papal Legates had arranged some apparent peace between Edward and his unruly subject. Thomas, Earl of Lancaster had been losing cards to play. The murder of Gaveston continued to reduce the number of his supporters - because it had been against his word, his safe-conduct. Further, Isabella had given birth to a new Edward, which established a future focus. Thomas returned the captured goods and jewels to Richard Damory, the King's Steward. He occupied himself in the North by building Dunstanburgh Castle, and in the Midlands by improving Kenilworth.

Alesia travelled with Thomas on an inspection journey to Scarborough; she stayed at the castle of Pickering. In a small way she insisted on some improvement to try to bring it to the standard of her beloved Bolingbroke.

"I have received a letter from Joan" said Alesia one afternoon. She sounded at once submissive and hopefully insistent. "She would like me to join her shortly, in Nottinghamshire, at their manor of Knesale. It is for the birth she is expecting."

Alesia awaited any reaction, which came as straightforward agreement.

"I am much away in the North these months. Since my refusal to attend Parliament last year I expect I will again this year. Edward will also have to pardon others, of course, even down to le Strange and Willoughby."

"Oh, Thomas, no pardons yet for that Gaveston affair colours it all. Anyway, surely you are safe here. Now Pontefract is the centre of your affairs it seems to be working well."

"Yes, as much as sheriffs follow Edward's orders. I understand he's going to appoint them, and stop their being elected."

"There is more in this letter... more but not about State matters, may I say. Just that Edward has taken Joan's lands away - she thinks it is because she married without a licence."

"And in haste!" Thomas laughed, in faintly jealous wonder. "Yes, go and see your stepmother, of course. As to the lands, young James has vast estates. What the devil is Edward going to do with Joan's? They really should be mine in that situation."

"de Spenser?"

He surprised Alesia by his response:

"I would possibly not object." He felt pleased about his man in the Royal Household having become so accepted.

Alesia had heard gossip about the relationship of King and his new official. Seemingly no-one had dared to tell Thomas, and this was not the moment.

"Oh, Alesia" were the first fervent words of Joan to her as soon as she arrived at Knesale Manor. The actual words were irrelevant in conveying relief and pleasure.

"A thousand thanks for coming. More than that in fact. I know it's nice to be quiet, but a friend is more than myriads of assistants. There's a whole gang of them."

"James? I saw him a few weeks ago further north."

"James? Yes, he came here with me. He will be back soon. Anyway, I am so glad you are here. Our talk can clarify the matters men use such force to arrange."

"I think you should worry most about that wee babe striving to be out in the open air."

"Not quite yet, dear Alesia."

There were a few weeks to pass before Joan was expected to produce the new Audley. Her own feelings were simply for her own comfort, and resentment at her being foisted on to the small manor of Knesale. It was particularly infuriating, because when her husband James had to travel further north with King Edward, she had quite airily assured him that she was perfectly capable of getting back to

London. Not so for Alesia:

"Dear Joan, I really do prefer manors to castles. You have seen as many as I have..."

"No, no Alesia, it is a bit different with me, for until I married your father I envied those who lived in the best castle quarters. My own experience is brief. Here I feel pushed aside. James has so much that I am ashamed to be dumped here, without him."

"I think, then, I must tell you what I know. I beg you, Joan, be assured that it is for your benefit."

"It all makes me want to see my husband now. I do not wish to understand."

"Dear Joan. Of course from my own experience I can tell you nothing. Nothing, that is, except the material background. That's all I have ever got to know."

"I know also that bit about it being safe here. But why? And is it true? Why cannot James leave the King?"

"Better not, Joan. Oh dear, what can I say? You do this birth for love. For love of James. Yet more than that, if your child is a boy, he is a symbol of the Audley future. That colours the future of the child."

Joan looked more directly into Alesia's face. Yes, it seemed that what she said she had believed. Was she having this child for James? She pondered. It seemed to be more her own desire, but she wanted it to be by James. Alesia was stating an idealistic theory. Bless her, let her so dream. In any case, it all seemed to be initiated - the power, the joy, the need, the pain - by a force outside oneself.

Collecting herself, Joan explained that James was at present neither drawn to nor repelled from either side. To be with the King when summoned was conventional. James would continue thus, until he had to choose his bit either way.

"Edward already suspects his choice. I understand, but I do curse the situation."

Alesia felt that she could say more, but that it was not necessary, indeed imprudent. Audley had not shown his hand very strongly.

Joan, continuing in conversation, stated how much she found Alesia's company to be so calming. Maybe, thought Alesia, but for herself any straightforward help which she could give was limited. The women in Knesale seemed most senisble in the situation, certainly they were experienced, to her relief.

"My contribution, Joan, has been only to accompany you on walks across the meadows, and reading to you. If that has been good, then I am happy to have helped."

At the right time it was all over; Joan was lying comfortably, a new James Audley close by. She laughed:

"Your company was my stay. There was also the daily news I gleaned from looking at my reflection in the pond down the hill. We must walk there again, but of course I cannot for a few days. And I did not mean going down there only to check on the change in my reflection in the water."

In those days, with Frathesancia being messenger and helpmeet, Alesia saw to the maintenance of the standards of the household. The excitement was over. The new life was the new focus. Adoring visitors from the neighbourhood followed the household in turning their eyes to the baby James, to the bewilderment of pets suddenly deprived of obvious affection. And to the beginnings of a depression in Alesia which she could not shake off. She explored her mind to eliminate jealousy, she essayed all she could to be pleased for the Audleys. No, it was not the fuss from others which matterred, for she generally had enough of that. She was troubled of herself. Perhaps it had been a mistake to be so close to this occasion. Thus was what she herself had been married for. She called for Frathesancia to accompany her on a walk.

It was to ease her mind, to be associated with what had occurred, that drew her along the path across the meadows to the pond. There it coolly lay, reflecting grasses and trees, and sun and clouds, in parts a shining varnish on the earth below its surface.

She knelt to give better reflection of herself. It brought her back to the mental acceptance of the childless state so long ingrained after visiting Mary of York. Why, of why then, did her body always try to bring her hope? By way of some rationale of this tarrying or this contemplation she just said to Frathesancia:

"James is a lovely baby."

There had been nothing connected with such a thought that had been obvious in this gentle walk, but Frathesancia tried to join her thoughts to the occasion:

"Yes, my lady. There's life in the family yet."

With a sudden bitter coldness that stultified her servant, Alesia pierced her with one word:

"Frathesancia!" and the shout emanating through the teeth transfixed her.

"Get me a switch from that hedge. There's one, break it off! On your knees, lean over that twisted branch!"

With astonishment at this new phenomenon, Frathesancia, terrified, got down. On her back came the lash of that switch. Alesia felt inside that she wished that she were stronger.

"Bare your back!... Quicker!"

It was satisfying that the spurs of the hawthorn now scraped red marks. What was that phrase in court, thought Alesia, '...until her back be bloody.' It stimulated her. It was a good, strong and whippy switch. She would have sought another if it had not been so. It crossed her mind to get an even better one, but her emotion began to tire. Most of Frathesancia's clothing was now so disarranged that it afforded no protection. She was ordered to stand up, and as her clothes fell to the ground she thus stood naked.

The view of her pretty body could at this moment elicit either praise or envy, cessation or further attack. As Frathesancia stood by the water, framed in a background of nature to complement her form, image of the poverty of her own feminine life came before her. Alesia whipped her into the pond, and Frathesancia fell.

Emotion expired, hysteria having no further force, Alesia collapsed upon the grass. She gasped for breath. She gasped for a role.

There was no-one to comfort them except each other.

Poor Frathesancia. All Alesia's anger evaporated. It had surged, and at its end she was calmer than before. All that remained was wonder, in the sort of peace that came from exhaustion, a peace tainted with guilt. Frathesancia had accidentally phrased a thought which released barbed unrequited tensions. Alesia comforted her the more. When they reached Joan's chamber, seeing her and James again, Alesia had become quite calm. She had had her maid, young enough to be her daughter, helpless in her arms. To Joan she said:

"The life I have to look after is Thomas's. No other. I have no other anxiety in life. We are of one family with King Edward, and all is bent for each other's destruction. Thomas still seems to want my support, or at least he needs it."

Some days later they parted, Joan to the south, Alesia travelling with her as far as Leicester, there to rejoin Thomas.

Any influence that she thought she may have had over him had, however, waned further. He was totally uninfluenced by Edward's pardoning him at last for his part in the beheading of Gaveston. Alesia spoke to le Strange.

"It included you, Ebulo, and Willoughby, so surely it is all a conciliatory gesture?"

"Not between those, Alesia, who think only in terms of gaining or losing points in a power game. Fortunately, you yourself are on all sides and none..."

Alesia looked anxious in being openly categorised in this struggle at all.

"...because of Thomas your husband; on the other flank there are your close family connections with Robert Clifford and Hereford who are still prepared to obey the King; then Pembroke who is urging a middle party to keep everybody apart."

"One must suppose that I will be linked with Thomas."

"Many know that you are not, Alesia. You have been heard more than once remonstrating with him. Excuse me for saying so, but you should know that your desire for harmony is well known."

"I have urged Thomas many times that he can only lose. Also I have tried to stop him throwing his patrimony away on life grants to so called supporters, which I imagine was why he brought all his administration here from Bolingbroke."

"Yet Thomas thinks he's influencing Edward. After all, Pembroke was allowed to give him New Temple and Ficket's Croft, which enlarged his influence on the law."

"We mustn't say too much further, Alesia, but this stalking game will go on until one side thinks itself strong enough to strike. Inconveniencing each other is useless. There is only one man on either side, in essence. Neither of them is likely to do anything directly to the other, and their supporters change constantly."

"Thomas is refusing to go to Scotland with Edward."

"Yes, and he is preventing me from going, but Hereford and Clifford will be there. Surrey also refused. It is a peculiar mix and it can go on for a long time."

The period of antagonism extended because Edward then lost the Battle of Bannockburn. With necessary but agonising patience he had to re-build the power base he had assembled.

Thomas was now the most powerful person in England. These should then have been happy years. He and Alesia were in their early thirties. While his present policy might have been achievable, the intimidation of Parliament was not the way. Incompetence was compounded in that the ultimate writ of power was still with Edward as King.

Thomas was appointed as King's Lieutenant and Captain of all forces aginst the Scots. It was the result of a conference called at Doncaster by him, with Archbishop Greenfield of York and a committee assembled by Edward to treat with him; all of it steering through the need to contain Thomas, and to prevent him getting underhand Scottish assistance. It helped to maintain Edward's powers, as had his enacting that sheriffs should be appointed by himself.

"Still jockeying for position, in my opinion."

"Is either side ever satisfied, Ebulo? I really am afraid things are getting worse."

"Yes. Edward has lost authority, and the lord Thomas has not achieved it, because he can only work through the Crown."

Some such statements had been urged by several barons and knights upon Ebulo le Strange to be made to the lady Alesia. It was all meant to get through to Thomas that the thousands of men under his command were no substitute for the basic power of kingship; that the orders of a puppet King would not, and already were not, being followed, whether they came from the Ordainers or not.

Alesia thought that they had conversed far enough, interested though she was in the subject, and more so in the persona of Sir Ebulo. She did, however, continue on one matter:

"Edward was much offended at Pentecost, and that does not help for peace, though it was nothing to do with Thomas."

"The Westminster Hall incident? I have heard something of it, probably at third hand. It does show how daring people can become, if the story reached me correctly."*

"I felt really sorry for Edward. The woman came into the Hall on a horse and with extravagant respect gave a note to him. He read it and found it nothing other than insulting. I was nearby, of course. It was an awful moment. She rode out quickly and will never be seen again. She was dressed as a minstrel, which was why she was allowed in, I suppose."

Thomas had also found cause for offence, by Edward. Alesia reluctantly spoke about it:

"For God's sake, Thomas, does it matter? He has a wife; if she cannot control him, how can you? She is closer to him, and daily. She dislikes him just as much as you do. You can do nothing. For the Lord's sake keep your interests separate. Hold on to your own, our own. The country is getting in a worse state every day. Now you've banished de Spenser. How does that help? You always said he was a good administrator."

"My man he was then. Now as Edward's he is as bad as Gaveston, receiving lands just like him, and taking authority away from us as before...."

With spitting bitterness Thomas continued -

"...what I didn't know was that he also has the same love habits as Gaveston."

From the mouthing of each word it was clear that any conciliation between the King and Earl Thomas was getting to be more difficult. To Alesia it showed equally clearly that she could persuade Thomas of nothing.

"I am sorry, my dear Thomas; I really am sorry."

He looked towards her more calmly, with a more communicative attitude.

"So, Alesia, am I. Yes, I am. I can say so with feeling, for you, for me, for us. I would much prefer peace. And normality."

Alesia noticed with developing warmth within herself that his eyes showed his words to be genuine. The dream of their being in harmony then shattered in moments; to their mutual regret, if the kindly tone of Thomas's next utterance was given their hopeful meaning:

"Alesia dear, I have to say that you should please travel south again. This time I suggest to one of your own manors, such as Canford..."

Startled, Alesia asked, briefly - "But why?"

She became afraid. She could not do other than rush to embrace him close.

"Thomas, what are you doing now? All this is useless. We can live in dignity without fighting unnecessary battles. Is this the end? Who against? Not Edward himself of course?"

He was not yielding. She disengaged herself from him. She turned to him again.

"I know. The de Spensers possessions. Just as with Gaveston. Pillaging land, killing peasants, driving off cattle. What the devil for?"

"Just that over thirty barons have put me into the lead for something like that."

"You're already scrimmaging with Adam Banastre in Lancashire. I warn you again."

"This time Hereford and Audley are coming..."

"Audley!"

"Yes, over that land matter of Joan's. Also he's got to know the real Edward."

"And Audley has such large estates I doubt if he could recite where they all are."

"Mortimer and Clifford are also..."

"The young Clifford, over on your side is he, after his father was for Edward. Just because of Edward's bad generalship, but..."

She was going to retort that it was no worse than Thomas's, but changed the sentence to:

"...as for Mortimer, I expect Isabella has persuaded him."

"You are beginning to understand."

"Very well, Thomas, I shall be moving to Canford shortly."

Alesia informed Thomas thus, in a cool manner, attempting to sound matter-of-fact. It was one of those occasions when they were together in the Savoy Palace, for a few weeks. Now it was after Christmas, heralding the New Year. They were together only in the sense that they occupied the same building, which in effect held both their households. They were both there because they had to be, to uphold to society that they were man and wife. Perhaps Alesia's moving to her late mother's manor in Dorset would not reveal too much.

Thomas, aware of little but coldness in her manner towards him, took the information as demonstrating the final future lack of warmth. He but asked:

"When?"

"It depends on the weather. As soon as the heavens promise some dry days."

"You will need escorting, and I will release le Strange if he would be suitable."

A quick inadvertent look from Alesia found no innuendo in his tone nor in his expression. She affected a nonchalant expression.

"Thank you, Thomas. He can seek you out afterwards."

This last sentence was indicative of trying to dismiss her own thoughts and growing love for Ebulo le Strange. It was not, however, that which was on Thomas's mind.

"I am doing only that which received your father's approval. Why is that wrong for you?"

"You are in revolt against the Crown."

"Where else could it all lead? You know perfectly well that nothing else will change the present state of things in this benighted land. Benighted because of him."

"Ten years have changed little."

"Edward has to be stopped."

"Very well, and what has to be started?"

"The barons..."

"Edward has no real power against us..."

"He takes lands on pretexts for his favourites."

"From those who revolt against him."

"So far."

"Never. Thomas, you are riding straight into danger. The cards are his, the people are his..."

"Those damned people! He fawns them to power against the traditional holders of office!"

"Nevertheless, they are too firmly established, and they do give strength. Once more I say to you Thomas. Stop. Wait."

"Wait! For what? Edward to govern properly? Through what council and what lords?"

Alesia sighed deeply. Thomas was running himself into a noose, almost figuratively. He could not win.

"For the last time, as perhaps it has to be, Thomas, let me say to you that you have not the strength, nor the support, to win. To be absolutely clear, you have neither the full aim of kingship, nor a majority of barons with you. Some time ago you were horrified when I asked why you did not kill the King. I say further that you will never influence him at all. I do not think my father realised that he himself was still considering the first Edward, who shared the same aims, and at least discussed matters. This one does not. He never will. You have sterilised his power once. It did no good. He is waiting. So you wait. Isabella is against him. There is a son..."

"The son is only about six years old. Even if he ever will be any good, as the son of this King, how long am I meant to play blindman's buff?"

"Preserve what you have, what we have."

"I cannot do only that. There are pressures, and supporters, too many to ignore."

"Not enough. A handful. The rest form a sluggish audience. There is not even from you a show of defence against the country's enemy, the Scots. Their influence reaches as far south as the Humber. Your castle of Pickering is in effect sterile."

Thomas had had the role of State protector forced upon him. It suited his traditionalist attitude. It fitted it the closer because he felt within himself that he had to prove the worth of his family line. Wife or no wife, his role had become conjoined with his self respect.

"The scots?" he said, with hesitation emanating from his conscience. He spoke loudly to insist his course to be right, and to avoid, even as it revealed, his attempted connections with them.

"Wait. Wait. Any more danger and others will join you. I know there is a slumbering disaffection, but you are too soon."

"Will you join me... us, perhaps?" Thomas sought personal information, for assessing their own relative position was one thing, but knowing it clearly from Alesia's lips would give or kill hope, would set his responsibilities, would perhaps free self-doubts.

"Sir. And I call you that. I am little or no help to you. For my own safety I must keep other arrows in my quiver. I am not prepared to be dragged down. You frighten me... no, not personally... with your public actions. I can be no part of them from now."

"Unless I fully agree with you and act as you direct" - which was uttered by Thomas with the scorn of feeling depreciated.

Alesia hesitated as to whether to proceed further, and remained for some moments silent. She could not deal with him. He commanded with bombast, with force because he could not assimilate any other point of view.

"There is that other reason, which I repeat" she attempted, and then her thought gathered momentum. "Indeed, more than one other. You are too soon with your opposing the King. You must not bring it to finality. He has not weakened one iota, in spite of all your efforts..."

"Ten years! Ten years it has been of Edward's reign! How long, then?"

"You will never be convinced, that is why I am no use to you. And because I will not share your ruin."

"Alright. You say wait. For what? There is in my opinion much strength to control Edward. That is as far as anyone can go. I am supported by Hereford, ...and ..." He must be thinking of Warwick's untimely death, after he had abandoned the cause. It struck Alesia with horror - was Thomas responsible? Turning more towards her, and moderating his attitude, Thomas continued:

"It is I who has to be the leader. A proper King and all this would not be."

"Give Isabella time to act in concert. She is more vituperative about Edward than you are."

"A wife, against her husband. She hisses but how can she strike? Except that is, by help from France. That threat is what this Edward is bringing upon us."

It was an interpretation which Alesia had not considered. In fact, all rested on the power of the King. No-one was prepared to remove that from Edward, nor Edward from it.

The silence which ensued, for lack of response from Alesia, was broken quite soon, by Thomas.

"I asked you to go to Canford for your own peace of mind."

"There was another reason for my agreement, which I have not yet mentioned."

Thomas just raised his eyebrows in enquiry.

"I know I have failed you in giving you no heirs. I am deeply sorry and I have prayed much and long for you in this regard. Never have I received back hope nor calming of my spirit. It would have helped you, though, Thomas, as well as me. You would have integrated with things as they are, and looked longer ahead."

"Heavens! Is that the result of such?"

He nearly aded that he hadn't noticed it among others, but held the words unspoken, for he remembered at once that here it was his wife Alesia to whom he was speaking, and that it had been Joan Ploucoun who had borne a son. Alesia was doing her best to think of some other matter, the only diversion coming to mind was, however, to run her fingers heavily along the surface of the table by her, as though rearranging items on it. But what had to be said would not be stopped. Her full emotion could have shouted it out loud and bitterly, but the words emanated in a penetrating softness.

"He did not have to be called John of Lancaster."

There was nothing that Thomas could find to be worth saying. What would give a suitable ring? That he was not there at that time, nor heard of it until it was all done. That it could be changed, but perhaps that would now make for general derision. Alesia had not objected to the fact, nor to the brief liaison.

"It makes me as nothing." Her voice gave the comment without colour, as an announcement without communication. It showed a state which could not be rebuilt together. For as much consideration of all the aspects of their present relationship that Thomas could give, he quickly gave. The sole outward sign was that his head lent on his hand, his elbow on the table. It was beyond him to change course, with all the outside persons who needed him. No succinct analysis or persuasive statement came to his mind. Without offering a different future no word of affection seemed to have point. Exchange of a look towards each other expressed and showed regret that it was now as it was. With lowered head Thomas slowly rubbed his chin on the back of his hand. He did not seem able to utter concerning 'of Lancaster'. Alesia could not bring herself to extend a hand to touch.

Thomas rose and slowly left the chamber, to continue what he saw as, and emotionally was committed to, his inevitable role as Earl of Lancaster, Leicester, and Lincoln, Derby, and Salisbury, and thereby the leader of the barons against the King his cousin. Leader, because in his office of great power he appeared strong, enduring, and secure against the outside world.

Alesia his Countess remained sitting for a very long time, harbouring much uncertainty as to whether she could ever rebuild herself as a woman with self-respect.

Before his departure in the morning Thomas sought Alesia, to approach her with a final question. It seemed necessary to convince himself that her determination was as clear and cold as its result would indicate. He spoke in a dulled tone which showed fear of inevitable despair. His wife's reply was as unequivocal as her attitude the previous evening, yet at its end it offered a solution.

"...I will not face these dangers which you bring upon us, by your own doing and by none other. All will be forgiven, with love, if you will return to the King's allegiance..." she saw his face begin to show anger

"...at the least to the principle of heriditary kingship."

"How, then. What happens then?"

"You can support the kingdom by taking arms against its enemies, instead of fighting the kingdom itself."

"I am an enemy of the King, am I, of the kingdom? It is he who will not support his realm against his enemies."

"My father supported the kingdom."

"Your father did not have the kingdom, nor his baronies and lands and honors eroded away by dandies and commoners behind his back, as lords have today. I have conciliated, and been ridden over for my pains."

"My course is clear," he added.

There was no point in proceeding further in conversation together, except.. Alesia looked up towards Thomas. She had known him a long time, certainly close enough to be now able to assess the basis of his demeanor. There seemed to her to be an absence of fear in his bearing. It was not like him to be totally secretive about matters which concerned him, certainly not to major ones. She had better have a further word:

"You have said nothing about Surrey."

"Should I?"

"Have you no spies?"

"Stop the taunts!"

"Thomas, you do not know! Or you ignore. Surrey has gone over to the King."

From his expression it was clear that to calm him it was vital to explain in full. Alesia went on without a noticeable break.

"Surely the gathering of Surrey's forces, with Edward's connivance, has come to your notice? They are to attack you. Edward has wanted to do this before, as I have tried to convince you. Leaving aside all the orders he issues which you disobey, he cannot have a rebel with such power in the realm."

"How in the devil's name can you say all this? Where have you come across this talk?"

"Thomas, Thomas, I told you years ago I would hear more than you would. I will start again - Edward has ordered Surrey to attack you if you take up arms. Obviously gathering men will take time. You know that."

"My question was - where did you learn this?"

Alesia had hoped that her information, and the concern in her warnings would have brought Thomas closer to her. There had come no attitude other than that of the organising of his received ambitions.

It was not for that, however, that Alesia became all obedience, and had agreed to travel to Canford within days. What she did understand was that Thomas did have a spark of consideration for her in that she should go to a place of safety. At the moment of bidding goodbye she saw in Thomas that he had embraced this whole mission to become part of himself. He had a self-important look, with little life in it, calm and firm - as though he was being venerated, a mast of a lying-in-state.

"Oh, Thomas," prayed Alesia in silence, "if you gave me all I would give you all and everything of me. My love has not been diverted to children; it could be for you alone."

Edward summoned barons, the acceptances indicating that his support against Thomas had grown. Warrenne, Earl of Surrey, had indeed gone over to the King, and was given the command to defeat Thomas's army. The commitment of minds and men to the King's cause did, however, withdraw at the point of decision to attack. Sufficient strength did not arise in purpose or in numbers. This should have been the time to cease all hostilities, but Thomas noted only the failure, and not that their numbers were greater than before. Nor could it be left at this juncture by the King. This shadowy struggle was at an intermediate stage. Sooner or later Edward would gather the power to act from his own personally safe position. Since Thomas was discrediting the King by despoiling de Spenser estates, Surrey and Edward decided to discredit Thomas, by doing something which did lie within their power.

They plotted to capture Alesia.

Ladies of the time of Edward I

# CHAPTER 20

At Canford life had little stimulus. Perhaps this should have been comforting, but the vacuum filled with no more than the mists and the clarity of weather and rumour.

"Come, be of better cheer, ma'am."

Frathesancia's request was the best that she could do. Even she thought that it was inadequate, but on that grey morning she herself was unable to be more constructive. The mist had surrounded Canford. Perhaps it came from the sea, for it was tangy and penetrating enough; perhaps it covered the County of Dorset. For whatever, Alesia had even prayed in an inhibited way before eating at all that day.

"Frathesancia", Alesia spoke in an explanatory tone: "Even the rumours of the last few weeks have faded into nothing. The anticipation brought by the sun's rising is before long turned into nothingness by its inexorable retreat down westwards."

"I am sure the Lord Thomas will fetch you, milady."

Unspoken as it had been, it was known that Alesia was still earnestly in hope of influencing Thomas to be loyal to the Crown, but she replied without conviction:

"If you want a prophecy from me, Frathesancia, there can be only one. It is that my lord Thomas will carry on as he ever did, and that is on the futile line of trying to force a change in Edward's mind and attitude. They co-operated once before only because Edward was not strong enough after the defeat at Bannockburn. The King is playing the lord Thomas as a salmon fish is fought with taut and slack line."

Alesia could only sit and wait for termination of this cumbersome insurrection centred on her husband. And in her isolation waiting meant simply not knowing of any communications until the messenger's horse's hooves were padding on the grass by the manor itself. Recreation came from intermittent entertainment of the knights and ladies of the county. Until one day, during one of these gatherings, there arrived one knight, and entourage, the size of which induced the staff to usher him into the throng without question. On meeting his hostess, Alesia realised that she knew him, slight though that knowledge was. It looked like some trickery, too. At least it would be enlivening, and there seemed to be no violent intention. The poor fellow was more than usually polite.

Richard de St. Martin, slightly deformed and shrunken in stature, was a retainer of the Earl of Surrey. What vain thoughts he had, made it appear that he thought he was unrecognised.

"I am on the way to nowhere but here my Lady Alesia, to speak to you on behalf of the realm."

"I was not aware that I had any power over such a cause, Sir Richard."

"Not yet, ma'am, but such can be given to you."

de St. Martin seemed pleased with that answer; at least, his face twitched to nearly a smile. Short lived as that was, he relaxed to some degree. It was still, to Alesia, an occasion to wait for some explanation of his unshared pleasure, at the same time to nod or gesture to others to maintain the atmosphere.

"I come from the King."

"And from Lord Surrey presumably" rejoined Alesia. She wished that she had not. It did not matter that de St. Martin was neatly taken aback; it was that in later course it might have had more effect, and it was knowledge which was protecting her.

"You should know that more than once I have seen you among his household" added Alesia. "Let us talk later, I have to be busy now."

So de St. Martin stayed silent. He had a task to perform, and being known was perhaps no detriment for it. His worry, indeed a strong feeling that put him off balance, was his suspicion that he always stood out only because of his deformity. He went outside, feeling at least accepted for the moment. The roasting oxen, the mulling ale, all the sustenance was there, and many guests collected it and stayed to consume it in the grounds. Strangely, he melted into the general hubbub, conversing with some, who did not seem surprised at his presence. Alesia's relief that he was fitting in to the scene was jolted severely at the end. Of course he could join in. When de St. Martin came to talk to her again, after the party had concluded, half a dozen knights remained standing by. He opened by saying:

"Lady Alesia, I have come to talk about your ability to help the King to rule. He has a request to make."

He improved his tone to what he hoped was persuasive and conciliatory.

"I am not here to rush any matters, nor to force you into any agreement that you do not wish to make. The Lord Edward knows full well the support of your family for generations past for the principles of authority...."

Alesia made to speak, but he had one more sentence, which he produced with some portent.

"... The King knows why you are alone down here, and thus is himself assured that you will listen to his message."

"Edward says thus that he knows much of me. Perhaps. I know much also of him. So tell me now what is this proposition, and you need not beat round the bush. I believe I have tried all that a woman can do to bring her husband to her way of thinking."

"It is read so, milady. I hope, however, that you will agree to more."

"You hope? Yourself? We'll see. And if I do not?"

"Ma'am, that is for King Edward."

"You have men-at-arms with you, more than befit your rank. Are those knights outside friends of mine or yours? In fact in number your escort is suitable enough for me."

"Ma'am, you go quickly on such a matter. Yes, I have been told to persuade you to come to London."

Alesia, stock still, could hope only that her fears had not become obvious. They had been growing as she had made guesses as to the visit's purpose. So she was not as far away from the turbulence of politics as she had hoped.

"What more, then, it cannot be just what you say, with all this detail preparation."

In order to conciliate, but more to hide what he thought might be a change in his approach, de St. Martin bowed. He knew that he was unlikely to be able to force the lady Alesia to travel to London, and she would certainly not go if she knew the whole purport. With an alertness which surprised himself, he simply lied:

"That is all of which I am apprised, ma'am."

His voice was more off-key than it had already sounded. Alesia preferred the long silence which followed. It was ventured to her that she could hardly refuse to show her loyalty to the throne. Alesia pondered.

"The court must be full of more news than I get down here at Canford."

"No doubt, ma'am, as among your friends. And rumours by the score. For myself I am somewhat down the line in receiving them."

With that last word, in this particular instance not true, Alesia decided that she might as well travel with him. Anything in fact, to improve the position she was in, being without husband, without status, without trust. Perhaps a voluntary gesture towards the King would work to stay Thomas's hand.

Out of fear and distrust she found herself saying:

"You may send away these conspirators of yours, de St. Martin. The sight of six Judas Iscariots is too much for me."

Alesia had heard from gossip at her party that Surrey had lost his courage on being ordered by the King to attack Thomas, and had withdrawn. She was beginning to feel elevated by growing contempt. With derision she turned to de St. Martin:

"So now you attack me."

"I do not like it, ma'am" was Frathesancia's clear opinion. "It's got a strange mark on it."

On being told to have preparations made for the journey, secretary Halton appeared full of doubt, but could not state his reasons precisely.

Alesia herself began to wonder when it became clear that she would be escorted alone with just her maid.

"After all, Frathesancia, I have not now the men here to do it, nor do I know the way. Surely I have only to talk and explain, and perhaps once again to urge Thomas to conform?"

It was not a question that the maid was likely to answer. It was her feelings. Maybe, however, they were wrong.

Two days later, with a gesture that was designed to please, and to hide what was really in his mind, de St. Martin ushered Alesia to a litter, bedecked in fine new curtains. Even the pony for her maid was clean and well chosen. It was too late to act on any suspicions. This preparation may be no more than fitting to her rank. It was even too late to demand to ride instead.

What was this business? The King, and Surrey, were they taking her for safety; or worse, as a hostage. She should have taken refuge in France or Italy - yes this would have been the prudent time to visit Saluzzo. Or would that have alienated Edward the more?

"Stay by me, Frathesancia." Then she whispered as best she could: "I wonder, has Thomas been captured? Perhaps it was wrong about Surrey retreating." Frathesancia gave a short nod, indicating thus that she would keep alert on that matter.

The constant attention and concern for Alesia's welfare and comfort would have done de St. Martin a great deal of good if in any way he had been an attractive character.

As it turned out, the journey was not difficult for him. The group attracted no more than the usual glances from villagers and any passers by. Even the local Canford folk had scarcely stood and looked with more than usual interest. The Lady Alesia was said to be off to see the King. Perhaps they thought that for that aim there should be more show, but Lady Alesia was like that.

She was, but friendliness went with it, and the soldiers of the escort were uncommunicative. No news could be reported to her by Frathesancia because they spoke of none. According to such folk as were around when they ate or spent the night, the Lord Lancaster was far away in the Midlands. Perhaps the North. Raising the country. Gathering the Scots. Recruiting the Welsh. The French were coming. For the people. When they were told that the Countess of Lancaster herself was here and would like to know more, or indeed as much, consternation halted the gossip.

Tired of profitless speculation, and for herself with no new thought over which to mull, it was a surprise to halt one day, and Frathesancia to open the curtain of the litter wide. At the same moment, she cried out:

"Look ma'am - nothing but us - they've gone."

"Impossible!"

"They've gone, ma'am, run off, ridden off!"

Still this seemed unbelievable.

"Impossible!"

Enough had been heard to arouse Alesia to look further round. She had been dozing, uninterested by the litter just halting. The muttering of a few men nearby had neither aroused her curiosity nor made her impatient. Those men, however, turned out to be her escort, and their subject had been her abandonment at the roadside. Frathesancia steadied the litter and helped her mistress to get to the ground, both of them the while looking all round in wonderment.

"Surely this cannot be what they mean to do, ma'am, to leave us here? Is it just a kidnap, to be abandoned out of devilment?" And with a second thought:

"They've left the litter horses, so we could go on. Or back to Canford" she added with cynical amusement.

"I cannot even think. Nothing to see except a hawk, a rabbit, and a hovel up that lane. Come, Sancy, which way did they go, and what were they saying? I was half asleep."

"In fact, ma'am, they gathered away from me, so I don't know what they were saying, nor what they were on about. It was sudden; one of them had started it with de St. Martin."

"They can't have had orders to stop here, though. It's nowhere."

"As to where they went, it was back there, into the sunlight, towards those woods. After that I was dazzled and I couldn't see much."

Alesia scanned again the hovel, the road in both directions, the fields, the trees. Nothing other than rural peace was apparent, except for - Heavens! - a phalanx of persons moving with standards unfurled. The sight of them caused her some anxiety.

"Would we be having a new escort, milady?"

"Nothing was said about that; at the beginning, that is. Nor before these men left. But surely they cannot have acted without instructions. Yet you say one of them spoke to de St. Martin, and then things happened."

"Yes, ma'am. He came from up front."

"Up front? How far ahead?"

"How far, ma'am? Well, a furlong maybe  Whispers, then they were off. Seemed anywhere from the direction of those people."

People? Not soldiers? To Frathesancia's amazement and relief her mistress began to giggle.

"It is the day of the Feast of the Ascension, Frathesancia."

Priests and people there were, moving slowly in a waving line, intent on plodding along the earthy lane and chanting the Litany. Content as they continued in their state, they scarce looked left or right, but only where their feet were next to tread. If a glance was cast to the two horses, the litter and the two women, then it was as furtive to be unnoticeable. Yet Alesia and Frathesancia both saw fit to acknowledge the passing of this procession by crossing themselves, standing quietly.

"I can see Surrey's men coming back, ma'am."

Alesia turned, having been examining the litter fastenings to see if they could achieve a horse to ride in addition to Frathesancia's pony. They couldn't stay here all day. She could now hear...

Her thoughts trailed off, diverted with the shock of the words...Surrey's men! Of course they were, and that she already knew; but the easy way in which her servant had uttered them brought them nearer to reality. How confident she had been, how now oppressed with doubt and fear. Where were they actually travelling? From the sun, north eastwards in general. Perhaps this was a genuine escorted trip to London and not a capture, then.

The doubt and increasing insecurity brought on an inner cursing that she had not made quicker from the start to escape. But whither? Sensibly to her husband. That would be to join his revolt. Was, however, it better with the King? What possible good could Surrey propose for her? Abducted! Just as one of her mother's forebears, Maud, and from Canford, too. That thought strengthened her, as being just something one had to get through. There was pleasure in her bitter emotion as the escort all returned.

"Your soul, de St. Martin is in poor order if you cannot abide the sight of priests in procession. Are all your men equally such sinners? That cortege certainly seemed more disciplined than that you have with you. Does the Lesser Litany especially upset you before the Feast of the Ascension?"

There was no rejoinder, only the greater busying about to restart the group in some order.

"If I do not wish to travel with you, what then? I do not feel safe with such a crew."

de St. Martin sat stilly on his horse, with an air of further visual checking that all was prepared. He was to make no remark. Unaccustomed to subtlety, he yet could think of no action except to await the initiative of the lady.

Alesia pondered, the while upon her feet. Frathesancia sensed that she needed assistance. A movement to prevent it by a trooper was waved aside by de St. Martin. They had to travel as before.

Hesitating while seeking for a clarification, Alesia had by now restored her own pride. She kept the feeling to herself. What had become so clear about the procession was simply that the escort had thought that they were men of Thomas's, patrolling in the search for her. This small moment of power-play having passed, Alesia now knew one thing only. This was an abduction plot; it boded nothing but ill; she was Surrey's prisoner.

So, having left Thomas so as to demonstrate her own loyalty to the Kingdom had not been enough. Alesia could not think her way through any other course, past or present, that would be better. She had for herself and her loyalty to the state to leave her husband; in France she would have had to urge the French against Edward, in concert with his own wife. In Italy she would only be tolerated as a failure by a distant Saluzzo cousin. If living quietly away from all the intrigue was wrong, then what was right? At an opportunity she asked de St. Martin:

"Where are we going?"

After some hesitation, which of itself confirmed her fears, he replied:

"You ask directly, ma'am. Just now to Reigate. My Lord Surrey's castle. But that is just a resting place on the route."

"Very well. Tell me again, why I am being taken."

"One understands, I say again, that there is some service that your ladyship can provide for the King."

If any relief could have been conjured from that arrangement with Edward, Alesia was aware at least that it did not mean service by her body.

"What service? I have not seen my lord Thomas for many weeks."

de St. Martin looked towards her, in sharp surprise. She had divined that connection, anyway. While he had some idea of the proposals in his masters' minds, he was going to avoid controversy as long as possible.

"We shall be informed, ma'am; at Reigate perhaps."

"Is the King on a peregrination in the district, then?"

"Ma'am, that I do not know."

The different tone was noted by Alesia, as one which rang true, and one which hoped to make all the previous answers sound genuine as well.

Men of the time of Edward II.

# CHAPTER 21

Having committed nothing against the state, the kingdom, the whole aura of these few weeks was the more frightening. There had to be an assumption that there was a purpose of high principle if the state was involved, yet it looked little more than a dirty game just to attack her with gutter methods to discredit her husband. Alesia would have wished much to hold her head high with disdain, but that would prevent her alertness to every signal of intent that there was. Mostly in the dull chamber she sat with her head drooped to her chest, or alternatively pacing restlessly, all the while looking, and especially listening, with intensity, where there was nothing to see nor to hear.

Where was Thomas? A message could surely have been smuggled to her at some time. Well, perhaps he had tried; or perhaps this really had to be a final break. Assuming she came out of here with freedom. But if sentenced - for what? There was, here and now, however, all the trappings of an incipient trial.

Thomas was not strong enough to defeat the King. Indeed not clever enough, because the King kept allowing him rope to proceed further downwards in the game of politics.

For herself, one day which should have improved her confidence only made the situation worse. Frathesancia was being allowed to bring her food, no more. Increasingly nervous protests were of no avail. Tension within her at an impossible pitch, Alesia just walked out of the door with Frathesancia. The guard was not quick enough in his mind to decide whether he should act or not. Together the women walked on, down through whatever arch or corridor lay open. Thus, unmolested because those who were met knew nothing of its irregularity, in the open air they came across an amiable looking rascal carrying some chain.

"Off a horse, ma'am."

A horse! A hasty thought for a horse, an escape, a dash away to anywhere. A bribe? Except that he would not believe it - nor at least that it could be paid to him in secret. There would be plenty of horses if that could be. With tremor of despair and false hope, both from depreciated morale, Alesia could not help but question:

"A horse?"

The man achieved a bitter expression, and a patronising attitude of mock companionship:

"Not, milady, your sort of horse. Our sort of horse."

The inference did not sink in.

"My work is over there, down below."

Down below. Some sort of cellar below ground? Alesia's face revealed her shock of understanding. The great fellow was amused, for he had achieved an effect from his calling. He passed on, his chains a'clinking. The horse. The torture horse for splitting bodies, weighted till confession or death.

"Back to my cell."

She was allowed in alone, her servant being forced away. In what Alesia now held to be her prison she fell, lay, desirous of nothing but human contact yet the working of her fingers and her nails, the pressures of her body, could not prise it from the stones.

Frathesancia was projecting hysteria on anyone of official appearance in the court and halls. She was not going to have any more of the treatment of her mistress which she already had seen. The Countess of Lincoln was a relative of the King and was to be treated properly if not released. She was not an ordinary prisoner. Surrey would pay. Where was de St. Martin? It all succeeded in inducing enough consideration in untutored men to stop their instinctive cruelty against a fallen aristocrat.

Information was set about that de St. Martin had had carnal relations with her before her marriage to Thomas, and was really the Earl of Lincoln and Salisbury. He bruited it around from the Council at Clarendon that he was prepared to sell rights to these titles, and further that Alesia had agreed with his statement. By the widespread acceptance of this gossip, Alesia fell from grace, became "a filthy harlot". Thomas attacked Surrey's castles in revenge, and he could only be stopped by the King taking them into his own hands. A civil war was averted by Pembroke's mediating efforts.

When the Pope heard of the situation he sent two cardinals, John of Gauselin and Luke de Flisco, to England to make peace between the King and his barons, who promptly levied a tax of fourpence in the mark upon them.

The cardinals in full retinue moved north, accompanied by a Bishop of Durham newly created at the Court of Rome, all to be pillaged by countrymen desperate after the Scottish depredations. Thomas sent forces to their aid, to escort them to York, and from there of necessity to safety in Pontefract Castle. The leader of the disturbances was Sir Gilbert de Middleton, later apprehended, his head then being fixed on Newgate. Malicious courtiers ascribed the attacks to Thomas.

With Alesia later under guard in her own Inn in Holborn, and Thomas disallowed from being in London, the end of her detention came when Edward deemed it reasonably safe. The guard was removed.

# CHAPTER 22

"Reconciled?" asked Alesia. "Again? Where's the change in either of your minds? Where is Edward's difference in his policy?"

Her thoughts and hopes had sprung alive within her, in spite of all. There had to be hope. The cardinals must have influenced Thomas to turn from his ways of rebellion. She did so wish to feel in a secure position again.

"Oh, Thomas! How can you speak of any expedient? What about my safety?"

"You appear to prefer this so called King to the old honour. No matter. I have to tell you this. The expedient is necessary, for the Scots are back in Berwick. There is danger for us all. You are surprised that I recognise that?"

"Thomas, Thomas," spoke Alesia, with soft chiding in her tone, far away from any wish to argue. "I can say no more than I have uttered before - but I will put it differently - how do you ever think for one moment that you are going to influence Edward? He is like that. He will never change. Nor will he ever tolerate again divers barons as his enemies."

"Relax, my dear. We are to attack Berwick together. We have agreed. He now refers to me as the Seneschal of England. All that was brought about by the new council."

"The middle men"

"Put it that way if you wish. At least it's a joint authority, not his. I am prepared to travel with it."

"For a time, you mean."

"Alesia, mistake me not. This realm is in shocking order, because the King consorts with the unworthy."

"Gains opinions from others, I would have said."

"Opinions from commoners, and decision from his lover. That is his government."

By now the situation was self-evident to Alesia, and it should have been thus to Thomas.

With a staccato snap in her voice, which was scarcely deliberate, Alesia demanded suddenly:

"Why don't you kill the King?"

"Madam! You have virtually said that before. For God's sake let it not be heard again, or ever should have been."

Thomas himself was struck as though by a blow. Partly because of the astounding nature of the question. More sensitively because within himself he knew that it was the fundamental of his unequal struggle. By instinct he could not. He did not have the detached power of politics urgeing it upon him.

"You have had plenty of opportunity, and there will be so again."

"Of course I cannot" uttered Thomas, strongly; as much to bury the idea as to salve his conscience before Alesia.

"You will not change him. So, instead of this formal sham reconciliation I suggest you give up rebellion absolutely."

What a mild way to put that point, she thought. How else? It would take root in particular circumstances, or not at all. Perhaps now was the last possible moment.

"At least Edward and I will be together on the nation's service."

"Oh, Thomas," with a great sigh, Alesia spoke from all her hopelessness. It was necessary to sit down, to rest, to see if she felt it worth gathering further argument. There seemed to her to be overwhelming proof of his danger to himself, and that his actions would not achieve any beneficial conclusion.

"It is still the King or you," she said.

Thomas had virtually stopped listening, but he turned to her:

"What does that mean?"

"God save me for uttering this. It is my last remaining vestige of hope for you, Thomas. Everyone knows you are near war with the King..." she held up her hand to prevent interruption..."of course everyone knows, and however you vacillate, that is the true and real situation. So what will happen? Your forces will meet his forces. What then? Men kill each other. You will be there, the King will not. The King will survive..."

Before her showed the image of the man Thomas, dead; desperate it had all become to try and help her man.

There were no interruptions in the silence that followed, no sound other than the desperate tearless painful sobbing of Alesia. She was more alone than if she had been alone. The Thomas who was with her had no communication with her heart, now none with her mind. The breach between them was illustrated as strongly as it could ever be by the very presence of his form.

"You read it differently..." Thomas began. The emptiness of their relationship now so clear, made him try to cross the gap between them, in some manner at least. Forcing himself, he spoke distantly, as though from a subconscious recess:

"There is this new middle party. I nominate one member only. Edward will follow that counsel. You should be proud of my position, the result of my efforts and power."

Alesia looked up at Thomas, standing before her. She had realised how rigid his mind was in the task that he had taken to himself. It was about what he stood for. It was for no more. His actions were just to return to what barons had been. He still believed that Edward's offensive actions could be smothered.

"Thomas, it is not you who are the cat, it is he."

"Alesia, I tell you now, most strongly, I can scarce believe that it is you saying this; I try to win for the good government of this realm."

There seemed to be no route on which to try further, so to Alesia it only remained to say something, to keep each other at least in some tune, in a little hope. She felt fear for some of her words, that they might reach the King, from some unguarded dissemination of what had passed between them.

"What next then, does this council do, apart from Berwick and the Scots? Deal with de Spenser again as it was with Gaveston? Against..."

She stopped. On the occasion of Gaveston's murder by Warwick it was Thomas's safe conduct by his word which had been abused, with him present. Many lords had opted for the King after that.

Thomas was so silent. No reply came. It was not a question of conscience at what his own should feel. It felt no pangs of personal emotion. It was a matter of expediency. It was politics. It was the constant personalisation of his actions for government and politics which was unanswerable by him. He worked by principles, maybe by defence of himself and his kind, but yet the emotional content was buried in the call for the saving of greater things. He would not explain to Alesia again the position in which his Council and he found themselves, because she would at once reduce it, to his mind, to emanating from his own personality.

They had the Council. The King was on it. And Thomas had only one vote of ten, so any proposition of his had to be confirmed. Yet it was in the King's name. Edward should not govern, and could not be his army's General. That was proved by disasters. Thomas felt that he had now manoeuvred his own supporters into a position of power, and had not antagonised those of the King. It had all given a picture of a group making decisions; people joining in, if not totally the Commons. That last he could not bear.

Edward had, by default, let the Scots in to the North; in East Yorkshire they were paying them for peace and handing over hostages.

"In this desperate situation" Thomas turned to Alesia, to inform her of his conclusions, rather than attempt persuasions, "I repeat, we are raising a force to retake Berwick. I will go with Edward."

He looked quickly at Alesia for any reaction. She was still awaiting any final point that may affect their relationship further. Perhaps that was, indirectly, it.

"Of course, Thomas, I support you in your person. Of course I do, but I feel for your safety. For now, what you are doing is of you, total and unbending. Your insistence for me is that I have no glimmer of right."

It was hard for both of them to know the interpretation of the somewhat off-key tone in which she spoke. Affection could not rekindle at that moment. Hope of normality and dread of more personal antagonism mixed her thought, to make a multiple feeling.

"I think, Alesia, that you had better stay here in London for the while."

Then he added, having his own hope for a stable relationship:

"It is my opinion that Edward will be alright. He has recognised that he needs our help."

Their minds were unable to come together. There was still the doubt with Thomas that his wife might be a supporter of the King. So many inner thoughts were buried in ordinary social communication that Thomas had long ceased to attempt to unravel such signs as there were. For the last year, in any case, the Queen had seemed cool to Alesia. That might have been because of the danger she herself could have run into by association.

Alesia spoke again, towards Thomas's retreating back. For some connection with him, she had dredged up another thought. To express it she wished, to put off with hope, or to heal the breach between them enough to give hope of its mending.

"Thomas!"

It was too late, for he was out of the chamber, and she could hear his steps afar on the heavy wooden flooring. It is quite possible that he himself did not wish to hear, and was pressing forward a little too quickly and noisily so as to prove to himself that he had not.

Half accidental, half deliberate, they came across each other within the hour. Thomas had not left yet, but half hoping to leave in peace of mind he delayed in the hall of the great Savoy palace. Looking through the outer doorway he received images of a happier kind of times past - the family riding out or returning after hunt, of the hope which they all had then in their power and in their ambitions. Strangely, all that had seemed to be positive, but a more anxious reality had now superceded all.

Alesia and Thomas met, because she too moved through the building, in hope that Thomas might pass across her way, or she pass his. In the hand of fate she placed herself; she felt the possibility of meeting, so she hoped; it was a quiet gamble. She saw him near the great window, about to move away. Interception looked accidental.

"Dear Alesia, please try and understand, not me, but my situation. I have not the constant ear of a King as your father had. Nor have we that previous monarch. We have one whom I think can now rule only as a group, who must therefore be curbed from his own weakness. More than that - after him his son - what can he be? There can be no-one like the first Edward. I support Kingship. That is the answer to the direct question you asked. What else can I do?"

By now their arms were embracing each other; they both needed that contact and reassurance.

Alesia was fearful that any words she might utter would undo at once the hope that these few moments had engendered. She must not be controversial. She must not give her reasons why she felt him wrong. She fought back her urge to tell Thomas that he was only fighting the Queen's battles for her, that it could only end in disaster when Edward had garnered his forces; that maybe Edward was no general but he had on his side barons who were, that just as in times previous Edward would give in, then strike back when ready.

In this frustrated spirit Alesia gripped hard her lip between her teeth; with that pain and the fear o'er mixed with hope of love rekindled she could only bring forth tears, silently.

To regain each of them their own composure they walked slowly round the garden.

"This council will endure. Do not worry, Alesia. There is no better way."

"Do please keep me informed." She had nearly added 'as you used to' but managed to prevent herself.

Thomas nodded, and looked calmer. Alesia's request did not fall on empty ground, as she had half expected. Thomas even replied, before riding away:

"Torkill. We can trust Torkill"

There was no disagreement from Alesia about that. Torkill, the honest man with his own confidence in himself, who envied no-one. Satisfied with his place, he would bring his own objective judgment to both parties. He was without the prejudice of the pride of the educated, and did not have to exert himself upon any learning to show proof of extraordinary ability to his superiors.

Before long, there was the first news that Edward and Thomas had opened the siege of Berwick side by side.

"Perhaps then, Torkill, the lord Thomas was right."

"In what, ma'am? He gave me no doubts on any question."

"No, I mean the council, of which he is one. The governing council that was to bring the King together with the Ordainers as one body."

"My lady, if you would like my observances, in addition to my messages, then I will try to give answer to any question. Before that, there was one suggestion from the lord Thomas. It was that you could now repair to Bolingbroke as he is to be so far North."

Alesia pondered only for a moment. Five years ago she had been at Pickering, which had seemed so safe. Surely this side of the river Humber would never suffer. In any event she must be seen to obey her husband, or at least so long as there was hope of long term reconciliation.

"Very well, Torkill, can you tell me what folk are saying about this council, about..." she trailed off, a little doubtful as to the obvious intimacy relating to her personal relations with Thomas.

"My lady," began Torkill, and in an instant hesitated. A further look at the lady Alesia, to see her as a person instead of a detached authority, and the anxious face he saw made him continue. Except for the office they held, all men had the same hopes and fears as he and his friends. Strange that he had never perceived that before, at the age of forty years more or less. Torkill recovered himself, and spoke less remotely:

"What we say is that, well, perhaps I should not, but it's fairly obvious..."

"Do, I beg you, say all you can. I will decide whether I agree or not, but the spoken thoughts are necessary."

"...not everyone is a supporter of the lord Thomas, but I think many of the people are. But above all, the King is the King. Barons, other ones, will support him. He has to be stronger than the lord Thomas."

"Yes. A King has so to be. That is the fear, as to what happens when he is."

"Ma'am, it is said that if the King had not lost Bannockburn, he would have acted against the lord Thomas after that. I do hope I am not..."

"No, Torkill, you are not..." and Alesia actually smiled "...for this was mostly realised, if not known." She added the last three words so as not to make Torkill think his reports were wasted.

"The only comment which we servants have is...if I may...that the weaker side is usually more careful."

"So, may it not be that there are two sides, and that we are the weaker one. Is that what you are saying? Then what about now, this council?"

"May I say now, ma'am, that I cannot presume to further than report; my opinions? Please, I beg, excuse me. I have not political experience."

"Yes, but I think I can guess them. There have been other reconciliations. But, one more point, Torkill. For myself I know the danger, but I cannot persuade the lord Thomas."

Alesia thought well that she should get her basic opinion into the circulation of underlings.

Some moments passed before Torkill was given leave to go. Alesia was pondering in silence, with frustrating effort to conclude the likely outcome of present events upon, above all, her married life. As to the state of the country itself, it was likely to be the Scots as the troublesome ones, even as in her early years it was the Welsh. No doubt it would get solved, but it was not for her to act upon. For all the signs were that she must continue to warn Thomas, the danger was increasing, and she herself must see him once again. There could be only one commander in a realm. She would go to Bolingbroke. The castle at Pontefract was too large and impersonal. Suddenly, without pre-thought she asked the attendant Torkill:

"If the lord Edward is planning to augment his supporters, as is only to be expected, what is it said that the lord Thomas is doing? He says that he is being influenced to lead this movement for the betterment of the realm."

Torkill shifted uneasily.

"Very well, Torkill, please tell what is said. Report, I mean."

"There is talk of...of other help, my lady."

"Oh?" responded Alesia, in a tone of encouragement. Then she continued in more of a note of despair, because it could only be the

Scots.

"For all the helpers there may be, there can still be no certainty of a peaceful conclusion."

It was as far as either of them dare communicate, even with a long background of confidence. Torkill was certain of being respected, but he was unable to be sure whether his lady Alesia was single-minded about his lord Thomas. It was said, indeed much was said, about her abduction by de St. Martin on both sides, but part rumour was that she had connived with Edward and Surrey to discredit her husband. If that were so it had turned against her, for she herself had a diminished position in society. There were many who were not involved in the King's Court, but who were not prepared to risk their opinions being known by association with those who were.

That was also in Alesia's mind, because nothing was happening to keep her in London. Contempt of Edward, widespread in all classes, was not producing much active help in England for Thomas. Except from those he could pay for, support was static. She would not tax Torkill to request the identity of the 'help' that he had mentioned. It was clear that Thomas was suspected of dealing with the Scots, for there was no other source of possible intrigue to strengthen his position. What on earth would happen at Berwick? In the only appropriate response she could muster in dismissing Torkill, she said:

"In these desperate events, it seems that I can do little more than sigh."

"It will be le Strange, ma'am who will escort you to Bolingbroke."

With a too obvious catch of the breath, Alesia had to believe that Thomas did not know of her love for Ebulo le Strange, the most civilised man she could hope to meet. And Ebulo did ultimately arrive at the Savoy Palace, with an escort of a few esquires and forty archers. The clatter in the Strand was hardly further increased by two more horsemen, in the livery of the King.

The escort made way, and le Strange moved his mount aside, the occasion by now effecting silence among all. Curiosity and anxiety about the purpose of the message that these men carried was relieved only when the King's men had received their answer from Alesia. They departed, and le Strange was admitted to the mansion.

"It was from Queen Isabella, asking me to stay in London a few days, and to visit her tomorrow. What is your interpretation of that?"

"There are rumours of Edward returning south, and presumably the lord Thomas as well?"

"The lord Thomas?" Alesia was surprised. "Ebulo, Thomas left a while before."

"Heavens! Not another breakdown between them!"

"It is very sad to have to say that it is just that. I weep for Thomas, indeed I weep for the foolishness of all this situation. Yet, what can you possibly expect, when Edward tells him that when they capture Berwick he is going to give it to Hugh de Spenser?"

After moments of silence, Alesia went on:

"Let us hope that we have a future."

Ebulo le Strange inferred with hope the meaning in its intonation - that they themselves would be able to remain in love. The plain words as such suited outside consumption.

It was somewhat embarrassing to Ebulo to receive this direct affirmation in what was an impossible dream, but nevertheless one that he too had sojourning in his thoughts. He had to veer away from taking this any further. Things like that could be said, but they could not be pursued too far.

"What, Alesia, do you yourself think Isabella wants? It might just be more news, perhaps some substance in the rumours."

"What rumours? I thought I had heard all from Torkill. He was up North." She turned aside, part in fear, part to hide a fleeting thought that - no she must not even have any speculation about what may have happened to Thomas in the attack on Berwick. It was relief to her conscience when she heard some more.

"I left the North after Torkill. Four score places have been devastated further south - all by the Scots. Northallerton, Boroughbridge, Scarborough. It is also said Skipton and Harbottle. So the King and your husband have to return. The York Archbishop's forces have been routed - he was meant to hold the County."

Alesia had begun to cling to Ebulo as much in fear as in affection.

"Bruce is not able to come all the way down here."

"Why not? We are able to go all the way up there. We often take an army right into Scotland. But Edward and Thomas are still on the move, and garrisons are being mustered in the Midlands. If that's not very comforting, then Bruce wants to negotiate anyway, for independence, recognition, and the end of his excommunication."

"It is all so slow, though. And it all stems from Edward. What do you really believe is going to happen?"

"Fortunately I am no good at foresight. One never knows who is doing what at what part of the country. Nor what they are thinking of doing when somebody's back is turned."

Alesia half laughed and told Ebulo he could do better than that.

"Well, then, if Edward would work with the right people there would be no trouble anywhere. If one is not homosexual one is not likely to have an appointment and Edward trusts no others. I don't mind him swimming, exercising, improving his body, but he should keep his mind objective, instead of... I am not going to continue that because it makes me sick."

After a pause, to clear the air for a better subject, Ebulo gave a brief reply:

"He'll not change."

"Thomas insists on the banishment of the de Spensers."

"That will not do any good. Actually they're needed."

"I have told him all that. He says if they don't go, then Edward will give them more and more, and will work through them and no-one else."

"Alesia, can't you tell him to bide his time? Edward can't go on like this for ever. Besides, with all respect, Thomas is trying to do things in a way that cannot succeed."

"I told him that too, many, many, times. And Gloucester's daughter is proposed for young Hugh de Spenser."

"Oh God! You know what that means. Why does Edward provoke so much? To place his friends strategically I suppose."

"Is that particularly serious, most of it is from estates in the King's hands?"

"Alesia, you are closer to these counsels than I."

"I should keep it that way."

The next day the meeting with Queen Isabella took place in her apartments in the Tower. All respect was accorded to Alesia, just like former times. Any direct result, or indication of the purpose of the meeting, was deciphered only by the happening itself. That it had occurred showed of itself that Alesia was cleared of any previous involvement, and that her friendly support was needed by Isabella. Although Alesia was so careful not to express opinion on Edward, she already knew full well of Isabella's bitterness in rejection.

"All was well, when Thomas was at peace in this country, and I am constantly trying to get him to see that" was as much as Alesia would utter precisely. Not on a side, but for a country. Alesia had to steer between the interests of Thomas, Edward, and Isabella. It was no time to be free in conversation with any one of them, but Isabella wished to know all there was to know. What did she have in mind? There was some underlying purpose. In sum, it was clear that she herself did not have a personal plan - yet.

Thomas, however, maintained his own policy: weeks later that was perfectly clear -

"Our group has attained its objective, Alesia, so I hope that you're convinced of our sincerity, and of our peaceble intentions."

"You mean, Thomas, that Edward has submitted to you, .... no, to the Ordainers."

"True." He ignored the hesitation. He allowed that it was no more than personal from a woman to her husband.

Alesia could think of no point in urgeing caution again. Thomas would have been furious with her, more so because of his basic weakness and doubt. Outwardly this time he was really proud of his success. She herself had always wished deeply to be at one with her husband in his endeavours. The emptiness in spirit which would result from taking herself away alone formed an invisible barrier, through which she could envisage the bleakness of the world outside. Fears came and faded, returned again, and this latest success of Thomas's was no different. Of course Edward had agreed. He took the pressure upon him as a sponge takes water, to be squeezed away at the appropriate moment. Besides, he was preoccupied in trying to stop the Scots again, which had doubled as a good reason to postpone a Parliament.

When it did assemble Thomas claimed the Stewardship of the Household, as a right of the Earl of Leicester. It was the next and necessary step after Edward's submission. Parliament was strong enough to refuse. Then Edward diverted Thomas and his brother Henry by confirming to them all rights in Provence, as under grant to them from the late Queen Eleanor. It was an impractical feudal devolution; Edward's action was almost a taunt. It set the atmosphere for the end.

With as much speed as was practicable Thomas and Edward stalked for their final positions. Over a couple of years the cumbersome arrangements of power, supporters, and the passing of intelligence of either side continued. The country waited for the result. With Thomas a powerful enemy antagonistic to the administration the body politic could not do any constructive act. Nor could Thomas. Nor did he expect more than that Edward should drop his habits and be a better King. Trapped as he was in his personality, to change was not possible.

Then there had been the great meeting at Leake in Leicestershire, to try and reconcile their differences. Attending the King were the Queen, the Archbishop of Canterbury, Bishops, eleven Earls, forces and attendants. Thomas, an individual in power, brought an entourage of eighteen thousand.

After having observed that King Edward strengthened his position by giving further estates and revenues to the de Spensers, including those of the de Clares. He continued to take estates away from Thomas's supporters. Even with the marriage of the Earl of Gloucester's daughter to young Hugh de Spenser, none of these actions had influence with Thomas.

It was left to Pembroke's busy initiatives to avoid civil war. Being in charge of Parliament at the next session he persuaded the assembly to defuse the situation by banishing the de Spensers.

Still supporting Thomas were Hereford, Badlesmere, and some lesser lords. Some of those who had been against Gaveston, such as Pembroke and Warrenne, had moved away from his cause. There was also moral support for Thomas, about as much help as that given by spectators. His half brother Kent supported him "through the Queen" - in principle, so did the Archbishop of Canterbury, the Bishops of Ely and Lincoln. Norfolk's backing was secretive.

Lady Badlesmere took part. She lived at Leeds Castle in Kent. Misled by her husband's confidence in Thomas, when Queen Isabella on a summer journey asked for lodging, in foolish ignorance of that lady's real opinions she refused her admission. Edward bestirred himself to this dishonour. He besieged the castle in November, and took Lady Badlesmere prisoner, to be held at first in the Tower, then with the Minorites. Her ultimate fate, nearly three years after her husband was hung, was to be released to live in the nunnery at Castle Combe. Edward's show of strength instilled confidence, and gained him more followers. Maybe the action had impressed the Queen, but it had been necessary because Thomas's power in the North had been increasing, by his calling assemblies to put his case. Through the deteriorating situation any hope would shine.

Attacking any King as anointed with the blessings of the Holy Church could be no light consideration. While emotions engendered by secular situations would override invisible powers they only activated the few. While the masses were helpless in the matter of the rights of barons, under Edward the Second they had had less taxation, and little disturbance by war. Edward had counselled with more of their representatives. Thomas's disturbance was an extra in an age of poverty, bad crops and animal diseases.

Edward himself was the fourth son of his father, the only one strong enough to survive. Fit he was, to the contempt of barons who did not swim and exercise. In that his position as King was not of itself being challenged he could shrewdly watch and wait. What he saw was Thomas now depleted of resources and increasingly ineffective. He himself was becoming the richest King the country ever had reigning.

The true situation was not realised by Berkeley, who joined Thomas. The young Warwick defected, which might have caused Thomas a moment's thought about any advice his father might have given. He had, however, a new son and heir. Arundel left him, being well informed. His father-in-law was the King's loyal Earl Warrenne. His eldest son had married a de Spenser. This was a definite turn around from his previous prejudice, occasioned by Gaveston having beaten him in a tournament. He had discovered much about the doubtful strength of Thomas's position by being Captain-General North of the Trent.

At a reception in London he met Alesia. She had remained in the capital since Thomas's last departure for the Midlands. In a less sombre period she would have been amused at all the cross currents and shades of opinion on the topic of the day. Some had changed sides, some had ensured neutrality; however, the committed to the King were in the majority, for this was a gathering in his base territory. Arundel had deliberately moved to speak to Alesia, then waited until no-one but they were conversing. His positive approach, its deliberation sensed from his demeanour, had caused her from memories to tremble with anxiety.

"We are sending le Strange overseas," he said.

Alesia reacted with astonishment, as much at the sudden and obviously deliberate interpolation into light chatter of a straightforward statement.

'We' - so who was 'we'? And why? And why tell me? Out of embarrassment she blushed. Yes, Ebulo was a man of Thomas's, but had been under Arundel. Alesia tied the remark to the apparent knowledge of the King and Arundel of her loving relationship with him. Of course they did, but for it to be implied so suddenly like this stifled thought. The fact of Arundel smiling as he spoke, indeed he still was so doing, might have been amusement at the effect it had had. It may also have been put on for public face here.

Alesia began to be frightened. There was a background to being told of this. It could be one only. They must have been very confident that it did not matter that she knew they were ready to attack Thomas. He must guess that, but could not change his course.

"Do not ask any questions. He will be away for a few weeks."

Then, in the interchange of such occasions someone was about to come close. He made his farewell in good time. Passing by her side he mouthed softly and clearly:

"Go...to...Bolingbroke." then loudly: "I look forward to meeting you again."

Alesia saw fit to obey the order so obviously emanating from her kinsman King Edward. Oh, dear God! Oh, Thomas! Ebulo? Was it done for her, or was it a way of getting at least one Knight and his men away from Thomas's army?

Proposed by the Earl Warrenne, the King's Council resolved that Thomas of Lancaster was in open rebellion.

Edward recalled the de Spensers. His army numbered 30,000 men, and was helped by Welsh Knights. He marched to the Welsh border and defeated half of Thomas's forces, on their way to join him. Their commander Mortimer was sent to the Tower.

By contrast Thomas's men broke out of the gaol and captured Warwick Castle and held it against the King. In desperation Thomas sent Robert Holland to raise more men from Lancashire. The situation was not unknown to them. They joined the King, stretching Thomas's morale to the limit, leaving only honour.

Thomas and Hereford marched away northwards, and clashed with an army under Sir Andrew de Harcla. Hereford was killed by a spearman hidden under a bridge. Thomas was captured and beheaded. de Harcla was created Earl of Carlisle. Before long he too was beheaded for trying to agree a treaty with the Scots.

# CHAPTER 23

The deepening grey of the winter evening across the flat lands to the south of Bolingbroke had no greater portent than ever before - in itself. Yet this night in March the silence seemed deeply profound. While night would fall with hint of terrors from unseen sources, and prayers would help the passage through to dawn, an owl or shrike would screech to show a greater whole on earth. This time the nightfall itself was paramount, and humans in the castle communicated in whispers.

For several days no soul had passed by. No-one, be it merchant, knight or friar had called at Bolingbroke to sell, to seek accommodation, to disseminate news or supposed news. Isolation began to prey on all. Something would have to be done on the morrow to bring reassurance and to frustrate imaginations. So messengers would have to be sent to Horncastle, or as far as Lincoln.

Alesia and Joan were used to most situations where calm had to be induced in others over fears based on rumours, gossip, or garbled facts, when belief in any true situation known to themselves was hard to sustain. This was different. They shared the fears over the complete absence of reality impinging from outside. With her young husband already dead Joan de Audley had come to stay with Alesia.

"It must be like this in a nunnery" said Joan. "Or, from what I hear, what it ought to be like. Prayer is the only calming influence."

Alesia gave a faint smile, remembering that a nunnery was once nearly her fate. Both Joan and she knew that it was at these moments hard to joke, to talk of the monks and nuns who had a jollier life than they were meant to.

Alesia's heart was heavy with the uncertainty of what she feared was happening. Soon there would be the final clash between the forces of Thomas and those of Edward. She felt the panic of desperation and uselessness. The last that she and Joan had heard was that the opposition to the King had divided. After Thomas had last summer accumulated more power he was conciliated by the banishment of the de Spensers. He completely ignored the signs that Edward was ready, by then, and had forces large enough to put down his revolt. Mortimer had one group, Thomas another. In the West Mortimer was defeated. Sir Roger de Mortimer of Chirk, and his nephew of Wigmore. They surrendered. That was the last that Alesia and Joan had heard. Their present fears were linked in their doubts for Thomas, for Edward had mustered greater strength than ever they had expected, divided opposition or not. And strength meant death or capture to the enemy, to Thomas, Hereford, Clifford, and others of their circle. Joan conceived her duty to comfort Alesia, though they were both connected with this struggle. Thank God, she thought, Ebulo le Strange was overseas. What agony of jumbled emotions that stimulated. Edward had needed a small force to go to Ireland, and he had ordered le Strange to be the commander. Whose doing was the choice? And why Ebulo? What was Alesia to believe? How could her conscience rest while her husband may soon die and her love survive? In all goodness she had to smother any twinge of hope in the fear of seeking a fulfilled future upon the death of her husband of Holy Matrimony. She must suppress the unanswerable question that her happiness in future might depend on a machination by Edward. She tried to speak again as she had before:

"If it's a matter of rights, Alesia, Thomas can dismiss the de Spensers as much as he likes - they started out as his own dependants. But in any case, if it's force that's going to decide this then Thomas is no fool."

"Joan, dear" Alesia spoke with an unintentioned patronising tone, "you never seem to believe me that Thomas has not got the proper resolve to fight to win. If he had, this would have been over years ago. He wants only a reasonable King who will rule and reign and he thinks he can get one by forcible demand." She added: "He is courageous but in fear of..." she hesitated and did not mention regicide... "killing and killing and taking things over. He cannot do it. So he has either to lose his head by defeat, or win and continue the stupid mixture as before."

Alesia felt a cold sweat over her. How she had managed to utter that straight truth she did not know. She could not contemplate the thought that in a straight battle between the forces the King would be a legitimate target if he were present. In the unlikely event of that, what exactly? Thomas as protector for his young son Edward? But Thomas had no such aim urging him forward. This was probably, she thought, why she had always tried to restrain him back to normality. To her, it seemed that he did not even want to know how to reach where his course was meant to be taking him.

"I don't think my father realised where this would get to."

"Obviously you know why Thomas felt it necessary. I always told Nicholas there were limits to what Edward could do. He couldn't give the de Spensers much more, not the whole country, one might say. They were bad generals, so is Edward. I kept telling him to calm down. Duty. That's the reply. Duty."

Waiting. Waiting. Tension as before a thunderstorm. Joan gripped Alesia's arm, tightly, for she felt that she may concede to fear and doubt, and come to wild conclusions about defeat.

"I do feel something is gone from me."

"Alesia, please. We cannot guess. We do not know. One must not force conclusions out of nothingness. I feel myself that he is still alive."

"Still?"

"We are both guessing, really. Let us not weep without cause."

"Nor smile without joy."

"It is amazing how women, given to emotion, have so often and for so long to stay themselves not knowing which one to show."

"I never know why my father urged Thomas on so much. But I know what he would do now. This minute, I mean. He would go round talking to retainers for his own comfort and seeking information."

So they did. Alesia despatched three men to Lincoln and beyond, to pick up news. And news it was to be, not rumours. They were to travel until they came across hard evidence of what was the situation. This order was eagerly obeyed, indeed considered overdue. Many of their friends, their brothers, fathers, menfolk generally were under orders with Thomas's rebel force, and some with the King from his manors.

Now some action had been instigated, the ladies felt better. For their own diversion and the occupation of the others, Alesia ordered a minor feast.

Nothing was known at Lincoln Castle, nor was there anyone there with authority until the seneschal returned. Or did not return, for he was with the lord Thomas. Such folk as they met in the inns nearby had small idea of the events, and minor interest in the import of them.

"They might have chosen better weather for fighting. I've done a bit, but summer's the only sensible time."

So spoke messenger William to messengers John and Roger. They rode on from Lincoln in the March wind and rain.

"We've got to cross the Trent and get up to Pontefract. Tonight it'll be an inn for us, or a barn."

"What about Tickhill?" demanded John, who preferred the freedom of castle kitchen supplies.

With a withering look based on experience of the world of affairs, he received his authoritative answer from William:

"Young man, you have to know these things, for your own preservation. Call at a King's castle now and you may never call anywhere again."

"I'd heard..."

"Whatever you've heard, it's not on our side, whoever it might belong to."

William's authority somewhat doubted, the rugged old soldier sped his mount to reachieve some initiative. Two hours and they were well beyond the river, soaked below and above. He knew Bawtry from of old, having more than once been there to escort lead for castle repairs. Now for the North he thought, on his old previous way towards Scotland.

"The lord Thomas was last heard of, by us at least, moving northwards, so we try this way. It would suit him, if he really wants the Scottish help they say."

"He wouldn't surely?"

"Don't ask me about these political things. I know nothing about how the masters think. You've just got to live as best you can with what they think up. I suppose they have their own reasons, but I'm damned if I try to follow much of them."

John, who spoke little in general, middle of age but available for these duties because of breathing trouble, was probably the most intelligent of the three. At least it was he who was first alerted. Down the slope of the road were men in attitudes that gave answer to the question yet unasked.

"William! Along there! Coming towards us."

The portent of the interpretation that William gave struck them with apprehension as to their own future. There was one horseman, and some shuffling men, on foot. Even at a distance not one displayed bearing.

"Defeated. There's no other word for it. A defeated army, at least, the front of it. I've seen that sort of thing before."

"Maybe it isn't ours."

William ran his sleeve hard against his face, as much to restore his thinking as to dry some sweat.

"One lord, I presume, and a few men. It must be ours. The beginning of hundreds, thousands maybe. It's not the King's men. Let's get up to them."

While William's deduction was correct, they discovered it had been based only on his simple idea of the colour and bustle of King's armies as he had known them. Not one of this unwelcome party was carrying a banner. The two groups met. William's hail and question was not answered. Neither who the first rider was, nor where they were bound, nor what had happened was revealed. From the exhausted men came no response, and their livery had been tampered with to avoid recognition. They trundled by with just a glance at William's posse.

Even William was lost for expression. It looked like the lord Maltravers, whom he had seen at the siege of Caerlaverock. But that had been among so many lords. This occasion was of such poignant importance that he was himself silenced. Whatever he said on any occasion he opined that he was right. Now he was down to something on which he could be challenged.

William urged his companions back towards the North, and said:

"There'll be more coming soon. Perhaps they can tell us something."

His initiative was soon regained by that simple prescient statement. More did come, on horse and foot, on their way to dispersing to whence they had left. The night's shelter for them was the nearest woods.

"Tired? Weren't you there?"

On seeing the scattered dishevelled men in the twilight William at once feared that there may be resentment, and that he was in error in not going about this job with subtlety, and with mud deliberately spread on his clothes. It was not the first man to whom he spoke who was interested enough to tell him much, but they seemed to harbour little rancour. This was not the sort of end-of-battle that William understood - except that it looked that a good number of them had kept well on the sidelines. At last he had found an archer who seemed to be in charge of himself. He first made his own excuse.

"No. Not at my age. I was not there..." and William deemed the man calm enough to further the matter "...I have been sent to discover the result."

"Pitch and toss. Who won, you mean. What does it mean to you, then, or me either?"

"Alright. I've been in battles. These men, you, you're Lancaster's from the looks of things."

"You know the tattered signs then. Were you for Lancaster? I hope you've fought better than we did..."

The message that the Lancaster faction had lost was now obvious without further conversation. In his sudden fear and worry for his future, William looked closer at the nearby men. Their minds were only on a brace of rabbits snared and now being smoked on a glittering fire. The archer was about to join them. He picked up his bow and quiver. The latter was still half full. No-one seemed much bloodied or torn, yet wearied and dirty with long marches and the paltry battle.

"I am beginning to wonder..." began William.

"Yes, I should think so. Who are you from?"

It seemed safe enough to mention the lady Lancaster.

"Bloody hell! You've got something to report. I don't envy you - who? - William - I'm Arno de Broc - your lady may well lose her lord. Hereford's dead. Lancaster's captured. A score of his friends taken..."

"Clifford?"

"...not certain; two or three did escape..."

"Maltravers? we thought we saw him down the road."

"Maybe, not sure. There were ten thousand on Lancaster's side. Or were they? I would say they walked round the country together."

"Is that really what it was?"

"Near enough. So you yourself would have had some orders. Maybe clear ones. So you had leaders who led and wanted to. What did we have? Neither. Not much of a battle I must say. You'd better stay here, rabbits are easy enough to catch. In the morning I'll pick off a deer."

While it was important to inform the lady Alesia of Thomas's defeat and capture, it was patent to William that there would be supplementary questions about things of which at present he knew nothing. He should have brought more men so as to be able to divide the party.

Because there was the battle lost, the rebellion over, William would not expect any one of Lancaster's men to move north. Such action would be misconstrued. The estates from which they came would be reallocated by the King. The loyalties of the men would be transferred, at least on paper. William's second silence that day came from the dilemma of the two possibilities of what to do next.

Arno almost laughed at the sight of William stunned with thought and little to resolve it. He tried to help.

"So, William, you've been in these things, you say. What happens to captured rebellious lords? Won't the same happen to Lancaster?"

William yet could find no words. Thomas was the King's cousin. No, that would make no difference; might be a greater threat to the King. Like so many lords in the past, he would have to be got out of the way, and permanently. The King hated him.

"How will the lady Lancaster take it? It's an obvious answer, you know."

"She's his wife, but she's been against him for years. I suppose like most women she'll be weeping for her husband, like him or not. But lord Thomas would not change his ways for her."

"Nor would King Edward change his ways for Lord Thomas, they say."

"Incidentally," added William on another line, "I didn't know the King was a good general. What's the real story?"

"Feller from up north, they say. No-one had ever heard of him. Not that he did much, it was just that we were doing less. Look, William, you've got your job now - why not send your two back and tell the lady her man's captured and you're trying to find out more further north. It's not for this reason, but if she'll pay me I'll come with you. No. I'll forget that. She won't have anything to pay with. I'll come anyway if you like. A day or two for me makes no difference."

"Arno, where do you come from? Which Lancaster place?"

"That's it. I'm from Tutbury and they might be King's men by now."

Perhaps Arno was just curious, but William could find no dangerous motive. In the misty dawn the two set off north. The messengers to Bolingbroke were told to hire a second horse at Bawtry.

The men in groups and the stragglers plodding, through and by whom William and Arno picked their course, must have numbered several thousand.

They were dismally returning home, including those who had not troubled to get as far as the battle. There seemed to be no Bolingbroke men among them, at least that William saw. The only news he gathered was of the defeat, followed by men departing, except that the King had ordered Lincolnshire men to go no further south than Pontefract.

The pair looked up at the gaunt and high forbidding stones of Pontefract castle, at which they were now cautious of the character of any welcome. They remained outside, attendant upon any passers by for whatever they may know. It was six days after the battle, or skirmish as William was now calling it, the twenty second of March. That day William saw his former great lord humbled into a being less than he himself.

"Arno, we'd better go."

"You've seen this sort of thing before, you said."

"You tease me. You know perfectly well that death is fearful. Five earls gone in one cut. A body in sackcloth. I could even see from here the look of glee on the King's face."

"How does it affect you, William? Telling the lady Alesia I suppose. You'll have to report about half. Let her guess the rest."

"God! What would have happened to her father! He was in support of Thomas, too."

"And there's Audley who was once with Lancaster. Lucky he died. His widow is with lady Alesia at Bolingbroke. Her step-mother. Anyway I've found out enough. There'll be more men assembling. Quick, let's move. I don't want to be recognised by any of our men."

"I agree," said Arno, as they turned and quietly rode away. "Besides, I see a couple of sections of King's men forming up. I bet there've been some escapes. Perhaps it really was Maltravers down the road. Nor can I see Badlesmere."

Living rough, eating such as they could buy, and keeping a lookout behind them, they progressed fast to Bawtry, where Arno saw fit to veer off for Tutbury. With prudence they had once ridden down a lane to let some King's men pass. Unknown to William they were on their way on the same road as was he. Arno and he grasped each other's hand for a moment; thanks from William, and a comment from Arno:

"Bad for the people, William, I think. The King is now free to exercise his petty licentious habits even more than before. Between them they were ruining the country....and each other. Is it now so different?"

William was advised to keep his mouth shut as Arno said was his own normal behaviour. It was more difficult for him, thought William, than it is for me. His worry was the impact that his arrival at Bolingbroke would have. He galloped, for he had to be first. His way was along the former Roman road to some four miles north of Lincoln, then forwards to make for Horncastle. Perhaps, if the night were kind, he could arrive without a stop, with part gallop, part canter, part trot, part walk.

Across the ford of the River Trent, and in a sense he felt much nearer home. Another mile, up the slope and there in front of him the distant view revealed a group of horsemen; at a guess the King's men he had seen before. At nearby Stow Park they had formed into some order, as an escort, and had no intention of troubling themselves with him. In their midst, tied to his horse, a prisoner. One whom William could recognise, a distant connection of the lady Alesia. The lord Bartholomew Badlesmere. The one whose wife had so insulted the Queen at Leeds Castle, Kent. Thus he was closely involved in Edward's final decision to put down the revolt.

William avoided showing that he recognised their prisoner. Were these lords fools, he had to wonder. Here was the Steward of the

King's household, castles and honours from the King and all that, and already having got his wife imprisoned in the Tower, the stupid bugger throws all the rest away. Sackcloth and a short ride on an ass for him too must be supposed.

William moved his horse aside and waited with heart-pounding patience as though the group were not in his comprehension. The escort was far too pleased with their capture to wish for more; Badlesmere was too dejected and morose to raise his eyes.

William waited, longer than he need have done, to try and prove that he was in no hurry and was not escaping from anywhere. It was with a sigh of part relief, and part in the fog of reassessing what was happening that William turned again to his journey. This time it was with the dread feeling that there was danger for the lady Alesia, if Lancaster's supporters were in defeat going to rally at Bolingbroke. The King's fury, mused William, would be such that Badlesmere would not now be one of them. He hurried on faster, now having his own life possibly threatened. By exhaustion of man and horse he rested before descending the hill to Bolingbroke Castle.

It had to be in the chapel, and quietly, that William had to relate the catalogue. It was confirmation to Alesia and Joan de Audley as much as news. Chaplain Beaurepair listened to William at the chapel side, then kneeled in prayer in front of the two ladies and their maids. The blessings of Almighty God were sought for the soul and spirit of Thomas, lord of Lancaster, Leicester, Lincoln, Salisbury, and Derby, and forgiveness for where he had strayed against the anointed King. In whispers to try and check the tears the prayers continued for such of the others that William had remembered: for Roger Clifford, Banneret; for Humphrey de Bohun, lord of Hereford; for Bannerets Henry Teyer, William Touchet, Sir Warin de Lisle, Sir Thomas Mauduit, John Mowbray, John Giffard, Sir Henry Wilington.

"And may our lord Edward spare we pray the life of Bartholomew Badlesmere," continued Beaurepair "and we pray that those others in this host may live and receive forgiveness on this earth in thy name, O Lord."

William bowed to his lady Alesia. As she looked towards him the agony in her eyes, the drawn pale face, was as he had never beheld before. He had to say what he had proposed, however, but it came out with much hesitation. Then he added:

"It is said, lady, that Sir Roger Clifford, your kinsman, was wounded, as being one of the few who fought."

In the subsequent silence William received a nod from Beaurepair and he left them quietly.

He marvelled at what he thought still held as an inner stolidity deep down in the lady Alesia. The lady Joan did have some palliative. Second wife and widow of Alesia's father she was Alesia's stepmother. Then she had made a spontaneous marriage to Nicholas, Lord Audley. Her nine-year old son James was safe in the guardianship of

Earl Piers de Joinville. Another Audley languished in prison at Wallingford. Nothing therefore connected her directly with Thomas's revolt except her refuge with Alesia.

William had long experienced by observation the antagonisms of his betters with each other. While the likes of him were assumed to be loyal to any command from the particular tenant-in-chief of their manor the lords practised the loyalty of opportunism. He felt that if the two ladies had seen the heads of Thomas and the others being severed then they would never erase the horror from their minds. As indeed perhaps he himself never would. Yet Kings, prelates, earls, knights seemed to be detached in their actions. Perhaps, he thought, it was like killing a pig with your mind actually on the food resulting. Their authority seemed to come from elsewhere, but surely not from God, though they often said so.

Alesia remained stock still. Joan and the chaplain were ready to leave, but sensed that it was not appropriate to utter a word. Nor did they feel that they should stay. So Alesia remained alone. Gazing at the crucifix, gripping her book of hours, she groped to find and expiate her own guilt. Lone helplessness in what she had tried to do to prevent all this, the resulting deep knowledge of her weakness -there was but one source to which to look for hope. Perhaps hope was yet again deferred. Yet how could she have been in this at her husband's side? Dear God, she would question again why had she not had a son, or any child, to divert her man from evil.

Should she have tried once more - yet Thomas would not see that he was only leader because of birth to that high position and that he did not have the resolve to try to win a war by killing. Poor Thomas. Perhaps his soul may be glad that it may be in peace. The noisy support of many barons expecting to be led to victory had thrust Thomas to a pinnacle on which he should not have been placed. O God, what of your servant, Alesia. What authority have I to live in peace upon this earth?

After a pause of many minutes in which she moved not one muscle she murmured:

"And yet my difficulties are of neither size nor shape as were those of thy son. It is I who have failed in my duty. Though it is not enough, I shall further help thine abbey of Barlings for further prayers to thy glory. I pray thee to guide me to greater acts within my soul."

The March day was chilly. The early evening grew colder. This did not loosen her tension, it insinuated and attacked her body, in her stillness welding her attitude of prayer. After long hours she began to tremble.

Next day the swaggering entry into Bolingbroke Castle of Peter Giffard, King's messenger, demonstrated to all that his master was in the ascendant, confident in his restored authority. Lady Joan Audley received him.

"My orders are to speak to the lady Alesia."

"She is ill. It will be a few days before she can comprehend any information."

"I wish to see her."

"I cannot prevent you from forcing your way into her chamber, but you have my word that she is in no fit state to respond."

"Is she in the castle?"

"Master Giffard, we are not on the terms you imply. Of course she is here. Ask anyone you like."

"That would prove something, but not necessarily that the lady Alesia is here. You must understand that it is imperative to do what I say. I have a summons to deliver. The King requires attendance, and madam, it includes you."

"I would go with the lady Alesia in any event."

"Now may I see her without force, or with permission."

Joan could do no more. Frathesancia conducted Giffard to the door of the solar, sufficient to show him Alesia asleep, and looking worth enough to tone down his attitude.

"How long?"

"Before what?"

"A journey to York, to the King. For you, lady Joan, for the Countess Alesia, for Hervey de Bury, Lewis le Clerk, and chaplain John Beaurepair. The King will not wait for ever."

"The point is, Peter Giffard, that the King has nothing to fear from us."

"I hope, madam, we can get off in a couple of days at most."

It was six days. When improved in health and fit, Alesia was not for being told by messengers. Nor did she appreciate the deliberate irony of Peter Giffard being chosen as the messenger, cousin of the John Giffard executed after being with Thomas at Boroughbridge.

Alesia looked round the escort, to guess from its composition what evidence she could of their status. Captain, archers, men-at-arms, much to whose relief the ladies were riding and not in clumsy equipages; and further to their admiration the ladies had dressed in smart and simple finery. One matter in everybody's mind - with Edward now in charge, and no opposition that dared to rear its head what would happen now?

"I always look down from the hilltop, Joan, whenever we leave. I expect Edward will go on as he always has whenever he had a chance."

"However do those two sentences tie up?" asked Joan, who had been restraining herself from mentioning Alesia's worried look.

"Ah. If Edward gives Bolingbroke to a de Spenser he'll get a piece of my mind."

"If, dear, we get to see him. It might all be between clerks. It might even be worse."

"Worse than what? I know. Yes, I am frightened. Yet I am entitled to dower, as widow."

"And other inheritances also, Alesia, but what are we dealing with? Revenge?"

"In the actual written order demanding our presence I was referred to as your daughter! You tell me, mother!"

It was an attempt at climbing from despond with jocularity. When Giffard was nearby next day Alesia asked:

"Master Giffard. Here we have some thirty archers. That is more than I can take on myself, though I am no mean hand with a bow."

Before she could also mention men-at-arms Giffard looked surprised, and made to reply. This was not about Alesia's archery as she had first imagined. It concerned the archers. In some hesitation as to whether he should reply or not, he did say that they were all there for her protection.

"Peter Giffard. I have heard that sort of thing before. I have travelled much, and I have had involuntary escorts before. Protection? Protective custody I think you mean, and that is a euphemism for you know what."

"My orders are in fact, ma'am, to protect you."

"Of course they are."

"No. I think you misunderstand me. There are dangerous men about. Thousands, maybe. There are lords whom the lord King has spared, and who may be your enemies."

"Spared? Spared? Who?"

"Ma'am, let it be known that nearly fifty lords and knights were with the Earl. Only, well, perhaps not 'only', but about one in five suffered the final penalty. It is said the rest may be fined or pardoned. Or, indeed, both. Surely that is clement of the King, ma'am? The King, in his authority anointed."

He did cross himself, the ladies assumed it was because of his cousin executed; they remained tactfully silent; their eyes showed enough thoughtful understanding.

"What is the danger to lady Audley and me?"

"Men in despair may seek revenge. Where else but upon what was nearest the one who led them to defeat. I am sorry to speak such of the dead, but surely, lady Alesia, you must have noticed such happenings in the past."

"I have noticed that men are always changing their loyalties, and what should be permanent, if not conventional, is so often blown away by a wind, and sometimes back again."

"Have you not heard, ma'am, of the capture of the lord Badlesmere?"

"Bartholomew Badlesmere? Yes. But his wife was stupid enough to anger King Edward."

"I know nothing of Badlesmere's intentions, but I followed the King's men on my way. We met after they had made their capture. It was this side of Trent. Where was he going? To Bolingbroke? For revenge? Or to hide? You could not, wisely, have tried to hide him."

"Revenge, on me?"

"To the view of distraught men, my lady Alesia, you are associated with the Earl Thomas. Whatever you may have done in private, as you suggest, is doubtless unknown to them. They think they've been deceived. With some, their blood is still up."

"And the King?"

"Perhaps he knows more, milady."

Peter Giffard knew nothing further to say. His job was to conduct the parties to the King in York, and any explanations or none that he would give were to make that end easier.

On the main tower of York castle there was a body hung in chains. It was Roger Clifford. Nearby another corpse, that of John de Mowbray. Justice was on view.

The apartment in which they were placed was large, plain, warmed by fire, and firmly locked and guarded. Visible through two high windows was the sky.

Day after day after day could be passed in nothing but idle speculation while they waited upon activity from the King. Their maids calmed them. Hervey de Bury and Lewis le Clerk attended them, as did padre Beaurepair. No-one, however, knew the mind of the King; his clerks had no information to give or even guess. It was true as Giffard had said that they were documenting fines for some of the rebels, and pardons for payment. They were taking lands and estates from the beheaded lords and knights, the measure of guilt of them and the survivors being decided by Edward on a mixture of advice and their known actions, and on his impressions gathered over the last dozen years.

The month of April passed into May. Edward revoked the Ordinances by a Statute called 'of York'. He was continuing on his previous course, for he appointed Hugh le de Spenser to expand the work of Parliament. The Bishop of Exeter, Walter Stapleton, was to reform the Exchequer, and domestic accounts were to be separated from it.

"Is this what Thomas was preventing? I verily think proud little realms of Earls within a kingdom are a hindrance. From Burnell's first Parliament forty years ago the Commons have helped the realm, but Thomas could not stomach them."

Joan may well at one time have liked to join in such a discussion. Now her health was failing and her spirits low. It had all been too much for her. For Alesia, unbeknownst, in trying to comfort Joan, she was taken out of herself and helped thus through these uncertain weeks.

"I cannot say Joan, that I am really used to this sort of thing. I at last begin to think a nunnery and the chastity in such peace would be better for our future."

"My dear, surely you will marry again. What are you, about forty? What about Ebulo le Strange?"

"You know about him? Yes, of course you can have done. I wonder, now, in these circumstances. Thank God he's in Ireland, otherwise he would have been with Thomas. Again, thank God. I may have, and I must repent to say this, that my conscience over my failure with Thomas is relieved that it is now all over. But I feel so deeply for poor Thomas, yet. Pushed by his office, what else could he have done? He was entirely unsuitable for the task; he got no proper support, and, well, I've said it all to him. God rest his soul."

"I wondered why you hardly listened to Beaurepair."

"After my brothers, mother, father, husband, dead? What words of comfort can chaplains ever utter? Look elsewhere. Look to God and his will. It is a real, real inside feeling, as you must also know - a wound that has to heal over."

"That sounds like Ebulo talking."

"Yes, I suppose it was. He put it much deeper, at a time when it was not so deep. Something also about God's purpose not necessarily being for happiness, but to build character and find purpose. He has rather a detached attitude."

"All I can say is that having one's character built is most unpleasant. Look, Alesia dear, what do you think is going to happen to us? Instead of arguing with Edward about dower, for myself I should be thinking about being looked after in a nunnery. Nicholas's grandmother is in Ledbury. On that, where do you suggest would be good and suitable? I should have gone when Nicholas died."

"You would want to be in Pembroke or Devon I suppose. Heavens, Joan, surely you could be looked after there. Your son will inherit huge estates there from your uncle William, and your sister Eleanor."

"I don't think I want to be far away over there. I would rather be near to you. Not even Ledbury. In any case his guardian is a collateral of Mortimer of Wigmore, and that may taint him."

Alesia thought that it was a tenuous connection, but a King could use it if it became convenient. She would say nothing - her own connection with Thomas was very close indeed. However hard she had tried to disassociate her own thoughts and presence from him, the outside world may see only her twenty-nine years of marriage.

Lewis le Clerk paid his daily visit, to give news and receive instructions. Week after week there had been little of either. The King's clerks now thought the King felt the country was under control at home, no other factions having arisen. Except that the Scots were beginning to move South again.

"Everything repeats itself in spite of all, does it not, master Lewis" stated Alesia.

"Yes milady, but it is also said, among my kind that is, that King Edward is turning his mind now to the disposition of lands. He has had long lists of manors, advowsons, fees and the like recited to him."

"de Spenser was there I presume," replied Alesia, and at once wished that she had not spoken the name in that tone, or at all. Lewis steered the subject away. Well-known as the thought may be, it was not for her to stimulate a source of gossip.

"You are being referred to, lady Alesia, as Countess of Lincoln, Countess of Salisbury, and Lady de Clifford. Lady Audley is also being mentioned. So far I know of no documents, for any of this."

Lady de Clifford? Oh, yes. Because of the corpse on the wall outside. A trick had been missed by their not making it visible from inside the chamber.

The de Spensers would come first. That was clear to them all.

"Anything about meeting the King?"

"I think, from my experience, that if it occurs, it will be some days yet, ma'am."

After Lewis had gone, Joan expressed her disbelief that she herself had been mentioned by the clerks at all. She had missed the point about de Clifford, as in fact had Lewis.

"Why do you say that?" Alesia hoped to bury the de Clifford circumstance.

"His tone of voice did not ring true. And in my mind these last days, and all that about the Scots, I see nothing but an awful future. There's Hugh Audley in the dreadful Wallingford Gaol. Nor have the Scots yet avenged Lady Mary Bruce being exposed as a public spectacle at Roxburgh, nor the Countess of Buchan hung in a cage on Berwick battlements."

"Frathesancia," said Alesia, "two things. We will have a special feast all together in a day or two, when you can get it arranged."

"Yes ma'am, for in two days it is midsummer day."

Alesia continued, blandly hoping that her secret would remain, though the only secret may have been that no-one had told her that they knew.

"And a soothsayer woman, in York; Mary, is it? Try and get her here. Find out whose permission we must have to let her in. It is time we had something to think about. I am bored with wool work. Our minds must get out of these stone walls."

They had been hoping with each dawn that they would know their fate. Every prayer at chapel times was for hope. They had hardly realised the passage of weeks till now, when their imprisonment seemed to have a chance of ending.

"Joan dear," spoke Alesia on looking over towards her, "I think perhaps we'd better not trouble about Mary of York. Let me get you to bed, and send for a doctor. Your colour is not what it should be. Tell me how you feel."

Joan was sighing, breathing too deeply, and thought that it was just the effect of being caged, with little fresh and moving air.

"No, I have not given up hope. I just don't understand these things. How can one deal with such a man as Edward? I feel ill because I can see no future."

"You will find, and it is my guess, that Edward..." and Alesia began to whisper "...is afraid of us, as Giffard said!"

"Alesia, really!"

"Oh yes. Oh yes. In his thinking it seems that he really could regard us as a rallying centre for other rebel causes. All right. You may say that's absurd, but men do need a name to follow. That's what Thomas always said, but he should not have taken so much notice, which is what I said. And I said it often. I'm sure he can't think that we are urging anything."

"But it was the insults from Gaveston and the de Spensers, and the power that Edward gave to them. That increased the enmity. I'm sorry, I'm feeling very tired. I'd better have that doctor."

The next person to request and obtain admittance to their presence was, however, Walter Stapleton, Bishop of Exeter. Alesia's thought immediately was that nothing was more likely to make them both feel ill. The gospel was not what Stapleton usually propagated.

"The lord Edward sends you his greetings Lady Lincoln, Lady Audley, and trusts that you are in good health."

"The formality of your opening is excellent sir," spoke Alesia, and as they both knew of their mutual dislike, her tone was appropriate, "but the lady Joan is in poor health, and we are just seeking a medical doctor. It does not seem to be a spiritual matter."

Stapleton ignored the innuendo on his spiritual abilities and continued:

"The lord Edward will be meeting you before long, and will disclose his plans. I am here to ask that you are prepared to discuss matters with him."

"On one point lord Bishop, I am surprised that the word 'discuss' is used. We are here under arrest. Are we to discuss our sentence? In any case excuse me, while I tell my servant to fetch a doctor to Joan."

Which Alesia then did. Stapleton then pursued his message:

"This is protection, ma'am, not imprisonment."

"That word again. We are protected by walls which seem the same for prisons. We do not need protection."

"The King is not vindictive."

"I am prepared to talk with Edward, my kinsman, and to look forward to it."

"And Lady Audley, of course."

"Joan is ill, and cannot discuss anything," which Joan acknowledged from her bed.

"There is to be a settlement madam, and the King will be seeking your seal and approval."

"I believe, my lord Bishop, that you mean acceptance rather than approval."

"Lady Alesia, there is one item to which I must have a straight reply, and it is this: Will you accept lands, dower, or as may be, but you to be subject to fine or penalty of twenty thousand pounds if you should relinquish them or part of them to anyone? To anyone at all?"

The bishop's repetition of the last few words caused Alesia to hesitate, to regret her own immediate taunting manner. Perhaps she wanted a fight after weeks of boredom. Perhaps she did want to avenge the death of her husband. She was now more in the position of a supplicant, however. With strong hereditary rights, of course, but they could be blown away as wind scatters the seeds of dandelion. The bishop had given the outline of Edward's proposals. For if the fine on relinquishment were to be twenty thousand pounds, then that value of lands must be involved. Instantly her mind modified her approach. To anyone at all? - Whatever were they worried about? So they were demonstrating some fear that she might use her power against the King. She actually smiled at the bishop, though he may have interpreted the lack of lustre in her eyes. So men do think on those lines; Alesia found it proved, with this inflexible set of masculine parameters.

"My lord Bishop, a man and a woman are not as Saul and Jonathan, who by death were not divided. The weapons of war were not mine. I mourn for the man, but I do not preach his office."

If the bishop looked surprised it was either because he was unaware of the precise basis of these remarks in the scriptures, and did not want such a line of conversation to challenge him, or he was hurt at the paraphrasing of the texts.

"Countess, I expect the King will ask you to see him tomorrow. I will inform him about the lady Joan."

So Alesia had now to decide what she had been constantly pondering almost since her arrival in York. She decided to look smart and not plain; confident and not beaten; equal, not obsequious; yet not to bruise Edward by appearing unaffected or superior. She would be attended by Frathesancia of course; and by Lewis le Clerk, the latter to make it look like an administrative meeting.

The lady Joan was just able to walk about in their chamber, but had to say that she felt no improvement. After lying down again and resting she was able to translate Alesia's feelings, and to proffer some advice.

"I agree with what you say about how you should appear to Edward. But, dear Alesia, first I am so very sorry I cannot support you. I will have to send to Edward and ask for leave. But you, how tolerant can you be, I wonder, and yet I know you have to be. Does it not help to speak of it? Thomas was after all your husband, murdered by Edward with all the petty excuses men believe for killing. Poor Thomas. His strong manner was of brittle material. Edward proved the vileness of man's fear. I wish I could believe that he will be brought to judgment, in heaven, for there seems no-one left on earth who can... Yet Thomas should have remained loyal. Surely he wasn't really afraid his power would be eroded?"

Alesia had listened, and she remained silent. Nor was there other sound inside this thick-walled room. Every thought of the basis of her life revived in her mind. There had been the period of hope of young marriage. The anticipated heirs had not arrived. With desperation and assumed joy she had tried elsewhere but it was she who had failed. Without love tears and fear had engulfed her; with developing communication towards love the upset of the emotion searing her life could not be faced. Strange that once she could have run away with that knight de Frene, yet now he figured in her mind above no other man. The consequences of barrenness had proved catastrophic. Her husband could not be diverted from the urgings of disaffected barons. With words of hers he had been unmoved. Yet her own father had encouraged him, but without stating a proper end to it all. They had grown apart not by those things that separate respect of man and woman for each other personally, but by outside forces pressing him to an uncharted journey.

"After Reigate, I cannot cry. Not here and now. In Reigate castle my lost and abandoned soul could see no other than stones devoid of feeling. There were solid unresponsive things wherever I would turn for mental balance, from imagining goblins and devils. I would like to cry - if only because all my small needs are in Edward's power..."

"Small needs? That surprises me."

"No, Joan, petty needs indeed. I have seen the jungle and its animals braying for territory. Understand I have had enough of prominence."

"I hope Edward believes that."

"You turn to sleep, Joan, it could be tomorrow before we know."

If Edward had made up his mind as to what to do for Alesia, at least he was ready to talk with her. Indeed, thought Alesia, it seemed clear that he still feared that she would support his enemies, and he wanted to range around the subject for proof either way. He was flanked at the end of the long table by Surrey, de Spenser, and the Bishop of Exeter. Clerks were in attendance. Lewis and Frathesancia were waved to be seated.

Alesia ignored a chair and draped herself as flowingly as possible, sidesaddle, some feet along, on the form by the table. It made her feel more free and outgiving. She had decided to talk to and listen to Edward only. Yes, there was tension in all of them.

The King spoke, with no special intonation. After the beheadings and the hangings, he was looking authoritative. Before he actually uttered, he appeared to be choosing from three or four beginnings, the while looking intently towards Alesia as though trying to penetrate her thoughts.

Finally:

"It were better to meet under pleasanter circumstances."

Alesia cursed inwardly. That had brought all the memories of good and bad out again. It undermined her from using her defences, and she had to wipe her eyes to stop the tears.

"Perhaps they will so become again."

"Cousin Alesia, Walter told you of a document, a surety, that it is required, that is, requested, that you seal and authorise, a fine if you should relinquish any lands which I grant to you, all now having been at this time taken into my hand."

Edward had spoken as one uncertain of her reaction. He was to receive, however, a clear reply, but longer and politer than Alesia would have instinctively wanted to give. Edward had not mentioned the figure of twenty thousand pounds. He himself must thus have some doubt after meeting her face to face.

"Edward," she began, feeling closer affinity as a kinswoman, also noticing the disapproval on the expressions of the others, "I am surprised to be so asked. I do not mind sealing such a document, because I know that it will never be called in."

The Bishop sought to ask a question and was nodded to by Edward:

"Since March, Countess, have you communicated with any one of the King's enemies?"

"Certainly not."

"Nor with any of the former revolutionaries, proved guilty or not?"

"No."

Who could they be, she thought; the King's summons arrived soon at Bolingbroke.

"I had neither the time nor the desire."

"Some were making from Boroughbridge to Bolingbroke."

"To, towards, to there or other estates or Thomas's lands, or where? They did not arrive at Bolingbroke."

All the while Alesia was looking gently towards Edward, and noticed that at the mention of Boroughbridge he had winced and closed his eyes. She continued to look at him during further exchange with the Bishop.

"We have to establish your loyalty, you who are recently - ah - widowed."

"I am not the Countess of Buchan."

"You are a de Lacy, and it is known that your father urged your husband to rebel."

"I urged him not to rebel."

"Are you not loyal to your parents and to your husband?"

"I was surprised at what my father said. I always thought he was urging influence, not death and destruction. I interpreted my loyalty to my husband as needing to try and stop his insurrection."

"He was senior Earl, surely, and had to lead. You must have known that."

Alesia crossed herself in respect of her memories of Thomas:

"You don't have to lead people just because they ask you. I do not know why he rebelled. He was in no particular danger. Nor did he have any special objective."

"No special objective! With two groups of armed forces, and trying to join the Scots!"

Alesia spoke directly to Edward, who was just letting the Bishop go on, knowing well that it was not making any difference.

"Edward, do I have to say this to your bishop, that Thomas had opportunities many times to kill you, but had no intention of doing so."

"Let me say, Alesia, that it did not look like that to me. However, there are other points to discuss. The documents, for example, are ready."

"I do not dispute what you propose so long as I retain Bolingbroke within it all."

Edward nodded.

"Lewis, my seal."

With the action taken to finalise the contract Edward relaxed. Alesia remained silent, waiting as seemed prudent with this serious set of frightened men.

"Perhaps it is I who should continue, Edward," Alesia went on, breaking into the quiet moments of the process of sealing the contract.

"It seems that because of my detention with little more than my own thoughts you consider I have some wish to influence affairs of state, to pursue some ambition of power seeking. Of course one regrets inability to live in harmony with one's husband. That is my regret and none other. It was a defeat for me, as for my designated task. Of course I have to weep, but that is not a condoning of wrongful leadership, for it could and should have been to preserve loyalty in dangerous times."

Surrey made to speak, but decided better of it. Exeter had begun to speak before he had assembled his thoughts. As they turned out to be on the same line, Surrey did not contribute at all.

"Madam, a fine could be exacted if in future you were to gather renegades about you to the detriment of the realm..."

Alesia drew herself up in fury:

"Edward, this is antagonistic nonsense. Edward, this attitude is far from any reality of mine. The bishop may believe that I am his enemy. The concept is laughable to me. I am in his terms a chattel, and inseparable from whatever circumstances are thrust upon me. To him I am no more than a fief to be bargained over. No, I have my opinions, and persuasions which failed in the face of persuasions by others. I say to you that I wish not for a highly prominent husband, nor to have other than security. There are lives other than preferments."

Edward understood. He had his love, and his commitment, though it was to Hugh de Spenser.

It had gone far enough in the presence of the others.

"You may marry whom you wish, of my allegiance," spoke Edward, "You may have for life as my Tenant-in-Chief Bolingbroke and much of your entitled inheritance, subject..."

There was no need to ask upon whom her lands would devolve on her decease.

Alesia looked up, expecting the continuation which Edward gave: "...to the ultimate interest of the lord Hugh."

Alesia once again wondered who was the specially manful one in Edward's liaisons. He seemed always to comprehend with feeling any talk on marriage relationship. Not so the Bishop of Exeter:

"You, ma'am, say you have no desire for elevation to your previous status in this realm. That is, perhaps your belief at this moment, but there are some who would seek such through your inheritances. Yet you say also that when you were consort of one who was seeking power, by the overthrow of the anointed King, you constantly attempted to persuade your husband into obedience."

By now Alesia realised with confidence that it was all over, and that Edward and she understood each other. She knew the documentation that she had disdained to read would be reasonable. Exeter could not get away from his inbuilt prejudices. Even de Spenser ceased to look towards her as though she was a competitor. Alesia replied in effect about her past, as to the four of them:

"My lord Bishop, the lord Thomas wished to influence, and no more. I have to repeat that. As to the rest, I have a fine collection of thoughts kept to myself."

Edward slightly smiled, looking as if he was pleasantly touched in weariness.

The summer months, so soon after Boroughbridge, saw much restitution of Alesia's rights. The sealing of her twenty thousand pound recognisance took place on the 27th June, for payment on the 1st of August, but void and of no effect if she retained all the lands she had or would be given.

By July she was being referred to on parchments as the King's kinswoman, Countess of Lincoln and Salisbury. John de Barton of Fryton had been mandated by Edward to spend his whole time upon her affairs.

Those affairs began to be assembled as:

Clifford in Wales, the castle, town, and manor; Bolingbroke castle in Lincolnshire, town, manor and soke; other manors, moors, markets and knights fees; all the lands and tenements in Holborn, London, as freely and fully as her father had held them. It was suitable to her household, now bereft of national duties which would have fallen to a male heir.

Alesia was also allocated 500 marks a year from Clitheroe, castle, town, and manor; other towns and manors, vaccaries, parks, chase, and forests. All of that was, however, as soon cancelled and surrendered, being diverted to pay for the auditors throughout the country who were sorting out the affairs of Thomas and the other rebels.

On the way home to Bolingbroke, Alesia with Joan stopped at Barlings Abbey. Abbot Thomas was relieved and delighted.

"It is a relief, lady Alesia, in these troublous times for you, and with our deep sympathy, to have heard that you were alive and well, and now to see you yourself. Rumours come out as news, and news insisted on as true, even witnessed, can be false."

Abbot Thomas hesitated there, realising that witness in his own vocation held a gravely different meaning. Alesia, however, was more intent on speaking. The relief she felt at passing through the ordeal of the past few weeks gave her the wish to give thanks to God. After worship she spoke to the Abbot:

"Thomas, in thanksgiving for our lives and mercy in danger, I will alienate some property for the better support of your work in conciliating our more than fearful God. King Edward has agreed to my proposal; I spoke with him at York and the licences were sealed. It is thus for you to accept the manor of Swaveton, and I added for your assistance the advowson of the church there, and licence for you to appropriate the church there."

With some humility, and at this unexpected new support, Thomas stood up with the initial intention of kneeling before her. Feeling that that might be too much for her to accept, and quickly realising that there would be an anticlimax in rising again, he stayed standing. He changed his attitude by bowing to her.

"This gift, lady Alesia, to add to others from your grandmother and yourself is more than I would have expected, particularly after - shall I say - the recent changes. May I add that a whim of a King can go far, and we have been much at prayer for you."

Alesia realised that they themselves had also been worried by the connections of Barlings Abbey with her and thus with her late husband Thomas of Lancaster.

She smiled, fully in control of her secret thoughts:

"Sir Abbot, also you, your men, and your lands are granted protection for life. The Exchequer will thus not harass you."

Abbot Thomas wished that he had knelt. The lady Alesia still had power and influence.

The King himself was now pleased to be in control, though not every deputy took notice of his new authority. Joan had not received her castles, lands, tenements and crops in Staffordshire, Cheshire and Shropshire, which had been ordered on 21st July. Edward's displeasure was remitted in August to Roger Corbet to execute his mandate.

"Well, de Barton," stated Alesia, "the lady Joan and I wish to be informed of any changes in our dispositions. In fact, I think you had better tell me, because the lady Joan is still not well enough to think of these matters. There will not be so much to do here at Bolingbroke as there was in my father's time, but nevertheless, I fully understand that these dispositions have to be kept tidy."

"You, lady Alesia, are still tenant-in-chief to a great deal of what there was, even though some of the benefit moves to - er - others appointed by the King. I speak of the de Lacy inheritance, of course."

"I am aware that the lord Thomas's Honor of Leicester was forfeited to the Crown."

"Yes, lady Alesia, it will take a couple of years to sort out, because only four manors remained in hand, all the rest went to knights for their service, as perhaps you knew."

"de Barton, I confess myself horrified. I did not know it had gone so far. It was the road to penury. I must have failed completely to have penetrated even the shallows of the late Earl's feeling."

"Lady, it is so often impossible with men to move off a chosen route. Determination sets in when obstacles appear. However, I understand that you wish to know the acounts of the bailiffs, reeves, park keepers, forest receivers, and so on."

"As widow, I must. I am not unused to schedules, rentals, rolls, and stock and grain accounts. You hesitate, or so you look, de Barton?"

"Oh no, not for anything you have said, ma'am. I have to introduce a sadder note that the King requests one more grant from you. A..."

"Oh. I thought that was all over. What? I note the word 'request'. To monsieur D. I presume. Again."

Alesia thought that once more she had been rash with her expression, but John de Barton did not react.

"Yes, it is so. Reversions, after the life of the lady Joan - part of her dower which was to have come to you my lady. Congleton, Whiteley, Ronkore, Constableship of Chester which were held by your father."

"And everything else she has in Cheshire, I suppose."

"It is so."

"I was not really expecting them myself."

"The law is that way at present. A document is required to change it. There will of course be a meeting."

Alesia's reaction had once again to be a movement of the shoulders, in feeling to clear from her mind an unimportant matter, or to make it so.

I will travel nowhere," she said,"but my seal can be sent."

"It will be used at Barlings, because I understand a party will arrive there to act with you."

"Oh, only at Barlings, so convenient. But who will be there?"

"One never knows, I'm afraid, who in the end will arrive, or just their seals by clerks. Some have documents taken to them. Possibly de Britannia, Richmond, de Valencia, Pembroke, Arundel, Basset of Drayton, de Bello Campo, Roger Beler, others, and me."

"No, de Barton. I am not sure of my reception. Take my seal."

"I am sure that is a good decision, lady Alesia, for it is so often left to us to search for such lords anyway. You have much remaining to consolidate..."

Before his last sentence was enlarged upon for clarity, Frathesancia appeared, to request her mistress's company on behalf of the lady Joan.

"Please, Alesia, I beg you," asked Joan, in some distress, "please do not leave me. I believe this to be my last summer. While I do not fear death, I am frightened to be alone on earth. By your expression you look as if you cannot believe this to be true. But I feel aches where there were none, numbness where there should be feeling. My energy is sapping away. I must seek atonement for my sins, and forgiveness."

"That may heal you, my dear Joan. It is hard to know what sins you may harbour which cannot be expunged."

"My menfolk have fallen foul of their anointed King."

"Not you."

"Not I, but it reflects on me. You ride a track between two precipices, it seems to me. I suppose your father did as well. Did you know he played a dangerous game - more for the King and law than for the people, yet the people thought otherwise?"

"Joan, yes, once or twice he may have practised a little duplicity. He had to, I suppose." Alesia evaded direct engagement on the subject.

"And so did you, I feel, in that affair when you were taken from Canford."

"Yet Edward is still a bit wary."

"But you play it all with such skill."

"Oh, Joan, please, be careful, be silent. At least on that subject."

Silent she became, but her lips were moving to find unuttered words.

Alesia lay a hand upon her and in a whisper spoke closely:

"Be at peace, I will stay with you..." and in response to an appealing look, "...yes, there will be a priest soon. Come, Joan dear, you have much time yet to live. Am I not your dutiful daughter now? Remember I was thus referred to on Edward's summons to York?"

A faint smile joined them.

*I will also send far and wide for your son James, again. Perhaps by now he is as near as Knesale."

"Look after him, please, he has only nine years even now. It did not turn out well for me to have put him in the house of Roger Mortimer, who is now in the Tower. But perhaps Edward can hardly worry about a boy."

She was reassured, but Alesia wondered how much longer she could continue with a fair expression and calm statements. Yet she added, at the same time attempting jocularity towards her young step-mother:

"After all, through you he is my half-brother."

The Mortimer household was, however, still under surveillance by King's men. James did not arrive. Joan, Lady Audley, died.

# CHAPTER 24

Apart from living and moving, thought Alesia, I have no role. I am but a flower with a shattered stem. There was no-one other than herself responsible for reassembling the pieces of her life. All which had passed prevented any outgiving. During her life with Thomas it was all very well to have dreamed of a future with another man, but the perils of the passage forward impacted hard.

"Abbot Thomas, my lady."

At least a visit from the Abbot of Barlings Abbey gave purpose to the grey misty November day at Bolingbroke. There was no feature other than the sun rising, and the maintenance of body and soul while it passed through the skies to fall once again below.

"Civilised company, Abbot Thomas. Thank you for coming whatever your mission."

"Not what you might expect ma'am. I ask for nothing, though I could have purpose alone in thanking you again for your support of Barlings, and of your and our faith in the power of our work."

"Thomas, you imply there is now something else to stir you."

"Yes. It is a solemn matter, but this time... well, let me not start at the end. No. I have brought a message to you from King Edward, or rather the content of a message which he has sent to everyone with authority in Lincolnshire. It is about protection for you..."

"That word again! To be so looked after, why should I worry?"

With some surprise, not knowing its previous applications, Abbot Thomas continued nevertheless. "The King has heard that some armed men are marching this way. They are awaiting an opportunity to harm you in some manner."

"Abbot Thomas! You were making me frightened. It is not your fault at all, indeed! I am grateful for your coming, but to what end, in all common sense, should I be attacked? Armed men? Lancaster's disappointed knights? Revenge on me? Who... But yes, I know the scenario. It has been whispered before."

"My lady, pray let me continue - I cannot say who these men are, but I presume something like what you say. Only they themselves know. The King addressed me among others, and I am here to tell you. The Sheriff and bailiffs have been sent to; the sheriff is authorised to use the posse of the county to apprehend these men, if necessary."

"So he will have a posse out?"

"Yes. I myself have brought extra men to hold the gate here if you wish to accommodate them."

"What on earth could these men want? I still feel incredulous."

"Only God does not change his mind. Men do so. There was Warwick, for example, then Arundel, first for your lord, then neutral, then for the King. Men have lost what they owned and may now think to please King Edward. Even now others who captured Warwick castle in the lord Thomas's name are being dealt with. Some may have escaped. The lady Badlesmere is still in the Tower. Lord Badlesmere is in Wallingford gaol. It is said that King Edward is considering pardon, but that would bring in a further group of discontented persons. Then there are the sons of the dispossessed."

"In the name of the lord Thomas, not in mine. But I did wonder whether Badlesmere was riding here when he was captured at Stow Park."

"Oh, ma'am, there are no aggrieved persons in your own name... Perhaps, I have just thought, they may want to rally behind your assumed leadership."

"In all event, they are not considering me as separate from my late husband." Alesia sighed.

"It is also said that the lord Henry Beaumont is becoming contemptuous and disobedient at Council. He is apparently veering away from the King. And Wells, for Edward has appropriated his lands. Wells supported Warwick, as you know."

Alesia had to smile.

"I have never known," she said "so much authoritative intelligence so briefly put on any previous occasion in my life!"

"Clerks madam, clerks. Clerks write. Clerks speak. Abbeys also communicate on secular matters with their parchments."

"And I rejected a nunnery for the nothing of oxen, crops and weather. Perhaps I too would have been nearer the centre of events than I am now. Yet what Edward commands is not necessarily done. He has to repeat his directives, to get his own sheriffs to carry them out. Even in Lincolnshire here I do not receive all the money from the county as ordered by Edward. I think people are expecting more trouble, even though Edward has stated his power shall not be restrained."

"I am afraid so. Winchester's defeat in the North by the Scots, and then Edward's a couple of months ago, in Yorkshire, has disgraced the country. It is a disaster. Edward is in despair, they say, and people bow only to strength. In Yorkshire they are buying immunity from the Bruce, in the Forest of Pickering certainly. The forest community have refused to pay to get their hostages freed from the Scots. Values of property are decimated. Skipton Castle is badly damaged from attacks."

"For certain? It has only been rumours here."

"Ma'am, again the universal church - universal in this case as far as Topcliffe, the rector of Seamer. It is said also, for our comfort, that Robert the Bruce desires no more than money. He does not want to fight, and evades a battle if he can."

The Abbot continued:

"Now, as to your safety. I feel we should talk of that again."

"I had almost forgotten. There is John in charge of the gatehouse. John de Lacy. Named from our name. His origin obscure. I have had a sudden thought - these armed men - could they just be Kyme, or

Willoughby, noticed as going home this way, but with, of course, no ulterior motive. Darcie, perhaps, though he would not have to come as far as here for Nocton. Yet he has been pardoned."

"Maybe, but I feel the information is about persons more ragtag. I do not think that mistake could be made. Can men be sent out, to keep in touch with the sheriff?"

Yes, Abbot Thomas, they can. Poor Edward. Nothing much goes right for him."

"You seem calm, lady Alesia, but perhaps unbelieving that there could be such danger. What you know and feel of your own actions and former attitudes will not be in their knowledge. In all Edward's problems and busyness he has found thought to act for your welfare. For ourselves at Barlings, we offer you safety there if you would accept."

"You are kind, Sir Abbot, and I might agree. I suppose I have to believe that many men's thoughts are not my own. If there is still fear at Christmas, then I would wish to do so, to celebrate with you. For now, let us be actively prudent."

Prudence. The starting point of prudence, thought Alesia, was to check on the present state of her affairs. Then to be around among her peers to see and know how the future was shaping, and that could only be done in London. Perhaps dear Ebulo would wish to marry her, though she could only note that so many after an illicit affair were abandoned upon the chance. Only Ebulo would anchor her in life and give it focus. She must wait. At forty-two it must be wrong to experience such skittish feelings as constantly arose in her. It was fun alternating with despair to work coquettishly with instincts.

Firstly, though, there could be no forgetting the past. Politically it was ever present in the previous form. The de Spensers now received lands of the former Knights Templars, so neither the King nor they had learnt anything about not creating resentment. For now, de Halton was asked to arrange a London visit.

"Before that it will cheer me to buy some clothes from Katherine de Lincoln. I understand she is carrying on after the death of her husband John. Why did your expression change?"

"I hope, ma'am it was indeterminate...it was just that she...oh dear, I'm sorry..."

"Come on, come on, I can guess. Let us not remind ourselves of these things. She is also associated with someone about whom you do not wish to remind me?"

"I am sorry, again ma'am, yes. The de Spensers."

"Let it pass, let it pass. Strange company, I agree."

"However, my lady, to London."

"Aye. And before that, what again are my absolute rights by now?"

"People seem to be waiting for something else to happen. King Edward's orders have constantly to be reasserted. However...as to places to live, for yourself, apart from manors if convenient, obviously Bolingbroke here is certain, and your Inn in Holborn in London as your father had. Then there is Clifford castle. As to Halton castle in Cheshire, I do not know if the Keeper Gilbert de Syngilton has acknowledged that. Then there continues your dower as assigned by the first King Edward at your marriage - the castle and revenues of Newcastle-under-Lyme. That is the one, of course, which if challenged successfully in court you would receive Hungerford town and manors instead."

"Revenue?"

"Well, ma'am, Lewis le Clerk could probably recite it better than I, but I can say that if pressure has to be exerted for its collection it usually works. It comes from many sources. Because most are those of your late father, so they are used to it. Some is now also coming in, surprisingly, as from the late Lady Joan. May I add that the five hundred marks from Clitheroe and revenue from the five other manors up there, and the vaccaries, chace and forest - which are now returned to you - that is being collected. Also the three hundred from Whalley Abbey monks for the gifts of your ancestors."

"You sound surprised, Henry. I suppose you're right to be so after the changing orders."

Clitheroe. Memories again; of Thomas and Joan Ploucoun. To hide them, she held on to a bitter point:

"Canford! I had to grant it to Surrey, including the new park my mother formed, and stocked with deer!"

With hopeful diversion and tact, de Halton rejoindered in a lowered voice:

"I remind you to Swaveton - you gave it to Barlings Abbey with its church, for the well being of the King, the Queen, your father and mother and your brother Edmund, and your ancestors. At present you are at a reasonably consolidated stage, ma'am, with what you have and what you have done."

Yes. Swaveton. Had she forgotten her late brother John in her dedications? Had de Halton forgotten to mention him? Not now, anyway. To the future. Perhaps she was ready to travel to London to see if Ebulo had returned there. Heaven must know that that must be all. It would certainly not be for the jangle of conversation about the disasters for new widows. Her future depended on Ebulo. There passed plenty of time on the journey to ponder on that future. Her circumstances had cleared in the same way as a bad dream ended. The manner of its finishing was more frightening than its continuance. Alesia was pitched into a personal freedom which conscience plagued with doubt. The new life offered had been desired, but not with this starting point. If only God had taken Thomas away by natural force there could be grief and then an end to inner tremors of responsibility. There would have been humble submission to unknown force and uncomprehended cause. Incipient guilt could not then have found any basis for his death, but only whether she could have made his life better. As villages and holdings were slowly passed Alesia observed much emptiness of life out there in the cold world to match her own circumstance. The crops were poor again this year, the clothes of the people unkempt, the horses and oxen underfed. This showed man's efforts to survive, always hoping and praying for decent wellbeing. Man's own initiatives frustrated, but not by man. For Thomas, how could she have stopped him bringing about his own destruction by another man? Ebulo was always telling her that she could do no more. Nor would she have married Thomas voluntarily. More than thirty years of her woman's life had been shackled, knotted into a social discipline which suppressed emotion. Thoughts of seeking a life companion, flirtations, open judgment of who would be right for herself, all that had been banned by its being purposeless.

Now she hoped that it would be Ebulo who would seek to marry her. Of course it had been mentioned, without daring to make a promise while Thomas was alive, and Ebulo mostly absent on missions since. Had Thomas thought like this of her? He had given no sign ever, leaving aside known and unknown manly excursions, of wishing to break with her. Of all their disagreements, none of them were personal. Poor Thomas. What else could Alesia think? It was, and had to be, 'poor Thomas'. For herself, it seemed either that the playful life she felt she should have had when young could now begin, or better that she would be beautifully entrapped by dear Ebulo. There was a contrast with Thomas! How rated it though, starting not from open choice, but peering through the bars as a bird in a cage? Let Ebulo decide as he may. Damn the man for waiting a descent interval. If he was waiting.

With feelings of hope in life reviving by her mind being full of thoughts of her dear love Ebulo le Strange Alesia was sought out by Geoffrey de Villiers. He was by now Receiver at Bolingbroke of her revenues, promoted from Constable of the Castle.

"No, lady Alesia, not money this time. Just a writ from the King, about Roger de Mortimer. No, no, not bad news for you, ma'am, just not to communicate with him or his adherents in any way..."

"He must have escaped from the Tower! How does one do that?"

"I am afraid it does not say, ma'am. But, as usual it says..."

"Read it all, please."

"It is addressed to all counties, their sheriffs, bailiffs, liegemen, and some individuals such as yourself..."

"How am I addressed?"

"As Countess of Lincoln and Lady de Clifford. It says that they and you are prohibited under forfeiture of life and limb from affording aid to Roger de Mortimer de Wygemor' or his adherents. No one is to communicate with them in any way, but to pursue them with hue and cry, as the King's rebels and enemies. Whoever adheres to Mortimer to be punished as the King's enemy. It also mentions his rebellion and, yes, his escape from the Tower. I do not think you need worry about it, my lady."

"No. Thank you Geoffrey. I have my mind busy on other things. Except I might enjoy the thrill of a hue and cry."

The marriage of Alesia and Ebulo was solemnized by Chaplain Beaurepair.

Life became a voyage of discovery of the oneness of two depending on each other in love. It was a home against the anxieties of the greater world. That outer world was Edward himself feeling and acting from his own new freedom.

"The most important factor, dear Alesia, is that I am not important," joked Ebulo on this matter. "Nor is Henry a rebel, or ever has been."

Ebulo had been transferred to Henry, the new Earl of Leicester, Thomas's brother.

"Yes," he continued, "Edward is still giving the de Spensers more and more. They are greedy, others grow in resentment. Same as before. It is not my place even to think of advising Edward."

"I do not want you to try," spelled out Alesia, with feeling. "I know it matters, but it is no longer, thank God, for us. You and I have scraped through. Leave it at that. Edward is disposed well enough towards us. Today's news is that Edward is giving me, us, Lincoln castle and bailey, and, so as not to anticipate too much, is taking away Halton castle and manor."

"For them."

*Of course."

"It's more strategic. Let us hope they run there to escape."

"Shh! Actually Edward has also ordered the Sheriff of Lincolnshire to pay us the last two years' arrears."

"Oh, well, well. I suppose the real position in the country is that the Queen is the only power other than Edward."

"Heaven knows we need, and welcome peace. And don't you dare get yourself into a high position."

"I will most certainly try not to, but are you not visiting Isabella next week? After that we can visit our manors."

Shortly it seemed prudent to go back to Bolingbroke. There was the need to act because the City of Lincoln had to be sued for the rents falsely collected from the castle bailey before it was confirmed back to Alesia. Judgment on that was ultimately achieved in the Court of the Fee of la Haye for the £57.6.8.

Then there were rumours of a French invasion.

King Edward seized Queen Isabella's estates.

"Interpret that, Ebulo," said Alesia.

"I'm trying hard. Do we believe this? What did Isabella say to you when you saw her?"

"Nothing outstanding to show that this was going to happen. Edward has invented the invasion theory. Certain, she is his enemy, but she's a long way from doing anything about it. I did think she was dissembling half the time. Just talking, trying to keep a friend. Those lands too will go to the de Spensers, of course, Edward's loves."

"Isabella, poor Isabella. What a life. Is she trying to do anything against Edward?"

"She's not succeeding, even if Edward fears that she is. What now? Does no-one take advice?"

"I think it's an act of a besotted man, and a false rumour. The de Spensers are fools to accept. It is also damn dangerous."

"For Edward."

"She's a French princess. Her brother in France won't like it."

"It's all starting again, but Edward won't see it. He's gone too far."

"My dear Alesia, he doesn't understand women."

"Ebulo. No. But you do."

Peacefulness descended upon them. Two years passed with their being left to themselves to live without great public duties, Ebulo not even being officially recognised as the Earl of Lincoln. It was a period of pleasant extended squiredom in the estates. The contrast with the state of the King was absolute. His French dominions of Guienne, Gascony and Ponthieu were seized. The next spring Isabella sailed for France on the pretext of settling the dispute. In the early autumn Prince Edward, as the new Duke of Aquitaine, the future Edward the Third, joined her, ostensibly to do homage to his uncle Charles the Fourth.

Edward's peace was now due to his accidental foresight about the lack of forces being gathered round his estranged wife. He resigned Guienne to his son in France. Edward was right in that France was not interested in invading England now. Isabella, however, had taken as her lover the escaped Mortimer of Wigmore. Feelings of the French took this excuse to urge her out of their kingdom. Relief for Edward upon this great news was shortlived. Financial backing from France withdrawn, it became more positive from the Court of Holland and Hainault.

"There is no pleasure but is muted by another factor. My dear Alesia, I was going to tell you of my forthcoming knighthood, and as a banneret. Also that of Montagu, Cantelupe, and Willoughby."

"Ebulo, so what's the muting by another factor? It's good, isn't it? What is not? Do look pleased!"

"There's more to be pleased about, really. But where does it come from. In the present situation. Shadows of coming events. More tightropes to walk. I have also been granted Sedgbrook Manor, yes; and Cardigan Castle."

Alesia looked speechless in inquiry. Ebulo put forward his fears:

"Don't you see the future arrival of Isabella? We receive honours under Edward. I was hoping to get through ignored by him. Anyway, I am now Supervisor of the Lincolnshire Array. All this comes through

Arundel."

"Ah! I understand. He never reveals which side he's on. My guess is Edward's... as Warden of the Welsh Marches he surely must be, with an office like that."

"I guess he hopes Edward will win when Isabella comes to England."

"Is it as certain as that?"

"At least Isabella is building up her forces, in Flanders; that is known. Ships are being gathered. Arundel has to be for Edward. When he was talking to me, though, he had the air of a man who was speaking without feeling. I do not think he feels safe. Though he is Mortimer's nephew, to him and Isabella he's probably a traitor."

"Oh, dear Lord!" Alesia failed to express despair any further, and tried to finish on a brighter note:

"So, what about us? Shall I call you Sir Ebulo."

"Yes, darling, when you feel especially respectful. In the meantime, as before, support the King, whoever it is, and hope the point is still recognised. For myself, I wait to hear more, because I cannot prophesy."

The horseman who arrived at Lincoln castle that September did not carry orders to array the eligible men of Lincolnshire. Such orders never did arrive. Information by itself there was in plenty.

The Queen had arrived in Essex. With her were Mortimer and Prince Edward. To raise funds he had been betrothed to Philippa of Hainault. The stated objective was to remove the de Spensers. Henry of Lancaster joined them. The forces sent to repel them joined them. Arundel was in flight. The de Spensers fled westwards with King Edward.

Arundel was captured, and beheaded at Hereford without trial, on the 17th November. The de Spensers were tried for high treason, and executed. King Edward was found at Neath Abbey by Henry, who escorted him to Kenilworth castle. The young Prince Edward was declared Keeper of the Realm.

"Should be interesting" remarked Ebulo one morning in mid December.

"What we already know must surely be enough?" queried Alesia.

"We have passed the test, my dear," he paused for effect: "I have been summoned to Parliament."

"Oh! my lord Strange."

"My Lady Strange."

"From Isabella. I know what you are going to say - keep in with the growing up of Prince Edward."

Parliament had a busy January. Declaring that Prince Edward shall have government of the realm and shall be crowned, it was resolved that the King was incompetent to govern in person, that he was controlled by others to dishonour, to the destruction of Holy Church and of all his people; unwilling to see or understand what is good or evil; would not listen to good counsel, nor adopt it, nor give himself to good government.

Different estates of freemen formed a deputation and compelled Edward to renounce the Crown. The demand was intimated to him by Henry of Lancaster. Prince Edward was crowned at the end of January, now of age, at fifteen. Three days later it was declared that Thomas was rehabilitated, and his sentences annulled; that his quarrel was good and just. Thus the last Edward was dispossessed by the agency of common men, whom his father and he had brought forward, to Thomas of Lancaster's great complaint. Then Thomas's good name was restored.

Alesia wept and wept. Where did this place her? For being against her former husband, trying to pull him away from that quarrel, she had now by implication been in effect pronounced wrong and unjust by Parliament.

"Sweet lady," pronounced Ebulo in a tone detached and understanding, "this is politics. Just wonder where these people were when you were in danger. Nowhere near you. And wonder where you would be if you had encouraged the rebellion."

He avoided mentioning Thomas's name out of sensitivity and his own feelings.

"No-one would have come to your aid," he added, "nor would they now..."

He stopped there. It seemed complete enough as a sentence. He was not, however, clarifying the confusion in Alesia's mind. It must heal itself. He would only try and bring calm to anything she might say. What Alesia did feel was again fear of the ruthlessness of those who were in power. It was luck which got one through this power play of ambition, of greed, intrigue, prejudice, hate, and murder. The new King Edward the Third looked as if he had a forthright mind of his own, even though at present he was submissive to his mother and Mortimer.

She could find no ambition in herself, only the need for wariness, and ingenious conciliation of those who wielded authority from time to time. The confidence in enduring loyalty to something deemed good and great on earth would always be to a temporary image. With the normal first Edward it would have been more straightforward. What now, from Isabella, Mortimer, and Edward?

Towards the end of February Ebulo returned to Holborn from Parliament.

"What is it?" asked Alesia after some hesitation. She could see there was something.

"Am I as transparent as all that? How do you know there's anything at all?"

"As soon as you walk through the door I can tell. So, please tell me... if it concerns me, that is."

"Oh, dear. Well it does. Parliament is now talking about... Thomas.

It is talk so far. They've got the bit between their teeth on the subject."

"Whatever are they considering now? He's been rehabilitated. Isn't the matter dropped? Let him rest in peace. Oh, I hope he can. Oh, I so hope with all my heart."

"I will tell you, since you've read my expression. Rest in peace? Oh, Alesia, I'm sorry, but they look like asking the new King to ask the Pope..."

"The Pope comes into it? To rest his soul?"

"To...I hardly dare say it. No...it's wrong to speak of it like that to you, I'm sorry. With no asides: The Pope is to be asked for canonisation."

"Oh Thomas?"

"So."

"Canonisation? You mean - Saint - Thomas?"

"Saint Thomas."

"Dear Heaven. Is it possible? I mean...in fact I mean...is there a case...a saint?...who can so consider?... What is this all about?...Surely...I cannot understand. Who started this? And why? Will it go through?"

"Well, it seems it would go through Parliament in a few days. Whether it will be passed by the Holy Father is another matter."

"A saint." Alesia was mystified. What she had said was neither a question nor a statement. It was an acknowledgment that the situation had not registered. It was only because it might have been upsetting to her ingrained religious principles that she managed to restrain herself from derisive laughter. She looked round the room, not for any assessable reason, except in hope of something upon which to cling.

"What do you think about it, yourself?" she asked Ebulo. "What can you think about it?"

"I suggest that the only comfortable way to live with this is to treat it as the Romans did when they sometimes made their dead Caesars into Gods. Plain political. For the honour of the family. A cleansing. I suggest, though, it is your opinion that matters. Except, Alesia darling, we may come to believe in time that there is holy power in their inspiration."

"My opinion? One may form when the shock has gone. And the insult to me. I have not been asked, and I presume the widow of a saint receives no recognition. Ebulo...do you realise that if they call upon Thomas to be in the gallery of Saints then I who opposed him must be in line for divine punishment?"

"Oh, Alesia, it cannot be. Go steady, please."

"I will tell you what it is like. It is like the only philosophy I ever came across: - 'women have no capacity to judge, they just believe what men say.' No, I remember a couple of others, from the East - 'men are superior;' and one from Aristotle I think - 'keep women in the house for their weakness.' If that is philosophy."

"I am conscious that Thomas was your former husband, my dear, but I must say I was, and am, more than surprised at this turn."

"My God, so am I. Perhaps in time I shall get some sleep. Or am I meant to stay awake with pride? For myself, I pray that I may be judged on higher beliefs within my spirit."

"Thinking further, I fear for the deposed Edward. Leaving aside Thomas's qualities or virtues. Why are they making him so superior? It must also be to build opinion against Edward, to stop any new faction arising."

With an attempt to bring herself nearer normal Alesia tried to be teasing:

"I am not going to believe what men say, just as the philosopher says. I accept that the family has been trying hard to cure the hurt of it all. They want to expunge the incident, and convince the people about them. They will pursue it to the end."

Whatever the truth of their speculation, summertime brought more. Ebulo had to report:

"A summons, dear, to Scotland."

He continued hastily to smother reaction: "Not the Scots. A small unit, to guard one of the ways to the north."

Alesia:

"Guard from what, then? Not Scots. I will guess. Edward."

"However can you guess that? Yes, to prevent Edward from escaping that way. There has been an attempt at rescue, and they're anticipating another. Thus, I am for the border."

"It was not a pure guess, actually..."

Ebulo showed considerable interest.

"...I wondered what it meant when I was approached the other day. About a week ago. I think they'd been waiting outside to follow me. I got in a press of folk in St. Paul's and a man near me whispered in my ear. He was brief. I was so surprised that I can't remember all he said, but the gist was clear. First it was something about could I help - no name mentioned - get him to Italy. Who else but Edward. From the south coast, I presumed. It was just a passing instant. Somewhere to wait was mentioned. I do not know whether I would have done or not. All I could say in that moment was just - 'Surrey has Canford'. What else could I say? It was so quick that I began to wonder if it had happened. Then I think I heard him say 'Cardigan', which we do have."

"How long ago was this, did you say?"

"I am just telling you now of the occurrence. It is best forgotten. It only confirms that there is support for Edward and some people, I know not who, are trying to get him out of the country. I can say no more. I have probably said too much."

Ebulo's mind searched round questions to be asked in a half-known situation. More than once he opened his mouth to phrase one. Then with an amiable grin and with respect for the resolve of his wife withholding any further point, he drew her to him, kissed her on the forehead and spoke on entirely another subject.

"Once again you have been caught by the sun, to liven your lights and shadows. There was that evening once when we met in the open field upon that hill, the westering sun full on your body. You stood there in its reddish light, stock still, your garments sparkling, a thing of dramatic beauty."

"I do remember, strongly, but there is more of me now, and less shape."

"I have heard, darling Alesia, of sins of the flesh, but I have never heard of sins of the bones."

Ladies of the time of Edward III.

# CHAPTER 25

After Ebulo departed for the North, Alesia was left in London, where she heard of events unfolding. To whom should she give her trust? Had much changed? The comparative unity in the country had already become challenged by those who would not tolerate rule by Queen Isabella and Mortimer. Thomas's brother, Henry of Lancaster, was the young Edward's nominal guardian. He was restored to Thomas's earldoms on petitioning Parliament. As Captain-General in Scotland, and Chief of the Council of Regency his power would have been considerable if he had had more than nominal authority. Quarrels with Mortimer soon developed. He and Isabella were uninfluenceable in their government. Their actions implicated the young King, but they seemed to harbour no inkling that he was growing up.

Isabella linked her cause closer with the Flemings against her brother King in France. Anyone who did not support her was her enemy. With her encouragement her son Edward added the title of King of France. He quartered the fleurs de lys on his arms. A campaign to discourage the Scots was abortive, by their misleading tactic of abandoning their camp fires at night. Bruce had won at last. Nevertheless a wool 'loan' from the clergy for a war with France was put in hand. The shadow of Edward the second dimmed every future action. Taken away from Henry's reasonable treatment, to worse and worse conditions, starved in foul circumstances, he was not dying. This would not serve for Isabella and Mortimer, for he could centre the opposition to them. He simply must die.

Ebulo returned south to Lincoln. His part of the mission was thought to have been accomplished, at least until any scares might come from Berkeley Castle about Edward the former King. He had been thought to be in Dorset, or in Ireland, or across the Channel. It was all guesses based on fears, though the talk of escapes never left peoples' lips. Berkeley, however, was surely safe, though it was close to the Severn estuary. The gaolers were surely brutal and trustworthy in the context of holding a prisoner for their own satisfaction. Whatever Isabella was ordering for the fate of that deposed King who was still her husband appeared unknown to the young Edward when dining at Lincoln Bishop's Palace. Ebulo spoke with him about his patrols up north, in result about nothing much except the weather and the people. Nothing about Edward's father. It was doubtless no more than he expected. He was fully aware of his situation, his mother's venom, political actions being forced upon him. He was waiting. He was not ready. He was observing, and gathering friends. It was easier away from his mother's court, as here.

"I am only glad" said Ebulo to Alesia one evening in their chamber in Lincoln Castle, "that we were interrupted, and he didn't embark on Arundel's execution. I wouldn't have known how to dissemble on that. My own superior. Gives one a funny feeling round the neck."

"Oh, darling, really, I beg you, please don't say things like that. It has to upset me." She continued:

"He wouldn't have let you dissemble. Fortunately he hadn't got round to that when the quarrel broke out."

"Yes. Disgraceful that was, Ministers Cephous, de la March, and Pirry arguing in public with that man Stephen de Clyveland, all in front of Edward. Although, he seemed quite interested and amused to see what would happen. I don't know what he would say now with Stephen being arrested and then rescued from the marshal by a gang. I gather they also assaulted the clerk of the Marshalsea at St. Peter at Arches."

"I think it is known who they are, so something must surely be done, because of the scandal to the King."

Ebulo sniffed a bit in doubt. He had seen enough malefactors in the last few months to fill any court for a long time.

Because of his silence Alesia changed the subject:

"I also kept my own counsel when they were talking nearby - Bishop Henry and Edward that is - about Thomas. They seemed to be speaking loud enough on purpose for me to hear. But I didn't fall for it. I simply cannot get it into my mind that Thomas had anything to do with religious spiritual matters in what he did. Heaven save me, and him, for saying so. God forgive me, but though I am not the judge, Thomas himself was not a Thomas Aquinas, now sanctified for his astounding influence in the church and its affairs. I fear what I say, but I have to speak - to you only, I add - that I do not understand the pressure for this upon the Pope. I say again, God forgive me."

"Dear Alesia, I suggest God and Thomas will both be forgiving and understanding of you. In any case, I shall be surprised if the Pope does anything about it. I had a long conversation, in fact conversations, with Henry..."

Alesia's eyebrows rose.

"... no, no, darling, not Bishop Henry, but your brother-in-law. He's thinking and waiting and also advising Edward. How I wish the King's getting older could be speeded."

It was on their way to London that from a passing messenger the news came through:

"Edward, former King, dead! Murdered!"

He passed on urgently. Perhaps his telling was from excitement, his mission to pass it to others up north.

"God, it's happened," stunned, Alesia managed. "I couldn't believe the whispers, certainly not the intention."

In one word Ebulo produced the total reason, instigation, and commander thereof:

"Isabella"

"But with Edward now pushng forward, she has been totally foolish. Certainly wholly unseeing. God! How scorned and bitter."

"As for Mortimer, what now? He must have agreed. Someone must be next, because this will create real enemies."

"Mention no names."

"Hmm."

"Don't you think of warning anyone whatever we hear."

"Alesia dear. I am not rash, but I'll deal with that if and when something may arise. I wouldn't stand by if I held any good information."

"Steady, steady. Can the news be really true? That's the first thing. With a son next to her, a woman murders her husband. Is that even tolerable in the senses? Leave alone the idea of politics. I fear for dead Edward's old friends. He had some; and not only those - some like decency, just like so many left Thomas when he had Gaveston hung."

"Such as..."

"We each know some, and doubtless the same ones. And his homespun relations antagonistic to the French princess. The less said the better. Once again."

It was an easy suggestion to follow. In shock, there may have been nothing to say, but after a while:

"It can't be true. Edward must have escaped and this is a cover-up. He must, must have been allowed to flee. As you say, a mother, ordering the death of her grown son's father? No woman can do that."

"Or, if they can, with the son gaining power with every passing season, it is extremely stupid..."

After a moment of thought Ebulo added in a lower voice, just enough to pass from horseback to horseback:

"... and dangerous for the son. It must have been arranged when young Edward was away up north. That's presumably why he was sent. At least he is detached from it, it seems."

"In body if not in mind."

"How does Isabella greet her son when next they meet? Just how?"

It was a moment or two before Alesia continued, indeed concluded, the conversation:

"I understand at last why Thomas would not go further than he did. He would not fight harder. He would not contemplate the killing even of his cousin. I can see there is some holy principle in that. Bless poor Thomas."

That Edward the second was stated to be dead was taken by the country without much emotion, even if it was only half believed that the noise of his death throes in the burning of his inside was heard through the high thick walls of Berkeley Castle. Isabella and Mortimer spent the summer solving the Scottish problem, in which they had little interest except what was not inevitable. Governing in young Edward's name they organised by treaty his renunciation of his claim to that throne, much to his unspoken disagreement. His sister Joanna was married to David of Scotland at Berwick, juveniles to close the Scottish connection. King Robert was asked to restore lands to the disinherited, but only those of Percy were returned. It was all necessary, to be free to protect the rear, for concentration on France. Edward was married at York to Philippa of Hainault, which closed the alliance with the Flemings. It was all reasonable and practical, except for Edward's own emotions.

Parliament was next called to be at Salisbury, so the usual preparations for departure to attend were in hand, for setting off from Holborn. Ebulo and Alesia were ready. Henry of Lancaster was not in London, but in the social round they had met Maud, his wife. Herself the heiress of Sir Patrick Chaworth, she simply had to speak with Alesia.

"I am ever so sorry to talk of this, because it will remind you of something I am sure you will have wished to forget. I really am sorry but I must."

Whatever might it be, Alesia wondered. Both her mind and that of Ebulo, standing by, raced through every possibility. Henry, guardian of Edward, disliked Mortimer to breaking point, but what had happened now?

"Henry's refused to go to Salisbury."

This was something, but not unprecedented. A strong protest, but not fatal.

"He's gathering an army at Winchester! Whatever does he mean by it? What should I do?"

Words of astonishment had to be smothered. It gave an interval for belief and thought.

Maud explained further that Queen Isabella's lover Mortimer was to be elevated to an Earldom. Why she was so sorry to mention it all in her distress for Henry was that it was Thomas's situation all over again. The immediate answer came from Ebulo:

"He must not act! He must do nothing. I am one of his vassals, and I have not been called. I know this is not that sort of campaign, but a word would have received consideration."

This was a tactful way of putting that point.

"To tell him not to, I presume" said Maud.

"Absolutely," interjected Alesia. "He has not the power to achieve anything. Nor has he gathered support. He must stop. Yes, I've seen it all before. A few years' patience would solve the problem. Edward will grow up and take over."

"You agree with me then, both of you" Maud sounded much relieved. "But what can I do? How can you help. Henry must be on his way to destruction."

"Yes, yes, yes" spoke Ebulo contemplatively, playing for time to assess the factors.

"You have told him everything you can?"

"Yes, except that when he left I didn't know how far he was going to get involved."

"He has no hope of success. Not a whit. He must ask for peace if it has gone that far. We shall find out at Salisbury."

"Yes, Ebulo," spoke Maud tentatively, "but is he not in rebellion? And his brothers Norfolk and Kent look like joining him."

"Maud, I know what you imply. So, King Edward must be approached. He is a sensible lad, and he will be at Salisbury. He must know the foolishness of this. He must also be considering his own position. He likes his cousin Henry. We will speak with Edward to calm attitudes, and try and persuade him to override our rulers. It must be before matters develop. Do what you can with messages to Henry. Make it personal from you. We must be detached and subtle with Edward. So, Alesia, we have to leave urgently."

Thomas and Edmund, Earls of Norfolk and Kent, always bore total resentment for those who had murdered their half-brother Edward the second. Now they were led into the open by their elder brother.

The situation would best be served by Henry of Lancaster himself dropping his plans for insurrection, before they had taken too much hold. Only persuasion was available to change his mind. No further magnates had yet joined him. It was a matter of urging that it must not be 'now', but that it remained a future possibility.

"I should see Henry," said Ebulo as a starting point of discussing a plan, "but that would make it seem that I had joined him in his gathering of troops."

"No, you don't" responded Alesia, firmly, "you would not be pardoned as you have been before."

"Right, darling. I don't understand Norfolk and Kent joining in this risk. They are not forthright characters. It could result in three powerful brothers asking for mercy. Our part is just to try and persuade young Edward to pardon them - if he can influence his mother and Mortimer."

"Mortimer, mostly. I am beginning to wish I had helped him to escape from the Tower. Then he might have a speck of gratitude."

"You didn't?"

"Isabella, I think, produced the bribes. For myself, I am sore through sitting on fences."

"Back to the business in hand, I'm sorry, but it surely must be you, dear, who whispers to Edward. I am by no means important nor close enough."

"How modest! I wonder, but I would not feel threatened. Just to say for heaven's sake forgive them when they stop their silly actions."

"It comes clearer from a woman, I'll say that. And you have more influence with a King than I do."

"I will do so, but will Henry stop? He must be the leader, though Norfolk's senior. Should I go and find him at Winchester? Or ask Edward first at Salisbury, then go when there's a nod of agreement? Or, the other thing." The prospect of a rescue began to excite

Alesia.

"I can see that Henry would not calmly ride into the lion's den without some assurance. Why is Henry being so damned impetuous?"

"Could we get Edward to endorse a message to him?"

"Hmm. Asking too much, I think."

"Henry's his guardian." Alesia pointed out. "Oh, no, perhaps was, now he's married. On another line of thought - would it be best to leave it to Maud?"

"I would have hoped so, but we must urge what we can."

"We mustn't ignore Isabella and Mortimer. They might act against the...rebels...without Edward."

"They would be very foolish to do too much in this line of country - armed forces, I mean. Isabella is no longer Queen, and he is just a hanger-on to her. It's getting into people's minds that way. Her husband was the basis of her authority, whom she killed out of vicious bitterness."

At Salisbury Mortimer was made Earl of March. As he drew near to the rebels with troops that he had gathered in the King's name Norfolk and Kent deserted Henry of Lancaster. The terms of peace were half their incomes, and a pledge of no further opposition. Peace it became. A peace based on having removed the horns of those who had any worthwhile power. King Edward himself, away in France for most of the year, did not provide therefore a focus for any dissent. The circumstances were easily misread. Social life became enjoyable, life was lived, by Alesia and Ebulo as much or more than other ladies and lords and knights. Upper clothes became fashioned into tighter fitting, pleats in shirts looser. Poor crops and high prices scarcely received a mention - except that in this period Mortimer planned his own further consolidation, cleverly based on what he knew of the discontent of the common people.

Alesia informed Ebulo one evening, in a voice of wonder and regret. "Kent's being a fool. Really, after his experiences.B amboozled by Mortimer's machinations."

Ebulo was shocked, being totally surprised. Uncle of the King, Edmund, Earl of Kent, was rumoured to be in a conspiracy to restore the late King to the throne, for they believed him to be still alive.

"Do you believe that, Alesia? I don't. We hear that Edmund thought he saw him at Corfe Castle, then weeks later we are told about this plot. Of course it's a put-up job by Mortimer."

"For myself, I am not sure whether Edward is alive or not. I am quite prepared to believe he did get out to Italy, that he must have been allowed to escape quietly. As a family matter. As to restoration, that is complete rubbish."

Ebulo was not certain what to say about rumour, now. If Alesia was considering believing the one about Edward's escaping to Italy, why not believe that he had been seen at Corfe by Edmund?

"I agree about the restoration notion being impractical, even if

Edward is still alive. Why do these lords, however, charge into these things, even including the Archbishop of York. I think it's a Mortimer plot to spread these things, to plan the Corfe appearance with someone who looks similar, and then to eliminate the conspirators."

"Heavens, not all of them!"

"Perhaps not to that extent, but some, as a warning that the reality of power lies with Isabella and him. With the volatile emotions of people like their opponents it's not too difficult."

"Well, what would you do? I'll add to that: if anything. But remember that there's a lot of unrest in the country about the extravagance of the Royal Princes. I would suggest that public feeling may support Mortimer."

"Perhaps he is behind that public feeling too, but he can't influence everything."

"May I ask again, then, what can be done, because Isabella and he cannot continue like this. Even so, surely, oh surely, not another murder. Not poor harmless Edmund of Kent? One must thank God that Henry is growing weary, and Thomas Norfolk also is not interested; at least I've heard nothing about them. Doesn't it rest upon King Edward?"

"Just yes, to that."

In the Spring of 1330 in Edward the Third's first Parliament a petition was presented by the Commons against the exactions of the Princes, based on their new demands in their estates to mitigate their financial position. More dramatically, Edmund, Earl of Kent, was apprehended. He confessed his complicity in the restoration plot. He was detained.

A few weeks later Edward repeated his request to the Pope that Thomas of Lancaster be canonised. A month after that a further demand was despatched. Pope John XXII continued the Papal indecision.

"Oh, dear, dear. The usual scenario. I will feel the King has grown up when he gets rid of that motto off his tunic... 'Hay, hay, the wythe swan by God's soul I am', and let others say he's sacred."

There was not all that long to wait. Alesia scarcely prevented herself from crying out 'now!' when Queen Philippa produced an heir. At Woodstock, on the fifteenth of June, a black-haired Prince was the first-born of the Queen. He was to be famous for military exploits, for his loyalty to his father, but he was never to be King, because he died the year before him. His first victory was as a baby, beginning to strengthen his father's attitude, whose potency as a man with status visited upon him.

Tension between the factions became such that Edmund, Earl of Kent, saw prudent to settle his castle and honour of Arundel upon his wife. In the scarcely expressed stalking war dance that was concentrating attitudes, Mortimer acted by September to improve his position by removing Edmund from prison to be executed. It should have been clearer to him that it was more than enough to have killed the King's father, and an uncle, all while living in adultery with his mother.

"We are to leave for the autumn Parliament in Nottingham in a few days, my dear Alesia. To Lincoln first, or perhaps Bolingbroke for a short while until it starts."

Alesia looked closely at Ebulo. His tone of voice had in it more than the announcement needed. With her lips pursed and her tongue pushing at her cheek she taunted with a pleasant intimacy of knowing and understanding:

"There's some background to that."

To Ebulo this was one more occasion when Alesia had interpreted a tension, a feeling, an unspoken thought, all from unexpressed communication.

"I have spoken" he said.

Any urgency of getting on the road northwards was assisted by Alesia wanting to resolve this question. She had also noticed a difference in the bearing of Henry of Lancaster. There was something going on. Both men had an air of solid confidence.

"You be very careful. I don't want you involved in any insurrection" was Alesia's statement to Ebulo at her first opportunity.

"It is not that at all. Please be calm, I beg you. Yes, there is something, but nothing great. Nor me personally. Even now I have said too much. Secret, my dear. Secret, please."

"It's through Henry. After Edmund. It's obvious."

Ebulo realised he had to go a bit further:

"He started the idea of improving things, yes."

Alesia laughed:

"What a brilliant way of saying nothing! How long do I have to wait?"

At Nottingham Castle the plot took effect. It was activated by the King himself, on the instigation of Henry of Lancaster, with the aid of Lord Montacute who learned of a secret way in to the castle from his friend the governor. Climbing through the dark and dirty shafts and tunnels of the sandstone bluff topped by the castle, King Edward led their sudden sally into the chamber of Isabella and Mortimer. Determination overrode Isabella's pleas for him to be spared. Edward regarded the past expunged after Mortimer was later hanged at Smithfield. His mother was moved first to Berkhamstead. The raiding party had included Ebulo, on duty with Henry of Lancaster.

"What does one think? What is there to believe?" Isabella, distraught with fear and remorse, found only anxiety in her position now. "The images in my mind haunt me in their fearfulness. Alesia, you... have you overridden all such memories? What does one do for this? It never seemed so serious when justice was done to a malefactor. But sweet Roger! We gave ourselves and the country peace, we thought; but enmity is continuous. What is Edward going to do with me? Do you think he will understand? Would it have been all right if we could have married? We would have done except of course for Roger's wife Joan."

"You are Edward's mother, Isabella. He has always been well disposed towards his family. You are part of it."

"Perhaps so, yet he is strong-willed like his grandfather. Nor am I even able to go back to France."

Within a fortnight, to Isabella's relief, Ebulo was ordered to escort her to Windsor for Christmas.

In their inner selves Ebulo and Alesia both felt pride in being chosen to accompany Isabella as guides, friends, and escorts. Reinstatement into social communication was complete, and in the new reign. Their demeanour had of necessity to be quiet, confident certainly, but it could only be relative to that of Isabella herself, her chagrin and guilt, mingled with grief. Between Alesia and Isabella silent communication developed. There was no need, no ability, to describe their inner images of their former men put to death. The cold and dreary late autumn day augmented the atmosphere of tensions. Queen Isabella's son had had her lover executed. Remorse at that, another forced death to clear away a presumed enemy, throbbed her mind in concert with the horror which had begun to grow within her over her long-standing liaison as the mistress of Mortimer. How unutterably foolish she had been to live on and on in that situation ignoring her sin that Holy Church constantly condemned to the people. Yet to her their purposes had been the urge to right wrongs.

What would be her own future? That remained her constant unspoken question. The day's journey was passed in silence, excepting only organisational detail. After all, Ebulo the Lord Strange had taken part with Edward her son in capturing her Roger, and casual free acquaintance could only be restrained. Over Christmas, however, it became clear that Edward would not speak about it, and would forever ignore his mother's liaison. She would live out her natural life at Castle Rising in Norfolk undisturbed, if not in mental peace.

Edward's new power was marked with other acts of leniency; restoring inheritances to the sons of those who had lately suffered, and to Mortimer's wife. He made cause with those who had hitherto been discontented. His benevolent actions to maintain the peace by reasonableness were extended to include the wife of executioner Gournay.

"Some will not understand all these actions" said Ebulo one evening to Alesia, "though I am sure he is right. It indicates strength, but those who did no wrong may wonder."

"And some will think more than that," responded Alesia. "Just consider; you say it shows strength. Yes, I suppose it does, but such forgiveness is rare, so they may believe there is little to forgive, that in the King's eyes their actions had been right and welcome."

"You look as if you are going to say more."

"Indeed. Yes, I was hesitating; Gournay was the murderer or supposed murderer of the King's father. So it seems possible to me that the rumours of poor Edward being still alive will grow again. More people will think that way than do already. They cannot believe a King can be murdered by his own. There are always plenty who wish to cling to such a belief. Even the one which names the abbey he's meant to be at in Italy."

"I didn't pay much attention to that with all the others. The abbey de San Burtio you mean?"

"It was. I think it's time the past was forgotten instead of all these actions bringing out everybody's theories and suspicions."

"Like the magnificent tomb at Gloucester?"

There came to be more effort to cleanse the past by King Edward's command. Ebulo and Alesia were invited to Pontefract, to attend the consecration of a new chapel built on the site of Thomas's execution. They had heard that it was in progress, but related it only to Edward's determination to have Thomas sanctified, about which Archbishop Mepeham had pressed the Pope once again. They lodged with the Court in Pontefract Castle. Inside Alesia bewilderment grew. There seemed to be one person, herself alone, who felt involved in the meaning of this gathering, as a proper blessing if not a funeral for her late husband. How could Ebulo believe in her love for him when all her flooding memories had to be controlled by private prayer? The throng there related to the future, with nothing apparent to mourn. Alesia related to thirty years of being linked with the man, whose honour failed to prevail with his assumed task, to end disgraced, humiliated, beheaded. When Alesia returned from the chapel she was always full of the piety of her prayers to bring the spirit of Thomas into the proceedings for opening the new chapel, and to call up the atmosphere of mercy which seemed absent from this new batch of courtiers. Ebulo broke into her state of dedication, perhaps from an unrealised jealousy.

He said "When you left Thomas, I think..."

"And I think you are wrong" interrupted Alesia "that is not the situation - he broke with me."

Ebulo was astonished at this; indeed what he was going to say was that she had been clever and percipient and had done it for her own good. Certainly in the material sense, because she had kept in with the King.

"But you parted, anyway."

"I parted because he would not see his own position and his abilities were not up to it, and so - alright, we parted on that. But he would not accept what I said. And what I wanted" she added.

"I thought it was your foresight of the disaster."

Ebulo had had to change his line of thought from congratulation to exploration and enquiry.

"Well it worked that way" said Alesia, wondering quite what had to be explained, "in effect he marched off. I was alone."

"I'm sorry, but I thought you had said..." he spoke deliberately for absolute clarity "...that you told him you could not back him up nor stay with him if he went once more against the King."

"As I say," repeated Alesia "I did say something like that, many times. And he went."

"So the responsibility is his" mused Ebulo, a little too loudly.

"What?" snapped Alesia "of course it is. But I pray for his soul. I pray also for forgiveness for my part, and for his rest to be in peace."

Ebulo decided he would press no further, since he was somewhat doubtful as to whether his original statement was worth uttering, or even held good. Of course, he thought at last, her talks to Thomas were as challenges as to her own worth and value.

"Thomas wouldn't accept your wisdom" he said, after a pause, believing that to be appropriate and flattering.

"I don't follow you" replied Alesia, "but at least I turned out to be right - unless, that is, being parted from me took away his interest in winning."

Ebulo wondered about her real feelings towards Thomas; though in logic they should never have been strong, indeed the other way round, they appeared to be ever-present, more than memory. But Thomas had been the man she had accepted, compulsorily of course, but for some years hopefully. That feeling will never die; particularly when it is cut short.

"Ebulo, dear" spoke Alesia, thinking that perhaps she had been contradictory when she should have helped him towards what he was trying to say. So she paused and began again.

"Ebulo, dear, is what you wanted to say when we got diverted that I have been clever in maintaining loyalty to the King for material reasons?"

Ebulo started with shock at this direct statement. He thought suddenly that that was exactly what he had been going to say. Spoken by someone else it sounded strong and dangerous.

"Alright dear," continued Alesia "nobody's listening; we can't be heard in the middle of this hall - so that is what you were going to say then."

"Well, more or less, that it turned out that way" responded Ebulo lamely. He gave a quick look round, and saw no-one. So he continued: "I was really trying to praise your judgment, and to say how difficult it must have been."

"Then let me tell you one more thing, and which you may not know, if you think that was good of me. Come nearer."

So Ebulo moved up the table, with another quick reconnaissance around, but no servant had yet re-entered to clear the remains of the meal. Nonchalantly, when re-seated, he whispered - "I am ready for a surprise."

"Since it is an evening when praise is to come my way for my mental abilities I can see what you are thinking, but this is about my mind, or what you believe it to be. So - not only did I somehow go against Thomas, but also..." and Alesia hesitated. Ebulo wondered whatever it might be, but Alesia had hesitated because she was still afraid she might have been wrong - in action - in honour.

Ebulo prudently remained silent, not wanting to divert her thoughts from this matter.

"I was also against my father" blurted Alesia hurriedly and holding her fears in check.

"Your father, Alesia; surely not! He died long before." Ebulo began to wonder if there were occult manifestations.

"Yes, in a way - but as he died, only just before, he spoke to Thomas. And I was there, of course. 'And when this Harry shall die' - that was my father..."

"Yes, yes." Ebulo nodded.

"Well, I'm sorry I can't just now remember the exact words, which I thought I could. But I have gone against my own father's urging my own husband - to carry on the fight against Edward."

They both fell silent then. Two servants came in to finish their work. Neither Ebulo nor Alesia could think of a light word to put on a front.

"Now I remember, yes..." spoke Alesia, when they had gone, after a few long minutes. "What he actually said was - and he asked Thomas to come close to him - he said 'stand with the right of the realm; resist the King; be governed by the counsel of Guy, Earl of Warwick'."

"My dear love, I think your father would have changed his mind; particularly if he could have seen what the Queen and Mortimer were doing. He knew better than anyone that when authority breaks down vicious people take over. You changed your mind. I suppose it can be put that way. Come to that, when Guy of Warwick changed his mind, Thomas himself did not follow."

Alesia pondered this. Perhaps she had only formed a new opinion, but her father had been the firm rock in her life. Her problem was that she had broken with her past. She had come out of the last few years tolerated if not fully accepted by the Court. Certainly in spite of all the changes in her manors and revenues by the second Edward she had not been cast aside. She supported loyalty to the monarch in rightful inheritance whoever he was. A strong desire for security of background it represented, which by her inability to persuade Thomas to the same loyalty had brought her to the insecurity of having a husband in rebellion. She had weathered that by Edward's knowledge of her and understanding, but on her part it had been emotion and instinct and not the product of deep consideration.

"I have found no rest and satisfaction in money contributions to the church; I have found relaxation inside one only when I am there alone" and while she was speaking she looked at Ebulo - sitting there calmly, she guessed he was trying to utter something helpful to her. He would rationalise the position, urge that she carried on with some task, and he would say that they should just continue with their ordinary life. Perhaps he would add a diversion if he could dream one up. Alesia relaxed, and continued: "without your calm reassurances I don't know where I'd turn... I'm lucky to have your steadiness."

"If it comes out like that, then it's fine. I suppose I have more tasks than you - so would you like to join me in a patrol tomorrow - I'm inspecting the district if the weather's decent. But that's not the point really, is it? Dear Alesia - you did right, your father would not stomach Isabella and Mortimer in charge. There's always the young Edward to put things..."

"Have you heard anything?"

"No, but it's his inheritance, and he will do something. He's a tough lad."

Alesia rested her head on her arms. They still hadn't left the table; her mind was full of her own situation. Ebulo had thought further.

"You, Alesia..."

"Don't preach, please don't."

"Sorry. Alesia..." in a lower tone: "you have acted personally and been right politically. Might one not also add that your father had been of course the greatest support to the first Edward, but also to the second. He never took any rebellious action. It was a bit early perhaps in the reign to see what was happening. But, but - let me go on a moment - isn't that the point? If your words are exact, he said 'resist'. That doesn't mean do as much as Thomas did. It was eleven years after when he came to defeat at Boroughbridge. I understand your distress but no-one can foresee that far." Seeing that Alesia had heard enough, and had relaxed enough, Ebulo decided to go on with his opinion, mixed with encouragement, about the situation.

"What the whole thing was about was Edward trying to balance the power of the barons by powers given to lesser folk. You can't tell me that barons rebel over nicknames and insults, however taunting. It was about power. The Great Charter has still only helped the baronage and free men."

Ebulo begin to realise that he was himself of minor status, but that he was talking to a representative of a greater. He had also realised that without Alesia he would not have been in charge of so many castles and manors.

By then they realised that they had no power in these matters, so Alesia returned to the patrol which Ebulo had set up for the next day. Yes, she would like to come too. Then a further thought occurred to Ebulo. After cautiously asking that he might say more about Alesia's father - he proceeded.

"I am not so sure that you need have the distressing feelings about your father and you, my dear, if I may say so. All right, he was sometimes for and sometimes against Gaveston. Mostly against. That's something, but not much. And he was appointed one of the Ordainers to control the King's affairs."

"So?" interrupted Alesia briskly, "I know all this."

Ebulo had recounted it to see if she knew the point to which he was leading. It seems that she did not. Then Ebulo thought he had better put it as a question.

"Did you not know tht he had a secret understanding with the King?"

"Impossible!"

Alesia was dumbfounded.

"Why impossible? he was a loyal tenant-in-chief," Ebulo replied.

"But who above all would know - me, surely?"

"Of course it is said and not written. I doubt if anyone dare mention it at the time. Even possibly, now, perhaps" he added, having shot the bolt.

He went on:

"It rather changes the position. About Edward's treatment of you."

Alesia couldn't nod, and she looked as though she had no response.

"And further, may I add that he, your father, was appointed about six months after the murder of Gaveston as Guardian of the Kingdom..."

"When Edward went to Scotland."

"...yes, and..."

"More?"

"... indeed. A few weeks after that he was granted the third penny of Lincolnshire revenues, back to the death of the first Edward. I don't suppose that was to help pay for his second marriage that summer."

Ebulo had almost forgotten why he had started this, but he had to conclude, somehow to clear the situation with truth: "No, it had been very costly to maintain a subtle war of words for holding the country for the King as crowned."

Alesia gave a big sigh, and felt more complex if not better, supposing she could take it in. For the moment it was more interesting that Ebulo was being granted Lincoln Castle and Bailey, and for Alesia her income from Lincolnshire county was withdrawn, to be replaced by receiving more manors and rent. It was not for maintaining Thomas's chapel. Isabella and Henry of Lancaster chose a monk from Pontefract Priory as an Ypres hermit and assigned a clerk to it. Those two would collect alms, keep an account, retaining fourpence a day as pay, for the clerk, and threepence for the hermit. The surplus revenue from the pilgrims was for the work of God. It was found out a year later that the hermit was married, so the appointment was revoked. The money was returned, and a new start made.

The rest of the year passed quickly, with enough incidents to occupy the minds and time of Alesia and Ebulo, though it really reflected only that life was going on as hitherto. King Edward began to dabble again in Scottish affairs, starting by repudiating the treaty which acknowledged their independence because he had had to agree to it when under age. England itself suffered rains violent and long, prices were high; to effect some alleviation Flemings were brought in to instigate weaving in this country rather than export sheep and import cloth.

Unrest might be diminished in the long term by the further employment created, but the countryside continued to be unsafe. Even Richard Willoughby was ambushed on the way to Grantham by the Folville gang.

By the next Spring, Edward had caused a few further changes in Alesia's land holdings, more particularly returning Builth to her so that she had now the traditional possessions of the Earldom of Lincoln, and none of Salisbury.

They finally won heir legal action in the Court of la Haye against the City of Lincoln over the revenues of the castle bailey. The £57.6.8 would be useful. For Ebulo, there came appointment as Keeper of the County of Lincolnshire, and thus a commission or two. Then, further a summons to Scotland with eighty archers from the county.

It was easy to be cynical about the future certainty of a stable situation in Scotland. King Robert the Bruce exiled some barons from Scotland. In August 1332 they returned, led by Edward Balliol. They won the battle of Dupplin Moor. Balliol took the throne. That was September. By December the Scots defeated him, and Balliol fled south. In March the next year Edward helped Balliol to capture Berwick, being assisted by William Crabbe. He was a siege engineer, now acting for Edward, because the Scots would not ransom him back again after his capture by the English. Then the battle of Halidon Hill was won, personally directed by Edward, and Balliol was promoted to the throne once more. Berwick opened its gates to Edward again. The threat by the Scots to Bamburgh, where the Queen was staying, was thus withdrawn. The disinherited were reinstated, and in February 1334 Balliol held a Parliament at Holyrood, with, however, little more authority than a puppet. In the Spring, David II of Scotland fled to France. Scotland became quiet for a short while.

The business of the Court was taking place at Pontefract Castle, now of Henry of Lancaster. Ebulo le Strange being under his command, he and Alesia were present in this case in surroundings so familiar, and with sad memories including her poor brother John. In this great castle there was space for vast numbers, with the consequent intertwining of personalities and tensions.

Civil talk never included the debt of over a hundred pounds that Henry de Beaumont owed to Ebulo. Nobody mentioned that Ebulo's Lincolnshire archers had been fighting the Flemish ones in York. Willoughby's and de Malton's men had joined in. It all concentrated on what was new.

Horses, colts, oxen, cows, sheep and swine worth about sixteen hudred pounds had been stolen in the Midlands from Thomas's executors. The commission of enquiry would not get very far, but in their joint interest it brought Henry and Alesia to a closer feeling. With some caution Henry spoke to Alesia on another subject:

"There is talk, my dear, of the King wanting to hunt at Pickering on the way to Scarborough. What is the castle like? I haven't seen it since it became mine. Can anything be arranged?"

"For all this lot? It's a matter of size. How many? We can house a small party of course, can't we, Ebulo? We could also put on some entertainment, I expect."

"It would presumably be for about three days," Ebulo answered, "but we should leave now, if this is imminent; I might add that we could not accommodate any part of the Court in Lincoln except by camping. That castle still needs a thousand pounds spent on it. Great Hall, brewhouse, stables, walls, towers, all in poor repair. So please don't let the King try there. John Beck would have heart failure."

They sent a rider in advance to Richard of Warrington. Ebulo and Alesia followed, accompanied by none other than Philip Darcie, retainer and counsellor of Henry of Lancaster. They all agreed that the situation had its piquancy.

"Ma'am, it was my great uncle's family who wanted the excitement, and the money I imagine. Arrest is now being prepared. I hope you do not think I am for anything but a quiet life - and even that needs some ingenuity."

"I was very cross at the time," Alesia rejoined, then warming to the acquaintance, "I'm afraid it was Bishop Oliver who was cut by my tongue, because he frustrated the Sheriff's action. Never mind, let us get to Pickering in good order."

Alesia then laughed and turned to Philip Darcie.

"If we meet any bandits today, you can attack them and it will be all evens. Incidentally Bishop Burghersh has got the right of sanctuary to apply to his palace and the canon's houses."

"For himself?"

A quick look from Alesia and Ebulo towards Philip Darcie was necessary to decide whether he was being humourous or bitter. Ebulo spoke:

"He hasn't been taking anything from you, surely?"

"No. Shall I say 'not yet'. He is a hunter for lands of poorer neighbours. They hope he will walk the earth after death with unquiet spirit, in Lincoln Green, with horn and baldrick, until they get them back."

"Deprivation of Treasurer and Chancellor of England has had no effect, then?"

"Indeed, no. Anyway, he is now Treasurer again."

"Let us not try to analyse that." Alesia spoke with memory of the doings of those in power.

"No, ma'am. However, let me be on your side. The gang from Nocton, though, were never as bad as the Folville brothers near Grantham. You know tht Richard Willoughby was ambushed by them."

"I do, but no more than that."

"Ah. Well, he was taken to a gathering of that criminal brotherhood in a wood. He had to pay over a thousand marks to save his head. All that, and the Folvilles were supposed to be gentry. One was in fact a Justice of the Peace. May I say that I am sent by the lord Henry to accompany you only to report back to the Pontefract Castle Constable Oliver de Stansfeud, to decide arrangements."

"I think that we shall please the King. The hunting is generally excellent."

"Not, I imagine ma'am what they do further north at Whorlton."

"Is it true then? I've heard strange stories."

"The nets? Yes ma'am. They string out great nets to trap deer and they call it hunting."

"Not, Philip, at Pickering. Certainly not."

"Nicholas de Meynell certainly upset the King by doing it in Whorlton Park."

King Edward did seem satisfied with his short stay. He had that day given Robert de Bridgegate 6s.8d. for leading him to a lost hound. Alesia de Whorlton sang before him, her name not apparently bringing up poor memories. Alesia, 'the red-haired' was doubtless unthinking in including 'Simon de Montfort' in her repertoire, but she was worth looking at.

The King gave money to the poor of Pickering, and the Court resumed its peregrinations.

"Was that alright?" asked Ebulo "it seemed to go quite well."

"My darling, you were charming with everybody. You made it a very friendly party."

"I must admit I prefer these smaller occasions. Don't they play fast here on the fiddle and rebec. Dancing the Trotto is exhausting, really lively."

Alesia veered to another topic:

"Ebulo, I have known three Kings in my life, and I wonder always about them. Their make-up I mean. The last few years have been horrendous for young Edward, with so much distress from his father, his mother, her paramour; and various relatives put to death. Can you tell me how he can now be open, bright, cheerful, and full of himself..." after a pause, and a hesitant grin "...you Ebulo, are you two people? Or how are feelings hidden from such dreadful happenings?"

The detail of philosophy or explanation of the compartmented mind of men, or maybe the necessary detachment of political thinking, did not seem to Ebulo to be as good a response as a diversionary statement:

"There is still that belief that the second Edward is not dead, but is in Italy."

"Yes, but does one have a tomb of alabaster, limestone and marble in a cathedral for no-one? What's more, Edward's chaplain, Richard de Potesgrave escorted the body to Gloucester from Berkeley."

As soon as Alesia spoke she realised that it could be just as the rehabilitation of Thomas, to give visible proof, however thin. There had been only de Potesgrave.

"Yes, yes," she said hastily, "we shall never know, though we believe. Though now they still say he's at the monastery of Sant. Alberto di Burtio in Lombardy. Why, oh why have I never been allowed to travel to Italy?"

Ebulo calmed Alesia: "I think you are showing why. Certainly on this subject."

Alesia envisaged the silken web around her.

Ebulo le Strange was now ordered overseas.

"But it's all over," complained Alesia.

Ebulo showed much relief in his agreement.

"One must suppose that this order has some purpose."

"Perhaps it's based on an old instruction. Check it with the Sheriff at least, Ebulo, my love. We've done our bit at our ages."

"Again perhaps - the war over - at least this one - maybe there's a little clearing up needed."

"It says overseas. That's not Scotland. Yet the messenger said he thought it was Ireland. The staff hear more gossip than we do."

Alesia paused. The only alternative was protest, which was impracticable. The situation would apply to others. It was compulsory in their position. After all, Edward had waited to call Ebulo until the war, this particular war anyway, was concluded. That is, she then thought, Edward had waited if he had thought about it at all. Contemplation on the matter turned to memories. Life had always been thus. It always hurt, on each occasion of the departure of the man upon whom she based her love and security of emotion. But no, not on each occasion. Sometimes she had felt relief on Thomas's departure. Then afterwards, a conscience at the thought. Ebulo, understanding the silence, waited for her next expressions.

"Duty, duty, duty," she uttered. The first one given with a tinge of contempt; the second questioning; the third towards male conviction of it.

"It has to be." Ebulo spoke evenly, joining Alesia in assumed equanimity. "I have been before. I will return as soon as I can, I assure you, darling Alesia. This time Edward may be right."

On Alesia's eyebrows being raised in astonishment, he continued:

"He has been impressed I think by people calling him the Justinian of England. He fancies the Roman Emperor idea. Always losing the next year the land he gains one year, he's copying Agricola, who stopped just north of Edinburgh. He's given up the Highlands."

This being greeted in silence by Alesia, perhaps because being impressed, perhaps believing that it made no difference, he then added:

"God gave them no decent weather when he located Scotland. That's why they are always raiding England, and Edward's wrong if he thinks there's any revenue there for him."

Perhaps Alesia could visit King Edward's mother. It was kindly meant, but it indicated the possible length of his absence, because the former Queen Isabella was detained at Castle Rising in Norfolk. Then Ebulo's departure from Bolingbroke was his smartest and tidiest ever. Their tension had spread through the staff, the escort; the commands to equip fully and to smarten the appearance of all were constantly repeated and checked for having been done. It was as though the total purpose was display in glistening panoply. It seemed that there was something to prove or reality to hide under a glistening surface. The latter was a facet of war; this time it betokened similarly reaction to fear and feeling. Ebulo surprised himself at how he, this time, had got his officers and men to a fine state, so long his aim in previous years. His own unexplained feelings had worked through as extra force and determination.

Alesia, as so often in her life, waved to the departing silhouette and banner as it topped the western hill. She had nearly ridden with Ebulo, to go as far as Barlings or Stixwould. There to pray, then to return to Bolingbroke. It was, however, her immediate return which she felt would depress, would emphasise loneness, would make her seem held trapped within stone walls of no breaking. It was better at once to stay where she could call home. She entered the chapel.

"Overseas." The word had been clear in the order to attend, with an array of knights and men from Lincolnshire. That word usually meant France, but that seemed unlikely, too soon after the Scottish adventure. So it could be Ireland. But to what end? By the time the County array had assembled in Lincoln, all that is, who could be found, and fit - by that time the advance platoons were well towards the west. To Ebulo the Lord le Strange it had been confirmed that his force was for Chester, for embarkation to Ireland. There to assemble and refit. From thence they would re-embark for assertion of force upon the Western Isles of Scotland.

Such later news of the plan as there was available told that Edward would set out from Carlisle, Balliol from Berwick. Juggling with dynasties had become ineffective, and Edward had ordered attack on the isles of Bute and Arran in the west, so as to detain Robert the Steward and his forces. It was expected that it was to be an occupation. No-one took much notice of that statement; cynicism of military and political persuasion had robust roots in experience.

By August 1335 Edward and Balliol had both reached Perth. That month peace was agreed. Peace in Scotland again.

On the eighteenth of August that peace was concluded in a face-saving formula with the help of David of Strathbogie. It at least disguised David's second change of allegiance. Then at the beginning of September fifty ships with fifteen hundred men sailed from Ireland to attack Robert the Steward's lands of Bute and Arran. With that force was Ebulo. His partaking in a sea expedition exhilarated him. The mariners' skill in maintaining a group formation across the moving elements of wind and water gave him aesthetic pleasure to watch. They were to land on Bute. Hopefully the Clan Donald fleet in Islay would not interfere. It was hoped that Robert the Steward, Robert the Bruce's son-in-law, would capitulate to this power, though thirty years before the English had been repulsed. It had been after the peace at Perth that it ws confirmed that they should proceed, after months of waiting.

Now for Ebulo, it was the end. The resistance on the shore was savage yet unformed. Such melee allowed Scots to penetrate to any special target.

On the eigth of September 1335 Ebulo was killed on the shore. Along with the others, his body was reduced in a cauldron to his bones. Coffined, boxed, or buried, arrangements were made for disposal in accordance with what was due to rank. Some reverence for the mystery of death was maintained by the presence of chaplains, amid the uncertainties of men who have lost their leader. By ship and carts Ebulo's Lincolnshire men accompanied their deceased lord and esquires over the long slow journey to Lincoln Castle.

English Ships of the thirteenth century.

# CHAPTER 26

Alesia awaited. She had lost her only love. Nearly fifty four years old, it must be the end for her. There must be some way of suspending feelings for what was left of her life on earth. The void of emptiness ahead had no form, and no response. There showed nothing to grope for in distress. It was abandonment once again. Nor was it certainly an Act of God. It was human folly. Because God had a purpose, however indefinable to a human, there had to be acceptance and submission to his acts. Desperation against such acts as this by man is no lead to any comfort. Give way to tears. Try and lean towards heaven, to rejoin Ebulo.

It was a morning long for the cortege to travel from Lincoln to Barlings. The journey was undertaken without delay for public display in the castle chapel of the draped coffin. The chapel was not in good structural order. Too many had feared to lose or lost their men in Edward's wars to expect the mourning of others. Nor was le Strange a local lord. At Barlings Abbey it was a short but earnestly expressed interment service, in deference to the dead, and in deference to the lady Alesia and her ancestors who had in the past shown such great material faith in its works and prayers.

Alesia was given support by the Lord Willoughby, who had been with Ebulo in Scotland. If there was any of the funeral routine that Alesia noticed at all there came but two conscious thoughts. She herself would lie next to Ebulo in death. That helped to compose her mind. And further, she was deeply sensitive to a feeling of guilt. She had not lived so purely in thought and deed that she could avoid belief that this her tragedy was divine punishment. Should it not so be then there was no reason for it.

"John, please take me back to Stixwould now."

Lord Willoughby understood her need, and without demur escorted Alesia to that nunnery a few miles eastward. Alesia had stayed there for the days of waiting for the burial. While it was convenient, another reason to be with the nuns was prominent in her mind. It was not anxiety about anything material, nor about Bolingbroke in particular. No, it was about recovery of equilibrium.

One week after Ebulo had died the orders had gone out from the King in Edinburgh to take his lands in hand. While the order included Lincolnshire Alesia was in no state to ponder on what would be for her estate. She had been in the situation before, and once again it must be assumed that she would be allocated suitable revenue. Gilbert de Leddred, escheator of Lincolnshire, Northamptonshire and Rutland had been able to essay a few reassuring words. The administration of Ebulo's estate was widespread, extending to thirty counties; also near London, and in three areas of Wales: North, South, and the Marches. The heir was Roger le Strange, Ebulo's forty year old nephew. All of that, subject to approval by the King, and to any greater priority he may have.

Edward had passed southwards, accessible enough for his next decisions. Gilbert informed Alesia at Stixwould that lands in the counties of Lincoln, Northampton, Nottingham, Oxford, Buckingham, and Berkshire had been returned to her. He was thanked for his trouble and kindness, and Alesia added:

"I will go back to Bolingbroke in a few days. In the meantime I have to make my peace here."

It was easy for de Leddred to interpret that statement. He uttered not a word; while he did not practise obsequience, he certainly absorbed with an objective interest the different characters of his betters for whom he acted, so as to deal with them effectively. Whilst he thought thus because he was so inclined for his own machinations, as much for his own preservation, he came to conclusions from observation, knowledge of Alesia's life, and all improved by rumour. His mien of outward expression covered his inner opportunist dishonesty.

Shattered was Alesia. Lord Willoughby had avoided mention of the truths of battle. In that short time before Robert the Steward surrendered Ebulo had received a death blow. However often a wife may half expect this end, the stark reality of its happening is the tragedy that concludes the life of hope. Alesia's drawn appearance showed inhibition feeding on itself. There was no outgiving, nor caring to communicate. Alesia's body was there, but not her mind, showing no sign as to what could make for recovery.

But was that all because of Ebulo's decease? So de Leddred pondered. That was the occasion certainly. And the lady Alesia's dire distress could be nothing other than heartfelt. Yet perhaps it might be compounded by conscience. de Leddred feared that he might show other than deep respect and sympathy, but his inner thoughts continued. It was fairly clear to him that the lady Alesia would be remaining at Stixwould until arrangements could be made for her to take her vows, to swear to chastity, and to be inducted into the sisterhood. That was just a matter of deduction. No doubt the great Bishop Henry Burghersh would arrive as soon as possible. For such an important novice, it could not be long.

From such a rich candidate endowments could be expected on a large scale, and a short period to full acceptance. Such support would continue contributions of generations back from Earls of Chester; and further, from the Saxon Countess Lucy herself. A haven of care for the rest of Alesia's life. To that end, in the same belief of the correctness of those surmises of de Leddred, the Bishop of Lincoln had made time urgently to settle the Countess. He too had assessed that the lady would have a troubled conscience to multiply her woes. Some of the gossip and rumours must have been based on truth.

Not one of the dozen nuns felt ill that day, nor for several days before, except with tremors of excitement. The bishop was to arrive mid-morning, having stayed at Barlings Abbey just three miles away. The nunnery was cleaner and tidier than had been known for some time. Sister Sara Bews, the Abbess, calmed as many as she could from her own tense state. Each one of them had gone through the ceremony of taking their vows, but not many under the scrutiny of a bishop.

The Bishop was assured that Alesia had spent the appropriate days in retreat in the Convent, right up to the night before still in prayer, and now in prayer:

"Lord Holy Father, confirm the resolve of your servant Alesia."

"Are you resolved with the help of God to undertake that life of perfect chastity chosen for themselves by Christ Our Lord and his virgin mother, and to persevere in it for ever?"

"I am."

Alesia so replied clearly without tremor to further questions by the celebrant bishop. She would strive steadfastly for perfection in the love of God; she had already died to sin; she asked for perseverance all the days of her life.

"Blessed is she who puts her trust in the Lord."

"Almighty God, by whose grace alone we are accepted and called to your service: strength us by your Holy Spirit, and make us worthy of our calling; ..."

"...bow down before his footstool..."

"...of steadfastness and justice...in purity of heart... crookedness of heart shall depart from me...the proud look and the arrogant heart I will not endure."

The collect and the psalms were loudly uttered, the bishop to the fore. There were sentences where Alesia's mind veered from concentration. Most of them she already knew, but had never used them in this context herself.

"...you too, when you had heard the message of the truth, the good news of your salvation, and had believed it, became incorporate in Christ and received the seal of the promised holy spirit..."

"...I believe nothing can happen that will outweigh the supreme advantage of knowing Christ Jesus my Lord. I accept the loss of everything...if only I can have Christ and be given a place in him..."

"Bless Sister Alesia who dedicates herself to your service, purify her from all sin and set her on fire with your love."

Alesia rose; with slow dignity in deep feeling she proceeded to the lectern to profess her vows. With the Abbess and the Assistant Superior General Sister she signed her vows on the parchment on the altar.

"Lord send the gift of your Holy Spirit on her..."

"Father, may her life reveal the face of Christ, your Son..."

"Lord, send your benediction upon this ring, which I bless in Your Name, that she who wears it may abide in your Peace, and ever live in Your Love."

The ring is sprinkled with water.

To Alesia:

"Receive this ring as a sign of your love and commitment to Christ. May he always be the first love of your life."

And thus Alesia:

"May He give me the grace to be truly faithful to Him...that I may bear the treasure of his mercy."

As, newly consecrated, Alesia stood before the altar, she was blessed, to be protected by God's grace. Then, kneeling at the Lady Altar, all intoned the Act of Consecration to Saint Mary.

It was stronger in its feeling than Alesia had expected. Her mind and conscience had been penetrated. Having heard of much of the ceremony before, when directed to herself the impact astounded emotion and memory. So what was to be her life to follow? The Prioress pressed her own assumption.

"We will improve your accommodation even further, my lady Alesia, now that you have consented to be with us."

There was no reply that Alesia could at that moment find heart to make. For herself she had never said that she was going to join the community. Perhaps she had been arrogant in assuming a short stay, maybe she had the very attitude that she was meant to cast away. It was to her but a haven for reassessment. She could not rationalise why she had gone to Stixwould, except that she felt the need for an anchor when her life had ceased to navigate. Her strength had, however, been returning. Soon, perhaps she would begin to think of tomorrow.

Yet she could easily succumb to the life. She would be looked after. Lesser nuns would serve her. She recognised some of them, as daughters of squires of Lincolnshire. She had forgotten so many of them as they had grown up over the years in this place. No. Not for herself did she even now feel that she would risk being physically hidden away in this place. There was fight for life still in her. She began to hold her head stronger. The narrow pettiness that magnified the slightest scratch above the mundane days routine was not for her. She had felt that in her mind all her life. While strongly influenced by the ceremony, she felt that the modicum of doubt remaining would urge return to her normal life, though in respect for her vows. She replied to the Prioress:

"Dear Sara, I may disappoint you, in the sense that I am not expecting to stay. I do not know whether my presence here would help you, even. Perhaps I may request to return, but for now, I must away. I am not quite ready."

Alesia stopped there. Perhaps she had uttered one sentence too many. Sara looked surprised, also personally upset.

"Lady Alesia. I am sorry. I cannot persuade you? I know we are humble here but there is for us the prospect of heaven."

Her feelings were mixed; with the fact of being wrong in what she said at first; then smothering her anger at the brighter future for the nunnery being whisked away; in her tone was some of her resentment at being used just as a meeting place between Alesia and the Bishop. Nor had she yet proof of her final hope of material reward, although it might well be forthcoming.

"Sara," replied Alesia, with a tone of conciliation, "for myself I am just as much held in vocation inside castle walls, as any vow can keep me anywhere. I am not as ready as I should be to feel that never again would I ride out or be away for some change. I should be, I know. My vows just taken are my protection; that I needed. I hope by them I will deal better with others. But closed doors frighten me. When they cease to do so, I hope that you will welcome me. As for now, I will pursue my contemplation, and I expect little more, in the strong confines of Bolingbroke."

How could she believe the Saints' advices of the wiles of women? That Eve deceived Adam? That woman's love is bitterness; her eye is a mirror of the devil? Inferior in spirit, physically, and ethically? Ebulo would have put it that these were thoughts of frightened men. If only those thoughts could never rise again.

Alesia pondered whether she would ever again be loved for human self alone. She knew what Prioress Sara's reply would be to that. Yes, there was God's enduring love which was the substance of nunnery life. It did not, however, stop Alesia from pondering the question all the way home. There was the relaxing sound of the age-old familiar squeaking of the lowering portcullis. A haven. Or a prison?

There was warmth enough these short winter days and long winter nights in the fire in her solar chamber. There was Frathesancia. That was all. For lack of a future memory took hold. It turned always to what had been unresolved in her life, to those incidents which seemed to have had no tidy conclusion. It veered on to events where she could have done better, or have been more kind. It developed a vicious strain in taunting her in recalling where she had over-exerted authority, had hurt others, or had had little consideration. In a nunnery was it conscience which they fought to subdue? Until they had none other than about trivia? Did trivia magnify, or once one had eliminated the larger feelings did one achieve peace? One might just as well try and do this in freedom.

"Frathesancia"

"Ma'am?"

"I whipped you once."

"True, ma'am. I had been foolish."

"Tactless perhaps. I should have apologised at the time. I was suddenly out of control. I was sorry then. I am now."

Not knowing anything about Alesia's thoughts leading to this remark, Frathesancia found difficulty in replying. It needed a totally original reply, which was hard to frame.

"I had either accepted it as just, or had forgotten it, ma'am."

"The bruises and cuts?"

"Sorry ma'am, but they cured quickly. It somehow cleared my mind too."

"I wish I could find others in my life to whom to show I did not mean to hurt them, by word or deed."

"Oh, my lady Alesia there can't be any. Surely m'am, how could there be."

"Incidents keep popping up in my mind. Memories are becoming unpleasant. I don't want to go back. Not to my life before dear Ebulo."

"Come, ma'am. Let us look forward, then. In humility, though, I would say that in this parish and on your lands there are many indeed who would be cheered by a visit from your presence and would find their own sorrows lightened."

Alesia sat silent. Frathesancia became afraid that she had gone too far. Her back did tingle again with the memory of that beating. In a sense it had been reassuring in that it had shown the animal in her mistress. It was all Frathesancia possessed - her body, and they had been closer since. She would have preferred to have fought back. At last came the reply from her mistress:

"You put that much better, Frathesancia, than did the priest when my brothers had died. Surely the fire in the Great Hall is warmer than this one."

While there was some comfort in human communication to maintain a balance in her mind, Alesia experienced little of hope for her own future. Her walks round the village, her interested looking into the barns and byres, accompanied by communicative talk - they produced little of companionship. There was all politeness, all subservience, but never the equality which could bring something to her for strength. Time may heal, and when it did her drawn and shattered appearance may yield to content and a recovered complexion. Initiative in all her doings had to come from her. The greater initiative needed to reorient her life waited for a prompt to start it.

The royal administrative service ground on, restoring to her the lands of her rights, but achieving from Alesia but the dull acknowledgment of a nod to Henry de Halton.

He should not have told her of the King's order that came through, despatched with Ebulo alive, received after Ebulo dead. He was to have Builth if he survived Alesia. de Halton could not have avoided her seeing another document: treasure had been found buried under a pear tree in Thomas's garden at her Holborn Inn in Shoe Lane. She could return no knowledge of it. Thus reminded of her two husbands violently removed from her, in her despond she felt no hope of any future dawn.

The news of the death of Ebulo le Strange filtered through the countryside as part of the talk of escheators taking his manors in hand. They had this task, and others, on the King's behalf. Avid listeners wanted all the stories available. Personal interest in any of it depended on who had gone to the war from that particular place. In

West Wales, however, a personal chord was struck in the mind of Sir Hugh de Frene. These times he was finding consolation when alone with Myfanwy. He never gathered her total name, alien to his Anglo-Norman basic thought. "Myfanwy" was sufficient for him, and indeed from him for her. What followed tripped off her own tongue easily enough, but the further several words of identification indicated a predecessor or two including their occupations, and all in Welsh. For Myfanwy and for Hugh it suited that the whole bundle of her seemed linked as one composition of intent - the lips and eyes and shape and attitude indicated a sensuous invitation. Intelligence may or may not have been present, probably just enough to serve her obvious needs in feelings and to project any necessary persuasive talk to that end.

He was de Frene of Moccas, only recently having become the heir to that small estate, plus appointment to Cardigan castle.

She was Myfanwy of Cardigan if described similarly to Hugh.

de Frene, now in his late forties, was a good enough knight, with an outgoing incisiveness. He was not expecting any special Royal summons which would improve his lot. There had always been hope, though unfulfilled. It was as well to settle for duties as demanded, and for Myfanwy between times. A knight lived on his allocation from the King or his inheritance. de Frene by inheritance and by grant was at least better off than most.

Both Hugh and Myfanwy persuaded themselves that they needed each other. From time to time they did. In present circumstances it was also true. Hugh had not settled down, though he was beginning to think that he should. Myfanwy, much younger, suspected that she was not the only one, and that she was trying or hoping to get out of her class. It was in essence a local arrangement of emotions, rationalised. de Frene had social importance in the context of Cardigan and of Moccas in Herefordshire, and nothing wider was in Myfanwy's ken, if indeed as much. She was the image closest to Venus of the willing ones around. If they had to marry, Hugh expected that he would do so. He could offer as much as any other lesser person, uncertain as he felt his position and life to be. Myfanwy did not really believe that such a future was likely, but did not break away, yet. She was often being asked by others.

There was no obvious significance to their own private situation in the arrival of Henry de Halton at the castle in December, 1335. It was occasioned by the death of Ebulo le Strange.

"We had heard rumours, but nothing firm. This corner is remote." Hugh further expressed his sorrow. He thought also of his own vulnerability for when he would be called again to some expedition.

Hugh added:

"The Lady Alesia?" The tone was as casual as he could make it, to exclude if possible any inflexion based on previous intimacy with her.

"Distressed. There is much to which to close ones eyes in this situation." Secretly amused at Hugh's controlled reaction, he continued: "I refer to the shock of the lord Ebulo departing for a war that appeared to have ceased, and yet not returning."

"Except his bones. A funeral service. A religious spell cast on the very air."

de Halton looked up to try and find any special deep feeling behind that remark. Protest or comment on any situation that was normal did not seem to him worthwhile.

"Let me tell you why I am here. It is firstly to confirm to you the situation, at the request of Lady Alesia."

Hugh began to ponder over that for as much significance as he could squeeze from it, indeed more.

Henry settled for interpreting Hugh's concentration as being sympathy for Alesia. He continued:

"Of course it is semi-official in addition. I thought I would report that all le Strange's lands are being taken into the King's hands, and that Builth will obviously not now be granted to the lord le Strange, as was being done. No, that's not the main item, you would have expected that. The main point is that the keeping of the castle and cantred of Builth has been committed during the King's pleasure..." he paused in this statement, having suddenly become cautious of its effect "...to me."

It was a jolt for Hugh. Builth to Alesia's administrator? And the district round it? Why not to himself? He was in the district. Henry de Halton preferred to make a quick effort to appease the surprise that showed.

"Whether this is temporary or not I cannot say. Most likely it is only to pay me for the executorship. For whatever time is required there, I thought you should hear from me that I would be your inland reserve at that castle."

de Frene rescued himself from the shock by asking:

"Is there much else? I thought most of the lands were with the lady Alesia?"

"Most, yes, but Lord le Strange himself achieved lands in thirty three counties. Also some in the marches, North and South Wales, and adjacent to London. He became, after all, an important tenant-in-chief."

Not expecting to have any sound of truculence in his voice, Hugh tried a mild self-defence:

"There's no land of his near here in this county, anyway."

"No, Sir Hugh. Perhaps I should not really gossip, but I have to say that the lady Alesia does not much like le Strange's heir being his cousin Roger. They do not get on well together. Roger has had the attitude of impatiently waiting."

"That does not say he will receive it, though?"

"No, no. There is a tendency, however, if an heir looks like doing his duty. I doubt if he will achieve it all. Half, perhaps."

"Now that you are here, will you stay and celebrate Christmas next week?"

Henry de Halton in his work had to be a reader of his superiors' minds, from reactions and attitudes. He had detected the dissatisfaction with his achievements that Hugh de Frene revealed in the unuttered background of his conversation. Upon this premise he felt that his reply should not aggravate matters.

"Thank you, Sir Hugh. I would have appreciated that. However, I must begin to travel back. My wife would have something to say if I did not. Builth needs checking up, and reviewing, and that will take more than a week.

He thought he had made as light a matter of it as could be done.

The next morning at dawn he and his escort departed, to be guided for two long days on confined woodland tracks towards the east, and Builth.

Subsequently and through Christmas, Sir Hugh de Frene spoke little, to the extent of Myfanwy's nerves tensing, and bringing her mind to speculation. de Frene's silence was the result of inconclusive thoughts, with the difficulty of assembling the components of the decision he was trying to reach. It was obvious to Myfanwy that the visit of de Halton had started this contemplation. That much was simple. With her, the rest would have to be intuition based on female parameters. What would her position be if Hugh did abandon her? In the long quiet moments she assessed her fall-back possibilities. With Hugh gone it would not be a disaster. She never hoped too much. She had acquiesced in this state of affairs. Looking back, great. But looking forward, blank - except for drudgery work like her erstwhile friends. Seemed she was not going to have children. Or was it Hugh. A bleak dark view, but she'd lived a bit better than others so far, and as for children, well, she was not bothered, from what she could see. It would be others who would be against her if Hugh went. Permanently, that is. Bit frightening really, but perhaps no more than life.

"Myfanwy Sara-Nellie-Tywyr" Hugh addressed her at long last.

Myfanwy had to laugh:

"Good" she said "There's one more on the end - Pant-y-Cefn." Then she added:

"I suppose you must."

After a pause, since both were hesitant she went on:

"My father once said that every relationship between man and woman will end in tears."

"I would love to know the rest of that discussion."

"You're leaving, then, Hugh." That was the longest sentence she could produce with any show of nonchalance.

Hugh saddened. Difficult it was to leave her, knowing also that there was no certain chance of it being a sensible thing to do. It was possible to settle with Myfanwy. There was basically no reason why not, in the ordinary course. For status and ambition, the lady Alesia was the one. It would be rather obvious. If refused, he would also lose Myfanwy. There were no other former acquaintances, friends, or lovers from whom he would wish to choose. Always assuming that agreement by Alesia was forthcoming. The matter was decided for him.

Suddenly Hugh relinquished touching Myfanwy. Something struck his mind; it was not a conscious act. He just on the instant moved away. Where he was leading her was wrong. All his doubts as to how he had been treating this girl developed into action. It was not a plan. It was immediate. It was a sudden instant clarification of mind. The instinct could not be altered. To his own amazement there remained no contrary doubt from which to frame a thought. He was empty of her.

"You are too young."

Leaving the lady Alesia out of it, it must have been correct to decide thus. The news about Ebulo and Alesia's widowhood were just the catalyst to resolve this situation. It might have worked the other way. Hugh had been stopped by a strike as of lightning.

Myfanwy submitted to the situation. To her it was obviously Alesia. The reason that Hugh gave meant nothing to her. If Hugh changed his mind she would be there.

Hugh, however, felt lighter of step. Free, he realised. Clear minded. With no encumbrances. Living his own life, as his own self. Yet after days of the calmness of castle routine and his duty inspections, desire for initiatives arose. So he would travel to Builth. To find Henry de Halton, if necessary to follow him beyond. Perhaps to cross country to the court, wherever that may then be. Henry de Halton would probably know the court movements. In any event, his presence might lead to something for himself, his absence would most likely not do so. He must climb out of his present blank state of mind. Myfanwy would no doubt marry Roger the Carter. Damn the look in her eyes which must mean she would return to him if she had the option. It was two mornings later that Hugh gave the final order to depart.

In a few days he was at Moccas, in Herefordshire. There was total absence of news there, in fact less curiosity. Helpful rumours confirmed matters. No, Hugh had not passed the Royal entourage on the journey; nor had he been granted any of the lands of Ebulo le Strange, yet. Of course not, said somebody, for young Kings grant to young people. These then, it impinged on Hugh, are my final short years, and they are those too of Alesia. Together, perhaps. He set off with his men to that destination, assuming that she would be at Bolingbroke Castle, but informing none.

It was about two years previously that Alesia and Hugh had last seen each other, at the tournament at Dunstable. Ebulo and she were clearly as much in love as ever. Probably that was what made Hugh realise the lack of future in his own style of romance. But his desire to be responsible always evaporated in a dream of the ideal, and of power. For much of the time on the journey Hugh was consumed in doubt as to whether he was going to look foolish at its end. Why had Henry de Halton made that tedious journey from Builth to Cardigan and back. It all sounded personal to him. These fellows, though, reported to the King anything that they considered may be helpful to him. Hugh thought that his management and alertness at Cardigan was satisfactory, so if it was anything to do with that, then there would be no criticism. So, was it more personal than that? If it had been just to report Lord Strange's death, then that could have been done by letter, though Hugh himself would perhaps have expected more. Alesia must surely know about de Halton's intention, and given permission for it. Likely, certainly. Perhaps without realising how far it was from Builth. At least, Hugh smiled to himself, he was found there, to be on duty. Again, was there a message between the expressions of courtesy? By the time Hugh had reached the narrow bank stretching across the fen to the river Witham near Tattershall Castle in Lincolnshire he had made up his mind. It was only a short day's ride from there northwards to Bolingbroke, so his attitude had by now to be composed. Hugh had become convinced that de Halton's visit had been opportunism on both sides - the courtesy, and the inspection report. He decided also that he himself was trying to move in far too hastily.

He revealed his intentions to Henry de Kirkton, a friend, and custodian of Tattershall.

There was no other way to explain his arrival in this eastern area. In fact de Kirkton would have conjectured something like it for interest and amusement. Hugh's plan to approach Alesia now being in the open, it strengthened his resolve, to the extent of being convinced of its total firmness. Part of this derived from de Kirkton's own situation. Hugh did not know whether to admire him or not.

"I could not emulate what you have done," he said to his host, "I would be expecting to be ejected from here, thrown out any day."

de Kirkton replied that he thought that the law had got tired of him, and that the result of a court action could perhaps be in his favour. He continued:

"Yes, 'perhaps' is the word. Actually I have not really relaxed. After a law case against me, which I won only six months ago, I was pardoned for acquiring this castle. So as to stop his sister getting it back again, John granted Tattershall to me. All his family were against him, even though he was the real heir. His mother's family had built it."

Hugh laughed:

"You look secure enough. Has de Driby anything else? I could help by receiving something."

John brought himself also to grin at that: "He has in fact died. The sister is also called Alesia. The lady Bernack. You wouldn't be after her, but she'd be after you - and not for your reasons. I can say that you were observed approaching across the fen, and we got on the alert until we knew who it was. You arrived at low tide in the river, and that is our dangerous time."

"Our convenient arrival was just fortuitous. It was easy to wade across. Thanks for not shooting arrows."

Then passed two days for refreshment, smartening himself, his men, and his horses so as to appear presentable at Bolingbroke.

"I hope" said Hugh "that there is no likelihood of a message going from here to Alesia, the de Lincoln one, of course, before I get there."

"Concerning that, you may stay here for a week and have no fear. The main doubt is whether you yourself will find the way round the edge of these fens. You got here along the causeys each side of the Witham - that was clever enough. Now you have to pass round the edge of the marshes - past Revesby Abbey. It's only a morning's ride. It is also so soggy off the proper track that it can take longer than that to move a yard. Let that not be your final destination."

Hugh raised his eyebrows in a question, but before he could utter de Kirkton was assuring him:

"Don't worry, I will send a couple of men so far with you; but you'll have to start no later than dawn, to give them a chance to get back in daylight."

And at the beginning of the day:

"Is this dawn here, and is this daylight?" quipped Hugh, with all assembled in the early cold grey damp December mist. I hope my welcome by Alesia is reward for all this discomfort, he thought. de Kirkton watched him fade away. Peculiar, he mused, that de Frene was not seeking a younger woman to marry, at least for his first. He had not seemed to be the mercenary sort.

At midday there was still the thin penetrating mist to the south. Trotting along made scarcely a sound padding along the soft track. Bolingbroke castle could now be seen after they had turned northwards, onto drier ground. It was an attractive focus as the sun lightly illuminated the bowl in the hills where it stood. It did not matter much now even if their approach was seen. There had to be such a moment, but surprise was important. Hugh doubted if they would expect any visitor at Bolingbroke, welcome or unwelcome, from the south. That was one thing. The other was how to get into the castle if permission was refused. In ordinary terms it should not be.

Having come round to the north side of the castle Hugh had proposed to halt his men, and to have his banner unfurled. It was red, with blue and silver indented bands, and should be recognised. He did, however, give a different order. The first few men, including himself, proceeded over the drawbridge and past the open outer portcullis, to halt within the gatetower. The halt was compulsory, the inner gate being shut. Hugh's idea was simply to act with charm in the notion that gaining access was a formality.

His men and the guard exchanged jocularities, one or two of them knowing each other from Scottish service under Ebulo le Strange. This seemed so friendly and easy that Hugh ordered that the inner gate be opened. A guard, however, came forward to hold his horse. Dourly standing there, the man stated that they had orders that the lady Alesia could not receive visitors, and that the castle was closed to all, to be regarded even as a private dwelling. They were sending for the bailiff because of Hugh's presence as a gentleman.

What Hugh did not know was that the guard had become suspicious of any purpose he might have in coming to Bolingbroke, which had induced them to call higher authority. By now nearly all his men had crowded into the gateway. With a calmness which surprised himself Hugh dismounted. He had noticed that the gate had been hastily shut, and a vertical gap of light showed that it could not have been barred on the inner side. Talking casually with his men he told them to crowd round to keep the guard from him, and between them he thought they could push open the gate to let him squeeze through into the castle yard. It succeeded. The melee, the shouting, the attempt to follow de Frene, all subsided when in haste he was nearly across the bailey, and about to move up the stairs to Alesia's quarters. He reached the door of the solar. He entered without rush.

By the window seat, looking outwards, stood Alesia, now turned to see the intruder. Hugh did not speak, because he could not. Whatever he had planned to say as an opening gambit could not reach his lips. Alesia was calm and still. Her shape silhouetted austere dignity. Pale of face, expression drawn. More than with that air of withdrawal, in this strength she impressed, in her stance and appearance, in the black long habit appropriate to her vow. Nor did she speak. What could have been an imperious gesture, but was really a gesture of defence, she held forth the back of her hand, to show her ring as a bride of Christ. Without meeting her eyes, and with a tact and a nerve reaction that he had certainly not premeditated, Hugh backed slowly, with dignity and humility, thus leaving the chamber.

Having seen the lady Alesia, and no instructions emanating, he overcame his doubts, and assumed that he was to receive hospitality. In a state of calm wonder at his own attitude he continued his visit as would a normal passing guest. It took much contemplation over the flickering flames in the Great Hall fire, the affection of the dogs and their total ignorance of his problems, and his constant silence through two days, to achieve assessment of himself, his position, and what should be his rightful aims.

Alesia, of course, did not know what had been his intentions. He must have been shallow in his thoughts to imagine that she would so soon throw off her grief about Ebulo, just because he himself had arrived. Yet she had given herself to him at Builth and in London. Heavens! That started over twenty years ago. Before Ebulo. During the marriage to Thomas. This may well be more vivid to Hugh than to

Alesia. There seemed to be no starting point now. All that could be done would be to wait and be sent for out of Alesia's curiosity, which must surely build up. Alternatively, go and say goodbye and thank you before departing, and thus to hope favourable conversation would develop.

One thing was sure - that short glimpse had stunned him as much by statuesque drama as she had stood there as by his own susceptibility to the aura of deep security shown in her state of mind.

Frathesancia did come with a message. Hugh was requested to talk with the lady Alesia. The beginning was not promising.

"You have broken into my castle. It seems that you are staying here. I did not say you nay to the second; but neither did I give permission."

"Alesia. May I say that I was indeed over-enthusiastic in my arrival. Somehow after travelling across the country just to see you I objected to the closed gate. It seemed in principle to be wrong. I came to see you, and not the works of stone and timber that protect you."

"But not from you, it seems. Nor mourning, nor vows, nor what attitude they bring to one."

"You are the same Alesia as ever before, though in these harassing circumstances, which I feel I understand. All of us are so temporary on this earth, so much in fear, yet always hopeful."

"No more. What I have seen and heard is now part of me. The cruelty of man, based on petty struggles which simple sense could render not required, is no longer abstract. Just in my mind, you may believe, not pain in my body. Yet I can tell you that it is a greater pain for its endurance. So I seek comfort in this structure of stone, and safety in its isolation. I try to be away from images of Thomas's dismembered frame. A man, a half of my soul, who had been near to me. With ourselves we essayed to create another life, but failed. And dear Ebulo, my kind love and companion. Now to heaven by the foul works of man. Yes, I dare say it now, the foul works of anointed Kings. I was born amongst it. My first remembrance is my grandmother asking the Archbishop to allow Llewellyn, my mother's great grandfather, a decent burial. Archbishop? Of what? He refused, for he was a man of politics and fear on this earth. You may think that this robe and this ring take me nearer heaven. There may be support from heaven, but there's little from this earth. You too have seen ghastly trophies exhibited, quarrels between cities to obtain parts of dismembered bodies, and mutilation and torture in cold blood. Don't look at me, Hugh, not like that. I have failed. A woman is for the constructive work of making families grow. For growth, not for destruction. Nor have I succeeded in that."

"Alesia. I look at you, whatever way it may be, from, I hope, sympathy; but more particularly, because I feel the depth of what you speak. It is all very well to remember; it has its agonising aspects.

Stray memories cannot die. Yet, in what do you take comfort?"

"Just and only in the everchanging distant view of the church at Boston. From here the tower is a representation pointing to heaven, from the base of human endeavour. The base cannot be seen from here. I think that that's a comfort."

Hugh was silent. His only effect here was his presence. He had no framework of words which would divert or change the situation. Perhaps his visit itself was helping.

"Go now," commanded Alesia.

Next morning, however, Hugh was requested to pass some time with her in the solar. It was apparent at once that she was climbing out of her despond. Dressed in grey, having at least for now relinquished the nun's habit, her air yet remained detached. Cares were indeed present, her face lifeless yet. Her perception was there neither for trouble nor joy. Her garment was itself, without adornment. It was also without usual diversion by jewellery. It was close-fitting. If it was meant to demonstrate the aura of her body it succeeded, as it thus struck Hugh. Did mourning and its accoutrements have an accidental sensuous appeal - the stressing of the basic human person, as here?

Hugh assumed that the conventional attire was meant to attach unemotional anonymity. It was not having that effect. In its simplicity it was tracing out the person underneath. The image at once appeared to promise closer communication, which would underlie any talk between them. The promise was not intended. That was made clear, without asking, for Alesia spoke in question:

"Well, Hugh, why are you passing to this remote part; where are you going?"

Perhaps, however, this was seeking clarification or confirmation of the circumstance in which she was involved.

"My reason for crossing the country to you was in hope to see more of you. I now know that by comparison your life has been full of hazards. Perhaps you have had enough of life's turbulence. I thought possibly you wanted now little more than peace. Yet I had hoped that you may join me. It was yourself that I was seeking."

Hugh noted a flicker in Alesia's expression rejecting her present state, her present demeanour being a surface upon her real self. Because of their former physical union Alesia's resistance had to weaken. By half calculation, half his felt need for Alesia, Hugh wanted to progress from this point.

"Dear Alesia, to take you away, with me."

Alesia's feelings developed towards him, part from memories as their foundation, and partly because of the possibility of the years of lonely silence that was the alternative. A glance outside convinced her - she glimpsed the cloudy mist carpeting the fen, with nothing but the empty flat surface of the world below. Thus by the fifth day of Hugh's sojourn there Alesia turned to him and stated:

"All my troubles have been put upon me by others, and it was I who had to contrive to keep matters even. It is like that at this moment. I myself therefore cannot decide this adventure. You broke in. How can I be demanded thus?" For a moment she hesitated. "It is not possible," she asserted, hoping for agreement.

It was the last moment that her willpower had the force to overlay her emotion. As soon as she looked up, reacting with a readiness to be told what to do, Hugh had accepted the form of her refusal. With a bow to untense his disappointment he turned and walked slowly away.

He ordered his men to prepare for departure, his melancholy telling them the reason. It was all hastened so as to escape soon enough this day. They formed in order in the village lane. From Hugh's mind fell the tension and uncertainty of unfinished decisions. So he turned and rode right back into the castle again to see his lady.

"You came back," which sounded as appreciation from Alesia. Her real position was that she had lost her anchor in Ebulo. She had no context now in her living days. She felt no association for her spirit. Into this state of mind Hugh broke, without elaboration, indeed being ignorant of its sensitivities he did not try to play upon it. Alesia would have appreciated a more subtle approach, but with what appeared to be as good a choice as any she concurred. At least Hugh held out his arms, ordering her in her weakness to leave with him.

And then at the dawn of a bright cold morning, they rode off. Her little prayers in the Christmas services, her attentions to those at the feasting, all helped to mark an end to what had been, to close it all, and the more to flee with Hugh, though as her insecure consort of the future. So it was with bright expression, any cares ignored, and refuge in the diversion, that Alesia, with Hugh at her side, travelled westwards. Their physical relationship already renewed, the underlying facts of their circumstances stayed conveniently unexpressed.

They crossed the river by Bardney, and along the narrow causey in single file to get over the fen. Neither was prepared to say their choice of route was to avoid Barlings where Ebulo was interred. It was as good a way as any to pass by the scattered religious houses. Hugh did not wish to ride by Tattershall. His unspoken reasons were simply that he did not want the coarse teasing from de Kirkton which would greet his success in riding off with Alesia.

And so to Somerton, the castle on the edge of the Trent Vale, below the hill some eight miles south of Lincoln. This was to be the first destination that was convenient. It was a King's castle, though built by Anthony Bek, warrior and prelate, some fifty years before. Bek, as Bishop of Durham, had left it to Edward II on his decease. Then it was transferred to the Royal House of Lancaster, thus to Thomas. Alesia's connection with it, however, was no more, for some dozen years. There was no guarantee that her request to enter would be accepted.

"We can get in one way or another" asserted Hugh.

"That I can believe" smiled Alesia. "I feel, however, that there should hardly be any snags."

Hugh was, to himself, doubtful. One never knew how the feelings and prejudices between King's men and Lord's men were shared, or even opposed. The party was now at the edge of the escarpment at Boothby, with the castle easily discernible a mile and a half in front of them. Beyond it, land now marshy, but dry enough in summer for grazing. The moat encompassed three islands; the castle almost rectangular, a round tower at each corner, and a gate tower in the northern wall formed the central one; the northern island, connected by a drawbridge, contained the outer bailey, with its further accommodation for bailiff, workers, barns, sheep, cattle, horses and fishpond. On the south island, over a footbridge, was a garden with an orchard. An outer moat also surrounded the castle and garden, with high banks outside. Further south, outside the whole, was an older grange, itself moated.

Since the grange had no strategic use for a flanking approach, Hugh looked more closely at the castle itself. He suspected difficulty, perhaps because of his own conscience. Discussion with guards could, however, give them time to close gates and drawbridges. There were two of the latter, and a sharp angle between them.

"Your aggression, my dear Hugh, has its uses, but surely it is not necessary here. Their sight of my banner should be enough. I have been here before, with Thomas. The custodian is now John Crabbe, the siege engineer, and I can't see you tangling with his methods."

She laughed lightly. Confident enough in her status, stimulated by irresponsibility, also knowing that there was at least one decent house in the outer bailey, which had only a palisade as defence inside its moat.

"Maybe," replied Hugh, "but we have to have at least a reserve plan."

He sent half a dozen men ahead to secure at least the outer drawbridge, which just crossed to the bailey. This was a wooden structure, more a hindrance than a final hazard to any determined aggressor. Yet by the time the main party reached it, nothing had been done. It was shut and fastened. Nor was there any defender. Nor anyone visible beyond it, at least not above the palisade. They came upon his men there, just standing awaiting instructions. These were straightforward.

"Get in that water, get across it, climb that fence, and open up from the other side."

They did. The moat there was not so wide, but it was by now cold indeed on this winter's day, itself lowering into darkening twilight.

It was just like waiting for hounds to draw a covert, thought Alesia. She and Frathesancia were waiting calmly with Hugh and the other soldiers, in anticipation of the drawbridge clanking down. Instead there were shouts. Hugh knew their purport, recognising the circumstance.

Six more men were sent. They helped each other over the palisade. There was now little time to express anxiety in the situation. The noise of a scrimmage ceased. The doors began to open. The bridge started to lower.

Hugh rode in to inspect the state of things. Some of the castle labourers had done what seemed reasonable to them, with resulting bruises and acheing bodies. They had then crept away into the lengthening shadows.

The total silence of this lone place was broken only by the sound which Hugh and Alesia least wanted to hear. The guards at the castle had lowered the portcullis, with a crash. Further noise continued as the drawbridge into the main castle structure was wound upwards.

"The bailiff's house, then" suggested Alesia.

"I have not yet given up. We shall be able to see for nearly another hour. The moon is getting up, over the hill in the east. Besides, we may get in with parleying."

"I did think so, but... well let us try then."

"Is there a postern gate, do you know?"

"Yes, Hugh. There's a garden gate in the south wall. There's a small bridge straight to it. There's also a lot of water to contend with, but there should be a boat the other side of this bailey. And remember there are arrow loopholes everywhere, high and low."

"Mm. We parley at the gate. I also send men to try that garden door. Right the other side from the gatehouse I understand?"

At the main gate it was understood in the calmest possible discussion that the castle custodian, John Crabbe, was not there. They could not be given entry, without permission. In the last rays of sunset Alesia called up for someone who recognised her to be brought. "I will speak for myself," she added. "It is not long since my orders were given here. I fail to understand your resistance."

York: Clifford's Tower of the castle.

# CHAPTER 27

Young John Poly, clerk to the reeve, insisted later that he had given his permission for their entry in view of Alesia's appeal, and the score of Hugh's armed men lined up behind them in the court of the castle had nothing to do with it. He said he had neither seen nor heard them. It might have been true, but with hospitality achieved it did not need to be analysed. The whole staff and inhabitants became friendly enough, and more than appreciated the excitement of the occasion. The gossip and approval, jealousy, condemnation, or amusement at Alesia and Hugh being out of wedlock improved the situation. Those who, for any of those feelings, felt that no good would come of it, were to be vindicated within the week. For John Crabbe was returning, riding across the great pasture, and was stopped by a yokel, who bore an unaccustomed authority for which he was scarcely suited.

"Sir John. There is a message for you. No sir John. Not at the castle. It is at the church.."

"What can you mean? How do you know? You're Roger Nunche, the carter, aren't you?"

"A moment, sir. Just passing, I was. There is a rider from the King. He insists on secrecy. He is at the church."

The wondering doubt, that anything such as this could emanate from a roughly clothed fellow as Roger Nunche, faded as the silhouette of a horse and rider could just be spotted. The skyline of the ridge revealed them in the distance for a moment as they moved, almost instantly being obscured again.

The meeting of John Crabbe with the messenger revealed that the King had heard of the abduction from Bolingbroke by Sir Hugh de Frene of the lady Alesia. The King, Edward III, commanded that they be imprisoned in the castle, and detained in different chambers. The King would further wish to resolve the matter in due course.

"With authority this can be done. So will you come down to the castle with me?"

"It is not necessary. I must return and report. Just to say that as you can see I come from the King, the sheriff de Trehampton will also support you if needed. Indeed, the information came through the Bishop, from the parson at Bolingbroke. I am glad to find you, and I will report success."

"So. I will do what is necessary."

It was a brilliant miniature operation, in Crabbe's mind. It was the most subtle act he could pursue, and it also amused him. Much more delicate than his usual siege tasks against whole cities. Firstly, behind the large stable on the outer bailey he assembled a patrol of horsemen, to wait there for orders. In the great barn enough men were quietly got together to form extra guards. To the watergate and into a boat on the moats a small party were sent to look as if they were fishing, and to watch the castle walls. For himself, Crabbe walked through the great gate into the castle courtyard, to see where his prospective captives were. Once discerned, his route took an unrelated direction. Nothing, in fact, could raise any suspicion, either in Hugh or Alesia, or in Hugh's men.

With the automatic falling of dominoes stacked in line, his orders as he passed out of the great gate again placed everything in position. The men on the water guarded the garden gate, the horsemen patrolled the outside, the foot men would guard for all hours. He passed inwards again, the gate then closed, the drawbridge was pulled up. All was now secure, and luck had kept half Hugh's men inside and half outside. All the small gates were now barred and bolted. The patrols would resume at dawn.

The separation of the couple could be done tomorrow, perhaps.

But no. John was more respectful of the King than he was of Alesia and Hugh. A room had to be prepared for Hugh. He would probably go quieter than Alesia, since he was in the wrong. Could be manhandled if not. By the variable and mysterious light of candles, John Crabbe presented himself to them in the Queen's Hall, with one man, and four outside the door. There were more changing shadows from the firelight, which helped the atmosphere, and lent unselfconsciousness to his authority.

"Ah, John," said Hugh, in no particular spirit of enquiry; just to start communication in an equable mood, with a military colleague whom he had seen in operation.

"There is news, sir Hugh. My lady."

John moved further towards them, now feeling that he could carry this through.

"I do have to tell you, though, that this news is from the King himself."

He was now being listened to with greater attention. There was silence, which he thus took as opportunity to continue. Caution began to creep in; much because of his general respect for superiors, but compounded by the delicate nature of interfering with personal associations.

"Yes?" enquired Alesia, after Crabbe had faded into silence himself. "I suppose you mean that the King Edward has heard of our ... travels. If that is all, why ...."

Hugh intervened. "I feel that there is more than that to it." He looked at John: "Let us know."

"Sir. My lady. I have had to order all gates closed, and guards to seal the castle. Then..."

He was not sure whether he would have finished that sentence, but he was interrupted by Alesia:

"Sealed! A prison? Guarded? Why?"

With haste Crabbe latched to her final question. He would give all the reason for the King's action. He would have done if he could have got it spoken. He thought of saying: 'For whose benefit I do not know...' - but that could be an aside personal to Hugh. 'It is a matter, I understand, of being unmarried, ma'am' - but that would cast aspersion on Alesia. With what he thought was inspired as it flashed to him, John uttered:

"The King is uncertain of your future relationship, I believe. Until that is resolved I have to guard you here as separated persons. With respect, ma'am, sir. And I hope you believe that I am unused to this sort of activity."

Alesia virtually laughed.

"No, no, not at you, Sir John. I am wondering what damage my personal life is to the King Edward. How kind of him to take such an interest."

"Separated persons means what?" asked Hugh.

"From now, sir Hugh. Apart... The south west tower is ready; for you, sir."

"Surely, it cannot be detention?" queried Alesia - "but I can name people who..." She did not continue. It was nothing to do with John Crabbe, and he could neither alter matters, nor would she look disconcerted in his presence.

"It is more akin," stated Alesia, "to some form of imprisonment."

It was. Next day the last move was made - both Alesia and Hugh found themselves prevented from leaving their quarters in the respective towers.

So Alesia had only Frathesancia to whom to turn. John Crabbe, however, visited his other captive, Hugh.

"Odd" he said "that we should meet in these circumstances. Saw you in the distance at Berwick. Been in Scotland also, not so?" He spoke with gutteral abruptness. From the Low Countries, a self-made man in naval and military ingenuity, he had now achieved constableship of Somerton Castle.

"Indeed so. Now I gather from looking out this morning that you are building and repairing and putting this castle into full repair. There are masons, carpenters, plumbers, all over the place. I didn't see them last night."

"They lodge a mile or two away in Boothby and Navenby. The days are short. For two years already, been working. The King agrees. He was here last year. Also improving the farming, and the grange."

Crabbe then added:

"You notice drawbridges in good order. Mending also doors, roofing.... everything. Walk the outer wall if you wish; no more. The top."

Crabbe, once a prisoner himself, felt at one with Hugh de Frene. The reason why Crabbe was working for King Edward was that the Scots, his previous employers, had not troubled to pay his ransom to get him back after capture near Roxburgh. Invaluable to the English, as a person he was equally desirous of making his social mark.

What Hugh reconnoitred, however, in his walk along the walls was more than the works. He retired dutifully to his chamber, having noted particularly what was but half completed. Masons and their assistants seemed to total about two dozen, and half that number of carpenters and sawyers. There were piles of timber, and heaps of small ironwork. With men on roofing, hoists for materials, and more important, scaffolding here and there, de Frene had enough to think about.

He was ready for the question brought to him from Alesia by Maurice, one of his own men, when food was delivered. It had to be repeated, however, for as Hugh listened his concentration left him suddenly. This man was Maurice certainly, but his identification was Maurice son of Edwin son of Maurice. Memory thrust into his mind Myfanwy's list of appellations. It also struck his conscience at what might be her plight, and whether he was in punishment for the pattern of his latest deeds. So Maurice son of Edwin son of Maurice resumed when Hugh's concentration returned:

"It is said that the Countess, Sir Hugh, expresses her concern for yourself, and her fears for both of you. She is anxious, I understand, and she hopes that you can clarify the matter."

"How, Maurice, do you know that?"

"Sir, there is the kitchen building, and there is the lady's maidservant Frathesancia, and so we met. I think the lady Alesia is hoping to communicate that way."

"Any other statements?"

Maurice lowered his voice and clattered the dishes. He quietly indicated that there was willingness to try and escape.

"It is the thought of every prisoner, Maurice."

Hugh's first question was whether it would always be him who would be serving him. Maurice assumed that it could be so. Hugh then had to consider his reply to Alesia.

He was quite aware that messages miscarry from person to person. That they must be simple. That they must not put the messengers in jeopardy. Presumably Crabbe would also be seeing Alesia now and again, so no message should change her demeanour to make him suspicious.

Hugh tapped a finger slowly on the table, as his hand rested there, contemplating whether he could ignore encouraging words of love and just let Alesia continue in her despond. Possibly the two of them were the only ones in the castle who knew any latin, but such a message would have to be written, and could be captured and have hidden meaning invented upon it. He was having to get words through two ignorant persons, so it had to be clear and not clever. In any event he did not yet have a plan.

"Hope," he said.

"Hope?" queried Maurice.

"Hope." If Hugh had added 'no more, no less' as he nearly did, then those words too might well have come out different the other end of the chain.

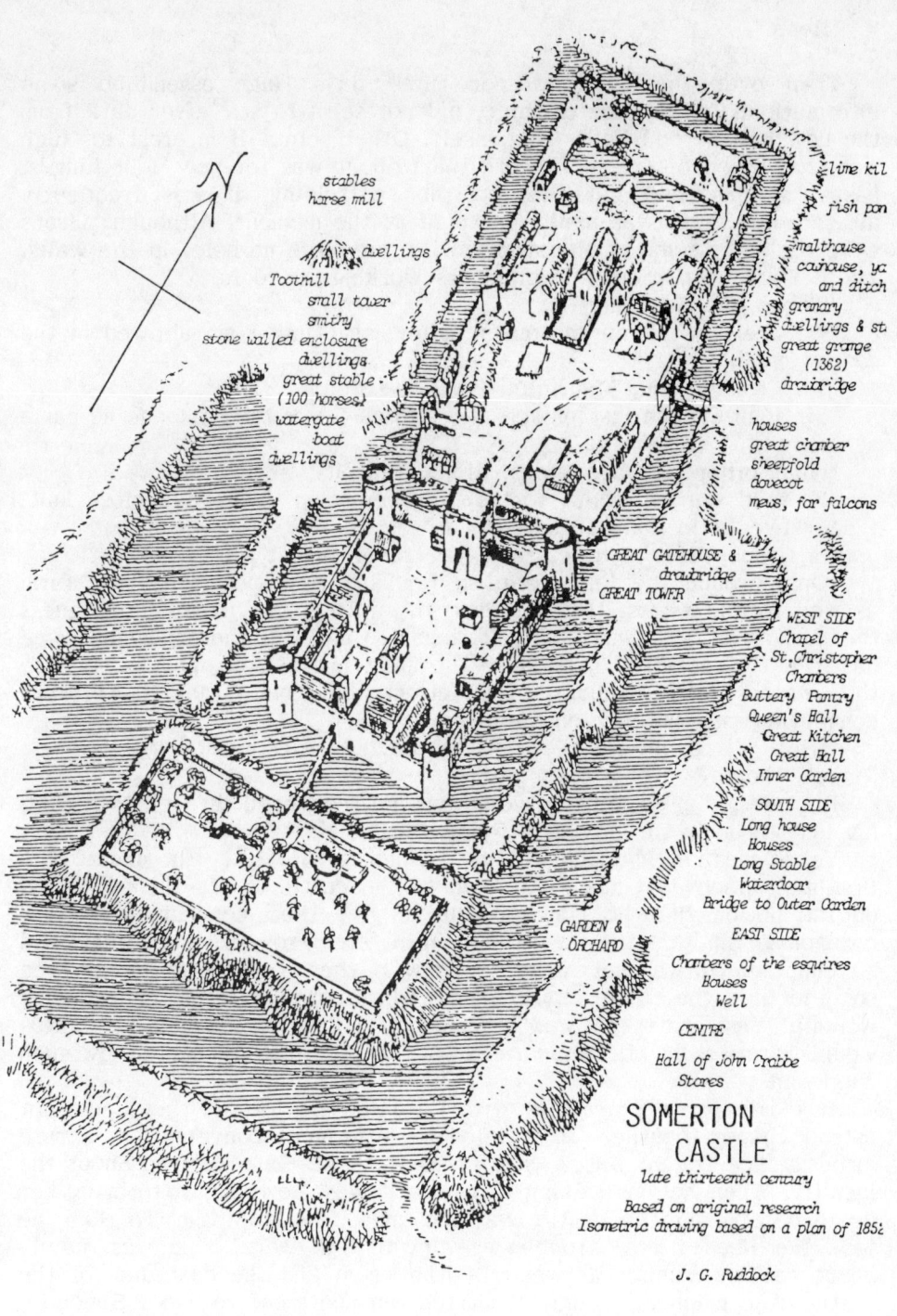

"Hope."

"Yes, sir."

Then over the next two or three days Hugh assembled some information. Crabbe, for example, did not seem to stir after dark from the new hall he had built for himself. Other points of interest to Hugh was that much of the metalwork lying about was for new door hinges, hasps, staples, and bars. As to the scaffolding, it was frequently altered, but there was none very high at the moment. Although masons were replacing some of the stonework there were no holes in the walls. There were carpenters and plumbers working on roofs.

"Where are my men?"

"We are now all on the outer bailey, sir. Only I am allowed in the castle itself."

"Why was it you, Maurice?"

"Sir John Crabbe just picked me. I think I was the first one he came across."

"What other men are there, armed that is?"

"I would suggest about forty, sir. They keep themselves close knit. I can have little contact with them."

"Is Crabbe always here. Does he travel out at all?"

"Only around the land here, so far, sir. He superintends the farm as well as the works. If I may say so, sir Hugh, obviously I can guess the purport of your questions. It seems to me that there may be some haste in this enterprise, because the moat is low now. This is because the masons are repairing foundations by the Great Gate, but completion may not be long delayed."

"'Hope' is again the message to the lady Alesia, Maurice. 'Hope', 'hope', 'hope?"

Doubtless Hugh's tone of voice was not conveyed through to Alesia, his last three words having a dying fall.

Yet it was not Maurice who gave Hugh the final key to escape. The Boothby parson de Gate rode down to the castle to see the prisoners, on the notion that he may be able to give them communion. It was common gossip that they were held in different towers, and Crabbe had no chaplain. It was necessary to know if they would ever be allowed together into the castle chapel of St. Christopher at least for a Sunday worship. Besides, there was his curiosity, and he thought his status would improve by the appearance of having been requested by such important people.

It led to private meetings with the two, because no, they could not attend chapel together. It also led to intelligent conversation, a rare circumstance for de Gate. As it progressed, de Gate chatted about the locality. When he was talking to Alesia it was, he thought, to bring her up to date about the castle that she knew from the past. To Hugh he took the line of how troublesome lower folk were. This was mainly about the antagonism between Boothby men and the custodian of the castle. It continued, though it started ten years before under Simon de

Spense. Common pasture had always been enjoyed in part of Somerton, when it dried out, by Boothby men and their ancestors, time out of mind. By ill-will de Spense deprived them of it. By Parliamentary Petition an enquiry had been held, but the Justices had died, and nothing had been done. They were in the same position now, and were seeking another enquiry.

"How exciting" agreed Hugh, as a way of being amiable and hiding his own thoughts. He also asked if there was anything in it, so as to hide any obvious joy at the idea that had occurred to him. With the importance of one not having to make the judgment, de Gate replied that there certainly was, because the part of which they were complaining used to be, indeed still should surely be, in Boothby manor. Thus, feeling better, de Gate left.

So, decided Hugh, it was Boothby men among the workers who could be bribed. He felt he had been slow in at least realising they would owe little loyalty to the adjoining manor of Somerton.

"Particularly the scaffolders, Maurice. Surely they can find some stones loose between these two south towers which need replacing."

The factors were beginning to emerge, to give real hope, to present something to plan upon. The last thing Hugh wanted to show was abnormal cheerfulness when John Crabbe visited him two days later. Apart from confirmation that his prisoners were both still in custody nothing was given away from either side. Hugh's men, with Frathesancia, had, however, been talking on the problem, all in an outward state of jolly taunting.

"Galfrid!" exclaimed Hugh, with shock and fear about his scheme, when Galfrid Postel arrived at his chamber with his afternoon sustenance. "Where's Maurice?"

Then, to avoid any suggestion that there was less trust between them, he quickly added:

"He's not been taken? Or injured or ill?"

"No, sir Hugh. But because of possible responsibilities after your escape, we all decided to take a little part. Not just Maurice. We have all wandered about and looked round, and there are important points to tell you. After me will come another, and so on."

Hugh invited Galfrid to continue, realising that it was trust all or none. People were always messing about with any plan.

"Sir. These facts. The lady Alesia's chamber is not at the height of the outside wall, and so she could not reach scaffolding or ladder, without first going out and down to the courtyard and then up the wall steps. She would be seen, or heard. But she does have a window facing outwards, which, if loosened, she could get through easily, and down a ladder. That's one matter. Another is that on the right night you yourself could be provided with a rope long enough to get down the wall.

Then there's the guard. Usually only one at night. The off duty ones are rather sleepy, and never expect anything..."

"...but would of course alert quickly."

"Yes, sir. But whoever brings your supper, will knock the guard out. There's a fine supply of iron all over the place."

"And any alertness all of you can deal with."

"Once you are out, we think so, yes, sir. It is also important that Constable Crabbe is going away the day after tomorrow. It is not known for how long, or where."

"Is it known why?"

"It is said that he is seeking yew wood, and that the castle is to be used by fletchers for making thousands of arrows."

Hugh congratulated Galfrid on his report. Soon he would produce clear orders. He waited two nights before he gave them. It was safer to have Crabbe away, even risking his return by that nightfall. To the shrewd Crabbe his men must remain full of doubt and frustration in his presence. In the meantime the building workers had been passed simple instructions. So it was Thomas de Burgel who was told that winter's morning, with Crabbe just gone, the word 'Tonight'.

With cheeky expression and ulterior meaning de Burgel passed the word to Frathesancia. Being part of the present castle activity, no notice was taken of builders erecting scaffolding against the south east tower. Plumbers had already worked on the roof leadwork. A long ladder was being assembled for Hugh, as more fitting for a gentleman than a rope, the builder men disbelieving that such a person would be skilled at lowering himself down one. The door in the south wall, which led by the footbridge over the inner moat, was barred from the outside. The carpenter who did this had the awful thought that maybe either the lady or gentleman would change their minds and try to escape from inside the castle instead. He would wait till it was all over, and have to tell from any noises whether it was they, or the castle people attempting their recapture. Scaffolding, ladder, and bar would all be gone by midnight and the workers all away. It led to excitement in the job and satisfaction against a foreigner, the custodian of Somerton, all helped in motivation by some having worked for the lady Alesia at Bolingbroke.

Hugh's men had their instructions, the most important and strict one being that none of them in the castle bailey on the north should react to any movement or noise. A foot messenger would wait with the horses to run to the far north end of the outer bailey to tell them that it was safe to move. There was one exception. If two of them could hijack the boat after its daily duties and get it to the steps on the far side of the garden, then they could ferry Alesia and Frathesancia across the outer moat. Within himself Hugh cursed this difficulty caused by his hardly expecting Alesia to wade across even at its low level, an ordinary hazard for a soldier.

In this season there was no route to the west over the marsh. To the east was the dry low hill stretching north and south for many miles, across the country. Further east was the River Witham in its fenny flat plain. So his men had been told to ride east to Boothby, then south, with rendezvous as soon as possible on the High Dyke road, a former Roman one, stretching three days ride to London. If necessary a rearguard action to prevent pursuit, or at Captain Walter de Aura's discretion, induce a false chase northwards towards Lincoln. They had permission for themselves to finish at Bolingbroke, if vital, either as a blind, or for personal shelter.

Hugh and Alesia would have horses waiting for them, south of the castle. Something had been simpler than expected - that fundamental requirement.

Only two days before their hurried departure, from his man as chosen for that day had come this information - "Captain de Aura says two things for you. Firstly we can leave horses out at grass for the night, because nobody checks whether we have or have not. Second, right at the far end of the outer bailey there is a fairly new lime kiln, to do with the works going on. Over the moat at that place is a good gangway used for stone and fuel, totally unhindered. It's only a single moat there. Going out for us could not be easier, sir."

"We go ahead. After nightfall. After it's quiet. By the moon, halfway to midnight. Round the south outer moat there is a high bank, then the Grange near it. Horses and men to be on the south-west, that's the corner nearest the marsh."

Men of the time of Edward III.

## CHAPTER 28

Thank God I am not always thinking of my dignity, thought Alesia. Frathesancia was more worried. The shadowy building men helping them through the window and down the ladder were in good mood. They certainly maintained silence, for their own sake as much as any reason, but there would be some future ribaldry. Alesia acted as friendly as possible, in quiet appreciation. Frathesancia's anxiety at her modesty being in danger was another way of avoiding fear at the unaccustomed climb down a hastily erected and wobbly structure. Hugh had already descended his ladder, with relief, and it was already dissected for quick removal. They met on the edge of the grass, hard up on the slope against the wall of the castle, along from the footbridge. The reflections in the dark water showed by their gentle movement that the moat was slowly refilling from the river on the east.

"I can't get up on to that bridge" whispered Alesia. Hugh hesitated. He looked up and found himself not sure either that he himself could do that. The waiting carpenter extended both his arms, but it was nowhere near sufficient. The nearest poor support which might have been useful to a lithe climber already had its foot in the water.

With a defiant grin, which unfortunately was glimpsed by no-one, Alesia lifted her skirts as far as she could gather them with one hand, walked slowly straight through the water; her other hand high, steadying herself on the underside timbers of the bridge. The other bank seemed steeper than it had looked in daylight, but it was possible to scramble up and grab the bridge timbers at the southern end. Hugh could never have brought himself to have led his lady to such an activity, but he was glad to follow. As did Frathesancia. By the time they had clambered into, and crossed, the garden the cold had turned to warmth in their legs, however temporary.

If the guard had recovered and was peering from the south parapets of the castle the escapees could not be seen as they crept quietly through the orchard trees, to the steps down to the outer moat at the far southwest corner. There was no boat waiting. Hugh was relieved at this. It could have created attention as it had passed the castle walls. He hoped that it was prudence on the part of his men. Who now cared about the water?

With relief, and an attitude of light dalliance, he handed Alesia down to take her through. After a faint noise of doubt and alarm from behind them, Hugh waded between both of them, and the mutual support was necessary. It was waist deep. Without their waiting soldiers helping from above they would not have got out. Wringing wet, on horseback, was most uncomfortable on a February night. The faster the more dangerous, but warmer, and the sooner to somewhere to cure the circumstance.

It was a wonderful relief to be out, in spite of all. What was happening at the castle? Had his instructions been followed, after their escape? Perhaps he should have ordered support from Bolingbroke, but that would have involved Alesia. There was also extra risk of detection.

In haste they mounted, and made off. In a few minutes they reached the old Roman Road and turned south. After a few miles of chasing in the shadowy night along the grassy rutted road it had gone on long enough for Alesia:

"Steady, steady, Hugh! Halt, please!"

They drew up.

"You're over-anxious, Hugh. At least let the men catch up. There'll be broken fetlocks if we go on like this. Go steady. Where are we going anyway?"

"Perhaps dark is sufficient, but I don't want the King's men from Somerton to get here first. All right."

They continued more slowly.

"Now, how uncomfortable are you, my dear?"

"Most of the discomfort has gone..." and looking round "... and for Frathesancia."

They were riding astride; for the convenience, and avoidance of contact with wet skirts their clothing was rolled up to their thighs, to the contemplation as much as possible by the few men with them.

So they walked their horses, but Hugh was still anxious -

"They are able to guess which way we are riding, for there's no other course."

Alesia did not demur. She was told that they were on their way to Moccas in Herefordshire. Her Clifford Castle was very near to there. Wherever Hugh had stayed on the way up had been friendly. All very exciting thought Alesia, beginning to wonder why they had left Bolingbroke.

The whole group reached the castle near Grantham of de Ros, a former constable of Somerton. He showed his interest, amusement, and hospitality.

"It may be best to go to London," expressed Alesia.

"Hugh, you forget that King Edward knows about us and is angry."

Perhaps she put the matter too obliquely, for of Kings she had more experience than had Hugh.

"Calm, calm, dear Alesia. When we are in peaceful residence and in a suitable evening sun, the warmth of any spirit shall equal it, and I shall ask you to marry me."

Maybe it did not sound genuine, but to resurrect their respectability it would have to be. With a little taunting Alesia replied:

"Good sir, how mature that sounds. I must wait for that good seasoning. Yet Eve de Clavering lived with James Audley for twenty years and no-one made a fuss. Perhaps Edward will stop his interference."

King Edward thought otherwise. On the twentieth of February, 1336, he issued two orders from his court, then at Walsingham in Norfolk:

- One of the orders set up a commission with Simon de Grymesby and Gilbert de Leddred to take into the King's hands the lands goods and chattels of Hugh de Frene and Alesia Countess of Lincoln in the counties of Lincoln, Northampton and Nottingham, and to keep the same until further order; the said Hugh and Alesia having escaped from the castle of Somerton where the King ordered them to be kept separately because Hugh took her from the castle of Bolingbroke thither and entered the castle of Somerton by force.

- Secondly, he appointed Nicholas de Cantelupe, William de Gray, and Richard de Gray of Langford, to arrest wherever found Hugh de Frene and Alesia Countess of Lincoln, on information lately received that the said Hugh, coming with a number of armed men to the castle of Bolingbroke where the Countess was staying, brought her thence to the King's castle of Somerton, and entered the castle against his will, and to cause him to be kept in the castle until further order.

- The King also ordered that the person of Alesia, Countess of Lincoln, is now attached to him under his own legal protection.

de Cantelupe and William de Gray arrived a few days later at Somerton from their manors in Nottinghamshire. Richard de Gray, from his estate near Newark, was already there. Leaving a message at home on the chance that the other two may call in on the way, he dashed off next morning to Somerton. His comparative youth, at age twenty eight, made him feel honoured at the comission. The other de Gray, from Sandiacre, a cousin of his late father, would doubtless join with de Cantelupe from Greasley in Nottinghamshire.

Crabbe was in a fury. All his men denied everything. All they knew was that one was knocked out by one of de Frene's men. He was the only man on duty on the wall. How did they get out? Somehow on to some scaffolding halfway up the west wall, they thought. It must have been the only physical way with both drawbridges up, and the portcullises shut. Then they must have gone by boat, but on what evidence for that? How on to the scaffolding? There are ropes everywhere, with the builders hauling up stones and lead and tools. They know nothing. They're not here at night, and it's dark early. All the prisoners and soldiers can only have escaped through the north end of the bailey over the temporary bridge to the new limekiln. Yes, also they'd left horses outside, which was only now realised. Not unusual, but this time a trick. No bribes. I think I believe my men. All of them.

Two days later de Cantelupe and the older de Gray arrived. Young de Gray had been getting anxious that he would annoy Crabbe by having to repeat it all, or be in trouble for his having started the questioning. de Cantelupe, however, just listened to a brief account. He had found Crabbe's mixed accents hard to follow. His interest was more in the actual state of things at this day, namely find Alesia and Hugh, to do what the King had ordered. He had decided purely to ask questions about what they had heard about a planned route. He just walked through the whole castle ground, from the garden, itself totally moated, across the footbridge into one of the halls into the courtyard. He took the steps up the wall to see the relative chambers. As he passed down again and through the Great Gate and across that moat there he remarked that he could see no clues at all. Noticing the water gate on the left in the outer bailey he asked to see the boat. Now hauled up and being repaired, he was told. It looked to de Cantelupe that it also needed cleaning, from the fish residues that still glistened on the timbers.

"Yes, yes. But where was it found?"

"Just below the steps, sir. Sunk as it was returned I should say."

Why return it, thought de Cantelupe, when the point of escape was at least a hundred yards away, diametrically across the outer bailey, with its clutter of buildings, compounds for animals, hovels for peasants, houses, barns and stables. No, sunk for some other reason. So that it could not be used to investigate the outside of the castle during the escape, he presumed. He did not expect anything useful to be learnt, however, and if any horsemen had to be despatched in search he had better get on with it, for the day was lengthening. Crabbe's men were trying to be free with any chatter they could think up, which might show ingenuous innocence, or that they were reacting from guilt. After all, if Mortimer could escape from the Tower of London by bribery, then Somerton must be simple. de Cantelupe had had to see what he had seen. It was time now to effect his instructions.

To Richard de Gray he ordered:

"You go across the heath up there, past Temple Bruer, to Ruskington - the lady Alesia has a distant connection there - Agnes, Lady Bardolf, related to the de Clares; then to Sleaford castle, then return here. Look for them, also as to whether they have been seen."

He then sent men checking north and east, planning himself with the whole party to go south-west, because he did not expect Alesia and Hugh to risk Lincoln, get involved in the Fens, or visit the obvious nearby relatives or friends. He knew that they had not travelled westwards, because his own party had ridden some forty miles from there.

The anger of the King was complete. A messenger arrived, carrying the information that further lands had also been taken from Alesia and Hugh - in Oxfordshire, Berkshire, Buckinghamshire, Cambridgeshire, Dorset, Wiltshire, Middlesex, Shropshire.

"These are not all, sir Nicholas," he said. "The written list is complete with any place or right however large or small."

"Have sheriffs been informed and given orders? I have power of arrest, but it is more likely that a sheriff would find them. Sheriffs are dispersed throughout the land, I have only myself, and general directions to surmise upon.

"I am certain the King would be pleased for you to take what action is required. Not everything can be written. However, my main information is that towards the end of March the Court will be at Westminster or at the Tower. A report is then required, sir Nicholas."

Was it, thought Nicholas. He fell into contemplation. South or south-west, yes. Possibly first to de Ros, to replenish. Or was Sedgbrook still Alesia's? Most likely then they would think about the far west, to a place of de Frene's. Oh, but by the time he got there he wouldn't have one. They would find that out somewhere in a day or two. Further south towards Dorset; but again, Alesia had nowhere to go. With the King moving east and south, to London, they would surely have to avoid that? He turned suddenly to Crabbe:

"Was it raining that night?"

Crabbe seemed to think that this was a deep question which would dredge up some final clue. But he had not been at Somerton at the time. He would be absent a moment, to find out. He did. It had been raining part of the night. By now the poise of the conversation had evaporated. On presenting his reply Crabbe looked askance for a wise projection to come forth. It was far too late to joke with his stolid person that the romance of the escape would only have lasted five minutes. de Cantelupe sadly only nodded thoughtfully, to avoid further reference.

"They would go to London;" he spoke aloud. Crabbe, a brilliant practical man, could but admire the decisiveness of the end conclusion, yet mystified how anyone could divine that from the state of the weather.

"To London!" His order took effect next morning.

"All right," asked Richard de Gray, "but how do you know that?"

"Alesia is female..." replied Nicholas.

"Very. Yes. But...ah!...security...rank...she will be frightened sooner or later, and will have to get back to where she was."

"Precisely. I think they'll marry, and bow before the King. They have no other way to avoid separation and penury. So it's London. First to Stamford."

"May I suggest, sir Nicholas, a spread via Leicester, as a second string."

"Why, William?"

"Well, first of all we don't precisely know which way they might go. They may have started down the road to de Frene's castle in Wales, then will change their minds as and when they find out about their lands. They should have visited at least one of her places by now. The lady Alesia is familiar with either route - Leicester, or Stamford and places between. Queen Eleanor's catafalque was taken through Northamptonshire, as you know."

"That makes it even less romantic" muttered Nicholas. "Very well. Beware of false information brought about by bribery. Meet in Westminster if not before. I wasn't really thinking we could catch up with them. We will get information as we go. They are prominent enough as they pass. It's no use their fleeing to the south-west or Dorset, so sooner or later commonsense must prevail. A pity, really."

He added:

"Don't look so excited. She's a relation of the King and he doesn't like having her abducted. She must know that because of what happened here."

"Yes, Nicholas. A question if I may. Arresting de Frene can be simple. What does one do with a lady if she - er - resists?"

"It would be an interesting experience," replied de Cantelupe, sardonically "let me know about it."

As they conversed over preliminary refreshment he clarified the runaways' status:

"It seems that until they marry they have no standing, and only the money they may have with them, though their credit could be good. That is why I say their only answer is to marry to conciliate the King. Maybe they were not expecting his reaction. They can find a friendly parson, and forget the licence, and the banns. They can get through that fairly easily, at least up to acceptance by King Edward."

"I would have thought they would have been better to have stayed at Bolingbroke and taken their time to sort it out."

"Excitable female? Abduction in her mid-fifties? Her first thought might not have been her second cousin."

"Of all the choices of destination I still choose the conventional one. Friends will drop away. No, there's no earth for this brace. However, we will proceed, and be seen to be joining the hunt. No animal mates on the run."

It was a convenient statement of spontaneous supposed wisdom. Animals, though without conscious thought, have instincts and reactions which cause exertion, and it might have been correct. Alesia and Hugh, however, were in need of proof of the rightness which could rationalise their action in fleeing. Excitement being one reason for irresponsible feelings was followed by another, self justification. During the day the outside world looked homeless and indifferent, their lives without aim. They had stayed on the way without hindrance, but after a night at Alesia's manor of Bicester the sheriffs, Thomas de Langele and Tolm de Benham, met them on the road towards Oxford. Both parties hesitated a way from each other, but walked their horses slowly on, the sheriffs' party then blocking the road.

"Greeting," commenced de Langele "I have information for the Countess of Lincoln, as I imagine you are, my lady."

de Frene made to move forward, but was restrained by a gesture from Alesia.

"I imagine that you are the sheriffs, from the appearance of your posse. What is your information?"

Colour began to return to Alesia's cheeks. The mystery of the information to be heard would prove their identity. Hugh was assessing the relative strength of the escorts.

"Ma'am," de Langele held up a parchment, "King Edward has ordered us to take your Oxfordshire lands from you into the King's hands. We do not know why."

The message was brief and clear. Its implications were not fully so. Alesia and Hugh were silent, expecting more. The sheriff therefore continued:

"I can assume, ma'am, that other sheriffs have this same order."

"Nothing further?"

Both sheriffs relaxed at this indication of their authority.

"No powers are given to us beyond that, Lady Lincoln. We shall, of course, have to inform the King that we have met. May I add that it was not difficult to find you, because we heard from a traveller that you were on this road. We are going to Bicester ourselves today."

There would be other statements added, thought Hugh. The adventure could only continue if it was put into proper social form. He spoke without much preliminary thought:

"Perhaps in your acknowledgment you would inform King Edward that we are on our way to be married, either in Wiltshire or Dorset, as may be convenient. Perhaps we should have told him first."

Three conversations took place after this encounter. The two sheriffs passed by Alesia and Hugh, the latter two riding on to Oxford.

Sheriffs de Langele and de Benham thoroughly agreed that the couple had received a nasty shock. They grinned together that at least some of the prevalent wave of corruption of morals may have been stopped. It would have been a triumphal entry into Oxford if they had had powers to arrest them.

Alesia and Hugh also conversed.

"Why is Edward so furious, Hugh? What else has he got in mind? Why not let's ride back to Bolingbroke and start life there again? In Heaven's name, I am not as significant as all that in the firmament.... certainly not with Edward having done his damnedest to bed his new Countess of Salisbury. Did you know the only way she could stop his persistence was by threatening to kill herself?"

"And here are just us, no rejections, no arguments, and no... I nearly said no scandal, but it seems to be manufactured. Clearly it is I who am wrong. Even so, shall we marry in Oxford? Will you still do so, or, Alesia, should I leave you alone?"

"Oh, a gentlemanly offer, indeed. But thank you only, and no, sir. We will seek a cleric. I married Ebulo without a licence, relying on the second Edward's authority to marry whom I pleased and within his realm. I please."

"You please. I will."

Then Alesia felt cold so suddenly that to try and conceal any change of expression she fell back a couple of yards. In case Hugh turned to question her she fiddled nervously with the bridle. Edward's reason for his repressive action had struck her as though it were terror. He was exerting effort, propaganda and money for the canonisation of her first husband Thomas, and she was showing herself to be wanton and irresponsible. Indeed they must marry, to be right with the Church. If the Pope heard about this present adventure before that... she would fear ex-communication. Alesia trotted forward to parallel her paramour. She loosened her hair from its covering and its ribbons, to let it flow in the breeze, the gesture distracting from her tension. It had all been too quick to alert either Hugh or Frathesancia. It resulted for them in appreciation of what looked like freedom and happiness.

The third conversation took place some three days later in Oxford once again between the two sheriffs. The order to arrest Alesia and Hugh now extended to include Oxfordshire, Berkshire and Buckinghamshire.

"We should have guessed. It was a long time arriving, but we could have taken a chance."

"I wouldn't have done. No, too risky to dabble there. Maybe those lands were taken away, but you never know, at the same time they might have been given some elsewhere. However.... where are they. Let's be off. South, I guess."

"Damn me for missing them. I'm sure they've gone too far. I heard that they asked the priest on Sunday to marry them, and he refused. They'll get someone to do so. Why not her own chaplain?"

"Left behind."

"You look amused."

"I am. Let the lady have her excitement."

"I'm going south."

"Where to?"

"Hoping for luck, but I'm only guessing."

"Hold. If an ordinary parson is cautious, where are they going to find anyone to marry them? Leaving out the conventional system, that is."

"She's got connections in Wiltshire. In Salisbury, and some manors. That'll be where they're going, even if not to a collateral in the church, a Saluzzo. Distant, but connected in their terms. If he's still around."

"It's all over, then. The order for arrest doesn't apply to Wiltshire."

"This is all damnedly frustrating. I was really hoping for a dramatic chase down the road."

"We can still go and look."

"'Countess! I hereby arrest you in the name of the King!' Good idea, isn't it? Or is it?"

- 351 -

"They might still be in this County. Let us ride to Abingdon and check."

Whatever unusual task the sheriffs were hoping for did not come about. Alesia and Hugh had been warned. Not by word of mouth, but by circumstance, at last. They also desired some comfort.

"Surely" said Alesia, maintaining as patient an attitude as she could "they will not prevent our staying at Holborn in a proper manner, to organise marriage."

There was no difficulty, after the straightforward decision to ride to London. Nor did their arrival at Alesia's Holborn Inn occasion much surprise, except for its short notice. No order had been received to remove it from her.

"It makes an astounding difference, dear Alesia," spoke Hugh with an abiding sigh of contented relief, "to have somewhere to live, someone to live with, and a position acceptable to a rigid society."

"I apologise, Hugh," returned Alesia "I did not expect the problem."

"Apologies to King Edward now done, no need for apologies to me, my dear, I beg you. I don't think he was sure whether he had had any effect on our progress or not. He was at least amused by our escape from Somerton Castle, equating it with his own secret entry to Nottingham six years ago. It has all been my fault."

"Not many ladies, Hugh dear, have knights galloping from one coast to the other to be captured... or captivated."

The clerks were set to work again, to return all that had been confiscated:

> On 23 March, 1336 - from Westminster:
> To Simon de Grymesby and Gilbert de Leddred: Order to deliver all the lands of Hugh de Frene and Alesia, Countess of Lincoln, whom Hugh married, in Cos. Lincoln, Northampton and Nottingham to the said Hugh or his attorney, together with all goods and chattels...
> The like to Thomas de Langele and John de Benham in Cos. Oxford, Berks. and Buckingham.
> John de Tothill in Co. Cambridge.
> Ralph de Middelneye in Co. Dorset.
> Gilbert de Berewyk in Co. Wilts.
> Richard le Ward and Thomas de Alta Ripa in Co. Middlesex.
> To John Crabbe, Constable of Somerton Castle: A like order with respect to the goods and chattels of Hugh and Alesia in that castle.
> To the sheriff of Salop: Order to deliver the castle and manor of Ellesmere... hamlets of Colmare and Hampton, together with issues thereof to Hugh de Frene or his attorney without delay although the King lately ordered the sheriff to take into the King's hands all the lands, goods and chattels in that county of

Hugh and Alesia, Countess of Lincoln, whom Hugh married.

"'Married', 'married', 'married'... what a significant word that is," breathed Hugh, in wonder; "Of course, his attitude might well have been reaction to your tight upper clothes, cross-coloured, and your pleated skirt."

"Well, well, you noticed. Perhaps Edward was thinking they were out of fashion."

> On 3 April, 1336 - from Eltham
> To William Trussel, escheator this side Trent: Order to deliver to Hugh de Frene and Alesia his wife, late the wife of Ebulo Le Strange, a messuage and carucate of land in Avyngton and rent from certain free tenants in Wenbury Co. Berks, together with issues thereof, from the time of Ebulo's death...

"I presume these were all the places he thought we were likely to get to," was Alesia's comment. "I would just say that Kings are alright as long as you agree with them."

"Even so, I am sorry to say this, but we must live a conventional life now, and get through apprenticeship again."

Before long Henry de Halton was ordered to deliver to Hugh de Frene and his wife the castle and cantred of Builth in Wales with Knights fees advowsons of churches and all belonging thereto, certain claims of the King to be discussed.

"What does that mean? Something to do with what it's cost him?"

"What else? But he's being very reasonable. In any case, he's in Scotland again with other business on his hands."

The castle and manor of Clifford was returned to them, manors in the counties of Brecknock, Radnor and Herefordshire, for life, then to Roger le Strange. Then the constableship of Lincoln Castle.

"He is in a good mood."

"Of course he is. Not only is he capturing castles in Scotland, according to reports, but better still he has rescued Katherine Beaumont and a bunch of lovely ladies from Lochindorb Castle."

"So you want to join him in Scotland, then? Dear Hugh, I do hope so much that Edward does not order your presence."

"It's going well without me, one can see; except that Montague has been defeated - Black Agnes."

This was meant to give a little amusement to Alesia, but she was still apprehensive. The campaign was taking a turn against Edward. He would call forward more men.

That autumn:

"Lord Frene, at your service, my lady."

"What?" asked Alesia, incredulous. Hugh was often addressed unofficially as Lord Lincoln, but what was this?

"I have been summoned to Parliament, and therefore that is what

I now am."

"Lady Frene" quoth Alesia, with a graceful curtsey, and a demure expression.

Within twenty-four hours it was Lord Frene ordered to Scotland.

It transpired that Edward was returning south, and Balliol was garrisoning Perth.

"'Garrisoning' means a steady base for government. There was meant to be peace last year, and this must mean it might be permanent. It's further north than before, so that suggests stability."

There was every point in making such remarks, Hugh was trying to comfort Alesia. She was silent, with foreboding. Once again, and at their time of life. It was not that many voluble expressions eluded her. They would make the whole execution of his duty more arduous for Hugh. That she was so quiet was from being stunned into fear she was refusing to reveal. It would happen a third time. Things did. What a silly basis of prophecy, but it wouldn't go away.

Hugh departed from a long long hugging embrace to give and take the warmth of life from one to the other.

Within a month Hugh lay dead in the House of St. John in Perth. It was just after King Edward had made him a further return grant.

"Yes, de Halton, I ought to know, so thank you for telling me. You may send back to the King the Grant of Cardigan Castle. He was not to know."

Death. How haunting, how unpredictable. As if nature's action itself was not enough, her tailor, Thomas de Gouuthorp, had been murdered by Alexander le Shephior. Why could one not sit and wait for eternal rest without feelings?

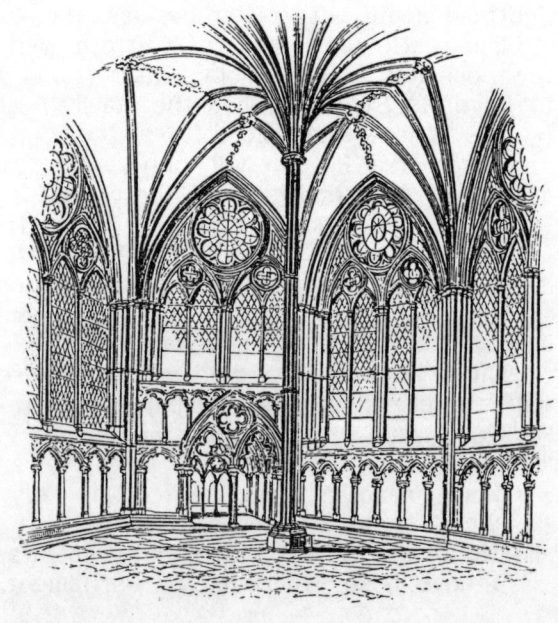

Chapter House, Salisbury Cathedral. The foundation stones of the cathedral were laid by William Longepee, 5th Earl of Salisbury and Lady Ela (Alesia's grandparents), and by Bishop Richard Poore.

# CHAPTER 29

"One can seek to the heavens for inspiration, Frathesancia, but one does fall down thereafter in not knowing what to do to gain one's aims."

They had been talking about Bolingbroke, the village, and the but faint improvement this generation.

"More of the soil is used more often, but the weather seems worse, and the efforts of man result in less than should be."

Frathesancia was these days on open terms with her mistress, who was now fifty four years of age, and relaxing into a peaceable life, with no plans to make, nor anyone for whom to make them. Frathesancia could by now speak as she wished, for Alesia had ceased to be the actress of an elevated social position. She appreciated the thoughts of all, of any station in life.

"It is not the same with me, ma'am; I know your life, your church. But I reckon our stumbling endeavours will always make for some improvement. They've got to. More and more people need feeding. It's bound to be. But most of the folk here, and anywhere I've seen, never think much. It is enough to keep the routine of life, and they're frightened of anything new. They have more than enough struggle some years, what with weather's droughts and storms. It's easiest to get through life without thinking."

Alesia thought how tactfully her maid had glossed over the increasing population thought. The instincts of women were rationalised in the urge to preserve the human race against all the pestilence and hunger, early deaths and dangers. Alesia had got over it all now. Children, children the future, everybody seemed to have that desire. Now she had lost it, and had preferred for years adult company. She was about to tease Frathesancia as to what had happened to the dragons of doom which so often were the bases of her conversation, but the woman had hustled to the window overlooking the court.

"Ma'am! Visitors!" and Frathesancia turned to the window again with haste almost before she had uttered.

Alesia sensed a frightening situation. Frathesancia had tensed, had turned again in fear: "They're pushing their way in!"

Disturbance and noise came from horsemen, horses, and shouting for attention, and from soldiers and men commanding those in the court to keep back. The guards of the castle had already been overwhelmed and held in the gatehouse. This neither Alesia nor Frathesancia knew nor could see. Nor was it the men's fault for lack of resistance. It was the brusque arrival of Roger le Strange, with his men. There was surely no need for this?

To bring order and peace to her domain Alesia moved outwards to the top of the stone stairs which led downwards. It seemed a simple affair to welcome a nephew of her late second husband, and the atmosphere below appeared peculiar and offensive. She saw her own staff, and wenches and urchins grouped, in bewilderment, standing well away from the visitors. There was no communication with those who had arrived, no horses were held, no assistance was offered. This was not how things were meant to be at her household.

Alesia was about to signal, call, or wave a command to those over whom she had authority, yet she could not find an effective method. Within moments she had the true position thrust upon her.

Roger le Strange and two knights had by now dismounted, and with a casual air looked towards her, but only with a glance. They had purpose, even authority. Alesia stood nonplussed, controlling a feeling of fear, but with no ability to do other than stare at those who clearly acted as though she were not there. Her mouth opened to speak, but there were no words to suit that would come forth. Her head turned away as if that would help to found a thought.

Instinctively, with no deliberation, Alesia moved down a few steps, which was at the same moment as Roger le Strange walked briskly to the staircase. He was flanked by two knights and followed by a handful of his soldiers.

"You will kindly go to your chamber" he stated.

Stunned by this peremptory order, her husband's heir, and supposedly a friend, it was his acid tone which clarified her mind. It was as though he owned the place. That was the attitude of his disdain. Retorts so flashed through her mind that it was a question of sorting out the immediate response. She was not dead yet. It was presumptious of him to assume that the castle would be anything to do with him even if she were. Soft words about his attitude looked as if they would make no difference. Why all this, when he would have been welcomed anyway.

It must have been, she thought in the end, just aggression against an unprotected woman. None of these background feelings came to being expressed. There was no time before le Strange walked up the steps right to her and repeated more sharply:

"Go to your chamber. We are staying."

With a surge of immediate fury the reply was strident, the tone was searing:

"I will do no such thing. If you are my guests you will stay, and that consideration you have forfeited. You will go out, and there is nothing here for you as even would be for any casual wayfarer. There is no behaviour..."

That was as far as she could get. Even with all her life's adventures, as never before she was turned, pushed and bundled up the steps by le Strange, his esquires and his men.

As she was felled to the floor of the solar she just managed a jab to le Strange's face with an elbow. The dirt from the sleeve of a soldier whose wrist she had caught with her teeth was still around her mouth.

Any satisfaction was compounded by fear as to how long this was to go on. Surely the news would travel soon, even if her own people were too fearful to send to Lincoln for the sheriff.

Frathesancia had been trying to follow her mistress, hopelessly grabbing at the necks of two of the men. They broke off from the general batch, and for pleasurable amusement held her arms and took her along with them. On being shoved through the door after Alesia, she was more torn than her mistress.

It needed some moments to just tidy clothing and regain calmness, yet remaining on the floor. Sheer astonishment delayed recovery. Breathing heavily awhile, Alesia sought to control her myriad thoughts as to what to do next. From all her affronted feelings the strongest need was to understand the arrogance of le Strange. While he had never been especially polite, such as this attack was a revelation. Simply that she, Alesia, alone, was to a man now of no account, and was in the way of territorial ambition. Contempt welled up in her mind - a fight was fair, but this was entry into her castle as an enemy, trading on the recognition as a friend. A shallow way of indicating that in his mind this castle was his by right. Alesia had requested to continue her life there, and the King had acceded to her desire; in fact, her right, as Countess of Lincoln.

Her next wish to the King would be that le Strange would never get the castle after her decease. After this unspoken train of thought it seemed paltry to Frathesancia that her mistress's first remark was:

"The man's a fool."

Frathesancia was never much in fear when alongside her mistress. Alesia had the power, enabled matters to be ordered or put right, and Frathesancia was protected. She was stimulated by the short wrestle with the soldiers, so she felt that there was not much harm to come.

"My lady, may I say I do not understand the lord le Strange. He is not a neighbour, but a lord with far extensive duties."

"Perhaps he asked the King for Bolingbroke and the King refused, so he takes it out on me - us. He has developed uncalled for arrogance in the matter of his relationship. Who knows? But I will let this matter be known."

If communication is possible, thought Frathesancia, but it was reassuring to know that Alesia seemed to think it would not continue long. With an unusual initiative, from a thought for their safety, she struggled to her feet. Standing a moment to recover balance from being somewhat dazed, she then went to the door and placed the heavy wooden bar into the brackets, to make an effective stop.

After looking through a window to the court, she turned to Alesia, who was sitting up, comfortably arranged yet with upset clothing, still on the floor.

"Ma'am. Oh, one moment! There was no-one there, not one person. Not anyone on the stairs. Now, someone's just coming, no, not here.

It's food being fetched, and carried across."

Alesia made no reply, purely looking quietly at Frathesancia.

"Ma'am?"

"I am alright, if that's what you mean. Except that I cannot accept this insult. And what of us? If they just go away le Strange must surely guess that I would denounce him to the King."

"Ma'am. For many years I have served you with the best I can give. I have learnt from you so much of people and of life. So may I now put forward one point to you - perhaps I have learnt something which you have not experienced."

"If it's about le Strange then please say - because I am beginning to worry about what seems his hysteria, and what surely must bring retribution."

"I would say, ma'am, that there is nothing to fear - on the one point that the lord le Strange is not thinking of any consequence at all."

"Why can you say that, Frathesancia?"

Alesia was beginning to tidy herself.

"I was brought up among the city alleys in London. If I didn't know a hundred turbulent people it was two hundred. They are unruly because they lose control. They never think of any consequence. It is a wild emotional expression. He thinks he's bigger than he is. High authority is far away...."

"Me?"

"Oh ma'am, forgive me - but authority to stop this sort of thing is not rank - authority is physical power. That's proved every day in London streets."

She curtsied a little and made to help Alesia to stand.

Alesia thought back to Thomas - he had certainly been urged too willingly to the disastrous course which he had taken, and it was only in the last weeks when he began to see that there was an inevitable end.

"You mean, I think, that we should get a message to Lincoln, for men to be sent. Where is our garrison, though, small as it may be."

"Without command, ma'am, without orders, bamboozled by this infiltered attack. Probably held, I guess."

"Like us."

"Can we escape ma'am?"

"You are thinking of Somerton" Alesia actually laughed. "I suppose it's possible to contemplate; but le Strange's men will be alert, not like those at Somerton. Even that escape took days to arrange. Also, my dear, they're probably less susceptible to a bribe than were those local builder's men."

She noticed the question in Frathesancia's eyes, and noticed too, that they had never been so bright. In a sense it was relaxing to see that calm submission was unlikely. Alesia was about to say more on the possibilities and differences in their situation compared with that of

Somerton - the freedom of de Frene's and her servants to move around and to communicate - the wish of the men themselves to help - when heavy footsteps stopped at the door, and an attempt was made to enter the solar.

With Alesia feeling no special reason to get off the floor, Frathesancia achieved information by both sides shouting to each other. It was le Strange himself, and he said he was alone. To that Frathesancia was emboldened to disagree, because she had not seen le Strange nor anyone ascend the outside stairs. When he had said that his word should be taken, Alesia prompted the reply that it should most certainly not be so. Because he did not want them to starve as prisoners, the point was put that they would be sent food, and then perhaps they would open the door to the servant. That was what his call concerned.

"Let him in." ordered Alesia.

After surprise, and with hesitation, unwillingly Frathesancia removed the bar. And when le Strange had entered, with no delay she promptly replaced it, to stand in front of it. le Strange was taken aback, and turned to see what she had done. He was strong enough to push past and get out if need be, so he did not comment. Indeed there was scarcely a second before he was being addressed. He was to hear a short sharp scathing remark from Alesia, in a tone that would distance them forever.

"Prisoner! I do not eat as your prisoner! Leave my castle!"

Noting that the stairs outside were indeed unoccupied, Frathesancia with alacrity made ready to release the door. le Strange just stood. He was near to Alesia, and what he saw was part of her undershirt exposed as a framing over her bosom, and her long cote draped over her thighs by the way she reposed on the floor. A sleeve was torn, to show an arm thus part-naked. The image had sensuous tones, which of themselves gave rise to his irritation, to justify the unjustifiable more.

"Your men also."

Alesia issued that as an order, from an instinct as to how a woman can influence a man. le Strange had no wit enough to make rejoinder, nor prepared sentences for this situation, much as, in part, he could have expected it. He noted further the saffron colour which Alesia wore, that of the Earls of Lincoln. Perhaps he felt out of his class. He turned, and Frathesancia smartly replaced the door-bar behind him, making as much noise as possible.

Alesia remarked to herself the strangely reassuring revelation that fighting from a lowly position and without apparent strength caused one to gather determination. She had spoken to le Strange with more power from these disadvantages. Even so, it was now time to dispose themselves to try and achieve some normality. It was a matter of waiting. Everything in the immediacy was portentuous.

For her own confidence, Alesia took refuge in helping to reassure

Frathesancia, as they sat simply enough, the one now in a chair, the other on a stool, with nothing to look at except the warming log fire, for which at least there was enough fuel for the evening.

"Do you know, Frathesancia, if this is imprisonment, for me it is the fourth time. By Surrey - that was dreadful - by the second Edward, either as a precaution against supporters of Thomas or against my continuing his rebellion..." she hesitated with the thought of those agonising days "...then by the present Edward..." she smiled with the memory of the escapade with de Frene. "The main thing now is that here we have the game played by one who hasn't any rules."

"Nor," she added, "do I know any cause other than his own overbearing nature. That is the part against which to have courage."

"If you ask me, ma'am, it's not so much a matter of what he wants; it's that he doesn't understand what he can't have. Send me out for food, ma'am, and I'll find out what I can. Even if I don't get any food."

"Well, all my staff cannot be completely useless, surely. But they are presumably disarmed. Can you get out, though?"

Alesia remarked the faint grin on Frathesancia's lips, and took that as the reply. It was back to interchange through a servant, just as at Somerton. In their substructure in society how much more free and intriguing must their lives be, compared with her own, she reflected again.

Alesia agreed that if she felt safe in doing so, please try.

"And fuel," she added, "we might have to sit this out."

In Frathesancia's absence Alesia would not only try and think of a plan, but would hope to attract attention outside the castle. Next to the garderobe there was but one embrasure; a limited way of looking out, and even less possibility of being seen from beyond the moat. The idea of throwing out a letter to a passer-by was but that of a moment, quickly rejected for the unlikelihood of its being found; and if it were, the greater expectation of its discovery by a yokel who understood little and absorbed nothing, maybe even one who would take a reward from le Strange.

Frathesancia had removed the bar from the door, to open it, thus attracting the attention of the guard a few feet off in the short corridor. Alesia thought suddenly that it might have been better if she had essayed this herself, in that a common soldier might not try to stop her.

She heard at once something which might have been a scuffle; then a shout from Frathesancia of "Oh no, you don't."

Hastening to the window, Alesia saw her servant descending the steps with comparative dignity. Oh! she should have given her a note, to give to some horseman to ride fast to the sheriff. Depressed by this, fascinated to watch whither Frathesancia would walk, Alesia did not notice that the guard was now standing inside her door.

"Get out."

And as he did so she smartly called him back.

"Young man. I do not quarrel with you, I presume you have orders. What are they?"

"To guard you, milady."

"To guard me....from what?"

"It means to guard the door. To do with escape, ma'am, so you don't."

It did not seem to be a tasteful task, because he went on:

"That's what I was told, ma'am, to guard the door. The bar is on the inside, so it is not easy."

"My servant has gone to get food and fuel. That is alright I presume."

"Ma'am, I do not know, but it is your castle."

Alesia felt that that was enough. Any more questions would make him take refuge in seeking authority from his guard commander. Yet scarce could anyone be seen, except two scouts on the towers. And they were not hers. Perhaps the gate was shut, the drawbridge up, and everybody eating. It was not the moment to try and command attention and assistance.

"Perhaps soon we too will eat," she concluded the interchange. The soldier retired, agreeing with that idea, hoping that the woman would soon return so that he would not be found with one prisoner only.

Frathesancia was noticed by several while fetching and carrying items across the inner court, no-one knew or asked what or why, assuming that it was ordinary movement in the castle.

So at least the two became warm, fed, and with comfort, safely barred in.

It was not, however, a good night. The physical comfort may have been available, but the whistle of the wind and the intermittent beat of blown rain emphasised the knowledge of the inhospitable world outside. It demonstrated her helplessness against this invasion of her home. Walls and windows may protect from natural elements, but against the entry of this man and his followers there was no defence. And his departure was in his own control. Any arrival of local authority would produce polite words, and a possible move, but no punishment. So the response for revenge was in her own hands, and if none there, then no retaliation was possible. Maybe some of her own staff were trying to reach her, but she could not know for certain, and she did not feel it.

"Milady, you need warming more; you shiver a little."

Alesia had realised with a deep felt chagrin that her only weapon of the past was now no longer of influence. Her opinion of a man just by itself had been a controlling influence on many occasions. At other times she had, or had been supposed to have, a power that was worth ingratiating. Then there had been many years of life during which few men would do other than behave at their best in the hope of her real affection, or just affection of her body. Now it seemed, she was nothing other than a hindrance in somebody's way.

"No. I am cold of the shock of this situation. Something more we must do, other than wait here upon le Strange's fair idea of time."

"There is a strong King, Edward three, ma'am, and he can be informed, at least afterwards."

Some of the sad feeling of losing force as age crept on came out with suddenness, from Alesia's lips:

"Edward! He has plenty to do without me! Remember I moved out of here once with the lord de Frene, and your Edward took my lands away..."

"Yes, ma'am, I did not mean... but now... has not this Sir Roger done enough to be deprived of his.. and not to have them returned as were yours." Alesia was, however, not concluded in her thoughts.

"Then this Edward creates a new Earl of Salisbury, as though it needed a younger actor for the part. But I am the Countess of Salisbury, as I have been in the right of generations, and as myself, and between thirty and forty years. I have nothing to expect from this Edward."

Surprised at her own bitterness, Alesia made to balance the purport of some of her words, but within herself she found insufficient feeling. So she remained silent. Continuation of the discussion was beyond Frathesancia's intellect, so she sought a further rug and lay it around Alesia.

Alesia sighed with weariness of mind. Too tired in fact to have more than passing thought of what might be their fate. She managed to request the fuelling of the fire, with a thought that the deep darkness of the night had to be endured before the welcoming dissolution of its blackness by the beginning of the day. She fell asleep. After gazing into the flames for relaxation, Frathesancia followed suit, half sitting up, supported by Alesia's chair.

"To live, ma'am, we need only food and fuel."

This was an abrupt and strange start to the new day, without preliminaries.

"I would prefer a bow and arrow at the moment, to get a message to the village, but anything useful on our side seems to be absent. I do not appreciate being locked up, nor the uncertainty."

"Ma'am, they can do nothing to you. We cannot worry too much."

"Men make spectacles of women when they wish for revenge."

"Oh ma'am, this is not a war! All they could do is to send us to a nunnery."

"At last, do you think. I have already gibbed at that twice in my life."

"Then we must go out, ma'am. I got out and back yesterday. I will go again today."

"All we need is to get a horseman off to Lincoln. Surely it cannot be too impossible."

"Yes ma'am. We could send for the doctor Colin. That could not be refused."

Alesia harked back once more in her mind to her poor state of anxiety and health when she had been in Reigate castle. That had certainly produced a touch of help and consideration from her captors. But they had wanted her to live, which was the undoubted source of their assistance. On this occasion she was not so sure that le Strange cared. Ordinary humanity was obviously not present, nor had she powerful supporters to take up arms for retribution.

"Even if they would send for him, can we trust him? Perhaps it's worth a try. I am prepared to do as you suggest in looking weak and harmless."

"Ma'am! Not that. Not weak, not harmless. I..."

"Continue please"

"...no... again from my experience in the low quarters where I first fought to live... it is not, ma'am, not the weak who are preserved, nor who are safe. Any cat stronger than another will see it off. Any dog with a greater jaw will bite the lesser to death. It is those who want nothing but peace who get the bully..."

Alesia had to be amused and to admire her philosophising, lecturing servant who had developed fire in her eyes, a throbbing heart, a heaving breast, and stood as though she were ready to attack. The real Frathesancia of the alley had come out.

"Your experience, Frathesancia is right for now, I'm sure, but do you propose to knock the sentry down the steps?"

"I would like to, and I could, but...Oh, ma'am, no, ma'am." This once her own self was not subservient. "What I say is that if you look weak, we are lost. Their urges are to attack. That is, anything or anyone who is lesser than themselves. That's the lesson of the streets. Ma'am, you must look beautiful, with authority, proud, disdainful. I didn't know I knew so many words."

"Sweet Frathesancia, do you say I should then wander untouchable amongst them?"

"I do."

There were knocks on the door, heavy and clear, perhaps made with the handle of a dagger.

"The lord le Strange wishes to see the Lady de Clifford."

Strengthened by the innuendo of the use of that title only, Alesia ordered that the reply be that she would see him in the Great Hall in the middle of the morning. That was regarded as unsatisfactory by the man the other side of the door. Alesia ordered the repetition of her message, and silence in reply to any further communication.

"It will cheer my own folk, if any can be about. So we will get ready."

"What if he doesn't let us out, ma'am?"

"We will not weaken now, just as you say. I expect that he will allow this, or he would look defeated in front of his own sentry. We even have time for a small dinner from what we have left."

Such calm appreciation of the situation soon dissolved in the hubbub which began to rise in volume from the court. It seemed very close, so both rushed to the window, to see, but not to comprehend, what a group of men were doing. It took some time to penetrate their initial bewilderment for Alesia and Frathesancia to analyse the actions of the men.

"It is absolutely beyond ultimate belief; that this could be - in my castle - by one such as he..."

Alesia could not in her cold fury pronounce the words to describe all she saw - it looked as though timber was being urged up the outer stair to act as a ram to bash in her door. At least it seemed too large to start a fire. And le Strange nowhere to be seen; an aide was in charge.

"I do not want angry words," gritted Alesia, "I want a weapon. The lord Ebulo used to say there was always something in a tight corner, always something to hand somewhere."

She paused to look round to find whatever might give her inspiration. Her eyes ranging to the fireplace from the door, the bed, the chest. Yes, the door could be blocked, but that was not consistent with her overflowing emotion, which had developed into hate. The bar on the door was too heavy to carry; a heavy fireiron would be useful, if it did not occasion derision when it was seen.

"Open the door." There was no disobeying nor querying, because of the cold determined tone.

The sentry was helping others below, so Alesia was able to go along the short corridor unseen. She was also able to throw his small sword, bow and arrows to Frathesancia, who had been told to stay by the door, in case of retreat. Perhaps it would be wise, Frathesancia hissed, to come back with these trophies. But Alesia wanted to use the fireiron, to test herself, to get even.

Silence fell at the sight of her at the top landing of the stairs; a dozen mystified expressions gazed upwards. Their total purpose would seem to have been frustrated.

The soldier at the higher end of the baulk prudently went down. Esquire Ronald de Burton moved up to speak to Alesia.

"For your safety, ma'am we are trying to prevent you leaving your quarters."

Alesia looked as casual as possible, and fingered the fireiron in the side folds of her dress. This man could not possibly know her anger, nor cared he it seemed. A contemptuous looking sod, she thought, and would need none of her remorse.

"Allow me to move round my own castle as I choose."

"No..." and Ronald looked round in hope of support, indeed a better authority. That inattention allowed surprise, and a satisfying swift blow with the iron right across the back of his head. Stunned, he fell, all the way down. Such remorse, such reaction, that she should have felt, much to her satisfaction she did not feel. She cursed to herself quietly because she had no further plan. Perhaps she could have walked through the astounded group, perhaps she could have walked straight out of the castle gate. If anyone further had come towards her she would have hit them too. But there would be no surprise. Perhaps she was as amazed at herself as were they.

The guard was looking towards her, from the gate. It cannot be said that Alesia's thoughts followed the logical course of weighing up any strategic factors. A run for the gate or a retreat to her solar were options, as may have been a storming into the Great Hall where she assumed that le Strange would be. He did not come out to discover what was happening, which was itself slightly unnerving. It was probably enough what she had done already, so instinctively Alesia felt that such reserve as she may have could come in useful later, and that she had possession of some weapons. Before anyone recovered their poise she backed up the top stair, and returned to the solar. Frathesancia's relief was considerable.

The latter's admiration was also involved, and some feeling that she herself should have done more. She promptly left for food, and, unmolested, returned in twenty minutes with a good supply, and was helped in with some water. She never knew that in her absence Alesia had collapsed in tears. The arrangement made to meet le Strange was not kept.

"My lady" ventured Frathesancia, after a comparative silence lasting a night and a day and into the next evening, "tomorrow we shall need more food and water. Is it perhaps not now the time for my plan?"

"For me to dress up, you mean? To look untouchable? Perhaps. It would have to be tomorrow, of course. I am a little doubtful because I am thinking more of what the lord Ebulo said once. Indeed it is appropriate. That there are three stages of life and I am now in the third. Just that the pressures of man and nature against us are always of the same strong power, but in the third part of life we ourselves are weakening against them."

Frathesancia raised her eyebrows as not fully comnprehending.

"In the first stage of life we are looked after by someone else. In the second stage we are equal to the battle. But now I am weary."

"Ma'am, I have only just remembered that you hunted with arrows and that you must be a good shot still."

"So?"

"There are twenty arrows here."

Alesia showed some interest.

"Ah, yes. By the time I had picked off twenty men in the courtyard, the others would depart! It is an attractive idea. Unfortunately after killing one I think there would be dire trouble from the others. It is not that I mind the first bit. But I feel safer in defence if they try and come up here."

It was not long before Frathesancia persisted on the subject. A stag, captured alive a week before, was tethered in the court. Alesia thought she could get it with a careful shot. At least it would interest and gain respect from the soldiery. With care and long consideration she installed herself, part on a settle, part on the stone cill, into position at the western window. There were four men by the stag, but it was not moving, so as a hunting shot it was easy, the only problem her beating heart.

Her shot was loosed:

"I am getting used to the incredulous stares of soldiers" she said, "my only problem now is climbing down from this window."

"You hit the stag, ma'am?"

Frathesancia as soon realised that there was no need to have asked, and regretted it. Alesia's lips twitched but briefly.

"What next, I wonder" she said, not meaning any rebuke at all, but only trying to assess what le Strange might do. At least she had shown some spirit and some strength, having concussed one of his esquires, and having made his soldiers think that an arrow might next be for them.

It was early morning, however, before there was any sign of communication at all. Alesia had decided that she might now take her maid's advice, and dress into finery. Hunting fashion, she thought, in case she had to use that bow again. Movement down below caused the two to examine the court again.

Two archers stood by the gate, taking moderate cover. Other men were moving, some with horses, along the western wall, and disppearing through the gate.

"It looks pleasing, ma'am."

"Are they really going? The archers are covering for any attack from inside. I was half expecting to do that on our own behalf; I think the sentry would have run down the steps."

Frathesancia was about to find out if she could whether they were still guarded, but was called back.

"Wait! le Strange is coming out. Yes, he's coming here. Wait. No. He's pondering, up a couple of steps. Open the door, dear."

"Ma'am"

"I will cover you. One move from any sentry and I shall shoot. I am not playing games."

There was no sentry. Alesia stood at the stair top, but le Strange had decided to move away, to where his horse was held. Alesia tensed and drew her bow, but she retracted, because an esquire moved forward instead. In some effort at a conciliatory tone he spoke:

"Countess, we are in these parts because there are strong rumours of a French invasion on the coast of Lincolnshire. Further, permit me to say that we are now to depart. With respect, ma'am."

He bowed, and turned away. Alesia thought of taunting their departing with the charge of retreating from the danger. Perhaps silence towards this young man would be of equal value. le Strange turned, and then turned back. She called out to him with some evenness and cold command in her tone:

"Do not inform the King. I shall do that."

It is doubtful if le Strange heard her words. She rather hoped not, their tired petulance was not impressive.

de Halton had suffered most. As her secretary the soldiers of le Strange had felt most to fear from his abilities. He had just been bound and left in a lower corner of a wall tower. Restoration of his body and spirit could be achieved only by rest, washing, and feeding. It would take a few days.

In the midst of the relaxation of those whose liberty had been curtailed, a cry went up from the top of the gatehouse. It was but a few hours after the departure of le Strange that there approached another party. This body, of some thirty horsemen, came right to the closed gate and lifted drawbridge. Alesia was there to look at them, for identification. From the parapet she gazed down at their banner, now unfurled.

An equerry called out: "The Sheriff! de Trehampton!"

"We have heard of trouble, Lady Lincoln. First yourself. Are you uninjured?"

"Indeed so, de Trehampton. We are now counting the cost of assault and imprisonment to my men and servants; also theft of goods, and apparently some horses."

"Can you identify the intruders, ma'am?"

"Why certainly I can. Roger le Strange of Knokyn."

"le Strange? Do you mean..."

"I do so mean. I know him well enough."

"My lady, forgive me. I did not presume to doubt. It was astonishment on my part. We passed him on the Lincoln road. Yes, there were too many horses for their party, but..."

"Yes, yes, how would you suspect anything."

"Thank you, my lady. Also there was Sir John de Lacy and Sir John de Rous in the party."

"Well, they kept out of the way. Arranging the theft of horses and goods I suppose. The de Lacy is no connection with me, de Trehampton, grandson of a former steward, though he did once hold office here. That is presumably why he was useful to le Strange. If you will produce a report, I will take it myself to the King. I have decided to depart to the Court."

# CHAPTER 30

The constant memory of the insult and disparagement to her by le Strange's violation of her castle home sustained Alesia's resolve to make complaint to the King. In person.

"Frathesancia," she stated, "we are to be ready for the first decent weather. I have confirmed it again to Mr. Halton. Yet do you know, last year I really imagined that the rest of my life would be all peace. I supposed that its ebb would be at my own command. Yet if it is not my person that is stolen, this next year it is my horses and material."

Frathesancia loved the matiness of journeys in the escorting group, the teasing and the jocularity.

"It will certainly be better to clear it up, ma'am. I am always ready to travel any time, and I don't think there's much that isn't already prepared."

Alesia looked thoughtful.

"Frathesancia, I have just begun to assess the reason for le Strange's actions. There must be one - more than that invasion rumour, which doesn't warrant it. That must be the excuse, but only that..."

Frathesancia began to fear that her trip to London might be called off.

"...Do you see the coincidence? le Strange expected more manors after my lord Ebulo's burial at Barlings. Perhaps even this castle. Then he was frustrated by my - er, link with Sir Hugh de Frene; again, he must have thought they were in his grasp. But Edward started returning them to me six weeks ago."

To Frathesancia's relief Alesia added:

"That must be his motive. He has no other. It so disgusts me that I am even more determined to act. Damn him. Damn the weather. Fetch Mr. Halton. We leave tomorrow."

Frathesancia scooted off gleefully, to disturb most happily Mr. Halton's cautious routine temperament. He retaliated to her with forceful doubts about the King being able or willing to do anything at all, with a war with France just sanctioned, Philip confiscating Gascony and helping the Scots again.

"She's a relation" retorted Frathesancia.

"Getting to be a thin connection" came the smart reply, "as a former daughter-in-law of the present King's grandfather's brother."

"Didn't seem thin with the fuss King Edward made over de Frene." Frathesancia managed the last word.

Mr. Halton made sure his gown hung tidily, and did as he was bid, arranging a suitable smile for the encounter with Alesia.

The manor in Holborn was still Alesia's residence in London, where any answer from Edward was awaited. The days were full enough of all the old stories about the Scots and the French, modernised. Edward had revived his claim to the French throne. He was closest of all to it, except for having a female in his descent. Not surprising that they were drifting into hostility. He had given up the idea of Scotland. He had just lost interest. Some said he should have concentrated on it and left France alone. No revenue there, said others, but there was in France. Warwick had been appointed Captain and Leader of the Army against Scotland, but he received no support. Edward's last brave try had been based on his realisation of the Roman idea of holding only the lowlands up to Agricola's wall. It was traditionally Celtic as far as there. The Bishop of Lincoln thought he himself would soon have to go to France to present Edward's defiance to Philip VI, but Edward's alliances with the Flemings, Germans and Bavarians were not yet ready. It was of personal interest to Alesia to know that Henry of Lancaster had been created Earl of Derby, a former holding of Thomas. Edward's six and a half year old son, nicknamed the Black Prince, had just a couple of months ago been created the first ever Duke, of Cornwall. It got the title above that former Earldom, so tainted by Gaveston's holding of it.

Alesia soon began to long to return to Bolingbroke, in full expectancy of her journey to London having been in vain. There was so much that she was left out of, however friendly were her old acquaintances. She did not feel inclined to get back into the social world. It was difficult when alone, and only the more enduring friends were left. And why should twenty five year old Edward be troubled in these times with fifty five year old Alesia? It was all renewal. Perhaps leave matters alone. She spent some of nearly every day in St. Paul's, close by her father's tomb and monument. For herself, she would prefer to be buried next to her husband Ebulo. Not to be separated, as was her mother in the Abbey of Lacock.

With Edward, or at least his staff, knowing of her mission she could not now depart without his leave, however insignificant it now seemed among all his other considerations.

She was not to know that Edward did want to meet her. The command came comparatively soon. His first words were regret at the delay, if she had been feeling impatient.

"Cousin Alesia, I would have imagined life was quieter at Bolingbroke than it is in political life. At least I was wrong on one point. Please tell me the whole story, which must be longer than the parchment which you sent to me."

Alesia narrated the attack by le Strange, and her later conclusion as to its basis. She felt that Edward brightened at the narration of the conflict.

"There were rumours about invasion," agreed Edward, "and orders to buy horses, but of course not to steal any. Certainly not yours. So I say that as soon as I heard from you I appointed a commission to investigate and report for action. A preliminary look at this does, however, make it seem that in law le Strange has a right to three or four manors round Ellesmere. They were held by Ebulo direct."

Edward turned to the clerk, and after whispers from him, continued:

"Yes. Nothing worse than that for you. For him that is the finish. By this he has incurred my displeasure. I gather the commission met the first week in May. le Strange should have claimed them in the proper way. Now he can never have any more, but that aspect of law has to be fulfilled. I started by hoping it would be the other way round."

Alesia nodded agreement to the last sentence, indeed to all, at having this attention as much as anything. It did not seem to have solved much. The King continued:

"The Bishop of Lincoln is now going to crenellate his palace at Nettleham, and Stow Park, - but it seems to me that after your experience it is not going to stop anybody."

A pause allowed Alesia to smile, as seemed to be required.

"Yes, I have wanted to meet you again. It has been a long time, but before more personal matters I have to talk about your position as Countess of Salisbury. I say at once that your revenues are secure, and as Countess of Lincoln and Lady de Clifford you will continue. You are doubtless aware, however, that the office of Salisbury is held by Service of Earldom. I notice, however, that you do not so describe yourself. Your heir in this is one of the Audleys. That's the ruling, going back to your great grandmother Ela, and forward again. Always just for when there is a person to perform the Service of the Earldom. What I am coming to, however, is my second creation of Earl of Salisbury. I thought it better to tell you personally when I could, that William de Montagu is to take up that service."

Alesia had to swallow this brief information without expression. It struck at her background, not her life.

"Thank you, Edward, for informing me. It is not an appellation the de Lacys have used much, if at all. The office must continue, of course."

"Ah! You show that the de Lacys have always been understanding."

Alesia smiled only. She felt that any remark might have upset the apparent genuineness of her reply, uttered blandly, but with difficulty.

"So, now," said the King, in a tone of gladness that that had all been concluded without fuss, "do join the ladies in the next chamber, and some social occasions will be arranged."

Later, to Frathesancia, Alesia's commentary included disappointment that le Strange had not been punished, except perhaps, and only perhaps, in the long term. More directly, about herself, she said:

"Edward wants an active Lord Salisbury, so he creates another. This is because he thinks I am unmarriageable, and certainly unabductable."

She noticed Frathesancia's quizzical look, so: "You, Frathesancia, would say: Peace be with you."

Next morning Alesia sent for Henry de Halton.

"It seems that meeting people in London here has opened my eyes to certain matters, Henry, and let us see what can be done to clear them up. First, I have heard things about Gilbert de Leddred, and his brother. Did we not have dealings with them a year or two ago?"

"Yes, lady Alesia, you obtained a royal writ delivered to Gilbert de Leddred at Boston. Yes, it was nearly two years ago. As escheator in Lincolnshire he was to certify lands of the late lord Ebulo le Strange, ma'am. Your attorney at Lincoln, Richard de Bolyngbrok, paid out about one hundred and sixty shillings to him, his brother and, I think Robert de Berughdon. They all later asked for more, and received it. Then they refused to hold the inquest. Then they made similar demands of the Abbot of Barlings before they would hold the inquest. The Abbot paid. They held the inquest..."

"Ah, yes, now I remember - most of it. How does it stand now?"

"My lady, Gilbert would not seal the record, nor send it to the King's Court until he was paid more by you, and the other two. They also took some rents and tenants' payments from your manor of Sedgbrook."

"So both the King and I suffered damage. Then Gilbert's brother John gave us some trouble, didn't he?"

"Yes, ma'am, he extorted, as I guess now is the right word, money more or less on the same lines."

de Halton waited for the explanation of these questions.

"Henry, I hear that he has been doing this to several people, and there's talk of a case being brought."

"Well, ma'am, I can say by recollection that if this is now actionable, the damage to you must be at least sixty or seventy pounds, and additionally some twenty marks. This can be investigated when we get back to Bolingbroke. I am afraid, however, it will take a year or two to get it to court. That is usual, of course, but what is not so ordinary is that there is further corruption about among the justices, and it is growing."

"Yes, that is also said. de Leddred was the Lord Thomas's bailiff for a time, and I did not trust him then, but the lord Thomas could not find anything of any note. I suppose it was very carefully obscured. Since then there have been more stories."

"Yes, ma'am, of matters like extortion from folk in Lincolnshire villages. What would you wish me to do, my lady?"

"This, Henry. If I do not take the lead, nobody will do anything, but you and Richard have the ability, and now you have my authority to get this man to justice."

de Halton remained silent for some moments. Alesia knew him well, so she waited patiently. It was his way of assessing a response, a deep commitment of thinking to the end before he pronounced on the more complex matters. At last, in a pronouncement which came out as though it was a judgment:

"My lady, I am sure that Richard and I can investigate all these matters, including the consensus of other persons. It must be done as secretly as possible, but it is bound to be talked about when we visit a village and seek witnesses. It may reach de Leddred's ears. He is a man with widespread power. He is escheator, wool collector, receiver of the fifteenth in Lincolnshire. He has bailiffs, clerks and grooms; his brother is his deputy; also he has keepers of the customs houses, and subescheators. So not everyone will be a friend of this investigation."

"He must be stopped and arraigned, Sir Henry."

"Please do not mistake me, ma'am. I am coming to the point that the law has to be positive in court. Not chitter chatter in remote villages. There are two things I am going to suggest. The first is that, yes, we will proceed, of course. We will find out what we can, and we will record it for use. The second point is that we must be on the watch for any further action of his against you yourself ma'am, which we will record as it may happen. This would add strength to the case."

"We can only wait and see. I understand you. If, or rather, when de Leddred hears about all this, then of course he may do nothing against me. He may feel himself impregnable."

"Or he can't get out of the habit, nor his staff. It is said that nowadays only half the revenue reaches the King."

"As little as half?"

"Corruption grows because of the King's ever increasing demands; it oppresses the lowest, because the powerful maintain their wealth one way or another. We have a very big problem to solve, ma'am. Our aim must be to provide the King with enough material for him to call a court together. Could you perhaps urge it upon Sir Nicholas de Cantelupe, Roger Bakewell, or Lord Willoughby? They all have justice experience."

"There will be a moment, and I will so do, Henry. At the right time we can inform King Edward. At least we must be ready. Sooner or later Edward must mete out justice..." and in retrospective thought on her own experiences, she added: "...one would think."

The hope and prospect of the case, and retribution for de Leddred, enlivened Alesia, though her mood would alternate between the effect of stimulus and despair. It was difficult to stay in either mood, for the one reacted upon the other. She was imbued with the various emotions and thoughts of whether there would be little more than an administrative check on the subject as in le Strange's case, or whether there would be proper action if it was judged as extortion as de Halton had suggested. With de Halton standing before her, awaiting a sign of dismissal, she waved him to the window seat. Once again memories were rising in her mind. Not those of her happier times; nor those of her hopeful times, but recollections of actions and utterances that with age were surfacing to trouble her conscience, to challenge her self esteem. She looked at Frathesancia, who alerted for any word. Alesia's thoughts were, however, that though her maid knew everything about her, at least of her latter years, the airing of her troubled thoughts to her would only bring them to stronger memory and leave no comfort. Perhaps this harking back to lapses of moral behaviour and to accidental hurts to others came to everyone with an ageing mind. Frathesancia admired too much, subordinated so much with loyalty, that she would probably not reply freely. Alesia smiled, which was cautiously returned by her maid, who did seem to sense that it was not a direct outgoing to her. Across Alesia's mind had passed the notion that it really was somewhat comic for her to compare Frathesancia's abilities with someone who should be in holy orders. That was it. Alesia must make every effort before she was called to account for her life that she was right for God. She was not even sure that she was right for this earth to which St. Michael had driven the devil from heaven. Others appeared to wish to do evil against her, and more than that, their own superiors seemed to condone them, and to enlarge their own power.

"Henry" - he stood and moved towards her, with an interested expression, intrigued as to the result of all this silent cogitation - "Two matters. Ask the Papal Legate for the Pope's permission to visit monasteries."

She ignored de Halton's total surprise. And: "How long do you think it would take to achieve the Pope's permission for a confessor?"

This caused de Halton to try to prevent himself revealing that he had no instant answer ready. He cursed inwardly for not having thought of this one before. He pondered that it was four weeks' ride to Rome. Then the weather at sea was a factor, unknown. The Holy Father may return a question, a negotiation, or have other business for some time.

"There are a few indeterminable factors, my lady, such as the weather. And the Papal organisation. So I would suggest perhaps a ..." he hesitated.

"A what?"

"I apologise my lady. I was going to utter 'a special dispensation from the Legate', but of course that is not the same thing."

He had changed his mind in mid-sentence when he realised that the confessor he had thought of had been that of King Edward the Second.

"You mean, Henry, that I don't look dead, yet. You feel that I can wait."

With de Halton feinting for an answer, he was not for reacting to this attempt at cheerfulness. He was in fact assembling a definitive reply:

"Ma'am, perhaps three or four days travel from London, again depending on the sea, to Boulogne; from there messengers and knights take about a month at best to six weeks to ride to Rome. For peace of mind, therefore, and after ordinary delay, one has to talk of about three months at least."

Then he added:

"I am sorry to speak of uncertainty, as in all travel, and waiting in Rome for the reply. Even so, if a clerical messenger is sent, it will be a couple of weeks longer."

"Why ever so?"

"It is a known circumstance, ma'am that they just do not rush."

"Perhaps they do not feel urgency in this world," rejoined Alesia, maintaining her respect for the atmosphere of heavenly forgiveness.

"Clerics also doubtless delay with friends on the way. It must also depend upon where the Pope may be found."

One God. A Pope away from the rock of St. Peter was not of the spiritual responsibility for which she felt. Perhaps that situation would clarify. She would rely on prayer.

"Just the monasteries, please, Henry."

There was no explanation. The only monastery that seemed applicable was Stixwould Priory, founded two hundred years ago, by Countess Lucy of Chester, her collateral, where Alesia had recently been; hardly for Kirkstead Abbey. Was it just to clear the Priory visit? Alesia thought that the permission would take as long to receive as that for a confessor. de Halton was now told to arrange their departure for Bolingbroke as soon as may be convenient. He found that they were to travel back to Lincolnshire via Oxford.

Alesia wished to call at Godstow nunnery. It was part of her task of clearing her past, to help her to complete her mind in this life. So, ultimately, the journey brought her party to Oxford. Interest was aroused, to seek to identify this lady, looking like a wealthy abbess. Surely nunneries had not got as rich as that? Why did everything to which her emotions led assail her conscience? She had taken the vow, but she had broken it; but now again in her habit for this part of the journey, did she need permission to readopt it? Chaplain Gregory thought not, and blessed her and the occasion, sending in the meantime, unbeknown to Alesia, to advise Godstow of her impending visit. So where could be her humility? Gregory only 'thought' a decision about her situation. Nothing firm. So perhaps a pilgrim's approach on foot, with physical discomfort. How much pain? Endurable? Unendurable?

Alesia was not inclined to try Gregory on this one. The only clarifications which shaped her mind were the impressions she received from prayer. She was to use her temporal power for entering Godstow nunnery, only half assuaging the Holy Church by asking for it, but knowing full well it could not arrive in time.

On arrival:

"...perhaps the Countess might have come for the next service. At

least for prayers with all of us?"
"Is the chapter house open?"
"Yes my lady. Can I..."
"Thank you. I wish to be alone there."

Whispers between Abbess Matilda de Beauchamp and the nuns about authority, and what the Bishop would say when he found out. The house had been in trouble enough in past years, with Bishop Hugh of Lincoln for their burying Fair Rosamund in front of the High Altar. Her body had to be removed to the Chapter House, even though King Henry the Second had given the order. They could no more in this generation challenge the Countess of Lincoln.

Alesia knew exactly where to go, having been here years before. This single minded determination caused Frathesancia to fall a little way behind, sensing that it was not her earthly companionship that was required. To maintain privacy, a sister tactfully stationed herself outside the chapter house entrance door. Alesia did not look round. She moved to a point which in the dim light seemed quite undefined. Nor was it more than shadows to Alesia in her unseeing eyes.

Frathesancia leapt to her side as she saw her sway, to move aside and sit faintly on the nearest form. Alesia was deep in the misery of tears quite uncontrolled. They hugged each other. To Frathesancia Alesia was her charge of years, her life, her anchor in the world, and now she herself was virtually the same to Alesia. Alesia wept freely. She had not yet explained any deep reason of conscience for their being there. Whatever it was, Alesia had too much emotion in her circumstances to hold under control. Her constant and long desire for emotional security had at every turn met, in a word, rules. They were either devised by men, or produced by men who said they were devised by God. She had maintained her inner self against her first husband she had wished to love; by her family record and her dissimulation, through the second Edward's reign; against the horror of the Queen scorned into vicious murder; found solace, and fulfilment, yes, with dear Ebulo, yet there had been years before their marriage of their behaviour contrary to the commandments of God, thereafter relapsed into sinfulness; overtaken by new enemies. The evils of the world never lost their power, but her resistance weakened with the years; now, opted out, shelved, to live as a shell, dead waiting for death, thinking of naught but preparation for the end.

"Do I really Believe?" Alesia broke her contemplation.
"Sweet ma'am, you live as though you do."
"I want your plain thought, Frathesancia."
"You have taken so much against you, my dear lady. These blows in life have come upon you. You are affected by communication with the Lord today, may I hope towards happiness."

Alesia looked up. "There is much in what you say," she told Frathesancia, "but more." She took several deep breaths. Trying to control herself, looking at the floor again, she managed to speak.

"I am alright. It takes a bit of getting used to. You know me well enough. I will pray. Aloud...if I can get through it."

"Ma'am, ma'am, please please tell, what's here? There is something here, more than your ancestor Rosamund de Clifford."

Alesia patted her on the arm.

"I will tell you" - she hesitated - "and God, in my prayers. Let me get through it, however I may. This day is the Feast of the Ascension."

Frathesancia settled her as well as could be done, upon the form, to sit near this mysterious place. It seemed to her for a moment that her mistress should sit upon the Abbess's chair, but she thought she would not say so. She moved away, but ever watchful.

Alesia spoke aloud. There were many hesitations for self control.

"God the Father, God the Son, and God the Holy Ghost."

She bowed her head, she moved so as to be upon her knees. She spoke the Creed of the Apostles. Then she spoke virtually another. Frathesancia then understood all. Alesia's living repentance was of a sudden clear.

"I pray for the soul of Rosamund de Clifford, cast into your care on the day of the feast of St. Margaret in the year of our Lord eleven hundred and ninety two. I pray for the redemption of her sins; used by the right and royal king Henry the second; thus I am of the fifth generation. I beg humbly upon my knees for the grant of thy peace to Rosamund. Her soul and my soul are met in feeling. Thus I pray for her soul and her redemption..." and before Alesia fell to the floor she managed to cry "and Lord, Lord, oh for mine."

Frathesancia's question was answered. In this place 'more than Rosamund' was Alesia. All that worldly power that had surrounded her status in life had scant influence on the welfare of her real being.

Alesia, since a year in line of inheritance, Countess of Lincoln, and Lady de Clifford. Perhaps the Salisbury title still there; but formerly also Countess of Lancaster, of Leicester, of Derby. Such an array of distinction and importance was now dispersed. To Alesia in her time it had produced activity, company, and an observation of people's pursuit of power through sycophancy and flattery. In all of it she had not had opportunity to reflect that she had been personally alone. She knew so now, alone, in life. Was the Fair Rosamund perhaps luckier to die with so many of her later years away from sin. Alesia was halted, placed aside. But blood still coursed and the mind still thought, and if her being could be stilled in this open coffin it would need more than time. Nothing she needed for calmness on this earth, alive, was there, and nothing and no-one was there to clear a new way. There were texts. That was all. And it was all that was immediate to lean on.

Alesia looked up at her maid.

"Sweet Sancy." she said.

In her disarray, they left the chapter house.

Some folk had gathered; they noticed her distress, and fell silent.

Alesia had not really thought about the possibility of being seen by the public. If she had, perhaps it would have made no difference. Some forty horses, and gentlemen, and attendants would always draw a minor gathering of children, idlers, beggars, and folk from any locality. The atmosphere pulled her round a little. Some of the player surfaced in her, enough to help her to walk past the silent groups. Strangely, to many of them, association with her was closer because of her human distress.

After the silent contemplative journey to Bolingbroke the more material affairs of life had to impinge upon Alesia's days. Centre of her exchequer, receiving point of her revenues, the continual need for her approval of the unfolding financial and estate reports occupied much of her time. It helped to take her mind away from herself. Then she took more note of the women and families left behind by King Edward's mustering of more and more men for overseas. Perhaps the parson at Denbigh had been right, after her brother Edmund's drowning in that well, to urge that mourners should share themselves with others to mitigate their grief.

Ruins of Audience Chamber, in the Old Bishop's Palace, Lincoln.

## CHAPTER 31

At every morning light a couple of pairs of her clerks rode from the castle on their exploratory missions to ride as far as they could in the length of the day to return that night. In contrived innocent moods their purpose was local gossip about de Leddred. Much had already gone the rounds, but it certainly appeared that more had not. At least the truth was beginning to be established. After some weeks of this Alesia sent for de Halton, and her attorney de Bolyngbroke.

"Gentlemen, if these stories are true, then surely there must be a time of de Leddred being brought to justice. We must continue with what we can, and prepare for a sheriff's investigation. Then the King can be informed when he returns to England."

"Countess," rejoined de Bolyngbroke, with his air of secret background thinking in the villages still influencing him, "the starting point should be with the sheriff, certainly. It may well be that the present one, Gilbert de Beaved is upright and honest. Yet I do have to say here that the last two would not carry out the King's orders. Except, that is, until they were specially paid for each one. Also, Trehampton has refused to pay tax, and has himself done some extortion from villages. Some of it in co-operation with the Abbot of Bardney. Then my namesake, John de Bolyngbrok, second sheriff with Trehampton, is thought to be worse. Even sheriffs can not be trusted just because of their office."

"I am absolutely astounded. Do they think they will never be apprehended?"

"Ma'am we are in essence preparing the way for a royal commission or court. That would be for Sir Nicholas de Cantelupe, but after the King himself has appointed him. I fully understand your grievances, and I am keen to continue to assemble cases. More particularly on your own behalf, of course, my lady. But where is the King? When will he be back in England? Can he not see that it is a countrywide habit to use every ounce of petty power for extortion from the weaker? It is indeed all in the feeling, if not conscious belief that they will never be caught. The King says he is King of France. So every official feels he has little interest left in England."

de Halton took the matter up:

"I do feel, lady Alesia, that Richard - perhaps we had better distinguish him thus from John de Bolyngbrok! - has a strong point here. We are on safe ground if we examine your affairs, but further than that may be dangerous."

"Dangerous. Are we to be afraid?"

"Ma'am. No doubt you would not be personally assaulted by a sheriff. Perhaps not us. But others, of course they could be. For us to go any further needs the King's authority."

"Maybe, gentlemen, but in the absence of the King Archbishop de Stratford has been given authority over the country. I suppose you are going to tell me that he is ineffective."

They both nodded in agreement.

It needed only a few weeks of suspended action before Alesia's resolve was forcefully reactivated.

"Your bailiff of Long Sutton, my lady, John de Shenfield. With your permission, he is here to speak to you. He arrived at the castle last night and stayed in the village. He has to report concerning an action of Gilbert de Leddred in your manor."

de Shenfield hardly looked as though he had recovered from his hasty ride of two days across the soggiest part of the fens of Lincolnshire, where a roadway was regarded as having a good bottom even if it was a couple of feet below the visible surface. He insisted that his news was more important than the trifle of his weary condition. His message was clear enough.

"My lady Lincoln, a few weeks ago there was a storm and on the shore next morning there was a stranded whale. It was not seen for some days, which is part of the delay in informing your clerks. We know that you and your ancestors have always had the right to wrecks at sea, and that a whale is no different. But the customs officer is a man of Gilbert de Leddred, and soon to his order action was taken. Ordered by John de Potanhale, the whale was removed by dragging it out of your domain, a few miles, to Fleet. That place is in the domain of the Earl of Lancaster..." he hesitated on the significance to Alesia of the last title, now held by the late Thomas's brother.

"Please continue."

"...thank you, my lady, yes, the whole was taken by mariners from Holbeach Hurn. It was cut in pieces, of course. It was in the charge of Peter Robbeson. He was paid by Gilbert de Leddred. We can thus find no profit for you from this whale."

Because Alesia was quiet and interested de Shenfield was uncertain of her reactions and the next point was difficult to express at this moment, his first ever audience with her.

So. Alesia smiled lightly in encouragement.

"Yes, my lady, the longer delay after that has been that the man of Gilbert de Leddred then took me, tenants, and servants for a whole month and held us all in custody. Our release was effected only after we had throughout the manor found twenty pounds to pay to Gilbert de Leddred. Ma'am."

Passing through the emotions of fury and self-control, of helplessness in the state of present law enforcement, of the desire to comfort this man in his oppressed situation, Alesia did feel reassured by the respect of her bailiff. He had even referred to Gilbert de Leddred by giving him his full name as a superior.

"I have men with me who will vouch for all of this, my lady."

"Yes, de Shenfield. Please refresh yourselves as you may wish. de Halton, the twenty pounds is to be reimbursed. This must be put right in time. We will meet with my attorney. There are, de Shenfield, other cases to make as well."

It was as much as could be said for his encouragement.

Shortly after, on the 12th April, 1338, Gilbert de Leddred was appointed as a Sheriff of Lincolnshire. He was to make use of the office for further thefts and extortions.

To Richard de Bolyngbroke Alesia was by no means calm.

"Richard," in wonder she spoke, "I have never much understood the purpose of blasphemism in speech, but by God, one can only demand, 'what in the devil's name next?' That man as Sheriff? It gets worse. There will now be no law case worth bringing. In fact, the cases that should be judged will be increased by the Sheriff himself and his gang of aides. So what now? How do we defend ourselves?"

After a pause, and before de Bolyngbroke had framed his reply she continued:

"In London Marie de Valence told me that this Gilbert had extorted money from four of her vills in this county. And something from her bailiff. That is what made me take the matter more seriously. de Leddred! Holding all those offices of responsibility! - God save us, how much more does he want?"

"Those vills of the Countess of Pembroke, ma'am, are a fair way from here. I had not heard of such incidents. We can of course help if you wish, by spending two or three days clarifying matters for her. It is all, however, getting to be a larger task."

"Does de Leddred know anything about us, do you think, Richard?"

"I can say only that we have received no sign of it, but I feel that he must have heard something, and is totally ignoring the matter. It is all so widespread, and some of his men must have been to the villages where we have asked questions. As we all know, he is increasing his oppression."

"But Bolyngbroke, what of the squires and villagers also, who have been robbed? What do they think, and what do they do?"

"My lady, there are several answers to your question. One is a further one - let us ask - 'what can they do?'. Through you, in your name, de Halton and I have some power. What do we do? We find out, but then where can we act to be effective?"

Alesia interrupted him:

"Of course, of course. There is nothing that can be done, even in my name, so they have no chance whatsoever. Until when? How long can this go on - until there is chaos?"

"My lady, you were right, and are right still to get us to gather cases. Kings do things, perhaps they have to, in great sweeps of clearing up what comes to their notice. They do it when they are able, and when they themselves feel affected."

"What a thought. So you think it must happen? I hope you are right. And in the meantime? Proceed? And the people? What is their attitude to these extortions?"

"Yes, ma'am. Proceed, with your permission. As for the people, well. Observe that in the hunt a deer is shot with the arrow. It has been attacked though it has done no more nor less than the others. It is culled. In seconds the herd is grazing at peace again. Doubtless each feels relief that it escaped the shot."

"No more?" asked Alesia, sadly.

"No more." returned de Bolyngbroke.

They both forbore to shrug their shoulders.

"What then, of the other sheriff, William Disney?" asked Alesia, all in an even tone, certainly not expecting any hope of forcible rectitude from him.

"Ma'am, whatever his attitude, he is a man of much fewer resources than de Leddred. Thus he can not be a restraint upon him. It is an office of trust, of course, in the authority it holds, and so often they treat it as a private affair..."

"A thought has just occurred to me," Bolyngbroke continued, "we never hear of these abuses in your manors elsewhere. Perhaps no-one feels like passing such information to us. All the same, we can start asking those who report here bringing your revenues from your sokes and boroughs and manors, ma'am."

"Well," returned Alesia, "if we have patience and endurance, then in a long time we may get some justice. At present, use the idea as a means of more detailed check on my revenues. Exclude of course those five which for no reason I know of I have had to give to Roger le Strange."

"The King's order which was sealed at Stamford, yes, ma'am."

From her further feeling of forever being of an insecure and weakening status Alesia brightened suddenly.

"Always when I am here in Bolingbroke," she pronounced with enthusiasm, "I seek an occupation of interest, instead of waiting through the days, restless to no purpose. So, in addition to all this background trouble I will consider a journey round all my old familiar possessions. I do not see why I should not inspect again my castle at Builth, and my borough of Blandford. There are my manors scattered on the routes. Let us work to that, for next summer. Travel has always been - oh, well, except for two or three journeys - enjoyable."

It seemed that her officials shared her pleasurable thought at the prospect of new scenes and different places. It was only the intercommunication of minds that provided stimulus, and Lincolnshire provided little. Next summer was worth looking forward to. In these present years they would only be on the receiving end of national news. From visits to Lincoln and Boston, it came for certain that Edward the third was virtually bankrupt. Gascony, last remaining English province in France, had been confiscated. So how could Edward in common sense start rebuilding Windsor Castle, and hold a re-enactment of King Arthur's Round Table? His revived claim to the throne of France boded no good, except that it gave a cause to his

Fleming and German allies. With drought in the country, and murrain in the cattle there was nowhere for more money to come from. It was quite a relief when the estates of the Lombards were seized; maybe they really were odious due to extortion, for no-one can pay forty-five per cent interest. Perhaps the new export tax on wool would help to develop home weaving, but Boston as a wool port and Lincolnshire as a producer would suffer.

Richard de Bolyngbroke arrived from Lincoln again, this time with a message from Master Ralph de Walgrave, sequestrator and commissary of the Bishop of Lincoln.

"Oh, him," responded de Halton.

"Yes. I have not mentioned our suspicions about his own behaviour."

"Same story everywhere. Nothing to do with the Countess, so far anyway. Right? So what is the message, and do we treat that with caution?"

"Seems alright. Just that the Bishop wishes to see her when she is next in Lincoln. Soon, as he is off somewhere, as usual. The request is written, but that's all, apart from the flowery beginning and ending."

"Which latter we may discount" stated Alesia with firmness, when she was informed. "I usually lose with Bishops on business. Money? Did he mention the cathedral?"

"No, my lady," replied de Bolyngbroke, "I did not of course see the bishop himself. Just de Walgrave."

"Of whom you do not approve..."

"Ma'am!..."

"...from your tone of voice. So, what other? But let it brighten up the autumn. What can you tell me further, then? Has he heard of our investigations?"

"If he has, my lady, I can only say that he would join with you in trying to pursue justice. He has had plenty of parsons robbed, and one or two unjustly imprisoned, as in Sleaford."

"Heavens, what for? No, of course I can guess. But by whom?"

"A couple were held by deputies of Thomas Dunstable, the victualler who collects food supplies for the army. His writ spreads through more than a dozen counties. Yes, they had to pay for their freedom."

de Bolyngbroke's brief explanation had left Alesia without reply, so he more lightheartedly told her of another occasion:

"There was a rather more amusing way of raising money tried on by John de Cotesmor, the bishop of Lincoln's bailiff in Sleaford. He revived the thurftoll for a week, for his own benefit. He levied it on all traffic; though it lapsed two years ago."

"Oh, well, to Lincoln then. On the way you can tell me of Bishop Henry's problems, in case he starts blaming me for something."

In fact, at their meeting in the Palace on the south side of the

Cathedral, Alesia began to think that Henry Burghersh was building up to something like that. He was distinctly respectful, he considered their meeting as persons to be a pleasant and important occasion. He thanked her for her contributions to Barlings Abbey tower, and for her other such help towards the groping for knowledge through the church.

At last, thought Alesia, someone has said this without mentioning previous generations of her family.

After these preliminaries the Bishop's tone changed. A strange re-modulation of voice made it recognisable as authority from above or afar, with an air of impersonal detachment. Alesia looked at his face more closely by re-focussing with intent. As much in surprise as with curiosity.

The Bishop was saying:

"...and I have this mandate sent to me by the Pope Benedict the twelfth on the Ides of July."

Mandate? Order to whom? Alesia tingled with worried alarm. The holy church? Herself?

The Bishop was wondering if he should soften his attitude and words. Right or wrong, he asked Alesia to kneel before him, and after a blessing upon her, he proceeded impersonally:

"You, Alesia de Lacy, are warned, and compelled by spiritual penalties, to observe your vow of chastity, which you made on your husband's death, and received in token thereof a habit and a ring. You having been ravished by the knight Hugh de Frene, and having consented to live with him in matrimony until his death..."

It had struck into Alesia's soul that she should be brought up to this rebuke. It destroyed any joy that there had been in the risk and the excitement. But the Bishop had not concluded:

"...Any who attempt to make you break your vow will be visited with ecclesiastical censure."

She was asked to sit.

"Alesia, while chastity is the brightest of female virtues, apart from the purity of the body, it refers also to the mind, and one's language, and the style of one's attitude to this life. Yet, through marriage unconsummated Etheldreda became a saint and founded Ely Cathedral; the Empress Pulcherea kept her vows through marriage; Lucy when betrothed made her vows, was denounced and could not get absolution from her betrothal, and was sentenced to live in a brothel, then died in prison. Celibacy and chastity are peculiarly acceptable to the Deity. For you, Alesia, there is dedication to devotion."

It seemed that no reply was called for; for whatever her thought, even her acceptance need not be uttered. Alesia nearly spoke a sentence to state that she agreed that she was still, or again, a bride of Christ. Before she was able to decide to speak or not, the bishop admonished her to Go in Peace. With a world like this, she thought that she would perish and die as though she had never been.

The bishop walked with her from his chapel to the main door of the palace. Some feeling prevented him from conversing even in light pleasantries. The occasion had affected Alesia, and with an air of remoteness in her bearing, turned in on her thoughts and contemplations, it was no occasion to mention any ordinary thing. Their footsteps echoed on the flagstones of the passages and corridors. They were the only disturbance in the air. The great door was opened, to reveal her escorts ready.

"Then farewell, my lord bishop" Alesia said, with a detached formality. The bishop gave his hand. She kissed it. Nothing else was spoken. Bishop Burghersh was more than satisfied that the ceremony had had effect. Alesia had arrived that morning to doubts in his mind that she could be genuinely brought to her vows, so mixed with rumour, and what was thought to be unpalatable fact, was her reputation. But by her reactions he thought that she was sensitive in grief for her late husband Ebulo, and fearful that her future could be unguided. He watched her depart; they acknowledged each other below anything personal in this encounter.

Never had her head been so light of earthly burden, but her body full of tensions, at once so encompassing her surroundings, yet disembodied with them.

She must return home tomorrow, to relate again to the comfort of familiar routine. Perhaps that included matters less than the ideal vision. At Baumber on the way she paused a few moments to contemplate her great aunt's grave in the church: Margaret de Lacy, wife of William de Mouste. The flat marble stone carried a straightforward statement in old fashioned characters: Ici gist Margareta de Laci: Qe fula feme Gwilleama de Mouste. There was nothing there to provide the atmosphere that she could have wished. Then four miles to Horncastle. Past the maypole, splashing across two small waterways, and in to the town from the north. A sudden inspiration, to lead her group past the market, down Church Lane, to south of the church. To the puzzlement of all the church was passed; Alesia led south again, across the river Waring and immediately west along its bank, to dismount on the Holmes where the rivers Bane and Waring joined. Alesia slid off her mount, to walk determinedly to the Julian Bower. To Frathesancia she whispered:

"I must concentrate on something; let's see if this maze repairs my will."

It helped. She set off walking along the rings of turf, often tripping along quicker to smother the temptation to give up, or to take short cuts to the centre of the circles. With her own people watching she could not possibly skip from one line to the next. She waved others in. Because of the maze, and them, or both, she smirked her way to Bolingbroke Castle.

"It has not been long, Sir Richard," Alesia complained lightly "before material affairs have overtaken my thoughts towards the next world. Here I am, overseen by Bishop Henry, charged with penance and inward thought, and you come along with a parchment from the King about the manor of Waddington. At least it's not another rumour of a French invasion. If there were, I would certainly close this castle against the enemy. Having lost three husbands in national causes I might just as well lose myself, and have the fears directly."

Sir Richard de Wllloughby had come over from the east of the county to clear a matter where a legal case had been started by Sir John, son of William de Ros of Hamelak, and Isabella, wife of William de Stopham.

"Please explain it to me again, Sir Richard, to see if I can understand the problem."

"Alesia, you and Ebulo were granted the manor of Waddington in Lincolnshire."

"Yes, Richard."

"You were also granted the right to compensation if it ever came out of your hands."

"Agreed. And is it now so coming out?"

"That is what the case is all about. John de Ros and Isabella de Stopham claim certain tenements, but the King is bound to make them over to you."

"Of pay me compensation."

"Exactly."

"Is this the de Ros who is taxer of the fifteenth?"

"It is, Alesia. Does that...?"

"No, it doesn't make any difference, except that he seems to be having trouble also with de Leddred, and the Abbot of Kirkstead. Possibly, however, as the innocent party."

"I do not know, Alesia, how you know that, but you are probably correct. His clerk, John de Colleby, however, is thought to use false measures in collecting tax by weight. As for de Leddred, I had better say nothing at this stage."

Alesia wondered if there really would be any other stage. de Halton, who was with them, was obviously relieved that she did not fall for the temptation of deepening that discussion. Instead she asked a question:

"Would I ever receive the compensation?"

de Wllloughby was one upon whom cynicism of the honour of rulers had not yet rested. His expression more or less controlled his astonishment, but not sufficiently to be able to compose a reply.

So Alesia relaxed by making a clear decision. With confident pleasure, and a feeling of command of her affairs, she uttered her verdict:

"Richard, would you please reply to this matter in these terms. With flowery sentences and loyal terms address me to King Edward. Inform him that he can forget the compensation."

"Alesia, he has requested in his order to be consulted of the outcome. So he will know of your generous answer, and will no doubt be grateful for your co-operation."

In her own mind Alesia considered that Edward would regard such action as no more than his due and would as promptly forget about it. At most she had saved the exchequer a minor embarrassment. Grateful? Gratitude? How is it shown? By reversing Thomas's attainder, by trying to cover him by urging his sanctification? Or by the Archbishop of Canterbury eulogising him to the Pope? As to that, Ebulo was more worthy. Not much concerning his sacrifice in the national cause. Hugh? Well. One husband taken away by man, and two taken away by God during man's works. Whom did she still love after their death, as she remembered the first Edward spoke of Eleanor? Was it Thomas? With him she soon had no meaning as a wife, not as a wife of his spirit. She had not been effective in shared companionship. She could not regret her parting, made fearful and full of self doubt. Yet, poor Thomas, thrust in the wrong walk of life. Oh, horror of his end. Cover the vision of that bloody failure with the love for Ebulo. Returned by him. Eleven happy years. But shortly afterwards she allowed Hugh to excite and invade her body. Maybe the Holy Church was right in its thinking; but of what are women composed that can practice obedience, when on earth ambition achieves pride and morale from bodily experience?

Alesia relaxed. Hugh had been necessary to her. She knew not why, but knew it was not love.

So, Ebulo. At once her mind eased, and as soon enlivened sadness over Thomas and Hugh. For they might meet in the hereafter. Her night was restless. The morning was decisive. Frathesancia was told to fetch her secretary.

de Halton was not averse to company lesser than himself. Such a situation relaxed him into a feeling of superiority, which he always, however, determined not to show. That would spoil the secondary reason for his apparent easy familiarity with all manner of persons. He had no desire for exchange of chatter with anyone at all, except that in any situation, monosyllables or a hubbub, he sought for information. He was just interested. Perhaps he was curious, but it was more for its background that he listened. This was for the advice, any advice, that he might have to give to his superiors. Yet he never appeared to be an intermediary. The people were simple, and association with the secretary seemed a satisfaction to most, so let suspicions be ignored. With the conglomerate way of living in hall, or in travel, and scant privacy ever, invisible barriers were crossed only by words, most of which were of trivia. Cooks spoke of cooking and the kitchen, a scullion of his scullery, a wheelwright of the strength of wheels, all of their own constricted field from where their impressions came. Secondarily they talked of their superiors, at once enjoying presumed knowledge of their association with matters greater than their own personal worth, safely imagining a life above their lot.

If most folk developed knowledge into gossip greater at each telling, there was one horseman, Jacques, promoted from boy in domestic livery, who adopted more the approach of a reporter. Cynical he may have become, but recounting he enjoyed, and accuracy too. By maintaining unaltered statements from one repetition to another, Jacques felt he achieved greater authority. This was indeed so, but on his part it was ingrained personality rather than conscious deliberation.

So what Jacques expressed, in whatever new company, gradually assumed a solid basis. Because he gave the impression also of reliability he was nearly always deputed on escort duty. Fair, tall, strong, quiet, he did not intrude in any measure on the affairs of his leaders, in effect just being around to do his job with a detached air. Jacques learnt much therefore, forgot a great deal, but would narrate when encouraged. So when Alesia sent a message by Frathesancia that the presence of de Halton was required, from the chat already spread from Jacques he had some idea of why.

The polite terms in which the message was given to her servant were not transmitted. de Halton was not one of Frathesancia's favourites, because she considered his eyes to be too far wandering in any company. He was but told with abruptness that he was wanted, and any guess as to the purpose Frathesancia kept to herself, as much out of not wishing to be a help as out of duty. Having achieved that reticence on the two counts, she maintained it in the face of a leading question by Hawisa de Curten, laundress, who desired gossip, and sometimes caused it. She then returned important in attitude to her mistress to say that her clerk would be on his way when he had gathered his materials. To her chagrin she was then dismissed so that she would not learn further details of the need for written work, and she had certainly not cultivated the only other source of learning it.

de Halton was ready enough to act for his Countess. Apart from generally checking or trying to check the tallies and accounts of others unwilling to reveal them, as he had not the direct authority for the purpose, he passed his time thinking over and over again what the next of his Countess's infrequent requirements might be. His mind was such that its clarification was best achieved by the need to write things down, and so often it did not come out as he had already mentally framed. Parchment had to be accounted for, and his written advice and composition sometimes had to be discussed and explained because it included so much further thought after a decision had been made.

It was time he ceased to take refuge in being called "young" Henry. It was because his father had been secretary before him, and such an appellation does not change. He welcomed the summons, in anticipation of the interesting task, and more especially that he would justify himself, improve his own morale, to feel secure and competent in his appointment. He gathered his clerk's effects and prepared himself for the interview with two thoughts in mind. He was to talk with the Lady

Alesia about a task which needed much thought, so he must avoid a nerve-ridden self-justifying immediate analysis but must make dispassionate notes for later consideration. He had but a few days previously returned to Bolingbroke from meeting and travelling from London northwards with fellow clerks and lawyers. It had given him knowledge of the more recent needs of the law. Also he had gained a deeper assessment of himself, which led to him returning in a profoundly depressed state of mind.

Never one to miss a general reconnaissance of the ladies, looking towards them in a mild imaginative way, just wondering, he had woven light and fanciful feelings around what he saw. He had travelled a fair way in his life, more than most in the nature of his job, and within his mind that was the way to lighten existence and brighten the scene beyond that evidenced in long sojourns in the home parish. There was always interest of people in each other, but looks toward those beyond his station had to be most brief and circumspect. His mistake had been in Stamford. A young lady of beauty and foreign extraction with her husband. The usual brief exchanges of the general company with each other, and his usual glances at her, who was worth looking at. But was it her husband or not? His last evening the man was not there. The lady had not been giving de Halton much response. The last evening she smiled broadly to him. Was it meant for him, or had she made a wrong identification in the dusk? He had frozen, sitting politely a little way away, and then gone to his chamber. She could not, surely, have meant that.

The next morning she was gone. The totality of her shape and dress and the pleasure there would have been in contact alone haunted him. What the devil was the use of his dreams if when they could come true he ran away? The abstract reward for moral behaviour was no compensation for the shattering of his image of what he thought he was. Given a week, yes, courage and acquaintance would develop, but he had not had a week. His mind inflexible, one which had to be prepared and ready, alert for preconceived opportunity. He was no good at steering in an unprepared situation. No use being ready for that young lady again. She had done what she could, but he could be on the alert for years and she or the like would never reappear.

Thus de Halton had learnt as much about himself as he had found out about new law. It was in this disappointed state that he entered the chamber of his Countess. He bowed, moved to the desk, smiled mechanically, and in case he was wrong, he waited for Alesia to denote the agenda.

"The matter we have to arrange will probably cause you considerable thought" was how Alesia opened their talk. de Halton jolted into alertness. Not only had she omitted the preliminaries about his wife and family, but had she seen through his personality and was humouring him along? In fact, while Alesia was fully aware of his hesitations at moments of decision, she took his reaction quite simply as interested special attention.

"You are fully aware of most if not all of my affairs" she continued, "I propose to make my will. I feel it is time. You no doubt have knowledge of the various formalities." He answered in the affirmative, relieved that here was the need for a document which would be drafted and revised and maybe revised again. While he awaited instruction, poised and ready, Alesia clearly wanted conversation to enlighten the occasion. There were few in these latter years with whom she could find tolerable communication. He opened up with pleasure and interest much tempered with wariness in his caution about giving away too much of himself. While unplanned, it may well have been on Alesia's part that the interchange was no more than the building of a relationship for the better consideration of her requirement.

"In thinking of my will then, Henry, what do you suggest I do? I wish to talk about it, to get it on the right lines. On the right lines for my circumstances, I mean."

He was constrained by this to get up from the desk and move to stand forward, in that he felt the authority and detachment it offered was now inappropriate. He gave a slight bow.

"Clearly on the spiritual side one commends one's soul to God as a commencement." He saw by the glance from his Countess that they had already gone beyond that stage, and that she really wanted equal interchange.

"Milady, of course I can say that this is a subject which in my duty I could expect to come forward. I am not unready with thoughts as to what your intentions may be. Again, I have reasonably full knowledge of your possessions."

He had indeed several times considered the possibilities. He had tried to think of his own wife as a widow with no family relations at all to try and achieve possible advice for his mistress. It was not quite the same thing, apart from the difference in wealth, because aristocrats had a further dimension. He had often realised the family background to be the obvious basis of wills, but for Alesia it was not there to work on.

Those items relating to the grants of castles, manors, and rights would be decided by the King, in the particular absence of a male heir. Alesia had no living husband, and no children. Ebulo's heirs should in affection come near to inheriting. de Frene had appeared, and he now dead had left in his brief embrace neither true love nor enduring deep memory. So it should thus be some le Strange who should inherit. Henry could guess that Alesia had hardened her heart against Roger le Strange getting anything - to be his just reward for his taunting derisive attack on Bolingbroke.

"You think much, Master Halton. I would hear you, even if you may be wrong."

It was just what always brought Henry forward - a quick question. He spoke what he had considered, and as he outlined this background, he divined the other dimension which might lead to the conclusion. Ordinarily it would be somewhere in the genealogy. Still with some caution he wondered how to put it. He posed it as a question.

"Does the answer lie, milady, with personal connections, or with the history of the lands? Not the lands themselves of course. Are we back to, and forward down a line again, to, say, the de Quincy's, or the de Clare's, ma'am? Perhaps not. Maybe to someone who has long connection with the land by duties?"

"You are getting there, Henry. In a sense you confirm my line of thought. Go a little further, though."

Henry knew that it would be so much in his favour and reputation if he could light upon her own tentative conclusion as to what she should do with her property. Apparently it was not to do with the church, because there was no direct personal connection. He began to realise how alone she was in the unfeeling world. He allowed a second's contemplation of the security he had for his own feelings in his own family. A person. One as near as she could get.

"There is a double connection," was Alesia's helpful remark. "Thin, but reasonable." She stood watching him. Henry's mind rapidly rescanned the de Lacy connections and their recent generations. He smiled at last. More relaxed, and almost with equality he asked:

"Are we, milady, talking about the connection with the le Strange Lady Tiphania?"

She was the only seemingly acceptable relative of the late Lord le Strange.

"We are. And then who?"

Caught in the spirit of clues and rejoinders, Henry spoke with some confidence:

"I understand, milady, why you smiled a moment ago."

"Well?"

A sudden response like this most often put him off from a reply. He struggled to utter his conclusion, his mind arrested at such moments. He was further encouraged.

"I think you must mean the double connection is the Lady Tiphania's grandson, ma'am, Sir Nicholas de Cantelupe."

He posed it as half in the manner of a question, for his own caution. Then he pursued this, because it had seemed to fall well, and added: "I know enough to frame the necessary paragraphs. Descended from the hereditary stewards of the Gaunt barony."

His last sentence was uttered with a tone of wondering whether it could be proper. The Gaunts had lost the Earldom of Lincoln by supporting Prince Louis of France at the Battle of Lincoln Fair after the death of King John. But it was four generations ago.

Alesia had to break into his contemplation.

"An appropriate and worthy conclusion. It includes stabilitry, tradition, and feeling."

With this settling the basic purpose of the will, Henry learnt that

Sir Nicholas knew nothing about it, nor did Roger le Strange. Alesia was assured that her clerk was of the appropriate mould, and thus requested a confidential draft.

"Yes, Lady Alesia, but may I put some questions, please? In essence, some matters often in wills, but which may or may not be appropriate. For example, upkeep of candles in the church, in perpetuity. Some small but enduring directions like that, or greater ones."

Alesia settled herself with interest, to listen.

"Pray proced, Master Halton. I will say 'yes' or 'no'. Firstly, not the candles."

"Milady; your Soul to God, the blessed Mary, and all Saints?"

Alesia nodded.

"I am sorry, but I mention candles agtain. Before the altar, or before the Cross?"

Alesia shook her head. Then she said:

"Let some of these items be for my executors, de Cantelupe, and de Bolyngbroke, and you."

"Priests to celebrate for your soul and the..." de Halton trailed into silence.

Alesia stood, reacting to move about the room in order to frame a calm expression.

"The usual phrase, de Halton, is, I presume, 'the soul of my late husband'. I will answer that shortly."

This would give her some moments to recover her poise. de Halton listed other possibilities with mechanical precision, a procedure which had to be effected: gifts to pious works, the Cathedral, Barlings Abbey, chaplains, friars, the poor, disposal of personal furniture and items. Alesia appeared to be taking no notice. At what seemed to be the end of the catalogue she turned to him:

"Thank you for your efforts. I picked out what I could of life; it has been a blank parchment like the one you have there, upon which my life has been written by others. The paragraph to complete it is all the remit left to me. So, Henry, I say this, and this alone:

"All to Sir Nicholas de Cantelupe. Everything. Secondly, I desire to be buried in Barlings Abbey next to the Lord Ebulo."

That cleared Alesia's mind; the finality relaxed her. She asked:

"Not many people discuss these things, so can you tell me what they do if they have sons and daughters, for example?"

"Family comes first, lady Alesia. There are not many variations in principle. The wills become public, of course..." he added so as to prove that he was not breaking any confidence; "...I can say for example that Adam de Welle included something to the boy's former nurse. This is, as you know, very recent."

*His daughters?"

"Lady Alesia, all three are to be nuns, at Bullington Priory. Their vestments to remain there after them."

Alesia looked contemplative.

"I think," she said, "I prefer the life that I have had."

To de Halton every question had now been answered. The executors would have to decide if wax should be burnt round her body on the day of burial. He would urge to them that she be clad in her best robe.

"No hurry, I feel quite well" added Alesia.

"Ma'am, a recent witness in a case was nearly ninety, and so let us not contemplate the final hour."

The desire for a confessor did not this time get mentioned.

He immediately and sincerely urged that in all life's uncertainty he hoped that she would have many years of life. He missed her quick glance by bowing again, and departing at once. He began to revise his knowledge and memory of her chattels; all those jewels, furniture, gold, silver, pictures, carpets, and money remaining from her several inheritances and their locations, all as amended by two Kings in the last twenty years.

The Countess Alesia then requested: "Arrange for tomorrow morning that I shall ride to Barlings, to return in the afternoon."

"Milady," de Halton replied, with the further intention of asking about smaller legacies, or something to the Abbey, or Bolingbroke church, or ... well, to those who had served her. Quickly enough, however, he noticed the tears forming in her eyes; perhaps for fear of death itself; maybe the realisation that with Cantelupe the only person to whom she could relate to follow with her possessions her aloneness had been emphasised. So de Halton concluded his response:

"Yes. I thank you. I will arrange your journey to Barlings."

It was to agree her place of burial.

In a few days the matter was ready to put before Alesia.

"So, Henry, my will is prepared and ready, from what I notice in your hands."

Alesia spoke to her secretary without expressing out loud her relief at this final clarification of her affairs. In the feelings of fear of death there was at this time not just her own health to consider. Subject to the unknown she felt so well. Recent years, however, had been of hard winters, incessant rains, unripened corn, and crops that could not be cut.

"I feel," she continued, "at last that the air I breathe is clear, and that I may relax. None of us know how long we may have in these awful years, nor whether the peace will be broken by the thuggery of roaming gangs..."

Alesia raised a hand in anticipation of de Halton's soothing talk, in order to prevent it.

"...I will read it now."

She mumbled through the words:

'Alesia de Lacy speaks health in God to all those who shall see and shall hear these writings... we have given and granted to our dear cousin the Lord Nicholas de Cantelupe all goods and chattels whatsoever in all our castles and manors throughout England and

Wales... neither we nor our executors nor any of our kindred shall have power to lay claim... excludes any goods and chattels of our very dear Lord Monsieur Ebulo le Strange whom God assoil.'

"Yes, ma'am."

There Alesia was silent. Straightforward it was. The situation was also clear, but in addition it was fearful. She would lie dead, buried, motionless, trapped from all impressions and feelings, for ever, in blackness.

"Witnesses, ma'am?" de Halton whispered softly.

"Witnesses, oh, oh yes. It would be easier if they were local, of those who can be gathered. It will shortly be better weather, one hopes. June? Send to ask who can come here to Bolingbroke. You will be included of course, also de Silkston, and de Falconbridge."

"I assume, lady Alesia, I should ask the lords Willoughby, Deyncourt, and ..."

de Halton hesitated, surprised then to find Alesia smiling broadly.

"Yes, him. Darcie" she responded. "He is not the same as his father. It would add a tang to the proceedings. What an excuse for a social gathering!"

Bolingbroke castle was alive on the morrow of the Nativity of St. John the Baptist, that June of the thirteenth year of King Edward the Third.

Two days later nearly two hundred hooves clattered outwards over the drawbridge, to let the castle be quiet again. All had left except the Willoughbys, Alesia's firmest local friends. Joan particularly felt that Alesia would prefer some company for a few days before the quietude of loneness in the castle descended.

"You can help me with this embroidery, Alesia. It's meant to be the latest thing of repeating panels with figures in them. There's too much detail to do it very fast, and I'm not good at split stitch."

"Joan, I date from Tree of Jesse patterns, and scrolling stems, but I will try."

It was but a start of conversation, update on life's news. Alesia had hoped again for a child when she married Ebulo, but then she was forty three years old. It had not of course happened before then, but one could not prevent hope again arising. Yet according to teaching it seemed that women were not meant to enjoy intercourse. How then could one exert one's feeling to one's purpose? Poor Thomas, Alesia grieved for him; his dying sadly; his living by the rigidity of honour, which brought him to the grave.

"But why should anyone want me now, a flower without a bloom."

"Oh, my dear Alesia, this air here is fresh and moist and keeps you looking young!"

"Well, maybe. Thanks, Joan. At least young girls don't - yet - protect themselves from me with holding up their crucifixes for fear of my being a witch. No, I am not sad, really. I must busy myself with something that endures. Somehow. I think my main disappointment is the lack of - well, I mean that if I had been able to support Thomas's cause I would have held a castle for him against all comers. I imagined myself as Jane de Montfort saving Rennes from Philip of France, by allying herself with England, assembling the people, and encouraging the whole of Brittany."

"I suppose the siege of Hennebont comes into this."

"Do I not wish I had been there!"

"Steady, Alesia, there may yet be such opportunity!"

"Why not? Like those ladies, I would shorten my skirts, and in armour gallop through the besiegers and burn the French camp."

Joan's mirth was loud.

"I am sure," she said, "that three hundred knights would follow you as they did that other lady warrior."

Lincoln Castle. *Left.* the Keep, *Right:* the Main Gate.

# CHAPTER 32

It was Joan de Willoughby who knew first that King Edward was to return to England from Gwent. From her husband who was with the King, and through Boston, the news reached East Lincolnshire. Edward's demands for supplies and money were not being fulfilled. Crimes variable in seriousness were usual, but now official misconduct had reached excessive depths. Edward had long been warned that his military adventures had stripped his domains, and that his officers were following his example in his absence. Local folk in their villages, farms, and Abbeys were not to know that the Collectors invented tax demands for their own profit. The King was blamed by the people. On 16th December, 1340, Justices were commissioned to hold inquests into oppressions, extortions and excesses of officials. Countrywide dissatisfaction, and his own policies and levies, were not included in the inquiry. Lincolnshire was to be in charge of Nicholas de Cantelupe; with Roger Bakewell; and John Wilughby, who took over the next October because de Cantelupe had four counties to oversee. Wilughby and his wife Joan stayed with Alesia. Commissioners were also Gilbert de Umfraville; Earl of Angus, being a prominent landholder in the county; John Kirkton of Tattershall; and Adam Welle. Two royal justices were also appointed, William Bassett and William Land.

"We will have to spend some weeks in Lincoln," stated Alesia, excited in the purpose now offered after several years of patience. "It is important to be there, I understand."

Richard de Bolyngbrok had been reviewing the evidence which they had collected against de Leddred. Now it had become a more serious matter because of its impending test in court. He replied to Alesia:

"Indeed so, ma'am. I am sure you refer to the law that if the appellant does not appear, then there is no case, but instead some trouble from the Court. I do not think that you need contemplate one of the sanctions available - namely, outlawry of the absent litigant." He paused, to a pleasant effect: "Incidentally, we will hand over all our notes of criminal actions to other attorneys."

"Good. Good. I take it that William de Hamsterleye has been told to have the castle ready for all of us, and as comfortable as possible."

"Yes, ma'am, even to the extent of camping perhaps for some of us. Dreadful affair about his clerk being murdered a couple of years ago. The man is caught. He will be one of the cases. Hugh de Loudham, a taverner, it was."

"He will be hung, perhaps. How foolish of him. But I have to say 'perhaps' in view of one of our cases about the sheriffs keeping prisoners to themselves."

Richard de Bolyngbrok, keyed up for this great occasion in his legal career, felt the whole challenge with keen confidence. It was to be quite soon, the tenth of January, 1341, when the pleas of the Countess of Lincoln were heard. After all that preliminary work he was confident. 'Of course the Countess of Lincoln will be heard first,' muttered the appellants who would not be called for anything up to the end of the year.

In the chapter house Alesia sat, watching with fascination as the story was unfolded of de Leddred's fraudulent demands it gradually influenced the tribunal. Firstly it was about proceedings after Ebulo died and obstruction of them, as reported:

Gilbert de Leddred, former escheator in Lincolnshire, was taken to respond, with John his brother and Robert de Berughton, his clerk, to the bill of Alesia de Lacy, Countess of Lincoln:

The Countess complained that she had obtained a royal writ, which was delivered to Gilbert on 2 Oct. 1336 at Boston and directed him to certify to the King's Court the lands in fee that had been held by the late Ebulo le Strange, Alesia's former husband, when he died. Henry de Halton, knight, John Bernard, knight, and Richard de Bolyngbrok (her attorney) made an agreement with Gilbert to expedite the proceedings and paid Gilbert 100s, John his brother 40s, and Robert de Berughdon 20s. Gilbert, John and Robert, however, on 5 Oct. 1336 came to Bolingbroke and told the Countess that they needed more money to proceed. She then paid Gilbert another 100s, John his brother 40s and Robert 20s, but later they left and refused to hold the inquest. The Countess on 24 Oct. 1336 at Stow St. Mary ordered Richard de Bolingbrok to complain and to ask that the inquest be held, but they refused. Gilbert then told the Abbot of Barlings that if he would make surety for the Countess to pay him 20 marks, John his brother 100s and Robert £4, they would hold the inquest. The Abbot did so and on 28 Oct. 1338 at Lincoln the inquest was held. But Gilbert would neither place his seal on the record of the inquest nor send it to the King's Court until he was paid the 20 marks, John his brother the 100s and Robert the £4. They ordered Robert de Hacthorn and Richard de Bolyngbrok to send the money to Lincoln by the Abbot of Barlings and Thomas Horne, the Abbot's servant. In addition, the same John took 16s from the Countess as a fee for his seal and Gilbert later took £4.8s.2d. in rents and tenants' payments for the following Michaelmas term from the Countess' manor of Sedgebrook. Gilbert also would give neither the King nor the Countess the profits of the manor in contempt of the King and to the Countess' damage of £50.

Gilbert appeared and did not deny the Countess' complaint. It was ordered that the Countess receive her damages and that Gilbert be imprisoned in the King's prison in the custody of the Constable of Lincoln Castle.

The Countess, through Richard de Bolyngbrok, her attorney, proceeded against John, Gilbert's brother, and Robert de

Berughdon, but the sheriff reported that they had died.

The Countess later asked that she receive all of Gilbert's goods and chattels, except oxen and plough animals, and that she hold half his lands according to the statute until the damages were paid.

They would hear the result in a few days.

"A good case," stated Alesia to Richard de Bolyngbrok. "A very good case."

That was spoken with feeling. Richard and she exchanged an understanding look; yes, a good case. It would have been especially interesting if a case were coming up against Roger le Strange. Perhaps Alesia had been too hasty in seeking justice against him that four years before - this time the King was in an aggressive mood.

Next case: Thomas Cok guilty of assaulting and stealing from Robert de Derlyngton, parson of Branston. 100s. damages; 1½ marks total fees for clerk and marshal.

The next one: William son of William Costard forced Joan, daughter of Robert de Kirketon the elder, to produce £40, whereupon he fraudulently freed Master John de Spauneby from a debt, against the peace. Damages £20; fee for clerk 20s; marshal 1 mark.

It was now obvious to the justices that Alesia and her staff were ready to proceed, and so her second case was called.

> Gilbert de Leddred, former escheator in Lincolnshire and bailiff of Henry, Earl of Lancaster, in the county, was taken to respond to the bill of Alesia de Lacy, Countess of Lincoln.
>
> The Countess complained that when a whale was beached at the Countess' manor of Long Sutton in Holland, where she and her ancestors had always had the right to wrecks of the sea, Gilbert during the night of 4 March 1338 paid Peter Robber son of Holbeach Hurn, mariner, and other unknown mariners to drag the whale out of the Countess' domain to Fleet Haven in the Earl of Lancaster's domain, so that the Countess lost the profit of the whale. In addition, Gilbert imprisoned John de Shenfeld, the Countess' bailiff of Long Sutton, and other servants and tenants of the Countess until £20 were paid, so that the Countess lost their services for the following month to the Countess' damage of £40.
>
> Gilbert appeared and did not deny the Countess' complaint. It was ordered that the Countess receive her damages and that Gilbert be imprisoned in the King's prison in the custody of the Constable of Lincoln Castle.
>
> The Countess, through Richard de Bolyngbrok, her attorney, later asked that she receive all of Gilbert's goods and chattels, except oxen and plough animals, and that she hold half his lands until the damages were paid.

"We appear, Richard, to have got him in custody in my castle. That is intriguing in view of our next plea. Very ingenious of you, asking for half his land on each case."

"It makes one much more cheerful my lady, when one wins. Again, we'll hear in due course about the damages. He will have to be released when he pays them, of course."

Any verbal reaction that Alesia might have wished to utter was prevented by them being called again immediately for her third case:

> The Countess, through Richard de Bolyngbrok, her attorney, complained that she had rights in fee to the constableship of Lincoln Castle, the King's gaol and prison in the castle and to all related profits, along with all profits related to prisoners arrested by the sheriff and his ministers, those sent to the castle in the custody of the constable and all those allowed bail. Gilbert, however, the entire time he was sheriff from 12 April 1338 until 25 December 1340, did not send any prisoners allowed bail to the castle, but always kept them in his house at Lincoln and other places in the county. He ordered his bailiffs to send all fines and redemptions to him and told the constable that he was not to take anything from mainpernered prisoners, so that the Countess lost most of the profits related to the constableship of the castle to her damage of £10.
> 
> Gilbert appeared and did not deny the Countess' complaint. It was ordered that the Countess receive her damages.

"Again, we wait, but a good day, Richard. Thank you a thousand times. That's all we decided to act upon, not so?"

"It is as far as we are concerned, my lady. Thank you for your remark. It is not de Leddred's day, however. He's got another five cases to come: thefts of horses, cows, oxen, and seizing wheat, barley, oats, beans, peas, linen, and woollen cloth, mostly by force of arms."

"My God, what a man! They really are so difficult to catch. Yet it does distress me to win like this to destroy a fellow human being. Oh, well, it's his fault... I think we should now leave."

On the walk back with her party through the Cathedral nave, through the market in the square, to the Castle, they all felt the people were much cheered and that they had achieved some popularity because of their actions.

Alesia relaxed, and turned to de Bolingbrok:

"Richard, I hope they don't start getting sympathetic with de Leddred by the end of the day."

"Not very likely. People have been wanting to curb him for years. He's been a wild predator without restraint, till now. Last December, when he was relieved of the sheriffdom I heard cheers in the streets."

"What else has the court for him?"

"His usual activities, in Gainsborough, Boston, and some other minor complaints I understand. Not the total, but enough to put him in your prison a couple of times more. The next sitting of the court is the middle of February, my lady, should you wish to see more."

"I don't know. What do you think, Joan? Since John has to be here, doubtless you want to see it through."

"A year? I don't know. I'll ask him," replied Joan, "I think my excitement's over. I just ought to see what happens to William, one of John's servants. He stupidly killed William Carleson at Somercotes last summer."

"May I suggest, ladies," de Bolyngbrok interpolated, "that we all should defer any move until it is seen what happens about the damages payable. They have to be personally acknowledged in court."

"A long stay here" returned Alesia, brightly.

A week later the justices confirmed Alesia's first case; two days after her second case. The third case having been decided at the hearing, she now awaited the money from de Leddred.

"I hope he doesn't pay" said Joan "then you keep all his lands, as in the two bites awarded to you. Anyway, do the damages cover all his winnings, and his previous seizures of land of yours for a time?"

"I don't think, dear Joan, that it quite works like that. Now I just feel that we must have some specially good meals to contrast with what he is now eating. I am feeling stronger against him."

"Let us hope de Hamsterleye doesn't let him escape. He's not many yards distant in his cell. I imagine he can afford the damages, though."

"Even when my life is nominally in my own charge" said Alesia to de Bolyngbrok, with a feeling more of wonder than of acrimony: "there still seem to be as many forces which need to be contended against. For myself, after all that success at last, I am informed that I have to give Sedgbrook back to Roger le Strange. It is an unreasonable form of organisation that hands revenue back to such a man."

"I am afraid ma'am that the estate itself counts for more than the man," de Bolyngbrok replied.

"Within limits, presumably" stated Alesia, thinking back to others who had fared worse, and to the de Lacy inheritances.

"Keeping to the rules in the wrong direction," she added.

"Whatever it was, my lady Lincoln, it has seen families through an astoundingly difficult and volatile century or two. I am sure that the King will always allow you enough revenues."

Alesia laughed.

"Richard, I suppose so. It is not that I need all this now. But they have been taken away and returned several times. In the end, whoever is the King is mostly forgiving as memories fade, or vassals change their minds. Although it's about time de Clifford was reinstated."

"There are whispers, my lady, that it is being reconsidered, for his son."

"I should think so too. It's been, what, twenty-five years or more."

"What we say, in administration and law, is that an estate is a parcel of revenue and duty looking for a figurehead, rather than a person seeking it. That is the royal point of view of course, not that of the dispossessed."

"I expect Edward needs all the money he can acquire. He spends it first and then - I was going to say collects it. But he doesn't now. Perhaps I had better say no more."

The gathering for the trials had served to exchange news, or hearsay, or hard facts, during all the periods of waiting around. Maybe Edward cannot repay the Florentine bankers. Maybe that had ricocheted into their being unable to finance the Pope sufficiently, but the English Court continued splendid, Windsor Castle was being rebuilt, campaigns against France went on when a professional army could be paid. Associated throughout her life with the visible insecurity of the realm the influence of the wife of a petty official brought Alesia sharply to realisation of her own state. The good woman clearly envied her, for her higher importance, her graces, her influence, and doubtless for her better clothes. The real position was, however, that it was her own security which was unassailable. Alesia had neither commented nor forwarded her own story as proof of disagreement.

She must not delay any longer dealing with the unknown time of being called to her Maker.

"I am now ready, de Halton, to request a Confessor. What next, in that circumstance?"

"My lady, it is convenient to start while we are in Lincoln, because under the present system there is a precise form of writing these requests, which will have to be done here. I will take your request now, and they will let me know what particular questions they would want to be answered."

"Do you yourself know these questions?"

"What I know may now be superceded, ma'am. I have studied them, but after the previous Pope, John the twenty-second, petitioning has become a skilled technique. For this sacrament, an important matter is whom you would choose, but that can be left open. The other questions refer to the attitude of the petitioner, if I may put that point to you..." He paused, but Alesia was not prepared to be brittle on the subject, though it trespassed on the personal. So he continued:

"...In fact, these can be taken care of by well known formal sentences. There are, of course, fees, but they too are now regularised, also by Pope John."

"I think, John, the Papal office needs the fees, with Pope Clement's problems over his crusade, and from what I hear of the state of the Italian possessions. Though as to that the lack of safety in Italy has always been given to me as a reason for my not travelling there. Yet he can lend money to the King of France, and send men to capture Smyrna."

"Indeed so, even if the locals did give it back to the Turks. Politics ma'am, changeable stuff."

"However, de Halton, this is not addressing the point. My attitude?

What else about that? Simple desire for absolution; surely it is straightforward, lots of people do it."

"Ah, but most locally, comparatively few through the Holy Father. Please forgive me for continuing. It is an emotional matter, and absolution should be sought from hope and not from fear. In general that is how I would put it. Again, for your consideration, my lady, may I put forward to you the point that it is unprotected from attention by the public, in theory at least, in whatever church or chapel it may be."

How glad Alesia was that de Halton had continued to speak by adding that last sentence. Perhaps he had noticed her tense momentarily and her expression become an unassessable mix. It was the possibility of fear being her motivation which had challenged her contentment in having decided at last to seek indulgence. Fear of forthcoming death, surely that is allowable? Her memories were growing upon her - of those happenings which she had infinitely regretted. Mistakes in personal relations, misunderstandings of which she had not recognised her perpetration of them until years later, these which crowded upon her. Surely it was conscience and not fear which necessitated for her the desire for mental comfort by their erasure?

So after reacting to the implication of what had been said, Alesia regained her composure. The image in her mind of her decision to proceed was strong. Confession in public may well attract many of the curious, but her reactions to such spectators and their opinions had become of no account. It carried the same depth and certainty of feeling that she experienced concerning marriage with dear Ebulo. Love, not fear. Fear was the experience when kidnapped by de St. Martin, to lead to desperate false admissions of revolting guilt; other incidents with her body seemed to emanate from a power outside herself. Every woman sought fulfilment, with love.

"Public, yes, as usual," Alesia replied, having taken a few moments to answer; not because she had not made up her mind, just for natural reticence. "I do know that point, even with a faculty from Rome, and it gives one to think. Strangely, however, I am composed. I am attuned to concentrate on my need. As to whom, or where, I will doubtless choose the bishop, or his appointee, and the place he may order. Also, I shall have to rehearse my memories," she added in a bantering tone.

At Bolingbroke Alesia waited for the Papal reply. She felt confirmed that she had requested a confessor none too soon, by the death of John the Huntsman. Older, sprightly, a short illness, and a sad farewell. News that Montagu had died, and that his Countess of Salisbury had taken a vow of chastity almost made Alesia relax with wry amusement. She would rather she herself had been the cause of the founding of the Order of the Garter. How brave that Countess had been to resist the King's advances with the strength of threats to kill herself.

"It is sad, John, to experience one's life unwinding, simplifying in anticipation of its close. Do you feel that too?"

"Ma'am, I expected little, I have no affairs to manage. I try and proceed straightway not thinking of the closure at the end of life. You, lady Alesia, have survived so well the difficulties placed before you."

"Well, thank you. Even so, I have just had another hint of my status, though. A few more manors removed from me. I can spare them, but it makes me think I am being watched."

"Oh, my lady, the King watches every one of his tenants-in-chief, throughout life."

"Ah. It is always so, but I spoke of how it now feels to me. However, all that aside, please write to the lady Joan de Willoughby to ask her to accompany me to my absolution."

"Indeed, ma'am" replied de Halton, quickly smothering his doubt of her immediate forgiveness by the bishop. Alesia's request had revealed a trace of her own anxiety and fear.

In Lincoln, awaiting the summons from Bishop Henry Burghersh, she had only one subject, however subtle the efforts of Joan to coax Alesia to some topic other than her forthcoming interview. Why was she so fearful? The forced jollity of Joan's last remark was not received in the spirit intended.

"My dear, Bishop Henry is not going to ex-communicate you."

This caused tears.

"Joan, I do thank you for coming with me. I am sorry to be so full of anticipation. But remember that the Holy Father reprimanded me only five years ago. I thought then that I might be ex-communicated, the way the bishop looked; not so much what he said. Perhaps I had better buy a corrody and have the right to live in a nunnery. If I am allowed, that is. Perhaps he would force me in at the twelve pence a week level. I want peace in my later days on earth. Where is it? Where is that peace?"

"Dear Alesia, these men do not comprehend the feelings, I mean the urges, forcing up from our composition. We are made like that. I think we have to be made like that. Where would Adam be without Eve? The serpent thing united them."

Alesia's lips marginally relaxed, and Joan carried on, from the basis of not having experienced her present situation:

"I am afraid I do not know all my sins. I cannot even remember them by the week. I suppose that's a sin by itself. But for you, Alesia dear, what else could you have done about any situation where you found yourself? Since we are pushed into marriage routine before we can assess ourselves we've got to try and find out later."

"When even Parliament voted for Thomas to be regarded as a saint, and these years after, what do I feel about my failure with him except despair? The King, the Church, the State, also the remarks and attitudes of some of the people - all contradict those twenty-eight years of my life. They do not ask me. I have never been approached upon it. Never, never. They demand glorification for him, but they don't seem to realise that the Pope so obviously cannot and will not agree until I am dead. My confession will be something, but not enough. What, therefore, of my own stature?"

"Thomas's reinstatement is more political than anything, isn't it?"

"It's probably the reply to the canonisation of Louis IX seventy years ago. I do not doubt the politics, but no such consideration enters every mind."

"Of course it doesn't, openly. My Uncle Antony had lots of private thoughts on such matters of state, which he sometimes spoke of."

"Yes, I met him several times, as you know, both as Archdeacon and as Durham Bishop, but of course in those years I knew at least as much politics as he did."

"Do you really mind about the situation about Thomas?"

"How do I know that, even? I found little in marriage to Thomas to make me feel wanted. I must have been wrong, but the second Edward would doubtless have died by now without being murdered, and we would have got the third Edward without all that bloodshed."

"Now here you are my dear, this must be the Bishop's Messenger who arrives."

"I will feel better if I walk to the Palace. I need some fresh air."

It was a relief that the bishop himself was in his chapel when Alesia was conducted into it, being in attitude of prayer by the altar. In a sense that alone relaxed her, whatever its purpose, for guidance, concentration or atmosphere. At least it showed that he was not going to breeze into her company for a secular and friendly talk. It was to be a serious and penetrating matter. Dressed appropriately in black, veiled in the older form of fashion, Alesia stood quiet, respectful. She hoped that she had eliminated any touch of femininity from her apparel. The bishop's own chaplain was the only other human being present. To make it public, Alesia assumed. He moved to the back of the chapel, so that the interchange need not take place in whispers.

The bishop rose and moved to his chair, and sat down. He beckoned Alesia to walk near to him but did not indicate that she should sit, nor was there any convenient stool. She stood directly in front of him. The bishop spoke:

"Alesia, we are met at your request and with the agreement of the Pope in Rome that with contrition through your repentance your confession can by satisfaction lead to absolution."

Alesia remained still and just waited for his total guidance. The bishop indicated a short prayer of blessing over the proceedings, particularly that he spoke not from himself but from God.

"Alesia. We will find whether some act of self-mortification or submission to some penalty is required as an expression of penitence.

In order to eradicate moral evil it is charged that we do all things unto the Lord, shortcomings being offensive and grieving to the Holy Spirit. As St. Paul said: 'a shortcoming must be perceived to be binding upon oneself.' Where the law is not known, sin cannot be imputed, though sinful conduct shaped from natural passions should be subject to the will. The will shapes, not the underlying tendency. Whatever the force of feeling, the will is responsible for actions, not temptation, not temptability, it is what one knows within oneself."

He paused. If Alesia began to feel a trace of self-confidence it was because he also hesitated. She had to assume that he was expecting her to speak without being questioned. Cautiously she looked at his eyes. To him through the veil she showed with mystery. From the movement of her shaded irises in their white surround he assumed a questioning gaze. He returned a slight nod.

Alesia stated that she acknowledged her sins, those of which she was apprised, and humbly by repentance sought absolution from the Holy Church for them and for those sins which she may have unwittingly committed. She narrated memories of incidents upon her conscience. She had disobeyed her parents and would not become a Bride of Christ; she had left her lawful husband Thomas of Lancaster of whom the Cardinal Archbishop of Canterbury had such a high moral opinion; she had submitted to a lover in her time of marriage to him; though she had later married him she did not feel that expunged the circumstance totally. She was open about her early and subsequent relations with Hugh; she should not have whipped Frathesancia at Kneesall. She could have done more in kindness, and had harmfully hurt others by her words.

It was the turn of the bishop to use his eyes in enquiry. Was it just to discover if she had completed her statement? There was apparently another matter of which he would hear, so she spoke again:

"No more do I know, though from time to time it comes before me that errors I have made and spoken have been reaction to some circumstance which later I should have corrected but did not have opportunity."

The bishop somehow did not look as if he thought all was complete. Alesia thus had to say:

"To you, lord Bishop, I say, and before God who knoweth it, that what has been uttered otherwise by ill-disposed people of my yielding to an enemy of my husband the Lord Thomas is without truth and has no foundation."

At once he requested her to kneel in front of him.

"Alesia, sacramental absolution can grant release from the guilt of sin to the sinner who is truly contrite and who confesses to a priest and who promises to perform satisfaction. Do you so promise?"

"I do."

"Alesia, I sentence you to Trentals, requiem masses for repose of the souls of the dead on all future days of Christmas and Easter until it shall have been said thirty times. Do you so accept this discipline and observance for your rest, repose, peace and quiet?"

"I do, with God's help."

The bishop placed his right hand upon her head.

"From divine judgment and divine forgiveness I absolve thee from thy sins in the name of the Father, and of the Son, and of the Holy Ghost."

"Amen."

Closed in upon herself as she had become, her mind filled with the mist of contemplation on the revived worth of her inner being, it was either fortunate or from understanding that the Bishop indicated that their meeting was concluded. Perhaps he too had passed beyond being objective and could not escape entirely from the spiritual atmosphere, based on Alesia's sensitive co-operation.

"So he thinks you're going to live for a good long time" said Joan on leaving the Palace.

It took a moment for Alesia to reply. The voice seemed to have emanated from a long way away. She heard the sound, but had to waken towards its reality.

"I could have added something if he had asked, but it was all to his bidding of course. I seem to have pleased well enough, but I would like to have explained that I myself cannot speak of or pray for Thomas's canonisation, that it is not a matter for me on this earth. It is a matter for the Church."

Joan let that pass. Clearly the mood was not yet appropriate. She then supposed that in due course she would have to consider the same situation herself:

"The Pope would not deign to consider my lowly soul, though. It would be a local...."

"Your uncle Bishop Bek - did he say that?" asked Alesia, at the same time wondering if lesser prelates produce lesser sentences.

"My husband John, thirty years ago a country squire."

Joan could not contain her curiosity, so Alesia had no opportunity to comment.

"Are you still considering the nunnery? Joan continued with her chatter. "Would it not be quiet, cossetted perhaps. I'm really wondering what I might do in such a situation. John often says I would have to, and if he dies first he would be more at peace if I did."

"But, Joan, I guess you won't," uttered Alesia with returning animation. "Do not follow me, necessarily. The answer in my case is 'no'. I couldn't stand the others, or some of them, looking at my behaviour and counting my masses. It is a thing one has to perform alone, or at least in the place of one's own choosing."

"It is all part of the church, though but don't let me try and persuade you. It is not my particular interest. I would rather rebel than conform; I've seen enough of that to last me several lifetimes."

"So what did your uncle Anthony think of that?"

"He was very fond of me. I think he was amused, and perhaps admiring. On the outward surface he was conventional without compromise. There were some questions he would never discuss. I am sorry he died so long ago. Well, over thirty years."

"What would you have asked him about?"

"Well, the official attitude to women. Or even to men sometimes. Once I was being a bit difficult about it. Your Ebulo thought it was more based on the Old Testament than the New. Also, no-one but monks and nuns, and lifelong ones at that, had much chance of salvation.

"Sounds like Ebulo, yet he kept to the rules, nonetheless."

Suddenly Alesia began to wonder in what mood and with what inner thoughts her mother Margaret lived her latter years. They did not meet so often then, never in fact did Alesia remember much except a confident, quiet, and unquestioning living in accord with what life provided. It must have been a less turbulent age, considering what events had since foisted themselves on Alesia herself.

"I shall say my masses; perhaps at last I can have some calm years. I mean, after those with Ebulo. On our way back I will say an extra one at Barlings by his grave. I'll rest, and do let us meet again before long..."

Alesia recalled that looking after others was a palliative for deep introspection. In these years of poor crops, disease, and deprivations association with the people of the locality itself alone reduced the tensions that arose.

"If you say so, Henry," she said to her secretary, on his talking of the benefits of her presence. "I am delighted to hear it. Sometimes I notice it to be so. I enjoy my tours around, and would so like to visit all my scattered manors. However, not now, most likely never. Please come with me for a moment."

de Halton felt some surprise at the unusual peremptory note which sounded the background of that request. Shortly, away from the others, forcing a strength in her voice to try and show a normality, Alesia stated:

"It is time for another petition, Sir Henry. I don't like going on like this and not being certain that I can complete these thirty masses..."

"My lady?"

"I do not expect to have the fifteen years needed, I do not always feel well; I do not feel confident of as many years as I require. For the security of my soul I want you to petition the Pope again..."

"Yes, my lady. For plenary indulgence... Well, ma'am, let us not go through the whole wording now. I can find it, and it will be done."

So de Halton began at once to organise a petition for remission of her sins at the hour of her death, to include forgiveness from any requiem masses which she had by then been unable to perform. It would be through her chaplain, or the parish priest.

Why had this petition been requested now? Henry pondered, and was not long in tying matters up so as to make a guess: The news had recently come through of the death of Henry, Earl of Lancaster, Thomas's brother. Alesia had been disturbed, and now she had shown that she needed the peace of mind by remission of the punishment that might be still due, for her peace in the Court of Conscience and before God.

It had to be, and it would be.

Alesia found that being in a state of obedience clarified so much in her mind. It cleared away the dross, to leave it pervaded with a calm sense of security. Into this aura, however, broke more worldly matters. It was certainly no continuance of the atmosphere of divine forgiveness when de Bolyngbrok arrived, rather abruptly in his audience putting a couple of questions:

"My lady, there are one or two further legal matters which I have to put before you...."

Because Alesia did at least look towards him he proceeded:

"...the first, and the most important, I think you will agree, is that de Leddred has paid the awarded damages to you. Against that is the order of the Court that acknowledgment is required. That means personally, in court; I am sorry ma'am."

Alesia just nodded.

"If I may mention another item, ma'am" de Bolyngbrok continued diffidently...and without receiving audible response he went on: "The opportunity could be taken to sue for some messuages which are being occupied by persons with no right to them. I believe there are three discovered so far, in the bailey of Lincoln Castle. It is not a difficult matter to sort out. Of itself it does not need your presence, just your permission to proceed."

It all seemed to stimulate Alesia. Perhaps after all it was life's variety which held its charm, though it all produced its fears and horrors. So now she began to consider what further she needed to tidy her last years, ranging through those memories which had kept pushing forward. de Bolyngbrok told her of some cases which would amuse her, he thought. In fact he expected that it would appeal to lesser emotions. The news of d'Arcies and some of their servants at last being charged with threatening travellers, assaults, and extorting large sums was only right, but the more recent assaults with force and arms by Sir John Darcie du Park's chaplain William occasioned Alesia shock.

"My next step will be to call again at Barlings Abbey on my return from Lincoln."

To Alesia it was better to perform her task there on the way back, leaving behind the foray into secular activities. It was another journey for Frathesancia, to whom the reason appeared clear, but viewed only from the facts of the court cases, and the location of Ebulo's grave. Alesia had, however, an inner motivation.

Frathesancia had rarely tried to advise her mistress on her affairs.

The social niceties for her Countess were routine, the aristocratic need to receive fortunes, and the greater difficulty of maintaining goodwill with changing paramount powers were beyond her; indeed beyond many who suffered rightly and some who suffered wrongly. It was not for her to trouble whether enormous sums were spent on abbeys and cathedrals and nunneries, castles and fleets and armies. When she heard that rents were proving difficult to collect and that there were disputes over land, it did not touch her. Certainly Alesia never seemed to have much money as such, but every door was open to her, and nearly always every courtesy. Frathesancia, of distant Italian relationships like her mistress, observed life as a show she was privileged to attend. Those, and there were a fair number, who thought that chat to her and a show of amiability would help a cause were disappointed. She reported nothing. If there had been any information of vital value she would have done, but it was the other way round; everyone always wanted something.

Calling at Barlings was not out of the way of things, but Alesia had sounded an extra insistence in her voice this time. By hearing conversation between Alesia and her present chaplain Hugh Frathesancia learnt little, just a review of the regret that the family was so dispersed in burials. Father in London, mother in Wiltshire, Thomas in Yorkshire, and Hugh in Herefordshire. Ebulo being and Alesia to be in Lincolnshire.

It was only in the Abbey that Alesia expressed her particular reason for rendering this visit special. It was for the final clearing of her mind from all but dear Ebulo. She uttered a mass for all those deceased. The rest was silent, only in her mind, yet fully impressed as if it had been shouted. She felt that Ebulo could rest at last. The sheer ecstasy of animal feeling with Hugh had led to her being envious of no-one. It had been wonderful; and temporary; and it had not been love.

"I will say, Frathesancia, that there is as much to observe in life as there ever has been. It seems never to slow down. The lord Nicholas de Cantelupe has been telling me of events this last year. They tally closely with what you relay from what is spread at the market cross. You had even told me that he and the lady Joan de Kyme had been allowed by the Pope to remain married, though distantly related, legitimising their children. The report of the cost of the two chaplaincies which they had to found was, however, somewhat exaggerated."

If Frathesancia wished to hear more she was disappointed, for Alexander de Ramsay, Abbot of Barlings was shortly due. He had to be prepared for.

"These days, guests do not follow each other so immediately," said Alesia. Her expectation from the Abbot was a letter from the Holy Father.

"My lady Alesia," the Abbot began, with such a tone of pleasure and importance that clearly he did have that letter, and its purport was good.

"I will say at once that I wish for and pray for your good health and wellbeing. As you are no doubt aware, the words I bring are unfortunately not to do with such a joyful circumstance..."

Alesia interrupted, to help a little:

"I know, Alexander, that my death must be, and that such is the occasion of a religious ceremony."

"My lady, I thank you for such a ... ah ... an understanding attitude. Yes, I have here the letter of acknowledgment of your confession, and the Holy Father's grant to you of absolution."

From that positive and clear statement Alesia felt exhilarated that her conscience need no longer nag at her, nor draw her further into misery and doubt. She had no words to frame. A chuckle escaped, just by smothering recollection of some of her former childish expressions of joy.

Abbot Alexander saw fit to continue.

"It is I who am enabled to give to you, my lady, plenary remission at the hour of death. I am confident, of course, that for many years I shall visit you annually to review your sentence. Let us expect that you will live well beyond the necessary years for completion."

Whatever ... Alesia ranged round in her mind for the appropriate question, just to ask herself, whatever else sinful was it feared that she might do? Could she not be trusted without being overseen to this degree? Why this strong invisible ecclesiastical cage?

She could not ask. The Abbot had not said; his air was that of carrying out straightforward administration, perhaps so as not to produce a reaction from her. Then suddenly the factors fell in place. The new Bishop of Lincoln of two years was a Doctor of Canon Law, from whom must emanate the exactitude of his training. There was pressure from King Edward about Thomas's canonisation, growing stronger if not impatient. The Pope must be willing, but he and they were frightened of her, naughty Alesia, starting another scandal. From the sweetness of secret personal amusement she smiled upon the Abbot, who, relaxing, responded:

"May I say again my daughter, that when that long delayed day may arrive, your resting place in our abbey will be dedicated with our sincerity in your memory."

"Thank you, Alexander. We are much amongst death of the body. Even before me, for example, has been Montagu, the first Earl of the second Salisbury creation. Let us believe, if the horrors of the plague reach here then by all that is heard one is but a frail being upon this earth. There are those who do not believe that we shall be visited by this scourge."

"It has been in France for some years, ma'am, though at present we are safe from it here. For our safety we need a pound of hard penance washed with tears of repentance. The danger can come from social intercourse, particularly from crowded, low society. Again, let us think pleasing thoughts."

He made a move for his departure, as he noticed the sun had about a couple of hours until dark.

Calling for Frathesancia, Alesia requested her to fetch the Steward of the Castle, Roger Cobeldick, to escort the Abbot to the bailey where his men and horses were in attendance.

"Dreadful about King Edward, isn't it?" was his parting chatter.

"Is it really true, then? Bankrupt?"

"Indeed so. The Bardi and the Peruzzi of Florence are toppled. This whole country does not possess the wealth to pay back what is more than a million gold florins."

It was not only she, was Alesia's immediate thought, who was preventing the canonisation of Thomas. Thereafter life's routine and patience for her end of life were all that occurred to her at Bolingbroke.

The morning of the twenty-first of September, 1348, dawned with the clear illumination of sunshine horizontally touching the fen to warm the day. As the shadow of the low eastern hill passed from the castle walls Frathesancia woke, to find her mistress no longer in this life.

Those who mourned personally included folk of all stations, but so many of them who had known her childhood and youth were already themselves deceased. Her body was made ready and laid in reverence in state in the castle chapel, for respects to be paid. Eleven days later, on the Feast of Saint Matthew the Apostle and Evangelist, Alesia's earthly remains were laid to rest in Barling's Abbey, next to those of Ebulo. Abbott, monks, nuns in attendance, archdeacon representing the bishop. Not the sheriff de Trehampton, previously caught in misdemeanours but the sheriff-elect Saierus de Rochford. Sir Nicholas de Cantelupe and Lady Tiphania, Willughbys, Dymokes, de Welles; respects and sadness were present in full. de Bolyngbrok, de Halton, bailiffs, staff, none more shattered than Frathesancia; strange how she had thought that she of lesser clay would die first.

The last amen was quietly said, and scarcely filled the abbey church. By then the interment was done, and the bearers had moved aside. By common consent the chief mourner was Nicholas de Cantelupe, and he passed forward to the grave. He reflected on the transience of the great de Lacy family, prominent for two centuries, to whom had passed by relationships not only their lands, and their titles, but also their very surname.

Most of the manors and liberties and markets and courts and mills and fairs and revenues which had supported Alesia were to go at once to the young Henry of Lancaster, the transfers already incorporated in the grants to her; he was a nephew of her first husband, Thomas. Just two manors were for Roger le Strange. Nothing passed to the possible Salisbury inheritor, Lord Audley, far away in connection through

Alesia's great grandmother, already with widespread possessions, but not "serving that Earldom", so achieving that title.

As the archdeacon passed by the open grave he gave a respectful nod, the while he made a mental note that he could report that Alesia had been returned to righteousness and lay next to her second husband correctly hers by the law of the church.

It cannot be said that Father Joseph, Abbott of Barlings, was without fair and humble feelings. He had taken an expressive service, for here was a soul who had returned to the true path. But for many years now an Abbott's duties had brought him so much work on administration and to the colder facts of the material needs of sustaining the background and foundation of their work, that other thoughts, indeed anxieties, would not be quietened, for it was Alesia's grandmother who had contributed so much to his Abbey, and Alesia had continued the gifts. The new church tower was nigh finished; the Abbey was not poor, but new people could tend to form new religious houses rather than support existing ones. And Alesia had left no money and no instructions for praying for her soul. But in conscience some of that must be done, for fear of ethereal ingratitude.

Walter was tolling the new great bell. Alesia had spoken with Walter on an occasion some years before, and he had not forgotten. He had been told how many times to ring that the occasion warranted, but he would go on further, from simple feeling in sorrow. It was already twilight; the river between the meadows was low and narrow, because the tide was out. That made a yard or so difference in depth, and a rod or two in width. In the afternoon sun the reddened sky gave a background to the tower. It all reflected on the water, and the light glistened on the gunwales of the boats leaning on the mud.

Peasants in the marshes heard the bell, as they had heard it oftentimes before. If they noted that it went on a little longer than was usual, the thought did not transcend their activity about their own primitive problems. Their food, and their warmth for the night, was their occupation at this time. The majority of tenants, villeins and bordars of Alesia's lands were far from Barlings. In their parishes the news of her death was to be received; where there was a church bell it had been ordered to be tolled. Where the orders were obeyed, indeed also in the places where they were not obeyed, there was talk of her, whether they had ever seen her, but everywhere talk of the new situation. The new lord Henry of Lancaster was likely to demand more discipline. But that never happened, for within a year their numbers were decimated by a plague and its deaths, and all efforts to maintain the old ways in the old manner were frustrated by the reduction of population, which increased their importance.

To follow came the redirection of the remaining honours and estates of the Lincoln inheritance. One connection was lost forever. Never again was the Earldom of Lincoln to be held by anyone with a relationship to a citizen of the city of Lincoln. Alesia's father, Henry de Lacy, had married Margaret Longepee, her grandmother being a daughter of Richard de Camville of the city, his line going back to the pre-Conquest Colsuen of Lincoln. Alesia thus had been the first and the only person ever to hold the title directly and to be descended from a citizen.

**END**

Barlings Abbey, Lincolnshire. Founded by the de la Haye ancestors of Alesia and enriched by her, and the families of Longepee and Clifford. Ebulo le Strange and Alesia were buried here.

Lincoln Cathedral